George Frideric Handel

A Life with Friends

George Frideric Handel

A Life with Friends

ELLEN T. HARRIS

W. W. Norton & Company

New York • London

For information about permission to reproduce selections from this book,
write to Permissions, W. W. Norton & Company, Inc.,
500 Fifth Avenue, New York, NY 10110

For information about special discounts for bulk purchases, please contact
W. W. Norton Special Sales at specialsales@wwnorton.com or 800-233-4830

Manufacturing by RR Donnelley, Harrisonburg
Book design by Lisa Buckley Design
Production manager: Devon Zahn

Library of Congress Cataloging-in-Publication Data

Harris, Ellen T., author.
George Frideric Handel : a life with friends / Ellen T. Harris
pages cm
Includes bibliographical reference and index.
ISBN: 978-0-393-08895-3 (hardcover)
1. Handel, George Frideric, 1685–1759. 2. Composers—Biography. I. Title.
ML410.H13H279   2014
780.92—dc23
[B]   2014008148

W. W. Norton & Company, Inc., 500 Fifth Avenue, New York, NY 10110
www.wwnorton.com

W. W. Norton & Company Ltd., Castle House, 75/76 Wells Street, London W1T 3QT

1 2 3 4 5 6 7 8 9 0

For Stanley, Charlotte, Harry, Eliza, and Nora

Contents

List of Illustrations

Dramatis Personæ

Grouped by affinity, with individuals in each group listed in general order of appearance

HANDEL
George Frideric Handel, died 1759

German associates
Friedrich Wilhelm Zachow, his teacher of music and composition
Johann Adolf von Kielmansegg, Baron, Hanoverian courtier who assisted Handel's career and patronized Goupy
Christoph Friedrich Kreyenberg, Hanoverian diplomat who managed Handel's dismissal from Hanoverian service
Johanna Friderica Floercke (in German, Johanne Friederike Floercken), his niece and residuary legatee of his will

Italian patrons of Handel's music
Ferdinando de' Medici, Tuscan prince who wrote Handel a letter of introduction on his departure from Florence (1709)
Gian Gastone de' Medici, brother of the above, later Grand Duke, who appears to have met Handel in Germany and invited him to Florence
Francesco Maria Ruspoli, Marquis, later Prince, Rome
Cardinal Benedetto Pamphilj, Rome
Cardinal Carlo Colonna, Rome
Cardinal Pietro Ottoboni, Rome
Aurora Sanseverino, Duchess of Laurenzana, Naples

London associates
John Christopher Smith (senior), his amanuensis and manager
John Christopher Smith (junior), his pupil and later his substitute as music director, a composer
John Walsh (father and son), his primary publisher
Peter LeBlond, servant
John Duburk, servant
Benjamin Martyn, friend on New Bond Street, secretary to Lord Shaftesbury
James Smyth, perfumer at the Sign of the Civet Cat on New Bond Street, last known person to be with Handel before his death
George Amyand, executor of his will
John Hetherington and Thomas Harris, witnesses to his will

Musicians

Georg Philipp Telemann, composer, Handel's lifelong friend whom he met in
    Halle c. 1701–1702

Johann Mattheson, composer, Handel's friend and colleague who wrote of
    their time together in Hamburg

Reinhard Keiser, senior composer at the opera in Hamburg

Antonio Caldara, composer in Rome, Venice

Arcangelo Corelli, composer and violinist in Rome

Margarita Durastante, soprano, primary singer for Ruspoli, who also
    premiered the role of Agrippina and sang for Handel in London

Agostino Steffani, composer and diplomat, Handel's predecessor at Hanover

Nicolini (Nicola Grimaldi), castrato who premiered the role of Rinaldo

Henry Purcell, English composer, most important English predecessor of
    Handel

John Eccles, English composer, Master of the Queen's Music under Queen
    Anne

William Croft, composer to the Chapel Royal, organist of Westminster
    Abbey

Maurice Greene, composer to the Chapel Royal after Croft, organist of St.
    Paul's Cathedral

Johann Christoph Pepusch, composer in London, musical arranger of *The
    Beggar's Opera*

Giovanni Bononcini and Attilio Ariosti, Italian composers for the Royal
    Academy of Music, competitors of Handel in the 1720s

Senesino (castrato) and Cuzzoni (soprano), leading singers with the Royal
    Academy of Music who later worked for the Opera of the Nobility in
    competition with Handel in the 1730s

Farinelli, renowned castrato of the period hired by the Opera of the Nobility

Nicola Porpora, composer hired by the Opera of the Nobility

Thomas Arne and John Frederick Lampe (in German, Johann Friedrich
    Lampe), composers of English operas in competition with Handel in the
    1730s

William Boyce, English composer

Matthew Dubourg, violinist in Dublin and London, only musician
    individually named in Handel's will

Librettists

John Hughes, poet from whom Handel first asked for English text to set to
    music, contributor to *Acis and Galatea*

Ambrose Philips, librettist of the Birthday Ode for Queen Anne

Alexander Pope, John Gay, and John Arbuthnot, colleagues and friends at
    Burlington House and Cannons (estate of the duke of Chandos)

Aaron Hill, playwright, theater manager, author of Handel's *Rinaldo*, advocate of English opera

Giacomo Rossi, Nicola Haym, and Paolo Rolli, opera librettists

Charles Jennens, Newburgh Hamilton, Thomas Broughton, and Thomas Morell, oratorio librettists

English patrons and impresarios

Johann Jakob Heidegger, impresario with whom Handel worked in London

Richard Boyle, Third Earl of Burlington, patron of Handel and Goupy

James Brydges, First Earl of Carnarvon, later First Duke of Chandos, patron of Handel and Goupy

Henry Furnese, patron of Goupy and Handel

Charles Sackville, First Earl of Middlesex, who failed to entice Handel to compose for the opera company he oversaw in London from 1739 to 1748

Margaret Cecil, Lady Brown, Baroness of Ranelagh, "enemy" to Handel from the late 1730s into 1740s

Jonathan Tyers, proprietor of Vauxhall Gardens

Sir Paul Methuen, art collector, patron of Goupy

Richard Houlditch, art collector who made manuscript copies of art auction catalogues from the first half of the eighteenth century

John Rich, manager of Covent Garden

English hosts of house concerts

Thomas Britton, a merchant in charcoal, who initiated the practice of public house concerts

John Wollaston, painter

William Caslon, developer of typefaces

Henry Needler, accountant and violinist

Doctors

John Gowland, apothecary on New Bond Street, Goupy's landlord for a brief period

Richard Warren, identified as Handel's doctor by Charles Burney

Francis Philip Duval, physician whose name is notated by Handel in his score of *Faramondo* (1738)

Dr. George Cheyne, famous physician at Bath, who advised Pope, Gay, Lady Percival, and perhaps Handel

Samuel Sharp, surgeon at Guy's Hospital who operated on Handel's eyes

John Belchier, surgeon at Guy's Hospital, named in Handel's will

William Bromfield, surgeon at London Lock Hospital, also operated on Handel's eyes

John Taylor, itinerant and self-aggrandizing eye surgeon, who operated on Handel's eyes at Bath

GOUPY

Joseph Goupy, died 1769
Lewis Goupy, his uncle, art adviser to Burlington, art teacher to Mary Delany
Dorothy Chaveney, his landlady and perhaps his mistress in the 1720s
John Hedges, treasurer to Frederick, Prince of Wales, and Goupy's patron
William Lord Bateman, son of Hedges's half-sister, separated from his wife on
     account of his homosexual practices
Dr. John Monro, a "mad doctor" consulted by Goupy for a woman in his
     household

Other visual artists

Marco Ricci, Sebastiano Ricci, and Giovanni Antonio Pellegrini, artists
     variously engaged at Burlington House and at the Queen's Theatre
Peter Tillemans, artist and set designer for the Royal Academy of Music
William Hogarth, painter, engraver, satirist, and social critic, a codirector of
     the Foundling Hospital with Handel, painted Donnellan with the Wesley
     family
Philippe Mercier, painted portrait of Handel, principal painter to the prince
     of Wales until replaced by Goupy in 1736
Rupert Barber, miniaturist who lived many years on the property of the
     Delany estate near Dublin, he painted miniatures of both Donnellan and
     Delany, and of Handel (now lost)
Louis-François Roubiliac, sculptor, creator of Handel's statue for Vauxhall
     Gardens and his monument in Westminster Abbey
Christian Friedrich Zincke, important miniaturist, whose work includes a
     painting of Delany
Thomas Hudson, painted two important portraits of Handel

DELANY-GRANVILLE

Mary Delany (née Granville, first married name Pendarves), died 1788
Bernard Granville (senior), her father
George Granville, Lord Lansdowne, her uncle, a playwright and leading
     Jacobite, who pushed her into an unwanted marriage at the age of
     seventeen
Sir John Stanley and Anne Stanley (née Granville), her aunt and uncle with
     whom Delany lived as a child and again as a widow
Anthony Westcombe, her maternal uncle who bequeathed a fortune to her
     brother Bernard
Bernard Granville (junior), her brother, a close friend of Handel
Bevil Granville, her brother
Anne Dewes (née Granville), her sister

John Dewes, her brother-in-law

Court, Bernard, and John Dewes, her nephews

Mary Port (née Dewes), her niece, married to John Port

Georgina Port, her great-niece

Alexander Pendarves, her first husband, a close associate of her uncle Lansdowne, died 1725

Mary Pendarves Basset, Pendarves's niece, his heir-at-law after he died intestate, and defendant in lawsuit brought by Mary Delany for her widow's portion

Edward Stanley, Delany's lawyer (no relation to her uncle Stanley)

Dr. Patrick Delany, her beloved second husband, protestant clergyman, dean of Down, died 1768

Margaret Tenison, Dr. Delany's first wife, whose family sued Delany after her death

John Wesley, with his brother cofounder of the Methodist movement, correspondent of Mary Delany

Jonathan Swift, author, essayist, dean of St. Patrick's Cathedral, Dublin, correspondent of Mary Delany

Margaret Cavendish, Duchess of Portland, one of Delany's closest friends, with whom she lived half the year during her second widowhood

HUNTER

James Hunter, third son of a wealthy Huguenot family, died 1757

Henry Lannoy Hunter, his brother, firstborn son

John Hunter, his brother, second-born son

Sir Harcourt Master, his uncle, director of the South Sea Company

Thomas Weston, Assistant Astronomer Royal and director of a school for boys in Greenwich

Catherine Hunter (née Cooke), Hunter's wife

MAYNE-BATT

Elizabeth Mayne (née Batt), died 1768

Christopher Batt (senior), her father, died 1739

Christopher Batt (junior), her brother, died 1756

John Mayne (senior), her husband, lord of the manor at Teffont Evias, died 1726

John Mayne (junior), her son, died 1785

Isabella Mayne (née Raymond, second husband: Archibald, Earl of Dundonald), wife of John Mayne (junior)

John Thomas Batt and Edward Pery Buckley, lateral descendants who inherited the Rubens oil sketch purchased by Christopher Batt (junior) in 1750

James Harris, philosopher, avid fan of Handel's music, hosted Handel at his house in Salisbury, preserved an important collection of Handel's music in manuscript first prepared for Elizabeth Legh, cousin of Lord Radnor (see below), who gave the collection to Harris; his son James Harris became First Earl of Malmesbury

Connections through the Harris circle

John Robartes, Fourth Earl of Radnor

Anthony Ashley Cooper, Fourth Earl of Shaftesbury, collector of Handel's music

DONNELLAN-PERCIVAL

Anne Donnellan, died 1762

Philip Percival, her stepfather

John Percival, later First Earl of Egmont, brother to Philip

George Berkeley, Bishop of Cloyne, close friend of John Percival, his proposal of marriage was refused by Donnellan

Samuel Richardson, author of *Clarissa* and *Sir Charles Grandison*, correspondent of Donnellan (and also of Delany and her sister)

Elizabeth Robinson Montagu, friend and correspondent of Donnellan (also close to Delany)

PALMER-PEACOCK-VERNEY

Elizabeth Palmer (née Peacock), died after 1764

Richard Peacock, her father, died 1737

Elizabeth Peacock, her mother

George Peacock, her brother, died 1740

Elizabeth Peacock (infant), George Peacock's orphaned daughter

Ralph Palmer (III), Elizabeth's husband, died 1755

Hamey Palmer, brother to Ralph Palmer (III), died 1771

Ralph Palmer (II), their father, died 1746

Elizabeth Verney (née Palmer), sister of Ralph Palmer (II), died 1686, wife of John Verney, first Viscount Fermanagh, died 1717

Ralph, first Earl Verney, their son, died 1752

Ralph, second Earl Verney, their grandson and childhood friend of Ralph Palmer (III), died 1791

Elizabeth Verney, sister to the first Earl Verney, died 1767

BRITISH ROYAL FAMILIES

James II, last Catholic king (from 1685), fled England 1689, lived in exile, died 1701, succeeded by his protestant daughter Mary II and her husband, the Dutch William III of Orange

Queen Anne, sister of Mary II, last Stuart monarch, died 1714

James Francis Edward Stuart, Catholic son of James II, after whose death he
was styled James III by his supporters, died 1766

Charles Edward Stuart, his son, died 1788

George I, previously Elector of Hanover and Handel's employer, first
Hanoverian monarch from 1714, died 1727

George II, his son, died 1760

Queen Caroline, wife of George II, died 1737

Prince Frederick, son of George II, Prince of Wales, died 1751

Princess Anne, daughter of George II, music student of Handel

Prince William Augustus, son of George II, Duke of Cumberland, leader of
government troops in 1745 rebellion

Princesses Amelia, Caroline, Mary, and Louise, other daughters of George II,
some of whom also studied music with Handel

ENGLISH EIGHTEENTH-CENTURY WRITERS ON HANDEL

John Mainwaring, author of biography of Handel (1760)

Sir John Hawkins, author of multivolume history of music (1776)

Charles Burney, author of multivolume history of music (1776–1789), and
history of the Commemoration of Handel (1785)

William Coxe, stepson of John Christopher Smith Jr., author of *Anecdotes*
(1799)

Prefatory Note

Spelling in the eighteenth century was largely phonetic and inconsistent, a practice which extended even to formal names. In all English eighteenth-century quotations, I have followed the spelling irregularities of the original without editorial comment or emendation. Dates given for Handel's works are, unless otherwise stated, of the first performance or, with Opus numbers, of the first publication.

George Frideric Handel

A Life with Friends

George Frideric Handel

ONE

Introductions

Handel and his friends

ON APRIL 11, 1759, George Frideric Handel lay on his deathbed. Blind for some years, he had been unable to conduct since 1753, had ceased any major compositional activity in 1752, and, since 1737, repeated episodes of illness—what newspaper and private accounts sometimes referred to as a "Paraletick Disorder"—had weakened his body as well. Nevertheless, he remained vigorous of mind. On February 24, the day after his seventy-fourth birthday, he visited his friend Thomas Harris, barrister and Master in Chancery, at Lincoln's Inn Fields and described his plans for the upcoming 1759 oratorio season that opened on March 2, and he was present at the performance of *Messiah* that ended the season on April 6. He had hoped to be able to travel to Bath after the oratorio season for rest and recuperation, as reported in the *Whitehall Evening Post* on April 7: "Last Night ended the celebrated Mr. Handel's Oratorios for this Season. . . . And this Day Mr. Handel proposed setting out for Bath, to try the Benefit of the Waters, having been for some Time past in a bad State of Health." On former occasions, his spa visits had sometimes effected astonishing improvement. Now, however, at his house, in Brook Street, London, Handel retired to his bed. He must have known death was at hand, and his thoughts turned to the close friends and associates he had made over nearly five decades of residence in his adopted English homeland.

In London, Handel lived largely in the public eye. Almost from the moment he arrived there, his music became an aural representation of the monarchy. In 1713, Queen Anne requested, when he was still only a visitor to Britain, that Handel compose the Te Deum and Jubilate for the national celebration of the Peace of Utrecht in St. Paul's Cathedral. In 1727, George II chose Handel, rather than the Master of the King's Music, to write the anthems for his coronation in Westminster Abbey, at least one of which has been performed at every coronation in Great Britain since that time. Handel also wrote anthems for the weddings of Princess Anne (1734) and Frederick, Prince of Wales (1736) and for the funeral of Queen Caroline (1737). The Te Deum for the victory at Dettingen was performed in 1743 in the Chapel Royal. In 1749, the *Music for the Royal Fireworks* to celebrate the Peace of Aix-la-Chapelle was performed out of doors to crowds estimated at more than 10,000.

Handel's compositions were hardly restricted to royal occasions, however. In London, the sound of his music reached from court to theater, from cathedral to tavern, and was performed by the greatest virtuosi of the era as well as the lonely spinster sitting at her keyboard. It served not just at coronations but as a background to daily life. His operas held the London stage for thirty years, from 1711 to 1741. In 1738, a marble statue by Louis-François Roubiliac, representing Handel as a divinely inspired Orphic figure, was placed in the very popular public gardens at Vauxhall, where his music was a staple: a remarkable tribute to a living composer. In 1732, the first public performance of Handel's *Esther* occurred at the Crown and Anchor Tavern, and from 1739, his biblical oratorios in English, commencing with *Saul* and *Israel in Egypt*, began to represent, even in some ways to create, the national Protestant identity of Great Britain. And *Messiah*, after the initiation in 1750 of annual performances in support of the Foundling Hospital for the education and maintenance of exposed and deserted young children, became indelibly associated with national ideals of charity. When Handel died in 1759, he was buried in Westminster Abbey in the south transept near the poet John Dryden, whose texts had been an important source of inspiration for him (*Alexander's Feast* and *Ode for St. Cecilia's Day*). His funeral was attended by more than 3,000, and in 1762 a larger-than-life monument by Roubiliac, showing the composer holding his manuscript of "I know that my Redeemer liveth" with a score of *Messiah* open next to him, was erected to mark his grave.

To a large extent, this funeral monument captures the image we hold today of Handel in life—an imposing public figure who consorts, even in death, with kings and queens, as well as with other artistic luminaries. In contrast, very little is known of Handel's own social milieu, and it almost seems as if the composer made a deliberate effort to keep his personal life private. Although he cared for his musical manuscripts meticulously and provided for their preservation in his will, very little of an intimate nature survives: few personal letters of any substance, no diary, not even any personal or professional account books. The lack of evidence has led some to suggest that Handel did not have the time, or perhaps the inclination, for active or engaged personal relationships. Offering a narrow opening into this largely unexplored area, Handel's will names many of those who played an important role in his life.[1] First written in 1750, with the last of four codicils added only days before his death, this very personal document shows Handel not only remembering surviving family members in Germany and close colleagues and associates in England, but also neighbors and friends.

In his initial will, Handel discharged his most pressing obligations. He remembered a number of his German relatives, singling out his niece, Johanna Friderica (Johanne Friederike) Floercke. The only surviving child of his late sister, she seems to have been named after her aunt Johanne (who had died in 1709 at the age of nineteen) and her uncle George Frideric. Johanna Friderica was not only his namesake but also Handel's closest living relative, and he made her his primary legatee and executor of his will. He also remembered his servants and gave a special acknowledgment to John Christopher Smith, the man who had worked most closely with him for more than four decades to prepare his scores for performance and to make manuscript copies for aristocratic patrons. He left a substantial bequest as well to James Hunter, a close friend. In a series of three codicils written in 1756 and 1757, he increased some of these gifts and brought the legacies to family and servants up to date. He also added bequests to two of his oratorio librettists, Thomas

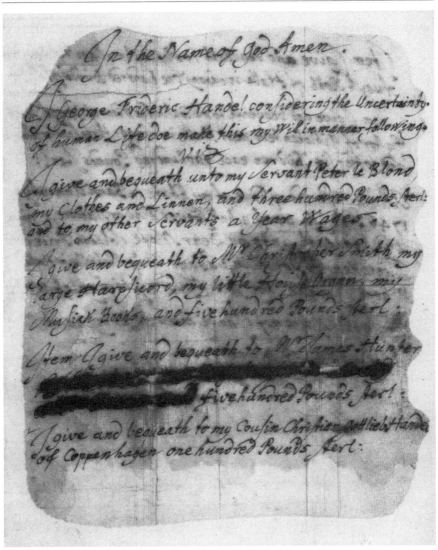

1.1 Handel's will in his own hand (1750), first page (The National Archives, Kew, ref. PROB 1/14)

Morell and Newburgh Hamilton, and named an English coexecutor, George Amyand, a wealthy merchant and Member of Parliament. He left paintings from his large collection to Charles Jennens, another of his librettists, and to his friend Bernard Granville, and a "fair copy of the Score and all Parts of my Oratorio called The Messiah to the Foundling Hospital," which gave them the freedom to continue after his death the annual charity performances for their benefit that Handel had initiated.

With the recognition that death was near, Handel turned his mind one last time to the state of his will. Once again, he remembered those who had done him service. He adjusted the gifts to his servants. He increased the bequest to Amyand and added gifts to John Hetherington, a law clerk, and to Thomas Harris, both of whom had witnessed earlier codicils. For the first time he considered his musical colleagues. He made a munificent gift of £1,000 to the Society for Decayed Musicians, which supported performers in their retirement, and specifically remembered the violinist Matthew Dubourg, leader of the orchestra during his Dublin season of 1741–1742 (which had included the premiere of *Messiah*) and arranger of performances of his music in Dublin thereafter. Beyond this, he began to focus on former and current neighbors.

The largest gift among this final group of beneficiaries went to James Smyth, the owner of a perfumery around the corner on New Bond Street. Perfumers at this time prepared cosmetic and medicinal fragrances (such as aromatic incense to sweeten the smell of a sick room or to ease breathing) as well as scents for personal use. Whether or not Handel used his professional services, Smyth was one of the last outsiders to be with Handel before his death on Saturday, April 14. In a letter he wrote to Bernard Granville three days later, Smyth explained that "Handel took leave of all his friends on Friday morning, and desired to see nobody but the Doctor and Apothecary and myself. At 7 o'clock in the evening he took leave of me and told me we 'should meet again,'" and "that he had *now done with the world*."[2] The apothecary was probably John Gowland, also of New Bond Street. The doctor may have been another legatee, John Belchier, a surgeon of Sun Court, Threadneedle

Street, and a mutual friend of Handel and the poet Alexander Pope. Handel also remembered Benjamin Martyn, a friend who lived, like both Smyth and Gowland, on New Bond Street. A writer who occupied various administrative posts, Martyn may have helped Handel in later years with setting up his oratorio seasons; in 1757 Thomas Harris sent to Martyn "to know Handel's scheme of performances."[3] Finally, Handel left bequests to a small group of women friends: two of these, Anne Donnellan and Elizabeth Palmer, were neighbors, Elizabeth Mayne resided in Kensington.

The eighteenth-century historian John Hawkins wrote that Handel's "intimate friends were few" and that "those that seemed to possess most of his confidence were Goupy, the painter, and one Hunter, a scarlet-dyer at Old Ford, near Bow." James Hunter, whom Handel treated generously in his original will, died before the composer, in 1757. Joseph Goupy and Handel, who had been close friends, had a serious falling-out in the 1740s, as a result of which Goupy published a cruel caricature of the composer. His resultant estrangement from Handel, according to legend, cost him a place in the composer's will. Another friend missing from the will is Mary Delany. She and Anne Donnellan were close, and it would have been Delany who introduced Donnellan to Handel. Although Delany first met Handel when she was only ten years old, it may have been through her brother Bernard Granville that she later entered the composer's social circle. That he received a bequest from Handel and she did not may have resulted from her having married and moved away from London to Ireland (see Chapter 7): the three women Handel included were all single and living nearby. The widows Mayne and Palmer are both described in the will specifically in terms of male relatives, and as with Delany, these may have been Handel's primary contacts—Mrs. Mayne as the sister of the late Christopher Batt, and Mrs. Palmer as the widow of Ralph Palmer. Donnellan was a spinster at whose home Handel continued to play the harpsichord for company even after he was totally blind. Mayne, according to family tradition, befriended Handel "at the time of his persecution,"[4] a probable reference to the early 1740s when he faced significant oppo-

Monument for me there and that any Sum nor exceeding Six Hundred Pounds be expended for that purpose at the discretion of my said Executor

I give to Mrs Palmer of Chelsea Widow of Mr Palmer formerly of Chappel Street One Hundred Pounds.

I give to my two Maid Servants each one years Wages over and above what shall be due to them at the time of my death. I give to Mrs Mayne of Kensington Widow Sister of the late Mr Batt Fifty Guineas

I give to Mrs Donnalan of Charles Street Berkley Square Fifty Guineas

I give to Mr Reiche Secretary for the affairs of Hanover Two Hundred Pounds.

In Witness whereof I have hereunto set my Hand and Seal this Eleventh day of April 1759.

G. F. Handel

This Codicil was read over to the said George Friderick Handel and by him Signed and Sealed in the presence on the day and year above written of us

J. Christopher Smith

1.2 Handel's final codicil (1759), last page signed by Handel (The National Archives, Kew, ref. PROB 1/14) sition from, as Delany put it, "the fine ladies, petit maîtres and *ignoramus's.*"[5] Palmer may have been another among the group of women who supported the composer at this time; Donnellan certainly was.

Goupy, Hunter, Delany, Donnellan, Mayne, and Palmer were among Handel's closest acquaintances, and, together with Handel, they are the co-protagonists of this book. That is not to say that they represent a group of friends. Delany and Donnellan were intimate, but otherwise there is no evidence that any of the others were close. Rather, each of the friends had an independent relationship with Handel. Except for Goupy, who is identified in the eighteenth century as an intimate friend, and Delany, whose correspondence details their close association, these individuals appear in Handel's will as recipients of friendship bequests, standing apart from the family legacies and the gifts Handel made in gratitude for service—such as those bequests given to John Christopher Smith, his librettists, medical and legal advisers, and servants.

The affinities among these six friends paint a striking picture, further distinguishing them from other legatees and known associates or patrons. Most lived close by in the neighborhood of St. George's, Hanover Square. With the exception of Hunter, their homes form a circle with a radius of less than a quarter of a mile.

Not surprisingly, all six friends possessed deep musical interest and talent, something that does not appear to be the case for other legatees who were also neighbors, such as James Smyth, Benjamin Martyn, and John Gowland, whose wills make no reference to music books or instruments. Most can be considered independent in terms of religion, few of them adhering literally to the normative creed of the Church of England but rather ranging in belief from Catholicism through dissenting protestant sects to heretical versions of Anglican doctrine, reflecting Handel's strong belief in religious tolerance. They also stand apart from the norm in terms of marital status. Only Mayne had children. The others who married, including Delany, Hunter, and Palmer, made matches strongly disapproved of by their families, resulting in various

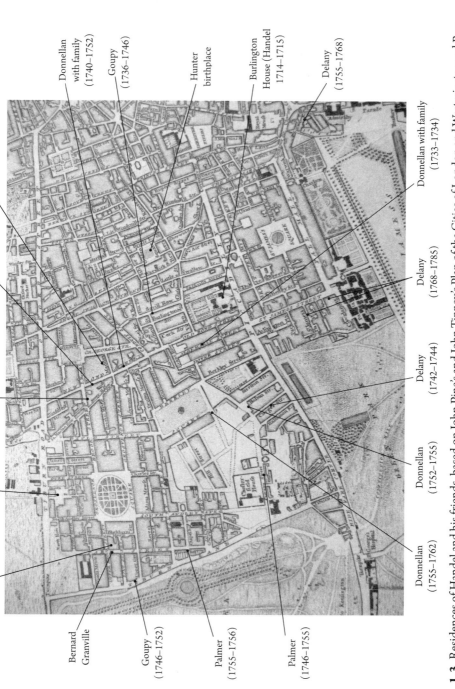

Chaveny's
(1723–1734)

Donnellan
with family
(1740–1752)

Goupy
(1736–1746)

Hunter
birthplace

Burlington
House (Handel
1714–1715)

Delany
(1755–1768)

Gowland's
(1734–1736)

Donnellan with family
(1733–1734)

Delany
(1768–1785)

HANDEL
(1723–d.1759)

John Hedges
(Goupy's patron)

Delany
(1742–1744)

Delany
(1734–1741)

Donnellan
(1752–1755)

Donnellan
(1755–1762)

Bernard
Granville

Goupy
(1746–1752)

Palmer
(1755–1756)

Palmer
(1746–1755)

1.3 Residences of Handel and his friends, based on John Pine's and John Tinney's Plan of the Cities of London and Westminster and Borough of Southwark, 1747 (courtesy of the Westminster Archives Centre, London) degrees of disinheritance. None of these marriages resulted in children. The others, not only including Handel, Goupy, and Donnellan but also, among a wider circle of acquaintance, Bernard Granville, Christopher Batt, and Benjamin Martyn, remained unmarried; James Smyth, who did marry, was childless. Like Handel (but unlike Granville, Batt, Martyn, or Smyth), all six friends experienced serious financial problems in the 1730s or 1740s, and many, as a result, were engaged in litigation or bankruptcy. Nevertheless, all, like Handel, were extremely generous and charitable with what they had.

The documentary evidence about the private lives of these friends, in some cases much more abundant than the surviving information on Handel, derives from multiple sources, including letters, diaries, personal accounts, legal cases, property deeds, and insurance records, and offers an intimate picture of London life during the first half of the eighteenth century. The lack of such sources for Handel means that his biographers have hardly any testimony from the composer himself. By examining the sources concerning his friends, one can glimpse Handel's personal interactions and posit motivations and threads of action. Although these conclusions often appear shorn of the cautionary "probably," thereby avoiding the constant repetition of this word, they are educated guesses based on extensive research. One of the most rewarding aspects of exploring these relationships has been the light it sheds on Handel's compositions. Put simply, the lives of his friends illustrate how Handel's music intersected with eighteenth-century London.

The music of Handel offers a tapestry of eighteenth-century culture and society. Woven with tremendous skill and imbued with vibrant colors, the images on its surface may tell of shepherds and shepherdesses, chivalrous knights, kings and queens, and biblical heroes, but the threads that make up the warp and weft derive from the interests, concerns, and desires of the world in which Handel lived. While it is hardly surprising to say that art is a product of its time and place, the relationship between Handel's music and its milieu goes deeper than most. In order to gain a full understanding of the extent of this relationship in both public and private contexts, it is not enough to touch on contemporary issues in a general way or to focus in depth on a single cultural issue, although both approaches can enhance (and have significantly altered) our understanding. Nor does an examination of the few surviving records of Handel's personal life offer satisfactory insight into his compositional and professional choices. Rather, in order to appreciate how deeply his musical scores resonated with his audience, one needs to look at the lives of individuals in that audience, lives in which Handel participated. Knowing about his friends, and in particular the friends to whom he left bequests in his will, extends our knowledge of Handel in his world and furthers our understanding of his music in the society for which it was written. Marriage, friendship, medicine, law, commerce, public relations, finance, religion, and politics all play a part.

This is not to say that Handel depicted his friends in his music, only that they offer an example of the public for whom Handel composed, and as such also served at times as a private sounding board for his new compositions. Handel's operas set in the Middle East (*Rinaldo, Tamerlano*), for example, would not have seemed remote to James Hunter, who was an international trader and later in life worked directly with the British East India Company. The tension between a forced marriage and true love (*Floridante, Imeneo*) was not limited to exotic or fantastical climes but common to many: Mary Delany had both experiences. False accusations and legal problems (*Solomon, Susanna*) plagued Delany and her husband, while Hunter and Goupy both endured long court battles. Issues of religious toleration (*Esther, Judas Maccabaeus, Theodora*) touched them all.

As a result of this refractory approach to Handel through his friends, the book is not strictly chronological but rather moves forward in layers. One of the most popular musical devices in Handel's lifetime was the fugue, where the theme (subject) is presented successively in all the voices (vocal or instrumental). A distinctive attribute of the fugue is that each statement of the theme overlaps with the continuation of the preceding one, somewhat like a simple round. Whereas a round (for example, "Row, Row, Row Your Boat") is inherently circular, however, and can continue indefinitely, the fugue has a distinct trajectory that provides clear direction and a conclusive ending. More complicated fugues sometimes have multiple themes, all of which interact with one another. Handel was well known for his fugues, which appear in his keyboard works, his overtures and concertos, and, most distinctively, in his oratorio choruses. In all cases he tended to treat the formal process freely, so that the eighteenth-century historian Charles Burney wrote of Handel that he was "perhaps the only great Fughist exempt from pedantry."[6] This biography of Handel is a fugue with four separate themes, following, of course, Handel's free style.

The first theme is Handel's life. It provides the overall chronological trajectory of the book. At points in the story, this primary theme is submerged while another takes precedence, but it always returns, frequently with stronger force. In developing this theme through an examination of Handel's career (and career choices), we learn more about his income, his sources of revenue, and the value of his music in terms of its composition, performance, and publication. Finance thus becomes important to the discussion, yet an exact conversion of eighteenth-century currency into today's monetary values is not possible. To get a rough idea of the value of eighteenth-century British pounds today, one can multiply by 200; for the figure in American dollars, multiply by 300. That is, the £600 Handel received annually from the Royal Treasury from about 1723, would today, in general terms, be worth £120,000 or $180,000. Appendix 1 explains the older British system of pounds, shillings, and pence, and provides examples of costs and fees in order to illustrate the relative value of money in the first half of the eighteenth century. For example, a ticket in the gallery for one of Handel's operas cost much more than a pound of salmon or a pair of kid gloves, but less than the imported luxury of a pound of good China tea.

The second theme of this biographical fugue encompasses the culture and context of the period. It provides the overall chapter organization in relationship to the chronology of Handel's life, but again, by necessity, themes reappear and intersect. Politics takes center stage in Chapter 3, but is never wholly absent in later chapters. Marriage and social status provide the focus for Chapter 6, but these topics also play a role in the treatment of legal issues (Chapter 7), and the emphasis on religion in Chapter 9 comes after many earlier appearances of the subject in previous chapters. To assist the reader in moving through this succession of topics, each chapter includes a brief timeline of events mentioned within that chapter. In terms of a chronological period or general topic, of course, none of these is complete. It would not be possible, for example, to include every event related to international trade in Chapter 4, or every private musical event in Chapter 5. But as the book moves from topic to topic, the timelines can provide something of a handrail.

The third theme consists of the lives of Handel's friends and legatees; it brings the contextual background to life by showing how cultural attitudes directly affected those closest to Handel. Given the range of ages among the friends and the differing amount of documentary material concerning each, the friends do not move through the book in a block, but come in and out where they fit chronologically and when the sources determine. Goupy, who was Handel's age, appears immediately in Chapter 2 ("Before London"), Delany, who was fifteen years younger, in Chapter 3 ("Politics, Patronage, and Pension"), and Hunter and Palmer, who were twenty-five years younger, in Chapter 4 ("Commerce and Trade"). Donnellan and Mayne make their debuts in Chapter 5 ("Music at Home"). Thereafter, the friends enter when appropriate to Handel's life and the cultural context. Because Handel's friends and acquaintances are not well known, and discussion of their lives also involves the inclusion of their family members and associates, the Dramatis Personæ at the beginning of the book offers a list of characters in the manner of Handel's operas and oratorios where, for example, the Romans and Egyptians in *Giulio Cesare*, or the Israelites and Philistines in *Samson*, are given in separate listings. The groupings in this book represent the social and familial circles surrounding each of the six friends and Handel, listed basically in order of appearance.

The fourth theme is Handel's music, the most substantive and extensive written testament that survives from his hand, which over the course of his life became ever more deeply engaged with cultural and personal issues. The shift is hardly absolute, as Handel's oratorios deal with issues of national religion as well as personal religious freedom, but there is a general movement from great questions of state concerning monarchical succession (Chapter 3: Politics) and international dominion (Chapter 4: Commerce) toward matters more cultural and personal in nature (such as friendship: Chapter 7, and religious tolerance and charity: Chapter 9). Although an understanding of Handel's music in terms of its London context is a significant aspect of the book, there are no musical examples. Rather than provide an analysis of the music's constructive elements, I have striven to create a vivid sense of its impact. For readers who would like to hear the music I discuss, Appendix 2 provides a discography of recordings I have particularly enjoyed.

Unlike a standard biography, there is no attempt here to provide a comprehensive chronicle of Handel's life. The biographies by Donald Burrows, Christopher Hogwood, and Jonathan Keates, all of which have seen revised editions in the past five years, do this very well. Rather, the book is an attempt to uncover the private person behind the public persona. Because the telling of Handel's life is reflected through the experiences of his close English friends, the book focuses primarily on his adult years from the time of his arrival in London at the age of twenty-five. What is known of his upbringing in Germany has been repeated many times: his birth in Halle in 1685, his early musical aptitude, his father's desire that he study law, and his matriculation at the University of Halle. With his move to Hamburg in 1703, Handel entered the world of professional music making. Together with his sojourn in Italy, from 1706 to 1710, these seven years formed the basis on which his musical maturity was built. All of these topics are touched on in this book, especially as they relate to the choices he made later in life, but the emphasis is on the fifty years Handel spent in England.

Over the course of the book's fugal structure, and the increasingly active interplay among its four themes—Handel's life, the culture and context, his friends, and his music—a picture develops of Handel's growing personal identification with the music he composed. At first, during the 1710s and 1720s, the composer reacted brilliantly to shifting circumstances (politics, commerce, music distribution). Overlapping with this, a more intimate view of cultural attitudes and mores (such as marriage and justice) appears in the 1730s and 1740s. Finally, Handel's music from the 1740s and 1750s, dealing with friendship, religion, death, and reputation, offers rare insight into his own deeply held convictions.

Handel's professional and compositional choices illuminate the composer in a far more intimate light than we might ever have imagined. Seen through the subjects and countersubjects of his life and the lives of his friends, his music speaks to us vividly of the man—not, of course, of his transitory mental or emotional state when composing, but rather of his ingrained values, attitudes, and beliefs. In the end, it is Handel's creative response to text and circumstance in his music that permits us this glimpse of the private composer, hiding in full view behind his public persona.

2.1 Miniature portrait of Handel by Christoph Platzer, c. 1710 (© Stiftung
Händel-Haus, Halle)

TWO

Before London

1685–1710
German training, Italian sojourn, arrival in England

AS A SMALL CHILD, Handel was not allowed to "meddle with any musical instrument"; none was permitted in the house and the boy could not visit "where such furniture was in use." His father, sixty-three years old when Handel was born, forbade it. The elder Handel, an esteemed barber-surgeon in the north German city of Halle who held honorific court appointments and maintained a flourishing private practice, had remarried in 1683 following the death of his first wife, at which time his new father-in-law described him as "the noble, honourable, greatly respected and renowned Herr Georg Hendel."[1] The one surviving son from his first marriage, Carl, had already followed in his father's profession and was serving at the Saxon court in Weissenfels. Georg Händel now intended the only surviving son of his second marriage, George Frideric, born February 23, 1685 (baptized Georg Friederich the following day), for "the study of the Civil Law." Nevertheless, showing the kind of independence that typified his adulthood, the boy managed at the age of five to have a clavichord (a small keyboard instrument with a very soft sound) "privately convey'd to a room at the top of the house," where he was able to practice unimpeded.

Because little documentary evidence survives about Handel's formative years, we are largely dependent on the biography by John Mainwaring published in 1760, the year after the composer's death. The anecdotal stories of Handel's youth, however, can only have come from

BEFORE LONDON: *Timeline*

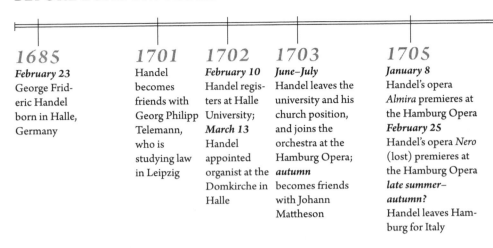

1685	1701	1702	1703	1705
February 23 George Frideric Handel born in Halle, Germany	Handel becomes friends with Georg Philipp Telemann, who is studying law in Leipzig	*February 10* Handel registers at Halle University; *March 13* Handel appointed organist at the Domkirche in Halle	*June–July* Handel leaves the university and his church position, and joins the orchestra at the Hamburg Opera; *autumn* becomes friends with Johann Mattheson	*January 8* Handel's opera *Almira* premieres at the Hamburg Opera *February 25* Handel's opera *Nero* (lost) premieres at the Hamburg Opera *late summer–autumn?* Handel leaves Hamburg for Italy

the composer himself, who frequently regaled friends and associates with accounts of his life. Even if Mainwaring did not hear the anecdotes directly from the composer but rather in some mediated form through one or more telling, he still offers the closest record we have of Handel's own words. The choice of reminiscence, and undoubtedly the adult shaping of the narrative, provides insight into what was most important to Handel's self-image. What stands out in particular is his sense of self-reliance and independence.[2]

In 1691 or 1692, when his father set out on a trip to Weissenfels, the young Handel resolved to join him. He had not been invited but wanted to meet his half-brother, who was thirty-five years older than he, and followed his father's coach by foot. Carriages, even when nothing delayed them, rarely traveled more distance in a day than a man could walk easily, and, in this instance, Handel, less than seven years old, was able to catch up. His father, "greatly surprised at his courage, and somewhat displeased with his obstinacy," reluctantly allowed the boy to join him. At the Weissenfels court, when his father was too busy to supervise him closely, Handel enjoyed "getting at harpsichords." He also played the organ, and on one occasion was overheard by the duke. When told the identity of the performer by Handel's half-brother, who may well have

MAJOR ITALIAN WORKS

1706–1710
Handel in Florence under patronage of the Medici; in Rome under patronage of Prince Ruspoli and Cardinals Pamphilj, Ottoboni, and Colonna; in Naples under patronage of Donn'Aurora Sanseverino; periodically in Venice

1707
spring
Il trionfo del Tempo e del Disinganno performed in Rome (text by Pamphilj)
autumn
Rodrigo premieres in Florence at Teatro del Cocomero

1708
April 8
La resurrezione performed in Rome at Palazzo Bonelli
July
Aci, Galatea, e Polifemo performed in Naples

1709
December 26
Agrippina premieres in Venice at Teatro San Giovanni Grisostomo

1710
by June 14
Handel appointed Kapellmeister to the elector of Hanover
autumn
Handel leaves Hanover for London

arranged an "accidental" meeting, the duke spoke to Handel's father about the boy's natural ability. Although he granted a father's authority to choose whatever profession he saw fit for his children, he also thought that a talent like Handel's should be developed. "He concluded with saying, that he was far from recommending the study of Music in exclusion of the Languages, or of the Civil Law, provided it was possible to reconcile them together." As a result of this encounter, Handel was allowed to study music with Friedrich Wilhelm Zachow (1663–1712), the organist at the Lutheran Marienkirche (St. Mary's Church, generally known as the Market Church) in Halle.

Handel made astonishing progress under Zachow as both performer and composer. By the time he was nine, he began composing concerted sacred cantatas for voices and instruments and did so "every week for three years successively." Though such productivity may seem doubtful for one so young, it is clear that the boy persevered and succeeded in music. In addition, he continued the study preparatory to a profession in civil law.[3] When his father died in 1697, it being common for close friends and family of the deceased to write mourning poems to be read at the funeral, the twelve-year-old Handel contributed one of his own and signed himself "Georg-Friedrich Händel, dedicated to the liberal arts." He thus referred to himself in a way that honored his father's wishes in terms of the broad humanistic study required of the law rather than the professional training of a practical musician.

Handel's growing musical achievements in Halle led his remaining family to think of a situation that would afford him better opportunities in this field, and a decision was made to set out for Berlin, at which court there was "a friend and relation . . . on whose care and kindness his parents could rely." It was here, in the court of Berlin, where Handel imbibed the critical importance of maintaining professional independence. His father and brother had already provided models in this regard, as they had made successful careers outside their court appointments, but the events in Berlin, pertaining specifically to Handel himself, must have had a more direct impact. Although few of the dates for incidents in Handel's childhood can be confirmed, the placement of the trip to Berlin in 1698 is particularly suspect. The visit probably took place around 1701.

Just as in Weissenfels, where the intercession of his half-brother played a role in the duke becoming aware of Handel's abilities, so too in Berlin the presence of a "friend and relation" appears a factor in having his talent recognized by Friedrich, self-declared King of Prussia and Elector of Brandenburg (and grandfather of Frederick the Great). When the king sought "the opportunity of patronizing so rare a genius" by taking him into service and seeing to his musical training, it was necessary to frame an appropriate, if negative, response. Although Handel's family recognized the honor of the offer, they also realized that, if he accepted a position as servant and court musician, he would relinquish all control over his career. That is, that "once engag'd in the King's service, he must remain in it, whether he liked it, or not; . . . and that if he happened to displease, his ruin would be the certain consequence." The imprisonment of Johann Sebastian Bach in Weimar in 1717, when he demanded release from his position, provides an example of the kind of situation Handel's father and half-brother had avoided in their own more flexible court attachments, and the kind the family now sought to avoid for the young

Handel.[4] Therefore, they declined the king's offer in as gracious a way as possible. Handel's independence preserved, they returned to Halle, where the young man "began to feel himself more, to be conscious of his own superiority." Having been taught from an early age the importance of "liberty and independency," he ever after "pursued the same maxim" and "refused the highest offers from persons of the greatest distinction . . . because he would not be cramped or confined."

It was at this time, in 1701, that Handel first encountered the composer Georg Philipp Telemann, who was studying law at the University of Leipzig, sixteen miles from Halle. In his later autobiography, Telemann wrote that Handel was "hardly sixteen" when they met; Telemann was then twenty. It is not known in which city the meeting occurred, but Telemann mentions frequent and reciprocal visits back and forth, as well as an active correspondence. Music was their primary topic. Telemann, according to his own testimony, "emulated the admirable example of the honored Johann Kuhnau [the cantor, or music director, at the Thomaskirche in Leipzig] in fugue and counterpoint; in the composition and analysis of melodic movements, however, Handel and I continually exchanged ideas both through shared visits and correspondence."[5]

Early in 1702, at the age of seventeen, Handel enrolled at the University of Halle and also took a part-time position as church organist for the Calvinist congregation at the Domkirche ("Cathedral-church") in Halle that served the Huguenot immigrant population. Although it would appear, therefore, that Handel was attempting to pursue two mutually exclusive careers, this may not have been the case. Employment as a church cantor (music director) in a major city typically required a university education, as the position included the responsibility not only for the performance and composition of music for the church services but also for teaching Latin and other subjects at the associated church school. Both Johann Kuhnau and Georg Philipp Telemann studied law in advance of taking on important cantorates, and for more than three centuries the cantors at Thomaskirche (St. Thomas Church) in Leipzig, with the sole exception of Bach, who needed a substitute to take over his nonmusical teaching responsibilities, were all university trained.[6] But Handel had a different career plan. Taking advantage of the freedom of choice that had been preserved for him at Berlin, he abandoned both the university and his position as a church musician in spring of 1703 to try his hand at a full-time professional career in opera. In doing so, he left behind a career in the law, to which he had never been attached. More important, he abandoned the tried-and-true path in Germany to becoming a cantor.

Handel's first stop was the public opera house in Hamburg, where Reinhard Keiser—the leading composer of opera in Germany and only about ten years older than Handel—was music director. According to his friend Johann Mattheson, he slipped quietly into this new world.

> Handel came to Hamburg in the summer of 1703, rich in
> ability and good will. I was almost the first with whom he made
> acquaintance.... At first he played back-desk violin in the
> opera orchestra, and behaved as if he could not count to five,
> being naturally inclined to a dry humour. But once when the
> harpsichord player failed to appear he allowed himself to be
> persuaded to take his place, and showed himself a man—a thing
> no one had before suspected, save I alone.[7]

After Handel put his real abilities on display, he moved quickly from a back-desk position and assumed the responsibility for leading the opera orchestra from the keyboard.

If Handel had not yet thought of London as a place that might offer him a lucrative existence as a composer, then that idea first took root in Hamburg, a flourishing center of finance and international trade with close ties to London. Mattheson introduced Handel to the British diplomat John Wych (whose son Cyril both Mattheson and Handel tutored in music at different times), and through their association with Wych, the two composers would have heard and spoken a good deal of London. Mattheson himself departed Hamburg for England early in 1704. In the same year, Keiser left Hamburg, due in part to financial difficulties, and with Mattheson now leaving for London, the young Handel found himself overwhelmed.[8] In March he sent an impassioned plea to Mattheson, who was in Amsterdam waiting for sea passage, to come back to Hamburg because "the time is coming when nothing can be done at the Opera in your absence."[9] Mattheson returned, but he continued at the opera house—in the threefold role of composer, conductor, and leading tenor soloist—for only about a year and a half: first he took over the full responsibility of tutoring Cyril Wych and then in 1706 was appointed secretary to the senior Wych, a position he continued to hold when Cyril succeeded his father. Mattheson thus spent much of his career immersed in English culture and language without ever having the opportunity to visit England, a situation that may have left him with a lingering sense of "what if." Many years later, after Handel had already experienced his first triumphs in London, Mattheson bluntly stated in his book on the modern musician: "He who wants to profit out of music today takes himself to England."[10] Mattheson may have wondered if Handel's compositional success could have been his, especially since, as he was quick to point out, Handel sometimes borrowed themes from his compositions. There is, perhaps legitimately, a tone of irritation in some of Mattheson's later writings about Handel, but this attitude did not begin with Handel's later success. It started with head-to-head competition between the two young composers in Hamburg.

Given the abrupt departure of Keiser and his acceptance of a commission for an opera from the court of Weissenfels, the opera house at Hamburg faced the difficulty of mounting the next season. Plans were already under way for a production of a new opera by Keiser, who left without completing his setting, and in order to make use of the sets and costumes that were in preparation, a composer had to be found who would compose a wholly new opera to the same libretto. Mattheson, who was finishing his score of *Cleopatra* for a premiere in October 1704, couldn't take on a second opera in the same time frame, so the raw newcomer was approached to compose his first opera, *Almira*. Keiser's departure, therefore, opened up opportunities for the young Handel, but it also caused tension between Handel and Mattheson. One evening in December, during a performance of *Cleopatra*, Handel refused to cede his position at the harpsichord to Mattheson (who was accustomed to taking over the direction of the opera after the death of his character onstage). When the two later met in the street, they drew their swords, and Handel was spared injury only because Mattheson's thrust was obstructed. Although the two men related the story some-what differently (Handel's version survives through Mainwaring), their accounts are similar enough to conclude that the event actually happened.[11] One difference in detail is worth mentioning. Whereas Mattheson wrote that his opponent's life was preserved because his sword broke on Handel's metal coat button, Handel claimed that it was a musical score he carried in his pocket that protected him. These descriptions are not mutually exclusive. Assuming that Handel had secured the score under his coat, perhaps pages from his very own composing score of *Almira*, its thickness would have served as a shield, even if the sword tip hit his coat button first. Handel's focus on the talismanic score emphasizes the narrative behind all the anecdotes he told of his youth. Not only did he see himself destined for a career in opera, but he now felt his very life had been preserved by music. Fol-lowing this happy outcome, the two men reconciled and continued working closely together.

Handel's *Almira* premiered shortly afterward, on January 8, 1705, when the composer was only nineteen. Mattheson sang the leading male role in this work, as well as the title role in Handel's next opera, *Nero*, also performed in 1705. Within the year, however, the lives of the two musicians would significantly change: Mattheson gave up his operatic career, and Handel left Germany for Italy. While in Hamburg, Handel had received an invitation to travel to Italy from a prince of Tuscany, identified by Mainwaring as Prince Ferdinando de' Medici, a known musical patron. More likely, the invitation came from Ferdi-nando's brother, Prince (later Grand Duke) Gian Gastone, who was in Germany at the time. Although the invitation to Florence gave Handel the impetus to travel to Italy, he declined the offer to join the prince's entourage. Rather, following the example his family had provided, he chose to make the journey independently—or, as Mainwaring put it so colorfully, "on his own bottom."[12] The lesson in Berlin, the entrepreneurial approach taken by his father and half-brother, and his own stubborn self-determination now began in earnest to play a role in Handel's career decisions. Over the next fifteen years or so, as he moved through Italy to Hanover and on to London in 1710, his engrained image of how a career should be formed helped to govern his actions while he depended on (and needed) the support of multiple patrons.

Having received an invitation from one of the Tuscan princes, Handel may have made Florence his first destination, but there is no trace of a specific route and neither is there any firmly documented compositional work from the middle of 1705 to the end of 1706. Instead, he spent a lot of that time absorbing the Italian style by studying, listening, and performing, and his early reputation in Italy was built on his virtuoso keyboard playing. While in Florence, he must have collected the "libretti," or "little books" containing the text, that were sold at opera performances: his operas *Radamisto*, *Rodelinda*, *Scipione*, *Sosarme*, *Ariodante*, and *Berenice* all derive from the librettos of operas performed in Florence between 1706 and 1710. In Venice, Handel, wearing a mask, was immediately recognized when he sat down to play the harpsichord as "either the famous Saxon [referring to Handel's birthplace in German Saxony] or the Devil."[13]

By late 1706 or early 1707, Handel was in Rome, where his virtuosity so stunned an aristocratic audience at his first public appearance that some, suspicious of his German Lutheran background, suggested there was magic attached to his hat.[14] He remained in Rome until early autumn, when he returned to Florence for the performance of *Rodrigo*, the first opera he composed in Italy.[15] He was then back in Rome for a similar stretch of months in 1708, taking time out to travel to Naples as the result of a specific commission from Aurora Sanseverino, Duchess of Laurenzana, to compose music for the wedding festivities of her niece. Mainwaring's dependence on oral sources is delightfully clear in his identification of Handel's Neapolitan patron as "Donna Laura," which must be how an Englishman heard the name Donn'Aurora—perhaps especially when spoken with a thick German accent. Handel's relatively

2.2 Lodovico Carracci, *The Dream of Saint Catherine of Alexandria* (courtesy of the National Gallery of Art, Washington, DC)

brief sojourn in Naples resulted in the composition of the serenata *Aci, Galatea e Polifemo*; two trios for soprano, alto, and bass (the same set of voices used in the serenata); and a group of solo cantatas.[16]

The majority of Handel's surviving music from Italy was composed during the many months of 1707 and 1708 when he resided in Rome, where his patrons included the marquis (later prince) Ruspoli and the cardinals Pamphilj, Colonna, and Ottoboni. It may be that Handel first met the painter Joseph Goupy, who would become one of his closest friends, under the auspices of Ottoboni's patronage. In later years, Goupy stated that he had spent "near seven years in Rome and abroad studying."[17] Given that he returned to London by 1711, he must have arrived in Italy before Handel, but their time in that country overlapped significantly, and the catalogue of paintings Goupy offered for sale in 1765, four years before his death, included a work identified as "*St. Catherine's Dream*, very capital, from Cardinal Ottobani's Collection" by "Ludovico Carracci."[18] This has to be a replica by Goupy, whose creation of unique copies of masterworks from prestigious collections was one of his greatest strengths and an important source of his income. As Carracci's original only came to London in 1798, Goupy's copy of the painting, based on his own identification, places him explicitly in Palazzo della Cancelleria, where Ottoboni resided, in the same period as Handel.[19]

If Handel and Goupy did meet in Rome, London would have been one of their topics of conversation. Handel's interest in that city had been awakened in Hamburg, and one can imagine the composer peppering Goupy with questions. Could we listen in on their conversation, however, we might be surprised to hear them speaking in French. German was not a language Goupy would have known, but French was the language of his family heritage. Handel at this stage did not know English; he made a point of learning it only after his first London visit. But his education had given him French, the true lingua franca, and the great majority of his surviving letters to his family in Germany are written in that language. After some years in Italy, Goupy and Handel probably also spoke Italian well, if not fluently. In the letter of introduction written for Handel by Prince Ferdinando de' Medici in 1709 when the composer was on the brink of leaving Italy, the prince notes Handel's "full command of several languages."[20]

In 1708 Ottoboni commissioned the great architect Filippo Juvarra to build a theater in his palazzo, a project that would have attracted both Handel and Goupy to the Cancelleria. However, a papal ban on staged performances in Rome between 1698 and 1710 meant that Handel wrote no operas for Rome. Instead, his Roman music includes his first two oratorios: *Il trionfo del Tempo e del Disinganno* (The Triumph of Time and Truth [the Undeceiver]), based on a text by Pamphilj in 1707, and *La resurrezione,* lavishly produced by Ruspoli in 1708.[21] A commission from Cardinal Colonna in 1707 resulted in an important group of Latin liturgical pieces, notably *Dixit Dominus,* and for a number of patrons Handel composed cantatas for solo voices and small instrumental ensembles based on Italian love poetry, in some cases written by his patrons.

Handel left Rome in the autumn of 1708 and did not return to the city during the remainder of his Italian journey. He traveled north, probably returning to Florence and Venice. The culmination of his Italian sojourn was the triumphant production of his opera *Agrippina* at the Teatro San Giovanni Grisostomo, the largest and most elite opera house in Venice, at the very end of 1709. Mainwaring wrote that "the theatre, at almost every pause, resounded with shouts and acclamations of *viva il caro Sassone!*"—that is, Long live our favorite Saxon![22]

It is not clear when Handel made the decision to leave Italy. He was "pressed very closely" on the matter of conversion to Catholicism, but these efforts only resulted in "confirming him still more in the principles of protestantism."[23] It isn't likely he ever planned on making a career in Italy. While there, he depended on Italian patronage and was housed in grand style, sometimes having "a palazzo at command."[24] However, Handel was never employed officially by any patron. Rather, maintaining his independence, he composed music in return for hospitality, and even before the performance of *Agrippina,* he had announced his decision to seek his career elsewhere: Prince Ferdinando's letter to the court of Innsbruck on Handel's behalf is dated seven weeks before the premiere. Handel traveled to Innsbruck early in 1710, drawing on Ferdinando's letter of introduction, but Prince Karl wrote back to Ferdinando that the composer had not needed his assistance. It may be

Ra Vrbinas jnu.   *N. Dorigny del. a Sculp.*

Sol

Planetarum medius et maximus. Domus ejus Leo.

2.3 *Sol* (Apollo), one of a series of eight prints of "The Seven Planets, and the Creation of Sun and Moon" by Nicholas Dorigny, based on the mosaics by Raphael in the Chigi Chapel in Santa Maria del Popolo, Rome (© Victoria and Albert Museum, London). Handel owned a copy of this set, probably from the time of his Italian journey.

that the only definite plan Handel had in mind during early November 1709 was to create as much of a success as possible in Venice with his opera. He knew that Venice attracted large numbers of foreign aristocrats for its art and music and could offer him many important English and German contacts.

Handel most likely visited Venice each winter he was in Italy for the opera season, which ran from Christmas to the beginning of Lent. Prince Ferdinando regularly traveled from Florence to Venice for the season, so Handel might have come annually as part of the Florentine circle. He was definitely in Venice for the performance of his *Agrippina* in 1709–1710, and the performance of Antonio Caldara's opera *La Partenope* in Venice during the 1707–1708 season leaves a trace in Handel's later setting from 1730 of a revised version of this text, suggesting that he was present that season as well and acquired the libretto at that time. If so, Handel may have met Charles Montagu, Fourth Earl of Manchester and British ambassador extraordinary to Venice. Although Manchester's official mission was to establish an alliance between Venice and Britain in the current European wars, his greater interest, it seems, was opera. At the end of the 1707–1708 season he wrote to the duchess of Marlborough that music had been "much in his thoughts," having "been in the midst of it all this winter, where there has been ten operas."[25] Manchester imported a number of Italian artists to England for the purpose of establishing a first-rate opera in London. In 1708 he sent ahead the castrato Nicolini (Nicola Grimaldi), whose singing and acting ability revolutionized the English taste for Italian opera. Later, in 1711 and 1715, Nicolini created the title roles in Handel's operas *Rinaldo* and *Amadigi*. On his own return to London later in 1708, Manchester brought with him the painters Marco Ricci and Giovanni Antonio Pellegrini, both well known for their operatic set designs. They were immediately engaged at the Queen's Theatre in the Haymarket, and may have prepared sets for some of Handel's early London operas.

Handel probably had met Ricci in Italy. It is thought that Ricci assisted his uncle Sebastiano in work at the Palazzo Marucelli for Prince Ferdinando in Florence between 1706 and 1707, when Handel was at this court, and that he may have visited Rome in 1708, when Handel was in that city, in order to study Juvarra's design of the theater for Cardinal

Ottoboni. Ricci's center of activity, however, was Venice, where he could have met Handel during the 1706–1707 or 1707–1708 season.

Ricci exerted a strong influence on Joseph Goupy. He was especially admired for his landscape paintings and caricatures, as well as for theatrical sets, and Goupy modeled himself on Ricci in all of these areas. Like Handel, Goupy may have met Ricci in Rome or in Florence. Just as the librettos Handel collected indicate some of his movements in Italy, the copies of paintings that Goupy later sold in London help to trace his Italian travels, and his multiple reproductions of *The Triumph of Galatea, with Acis Transformed into a Spring* by Luca Giordano, place him in Florence.[26] In 1710, after quarreling with his colleague Pellegrini in London, Ricci returned briefly to Italy, but moved back to London with his uncle Sebastiano Ricci in 1711, according to one authority, "in order to put Pellegrini out of business." He stayed in London until 1716.[27] Goupy and Ricci remained close friends until Ricci's death in 1730.

Without listing all the acquaintances Handel made in Italy, it is clear enough that he was collecting not just librettos but also personal contacts. He subsequently engaged singers and musicians whom he had met and worked with in Italy for the London stage, among them Margarita Durastante, who had sung the title role in Handel's *Agrippina* and had been the principal singer in Ruspoli's household. In Venice, Handel met Baron Kielmansegg, the deputy Master of the Horse to Georg Ludwig, Elector of Hanover (later George I of Great Britain). Their conversations must have led Handel to visit Hanover, arriving in that city in June of 1710 after passing quickly through Innsbruck. On June 4, 1710, the elector's mother, the dowager Electress Sophia, wrote to her daughter that the court was being entertained "by the music of a Saxon who surpasses everyone who has ever been heard in harpsichord-playing and composition" and that "he is going to Düsseldorf to compose an opera there." Ten days later, however, she was able to report that the elector had hired Handel as his Kapellmeister—that is to say, as his court composer.[28]

The terms of Handel's employment in Hanover need to be reconstructed.[29] According to Mainwaring's narration, Handel accepted the position at Hanover with the stipulation that he be allowed the liberty to fulfill "the promise he had actually made to visit the court of the Elector Palatine" in Düsseldorf and "the resolution he had long taken to pass over into England, for the sake of seeing that of London," and that, as a result, the elector immediately gave the young composer "leave to be absent for a twelve-month or more, if he chose it; and to go whithersoever he pleased."[30] Many years later in London, Handel may have told the story this way for a variety of reasons, but it provides a rather one-sided and improbable account of the agreement.

As a result of the British Act of Settlement of 1701, the dowager Electress Sophia of Hanover, the granddaughter of James I by his daughter Elizabeth and first cousin to James's grandsons, Charles II and James II, had been named heir to the throne of Great Britain. After James II vacated the throne during the Glorious Revolution of 1688, he was immediately succeeded by the Protestant daughters of his first marriage: first Mary (jointly with her husband, William, Prince of Orange) and then Anne, the reigning queen from 1702. The Act of 1701 ensured a continued Protestant succession by rejecting the blood claim to the throne of James II's Catholic son by his second marriage, James, who, following the death of his father in that year, had publicly been proclaimed James III of England by King Louis XIV of France. This legislative legerdemain—Sophia was fifty-sixth in the line of succession, behind fifty-five Catholics who ranked higher—not only aggravated tensions between Protestants and Catholics but also aggrieved those Protestants who believed strongly in the divine right of kings—as opposed to having them chosen by parliamentary election. Those who resisted the Hanoverian succession were called Jacobites in reference to the Latin for James, and throughout the first half of the eighteenth century, they sought to reinstate the direct descendants of James II.

Handel, although he may not have known all these details, surely knew that his new employer, Georg Ludwig, Elector of Hanover, was second in line to the British throne after his mother. Given his determination to travel to London, this knowledge may have been part of what attracted him to Hanover in the first place. Moreover, Handel's interest in England offered the elector a special opportunity, and he must have eyed the young composer closely to gauge his potential to serve the Hanoverian court abroad.

Because of his place in the succession, the elector had a great interest in the affairs of the London court and also in reports that circulated in London about Hanover. He was, however, dependent on envoys, for Queen Anne opposed having the electoral family take up residence in London during her lifetime. Georg Ludwig took care to monitor his London representatives closely. In 1707, for example, he sternly censured a former employee of his mother for attempting to negotiate separately for the dowager electress, making it clear that only those ministers who were "instructed in my intentions" would be allowed to represent the Hanoverian court in London.[31] It is extremely doubtful, therefore, that he would have permitted Handel, who from the outset was publicly identified as "the famous Mr. *Hendel*, a Retainer to the Court of *Hanover*, in the Quality of Director of his Electoral Highness's Chapple," to travel to London without providing specific instructions. Most likely, Handel traveled to London with orders from the elector, having been "instructed" in his "intentions" and chosen to carry out specific diplomatic tasks.

Surprising as this may sound, the composer-diplomat was a common fixture of eighteenth-century courts. Composers typically had facility in multiple languages, and their musical gifts gave them access to private areas of court not open to other ministers. Handel's predecessor at Hanover, the composer Agostino Steffani, had assumed diplomatic obligations for that court as early as 1693. Indeed, the use of artists as informants reaches back centuries and perhaps still continues to have currency: recently released files (August 14, 2008) of the Office of Strategic Services (the predecessor of the Central Intelligence Agency) reveal that many celebrities, including Julia Child, Noël Coward, and Sterling Hayden, gathered intelligence for the United States during World War II.[32] Handel was a strong candidate for such a position. He already knew

German, Italian, and French, and he had learned court etiquette from his father and half-brother. Ferdinando de' Medici clearly recognized the composer's suitability for a diplomatic post; he described Handel in his letter of introduction firstly as a man of "honest sentiments, civility of manners, and full command of several languages," and only secondly as "a talent more than mediocre in music."[33]

Whatever the specific terms of Handel's employment, the one thing they did not include was the freedom "to be absent for a twelve-month or more, if he chose it; and to go whithersoever he pleased." Handel arrived in London sometime during the autumn of 1710, and on his return to Hanover in June of 1711, after stopping in Düsseldorf to fulfill an earlier promise, he was concerned enough about being delayed to bring with him a letter addressed to his employer from the elector palatine at Düsseldorf, Johann Wilhelm.

> Most Illustrious etc., Your Highness,
>
> I have kept Capellmeister Händel, who will kindly hand over to you this note, for a few days here with me, in order to show him several *Instrumenta* and other things, and to learn his opinion of them. Therefore I entreat your Highness herewith, with cousinly cordiality and earnestly, that you may deign not to interpret amiss this delay, occurring against his will, and not to lay it to his charge, but to grant him your continuing grace and *protection*, even now as hitherto.
>
> I am again, etc.,
>
> D[üssel]dorff 17th June 1711

Indeed, the infraction seems to have been of such significance that the elector palatine sent a second letter to Electress Sophia to entreat her intercession on Handel's behalf with her son, so that he "may be yet again established and *retained* in the grace and protection of his Prince Elector."[34] The letters did their job. As soon as Handel returned, he received his full salary for the year (1,000 taler).

Although his acceptance of a court position at Hanover, and its requirement for his presence at a specific time, might indicate that Handel had succumbed to exactly the kind of employment he had been inculcated to avoid, the diplomatic requirements of the position and the opportunity to be away from court for long stretches gave him the flexibility he desired. The full year's salary he received from Georg Ludwig, even though for the past seven months he had spent no time at, nor composed anything for, the Hanoverian court, underscores the special nature of Handel's appointment and helps to explain some of his actions on arriving in London.

3.1 Anonymous, portrait of Handel after Bartholomew Dandridge, c. 1725 (Fitzwilliam Museum, Cambridge, Object 693)

THREE

Politics, Patronage, and Pension

1710–1727
Birthday Ode for Queen Anne to Riccardo primo *for George II*

ONLY A FEW MONTHS after his arrival in London, Handel had the privilege of having his music performed at court when the queen's birthday was observed on February 6, 1711, "with great Solemnity."

> The Court was extream numerous and magnificent; the Officers of State, Foreign Ministers, Nobility, and Gentry, and particularly the Ladies, vying with each other, who should most grace the Festival. Between One and Two in the Afternoon, was perform'd a fine Consort, being a Dialogue in *Italian*, in Her Majesty's Praise, set to excellent Musick by the famous Mr. *Hendel*, a Retainer to the Court of *Hanover*, in the Quality of Director of his Electoral Highness's Chapple, and sung by *Cavaliero Nicolini Grimaldi*, and the other Celebrated Voices of the *Italian* Opera: with which Her Majesty was extreamly well pleas'd.[1]

It is now known that this account by the journalist Abel Boyer is garbled: the birthday ode in "Her Majesty's Praise" was a dialogue in *English* by Nahum Tate that was composed by John Eccles, and the Italian music

POLITICS, PATRONAGE, AND PENSION: *Timeline*

1701–1714	*1706*	*1708*	*1710*
War of Spanish Succession: allied forces, including the Holy Roman Empire (incorporating Hanover), Great Britain, and the Dutch Republic against France and Bavaria	*February 21* The British Enchanters premieres in London (revived 1707), a dramatic opera by George Granville, Lord Lansdowne (and a model for Handel's *Rinaldo*)	*September 9* Handel's serenata *Oh, come chiare e belle* commissioned by and performed for Prince Ruspoli (Rome) to celebrate Ruspoli's financial and military support of France and the Papal States against Austrian forces	*February (?)* Handel leaves Italy, traveling through Innsbruck, arriving in Hanover by early June *by June 14* Handel appointed Kapellmeister (master of music) to the elector of Hanover, heir to the British throne *autumn* Handel arrives in London as an employee of the elector of Hanover; Handel's serenata *Echeggiate, festeggiate!* performed *c. December* Handel and the impresario Heidegger visit Sir John Stanley, whose ten-year-old niece Mary Delany (née Granville) is living with them

by Handel, performed by Nicolini "and the other Celebrated Voices of the *Italian* Opera," was an entertainment within *The Jew of Venice*, a play adapted from Shakespeare's *Merchant of Venice* by George Granville, Lord Lansdowne, that was performed on the same occasion.[2] Nevertheless, the content of the report, even with its errors, is revealing. It shows that soon after his arrival in London, Handel had begun to collaborate with the performers of Italian opera there, including Nicolini (the castrato who had been brought to London by Lord Manchester) and, in the memories of at least some auditors at this important celebratory court event, his music effectively displaced that of Eccles, Master of the Queen's Music.

It is not clear what music by Handel was performed on this occasion. In the collected works of Lansdowne from 1732, the direction for the

1711

February 6
Handel's music (possibly excerpts from *Echeggiate, festeggiate!*) performed at court for the celebration of Queen Anne's birthday, probably incorporated into *The Jew of Venice,* a play by George Granville, Lord Lansdowne
February 24
Rinaldo premieres, Handel's first opera for London; scenario by Aaron Hill
May
Handel leaves London to return to Hanover

1712

summer
Handel writes (in French) to a German friend in London that he has "made some progress" learning English
autumn
Handel returns to London, still in the employ of the elector of Hanover

1713

January
Handel commissioned to compose a Te Deum and Jubilate to celebrate the Peace of Utrecht, a unilateral peace not supported by the elector of Hanover
February 6
Handel's *Ode for the Birthday of Queen Anne* (his first sustained work in English) performed at court
May 5
Peace of Utrecht officially declared
late May (?)
Handel fired from his Hanoverian position
July 7
The Utrecht Te Deum and Jubilate by Handel performed at St. Paul's Cathedral
July
Handel is told he will be "all right" when the elector comes to the throne of Great Britain and promises to continue telling the Hanoverian agent "all he knows"
December 28
Queen Anne grants Handel an annual pension of £200

entertainment is for "a complete Concert of Vocal and Instrumental Musick, after the *Italian* Manner."[3] Handel's serenata *Echeggiate, festeggiate!* (Resonate! celebrate!) would seem to fit that description best. It is a large-scale serenata in Italian with orchestral accompaniment and definitely one of the first pieces Handel composed in England.[4] Given the length of the work, however, it could also be that excerpts were performed: Handel's alterations to his autograph (and its jumbled and incomplete survival) suggest that it was revised, and perhaps shortened, by him at some point after its initial composition.[5] Its text relates directly to the Spanish War of Succession, a conflict over the inheritance of the Spanish throne after 1700. France and the Electorate of Bavaria, known as the Two Crowns, supported the accession of Philip, Duke of Anjou and grandson of Louis XIV, while the Grand Alliance, including Brit-

Politics, Patronage, and Pension continued

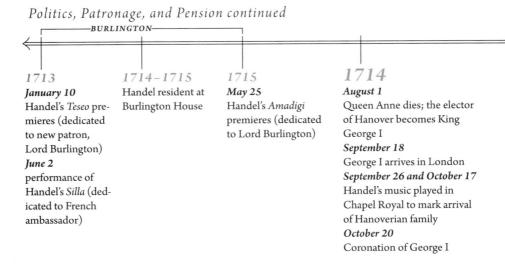

1713	1714–1715	1715	1714
January 10	Handel resident at	**May 25**	**August 1**
Handel's *Teseo* pre-	Burlington House	Handel's *Amadigi*	Queen Anne dies; the elector
mieres (dedicated		premieres (dedicated	of Hanover becomes King
to new patron,		to Lord Burlington)	George I
Lord Burlington)			**September 18**
June 2			George I arrives in London
performance of			**September 26 and October 17**
Handel's *Silla* (ded-			Handel's music played in
icated to French			Chapel Royal to mark arrival
ambassador)			of Hanoverian family
			October 20
			Coronation of George I

ain, the Holy Roman Empire (House of Habsburg), the Dutch Republic, and most of the German states (including Hanover), supported the Habsburg claimant, Charles, younger son of Emperor Leopold I. The war was fought by land and sea across much of Europe (but not Britain) with major military confrontations in the Spanish Netherlands, Germany, Hungary, France, and Spain, and naval battles in the Mediterranean. Italy, too, was drawn into the war because of territorial disputes between Austria and Spain, as well as by alliances of various Italian courts with either France or Austria.

Handel already had firsthand experiences of this war. When he traveled from Hamburg to Italy in 1705 or 1706, he must have planned his route in part to avoid active fighting, and while residing in Italy, he needed to be mindful not only of military action but also of the loyalties of his patrons. More than once he was called upon to compose works relating to the war. Most obviously, his serenata *Oh, come chiare e belle* (Oh, how clear and beautiful), written for performance in Rome on September 9, 1708, celebrates his patron Ruspoli by name for the recruitment and financing of a regiment to support Pope Clement XI in his defense of Ferrara against Austrian forces. Handel himself was clearly not a partisan; even in Italy he seems to have gone back and forth between patrons of different allegiances. When he arrived in England and was asked to

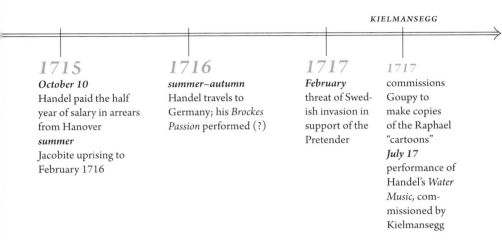

KIELMANSEGG

1715
October 10
Handel paid the half
year of salary in arrears
from Hanover
summer
Jacobite uprising to
February 1716

1716
summer–autumn
Handel travels to
Germany; his *Brockes
Passion* performed (?)

1717
February
threat of Swed-
ish invasion in
support of the
Pretender

1717
commissions
Goupy to
make copies
of the Raphael
"cartoons"
July 17
performance of
Handel's *Water
Music,* com-
missioned by
Kielmansegg

set texts relating to the war (on the opposing side from Ruspoli's regiment, but on the same side as his employer, the elector of Hanover), it
must have seemed a familiar subject. All of the music he wrote for Queen
Anne refers directly to this European conflict.

By 1710, English support for the war was waning, and efforts were
under way to find a peace settlement. Great hope had accrued to the
negotiations at the Hague in 1709, but although Louis XIV had been
willing to cede the Spanish throne to Charles, he was not willing to
use his own army to oust his grandson. On this point, the negotiations
foundered, and the war continued. Handel's serenata *Echeggiate, festeggiate!* celebrates allied victories and looks forward to an end to the war. It
brings together various Olympian gods and goddesses who continually
rejoice, "Charles alone is King of Iberia." Jupiter announces an end to
warfare, declaring that the Grand Alliance will rule the world and that
the "French Titan" (Louis XIV) and his Spanish allies "must bend their
necks to my commands." The final movements contain encomiums to
the "valorous champions" who fought successfully for a peaceful outcome, but, at the birthday celebration especially, Anne's dual role as conqueror and peacemaker could have been implied in such lines as "lovely
peace and noble piety shall reign *here*" and "Show me where there is a
single corner of the world which does not utter *your name* with admira-

Politics, Patronage, and Pension continued

┌─DUKE OF CHANDOS─┐   ┌─────────────ROYAL ACADEMY OF M

1717–1718	1718	1719	1720
Handel at Cannons estate of James Brydges (later Duke of Chandos); composes "Chandos Anthems," *Acis and Galatea,* and *Esther*	*early* Chandos buys Goupy's copies of Raphael cartoons from Kielmansegg's widow	*July 27* Royal Charter for establishment of the Royal Academy of Music *November 30* Handel appointed "Master of the Orchester"	*April 24* John Percival qualifies himself as a director of the Royal Academy by taking Oaths of Allegiance, Supremacy, and Abjuration, after obtaining a Sacrament Certificate

tion and rejoicing" (emphasis added).[6] Similarly, in the text of the Birthday Ode by Tate, an end to the war is imagined, now as a direct result of the power of "the gracious Morn, the Holy-day of Nature," Anne's birthday: "Europe bless the Royal Day, / All your Storms are blown away."[7]

It was at the queen's request that *The Jew of Venice* was presented as part of the birthday celebration: the play had first been performed in 1701. Handel would have encountered its author, George Granville, Lord Lansdowne, an uncle to Mary Delany (née Granville), at the birthday celebration, but given that his music was being incorporated into the play, replacing the entertainment Lansdowne himself had written for the original production—the masque of *Peleus and Thetis* set to music by Eccles—he could have met and worked with the playwright during preparations for the event. In fact, Handel had first paid his respects to the Granville family months earlier by calling on Sir John Stanley, commissioner of customs and secretary to Lord Chamberlain (whose office regulated the London theaters). The purpose of this visit, which Handel made together with the Swiss impresario Johann Jakob Heidegger (who had been overseeing the production of Italian opera in London since 1707), must have been to help pave the way for Heidegger to produce an opera by Handel.

Stanley was married to Anne Granville, Lansdowne's sister, who

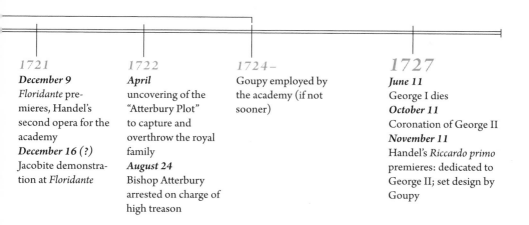

1721
December 9
Floridante pre-
mieres, Handel's
second opera for the
academy
December 16 (?)
Jacobite demonstra-
tion at *Floridante*

1722
April
uncovering of the
"Atterbury Plot"
to capture and
overthrow the royal
family
August 24
Bishop Atterbury
arrested on charge of
high treason

1724–
Goupy employed by
the academy (if not
sooner)

1727
June 11
George I dies
October 11
Coronation of George II
November 11
Handel's *Riccardo primo*
premieres: dedicated to
George II; set design by
Goupy

before her marriage had served as maid of honor to the previous queen, Mary II. Another sister, Elizabeth Granville, was currently serving as maid of honor to Queen Anne. The ten-year-old Mary Delany had lived with her aunt and uncle Stanley since 1708 in order to be groomed for a similar court position, and she later described Handel's visit.

> In the year [17]10 I first saw Mr. Handel who was introduced to
> my uncle Stanley by Mr. Heidegger, the famous manager of the
> opera, and the most ugly man that ever was formed. We had no
> better instrument in the house than a little spinnet of mine, on
> which the great musician performed wonders. I was much struck
> with his playing, but struck as a child, not a judge, for the moment
> he was gone, I seated myself to my instrument and played the best
> lesson I had then learnt; my uncle archly asked me if I thought
> I should ever play as well as Mr. Handel. 'If I did not think I
> should,' cried I, 'I would burn my instrument!' such was the
> innocent presumption of childish ignorance.[8]

Heidegger was an important contact for Handel to have made. At least by the late 1720s, the impresario was residing at Barn Elms (modern-day Barnes), about four miles southwest of Kensington. The local community there was known for its support for the Protestant succession, and as a Swiss Protestant Heidegger could have been drawn to the neighborhood for that reason. Similarly, the area would have offered Handel, as a Hanoverian retainer, a congenial environment, and he is said to have lodged here in 1712 and 1713.[9] The two men could have been introduced there, or they may have met through theatrical contacts in London. Handel had much to offer Heidegger in his quest to satisfy and increase the demand for Italian opera in London.

Although their sympathies and allegiance were more naturally aligned with the Protestant succession and therefore the Whig Party, Handel and Heidegger needed to solicit support and patronage from members of the governing Tory Party in order to fulfill their hope of producing an opera. This explains their visit to Sir John Stanley. Perhaps reflecting deference to the Granville family, who were ardent Tories and able to open doors for the pair, Handel's first opera, *Rinaldo*, produced only eighteen days after his music had been performed at court in conjunction with Lansdowne's *The Jew of Venice*, appears to have been modeled, at least in part, on Lansdowne's most successful theatrical work, the English opera *The British Enchanters*. Set to music in 1706 by John Eccles and Bartholomew Isaack, Lansdowne's play had been revived as recently as 1707 (and possibly again in 1710).

Rinaldo represents a milestone in Handel's career, and its libretto and staging deserve close attention. (A more detailed discussion follows in the next chapter.) It premiered at the Queen's Theatre in the Haymarket on February 24, 1711. Aaron Hill, manager of the Queen's Theatre since the previous year, prepared the scenario in English; Giacomo Rossi, the librettist, translated it into Italian and operatic format. It was standard practice for opera texts to be printed and made available for sale in advance and at the theater, and as we have seen, Handel collected such librettos in Italy. In London, where operas were not performed in the language of the audience, these librettos (or wordbooks) were particularly important, providing both the Italian text of the opera and an English translation. The libretto of *Rinaldo* includes a full English synopsis of the story:

Godfrey, General of the Christian Forces in the Expedition
against the *Saracens* [non-Christian Arabs], to engage the
Assistance of *Rinaldo* a famous Hero of those Times; promises
to give him his Daughter *Almirena*, when the City of *Jerusalem*
shou'd fall into his Hands. The Christians with *Rinaldo* at their
Head, conquer *Palestine*, and besiege its King *Argantes* in That
City. *Armida* an *Amazonian* Enchantress, in Love with, and
belov'd by *Argantes*, contrives by Magick, to entrap *Rinaldo*
in an Enchanted Castle, whence, after much Difficulty, being
deliver'd by *Godfrey*, he returns to the Army, takes *Jerusalem*,
converts *Argantes* and *Armida* to the Christian Faith, and Marries
Almirena, according to the Promise of her Father *Godfrey*.[10]

While the original source of the plot is the Italian Renaissance epic *Gerusalemme liberata* by Torquato Tasso, the magic elements of the story are
modeled on *The British Enchanters*. A comparison of the scenic requirements of Lansdowne's opera and *Rinaldo* shows that Hill largely based
the magic scenes in Handel's opera on the specific machinery available
to him at the Queen's Theatre and used in the earlier work. In *The British
Enchanters,* the sorceress Arcabon enters in a "Chariot . . . swiftly drawn
by Dragons"; in Hill's *Rinaldo* the sorceress Armida enters "in a Chariot drawn by two huge Dragons." Both dramas contain "a dreadful Host
of Spirits" (*Rinaldo*) that "descend in Clouds" and "continue in the Air"
(*British Enchanters*) or "rise and fill the Stage" (*Rinaldo*), as well as dae-
mons, dreadful monsters, dark clouds, fire, smoke, and a shape-changing
sorceress.

Lansdowne considered magic and spectacle essential to the success
of opera, making a statement to this effect in the collection of his works
published in 1732:

The nature of this [operatic] Entertainment Requires the Plot to
be formed upon some Story in which Enchanters and Magicians
have a principal Part: In our modern Heroick Poems, they supply
the Place of the Gods with the Ancients, and make a much more

natural Appearance by being Mortals, with the Difference only of being endowed with supernatural Power.[11]

Hill stated the same view in *Rinaldo*'s libretto, maintaining that to be successful in England opera needed to make use of magic and spectacle, and that the lack of "Machines and Decorations" in previous London productions of Italian opera had meant that those works had "been heard and seen to very considerable Disadvantage":

> At once to remedy both these Misfortunes, I resolv'd [in *Rinaldo*] to frame some Dramma, that, by different Incidents and Passions, might afford the Musick Scope to vary and display its Excellence, and fill the Eye with more delightful Prospects, so at once to give Two Senses equal Pleasure.

In the operas Handel wrote shortly after *Rinaldo*, the use of fantastic scenes and machines and the availability of specific machinery in the Queen's Theatre continued to play an important role. The chariot drawn by fire-breathing dragons reappears both in *Teseo* for Medea (1713) and in *Silla* (a privately performed opera, discussed later in this chapter) for Hecate (1713). Furies appear in *Rinaldo*, *Teseo*, and *Amadigi* (1715). In both *Rinaldo* and *Silla*, a principal character is conveyed offstage in a rowboat, and a cloud machine is used in *Rinaldo*, *Teseo*, *Silla*, and *Amadigi*. Only *Il pastor fido* (1712) eschewed such effects, and, as Lansdowne or Hill could have predicted, it was the least successful.

Rossi, who prepared the Italian text of *Rinaldo*, claimed that Handel composed the opera in two weeks. This statement, although it may be exaggerated, nevertheless indicates the speed at which the production was put together. Word of Handel's abilities had preceded his arrival in London, and "many of the nobility were impatient for an Opera of his composing."[12] The performance of a work by Handel by singers from the opera house, on the queen's birthday, must have added enormously to the buzz. The artistic collaborators undoubtedly wanted to capture this interest while it was still at its peak, and they did. The only problem was that the time limit placed by the elector on Handel's visit to London was running out, and the looming deadline was probably one reason for the artists' haste.

The letters of the elector palatine of Düsseldorf (quoted at the end of the previous chapter) excusing Handel's tardiness in returning make clear the seriousness of that deadline. Not only would Georg Ludwig have expected his employee to be punctual, but he also would have been eager to hear firsthand what the composer had witnessed and learned in London. Because Handel needed to return to Hanover, the thirteenth presentation of *Rinaldo* on May 9 was advertised as the last of the season. The opera, however, had not yet outrun audience interest. In the end, it was presented twice more, on May 26 and June 2, after Handel's departure from London. The demand for more performances coupled with Handel's impending absence left the position at the first harpsichord vacant and must have necessitated the preparation of a new score for the person replacing him.[13] An agreement dated May 5 lays out the cost of this score as £26 and shows that all was in train to continue performances without the composer present.[14]

Assuming that Handel left London shortly after May 9, he could have made his way to Düsseldorf, by means of a North Sea crossing to Rotterdam and then down the Rhine, in about three weeks, depending on the weather conditions. The elector palatine's letters excusing Handel's stopover in Düsseldorf are dated June 17, but this gives a misleading sense of the chronology. Britain and continental Europe followed different calendars, Britain adhering with Protestant stubbornness to the old "Roman" Julian calendar long after most of Europe had made the conversion to the modern "Catholic" Gregorian calendar. Although many European countries had been using the Gregorian calendar for more than a century and most had converted by 1700, Britain held out against it until 1753. Thus, for most of Handel's life in London, there was an eleven-day difference between Britain and the Continent. The letters from Düsseldorf dated June 17 were written on what was June 6 in London. If Handel left London shortly after the performance on May 9, he could have arrived in Düsseldorf in early June (in the British calendar), and visited for the "few days" mentioned by the elector palatine in his letter to Hanover of June 6/17 (as dates are given when showing both calendars).

When Handel finally arrived back in Hanover, his account of London probably sparked the elector's interest in having him return, and Handel himself, apparently concluding that he would return sooner rather than later, set about improving his English. In July, he wrote (in French) to a fellow German musician in London, Andreas Roner, expressing his desire to set to music a poem in English by John Hughes, reporting, "Since I left you, I have made some progress in that language."[15] Roner contacted Hughes and offered to forward to Handel whatever the poet wanted to send. Handel's only English cantata, *Venus and Adonis*, has a text by Hughes and can be connected to these months Handel spent in Hanover. By autumn of 1712, however, Handel was back in London, apparently charged with remaining close to Anne's court.

In February 1712, during the year of Handel's absence from England, the music for the celebration of the queen's birthday had not been a new work, but "an excellent Consort collected out of several *Italian* Operas" put together by Nicolini and performed by him with other singers from the opera. Very probably the selection drew on one of the latest and most popular of operas, *Rinaldo*. Given that Handel's music had been heard at the queen's birthday for two successive years, it is not surprising that soon after his return to London, Handel was asked for a new composition to celebrate the queen's birthday in 1713. There was an important difference, however. The text he was given to set, "Eternal Source of Light Divine," would mark his first work in English for the court. Unlike his later practice, Handel did not date the autograph, so there is no accurate guide to the period of composition. He seems, however, to have taken time to study the text carefully and to examine models of English musical odes by John Eccles and the late Henry Purcell. It is difficult to imagine that he could have succeeded so well in this first outing in English without serious preparation.

The text of the Birthday Ode is by the poet Ambrose Philips (1674–1749). Philips himself never acknowledged authorship, but Charles Jennens, the librettist of Handel's *Messiah,* among other works, attributed it to him in the margin of his personal copy of Mainwaring's biography, and the attribution is credible.[16] Like *Echeggiate, festeggiate!* and Eccles's Birthday Ode from 1711, it celebrates an impending peace in the War of Spanish Succession, again giving Queen Anne credit for bringing it to fruition. Laid out in seven stanzas of four lines followed by the two-line refrain, "The day that gave great Anna birth, / Who fix'd a lasting peace on earth," the Ode's first four stanzas call upon the different parts of nature to sing Anne's praises, moving from the sun, to the birds of the sky, the lambs and wolves together, and the rolling streams and wild meadows. The last three focus more on Anne herself, asking that "kind Health" descend upon her, that "Envy" conceal itself, and that "united nations" rejoice together.

The birthday celebration took place on February 6, 1713, at St. James's Palace even though the queen was ill: documents attest to her being carried into the Great Presence Room. It has been suggested, given the queen's illness, that performance of the Ode was postponed for a year to 1714, but that year the queen's birthday was celebrated at Windsor, and payment records clearly indicate that the music was once again by Eccles.[17] After 1713, Handel's Birthday Ode was not heard again in the composer's lifetime. It had been written as an occasional work, and any opportunity for additional performances died with Anne on August 1, 1714.

The vivid depictions of nature and descriptions of actions played to Handel's strengths, and his score announces his musical and dramatic sensitivity at the outset. Eschewing the typical opening symphony (though an independent instrumental movement or work could have prefaced the work in performance), Handel begins directly with a fanfare initiated by the countertenor and repeated by trumpet. There is some wit in setting the long opening flourish to the word "eternal," but maybe, more seriously, the movement was meant to provide an immediate sign of Handel's knowledge and respect for the genius of Henry Purcell (1659–1695). Known as the "Orpheus Britannicus," the late Purcell was considered the epitome of English composers, and foreign musicians were well advised to pay homage. When Handel's compatriot Johann Sigismund Kusser arrived in London in 1704, he kept a list of do's and don'ts to assist him in acclimating to his new cultural surroundings. One of these read: "Praise the deceased Purcell to the skies and say there has never been the like of him."[18] The opening movement of the Birthday Ode may have been both Handel's public obeisance to Purcell and a sign of his independence. He could have borrowed the general sound and shape of this movement from the interior of Purcell's Ode for the sixth birthday of Queen Anne's son, William, Duke of Gloucester (1695), "Sound the trumpet and beat the warlike drum."[19] If so, he then deployed these features in a very unusual way, by using them in the opening movement. Purcell's standard practice was to begin with a symphony, and when he side-stepped this convention, as in his Welcome Ode for James II (1685), the rarity was tied to the text: "Why are all the Muses mute?" And even here, the symphony was not omitted but simply displaced to second position, its signal to start also cued by the text: "Awake, 'tis Caesar does inspire."

In distinct contrast with the Purcellian examples, there is no narrative basis for Handel's choice to forego a symphony and open with a vocal flourish, but his setting of the word "eternal" reaches beyond simple text-painting to create the sense of a summons to attention imbued with a hint of military signal. Martial overtones, however, are quickly dissolved in the dancelike setting of the refrain celebrating Anne's peacemaking, first for countertenor solo and then for chorus. The musical setting of the first stanza and refrain, therefore, ingeniously depicts the general trajectory of the peacemaking, from military preparations to joyous celebration. Thereafter, each stanza is presented by one or two soloists in a distinct stylistic idiom. In "Let all the winged race," Handel uses a favorite technique of a pervasive, rhythmic motive in the accompaniment that releases the voice to more lyrical motion. Here the motive is a quick, repeated pattern of three descending notes played by treble instruments untied from the underpinning of the bass, first heard in threefold repetitions, but later in longer passages moving both up and down, representing the fluttering of beating wings. "Let rolling streams" makes use of a rollicking four-measure bass pattern (Handel's facility with a repeating bass again demonstrating his ability with a very Purcellian idiom), while "Kind health descends" presents a lilting pastoral, and the fast tempo and rushing scales of "Let Envy then" for bass voice approaches the style of an operatic rage aria. Although every stanza ends with the same textual refrain, Handel, in a stunning shift from convention, chooses not to repeat his musical setting but rather recomposes it each time in the style of the preceding stanza, waiting until the final refrain to bring in a return of the original setting. Indeed, the continually different settings of the identical refrain text are so distinctive that Handel's nineteenth-century editor, Friedrich Chrysander, felt the need to provide a different German translation for each one. It is almost as if in Handel's hands not only all of nature but also the whole range of Baroque music sings in praise of Anne.

Even before this wonderfully vibrant piece could be performed, however, another royal commission came Handel's way. If, as seems likely, his instructions from the elector were to penetrate Anne's court, he must have been particularly gratified when the queen asked him, rather than one of her English musicians, to compose the Te Deum to celebrate the Peace of Utrecht as part of a national day of Thanksgiving. The Hanoverian envoy Thomas Grote was so pleased that he independently authorized an extension of Handel's time in London, as he reported to the elector in a letter of January 13, 1713:

> My lord Bolingbroke told me in the name of the queen that Her Majesty had commissioned Your Highness's Kapellmeister, Handel, to compose a piece of music for her. Because she would like him to remain here until this is done but has found out that Your Highness's permission for him to remain here has come to an end, I would like to inform Your Highness in confidence that Her Majesty wishes Handel to remain here for a while. I have promised that with pleasure and herewith report, as I didn't doubt that Your Highness would be pleased that one of your servants would have the honour of serving Her Majesty in some

way. This music is, as I understand, a Te Deum, which shall be sung in St Paul's Cathedral when peace is proclaimed, and more than a hundred musicians are going to be employed for this.[20]

Handel finished the Te Deum on January 14 and probably completed the Jubilate after the queen's birthday. The finished work was publicly rehearsed at St. Paul's on March 5 and 7, and at the Banqueting House at Whitehall on March 19, affording repeated opportunities to present what was planned for performance "on the Day of Thanksgiving," and to promulgate both the composition and the peace.[21] Once the peace was officially proclaimed on May 5, preparations for the thanksgiving increased, including further rehearsals. Georg Ludwig, who strongly opposed Britain's unilateral peace with France, could not have been pleased with the prospect of his own composer being used to celebrate its success. Shortly after the official proclamation in May, he took the only step he could to separate himself and Hanover from the thanksgiving service. He fired Handel, effective immediately.[22]

More savvy than his envoy, Georg Ludwig seems to have recognized that the choice of Handel to compose the music for the thanksgiving service was a political maneuver on the part of Bolingbroke or the queen herself. The elector had privately urged the queen not to negotiate unilaterally but to work in concert with the allies, and at an earlier stage he even had taken his case to the public in memoranda published in British newspapers, such as that in the *Daily Courant* on December 5, 1711:

Nothing but a perfect Union between the Allies while the general Peace shall be treating, and the mutual Guarantie they shall give each other upon what shall therein be concluded, can secure them for the future . . . 'Tis not doubted therefore, that her Britannick Majesty proposes to act in this whole Affair joyntly and in Concert with her Allies, conformably to the Assurances which she has given them. But to banish all Distrust, it would be necessary that there should be no secret Negociation, which might give Ground for Suspicion that one or other of the allies

might make their own Treaty . . . And this way [of working in
Concert] appears to his Electoral Highness to be more sure
for procuring this End [of peace], and for preserving such
Advantages, than if Great Britain should endeavor it, without the
concurrence of the Allies, by a separate Negociation.

After Anne successfully pursued a separate peace nevertheless, her
choice of Handel, a servant of the court of Hanover, to write the Te
Deum implied an international accord that did not exist. The notion of
"united nations" combining to praise Anne for her peace-making, which
was explicit in the text of the Birthday Ode, was far from the truth.

As is clear from surviving letters, Handel was blindsided by his dismissal. When notified in a missive from Kielmansegg in Hanover of
his dismissal, he immediately contacted the Hanoverian resident in
London. Christoph Friedrich Kreyenberg was no music lover—as he
wrote to Georg Ludwig on June 5/16 (giving the dates in both calendars to clarify the timespan of the correspondence), "I will admit to you
frankly that Mr. Handel is nothing to me"—but he understood what was
at stake. He reported that he had advised Handel, who had found the
terms of his dismissal "mortifying," on what to write to Kielmansegg
in order "to extricate himself gracefully," and also gently reminded the
elector, in the guarded language of a diplomat, of Handel's value in
gathering information for Hanover, especially on the queen's health,
and in providing "stories" of the Hanoverian court to the English.
Although he was careful not to name him, it is from Kreyenberg that
we first learn of Handel's close friendship with the author and physician John Arbuthnot: "The queen's physician, who is an important man
and enjoys the queen's confidence, is his great patron and friend, and
has the composer constantly at his house." He was cautious to emphasize that the information Handel passed about Hanover only served the
purpose of supporting the Hanoverian position and Protestant succession (thereby assuring the elector that the composer was not also acting as an informant to the queen—although we cannot know whether
this was the case) by adding, "you understand the stories to which I

am referring." These reports, he wrote, were later "passed on to some serious ecclesiastical gentlemen, and this has a marvelous effect." He commented that Handel's information about the queen's health was very general—unnecessarily, as the elector would have known exactly what information had been passed. Once again, the statement was protection in the event of his letter being intercepted by English agents. He reported that "since His Highness was determined to dismiss him, Mr. Handel submitted to that wish, and that he desired nothing save that the affair be conducted with a good grace and that he should be given a little time here so that he could enter the Queen's service."[23]

The written response from Hanover has not survived, but on July 3/14, Kreyenberg wrote again. He acknowledged the elector's letters of June 19/30 and June 23/July 4, relieved that the elector had "finally received all of my letters." Having grasped Kreyenberg's point about how Handel might continue to be useful to the court of Hanover, the elector relented from cutting the composer off completely. Kreyenberg responded:

> I am pleased that you have written to me about Mr Handel. I had
> not expected that he would remain in His Highness's service, nor
> was I considering that but merely the manner of his dismissal;
> I have done it in a way that he is quite content, giving him to
> understand that he is by no means in disgrace with His Highness,
> and dropping a few words to the effect that he will be quite all
> right when the elector comes here. He will continue to tell me all
> he knows.

The phrase "he will continue to tell me all he knows" is written not in words but in cipher code.[24]

The performance on July 7 of the Utrecht Te Deum and Jubilate at the Thanksgiving service in St. Paul's was in many respects Handel's compositional epiphany. He had previously achieved great success with operas in Hamburg and Venice, and his opera *Rinaldo* had been a hit in London during his first year there, but opera attracted a relatively small segment of the population, whereas the thanksgiving service was planned to capture the entire body politic within the cathedral: the monarch, lords spiritual, lords temporal, and commons. The sound in St. Paul's, as in most cathedrals, is very reverberant, and Handel accounted for it from the very opening of the Te Deum with loud, separated chords for strings and woodwinds followed by a soft, descending echo in the strings. The long, sustained notes on "we acknowledge thee," against the fabric of more active sound, would have resonated throughout the cathedral, as would the punctuated full-choral repetitions of "all" in "all the Earth doth worship thee," the reverberation emphasizing the meaning. In the softer sections for soloists, the contrapuntal intertwining would have wafted more gently to envelop the listeners, as in the opening of "Vouchsafe, O Lord, to keep us this day without sin." In the final movement of the Te Deum, the block, choral repetitions of the word "never" in "let me never be confounded" resound with absolute conviction, the music emphatically supporting Anne's peace. An attack of the gout prevented the queen herself from attending the service, but she surely was told of the music's powerful effect. The Utrecht Te Deum established Handel as an English composer, and his setting of the Te Deum became the template for English settings to follow. On December 28, Queen Anne granted Handel an annual pension of £200, essentially replacing what he would have received from Hanover had he not been fired.

That Handel successfully "entered the Queen's service" and received a handsome pension (allowance) without specific, attached obligations, was perhaps the single most important moment in his career, although he may not have known it at the time. When, in 1714, following the queen's death, the elector arrived in London as George I, Handel was, as Kreyenberg had told him in 1713, "by no means in disgrace with His Highness" and "quite all right." George not only continued Queen Anne's pension of £200, but in October 1715, saw to it that Handel received six months of salary from Hanover to cover arrears from the second half of 1712. In 1723, George added a further £200 to Handel's pension, along with the largely honorific court title of "Composer of Musick for his Majesty's Chappel Royal" (Handel was never given an official appointment

3.2   Engraving of Richard Boyle, Third Earl of Burlington and Fourth Earl of Cork (1734) by John Faber, Jr. , after portrait by Sir Godfrey Kneller, Bt (© National Portrait Gallery, London, NPG D33107)

in the chapel). Around the same time, Handel was appointed music master to the elder children of the prince of Wales (later George II) for still another £200, a position he also held for life, despite the "children" growing up and in some cases moving away.[25] Handel's annual receipt of £600 from the Royal Treasury gave him freedom to experiment artistically and freed him from the necessity of restrictive patronage (employment), affording him the unusual opportunity to become entrepreneurial later in life. In the 1740s, it played a role in his ability to dispense altogether with subscriptions and to rely exclusively on box office receipts.

In mid-1713, however, Handel must have been concerned for his future. In his first two years in London, his primary obligation had been to his patron and employer, Georg Ludwig. Having been dismissed by the elector, and not yet having entered the queen's service, he was without patron and without income. One revenue stream he had pursued, however dubious it may have been, was opera on the London stage, and this would have become more important to him following his dismissal. *Il pastor fido* had premiered in November 1712, the libretto based on a pastoral drama of the same name by the Renaissance poet Giovanni Battista Guarini. It was prepared for Handel by Giacomo Rossi, the librettist who had prepared the Italian text of *Rinaldo*, but unlike that opera, it lacked magic and enchantment and did not please the public. Working with a new librettist, the Italo-German cellist Nicola Haym, Handel next turned to the mythological story of Theseus and Medea, adapted by Haym from a text previously set to music by the French composer Jean-Baptiste Lully. Like its French model, but unlike traditional Italian opera, Handel's *Teseo* is in five acts. With its inclusion of magic and spectacle, it found more favor with the London audience, receiving thirteen performances between January and May of 1713. More important, perhaps, it marked the beginning of Handel's relationship with a new patron, Richard Boyle, Lord Burlington, to whom it was dedicated.

Burlington, who succeeded to his title in 1704 on the death of his father, was only nineteen years old in 1713. His artistic patronage, which would later become highly celebrated, was now in its infancy. Handel, who had first experienced the dynamic nature of the patronage system in Italy, where an interrelated set of patrons supported him and gave him access to the highest levels of music making, would have understood the necessity of harnessing the system in London as well, even before he was fired from the elector's service. By choosing to dedicate *Teseo* to Burlington, Handel signaled his interest in the young lord's patronage. He may have secured introductions from colleagues and acquaintances who had connections to artists already in Burlington's circle, among whom were the authors John Gay and Alexander Pope. Both Pope and Gay were close to Dr. Arbuthnot, at whose home the Hanoverian resident Kreyenberg reported Handel as being at "constantly." The three men formed the core of the literary Scriblerus Club that took shape in 1714 and also included Jonathan Swift and Robert Harley, First Earl of Oxford. Arbuthnot, therefore, is a likely point of contact between Handel and the Burlington circle. It also may be that Handel's association with Aaron Hill, with whom he collaborated in the creation of *Rinaldo*, and who had been a schoolfellow of Gay and was serving as Gay's literary mentor in London, helped smooth the composer's entry into this group.

Goupy, too, could have played a role. After returning to London in 1711, Goupy immediately set about seeking patronage. Unlike Handel, he did not arrive in London with a salaried appointment, or with introductions to the highest levels of court. However, his uncle Lewis Goupy was Burlington's artistic adviser, and there may have been further connections to Burlington House for both Goupy and Handel through Marco Ricci, who also had returned to London in 1711. Between 1711 and 1715, while Antonio Pellegrini, with whom Ricci had collaborated in London, and Ricci's uncle Sebastiano Ricci executed large canvases for the entry hall and staircase of Burlington House, Marco Ricci resumed designing sets for the opera, probably including some of Handel's. From May 1714 to May 1715, Burlington made his first grand tour to the Continent accompanied by Goupy's uncle Lewis. It was in Paris during this trip that Burlington purchased *Belisarius Receiving Charity*, then attributed to Van Dyck, which Joseph Goupy later copied for a number of patrons, including John Hedges, treasurer to Frederick, Prince of Wales; Edward Harley, Second Earl of Oxford; and, finally, for Prince Frederick himself. This last copy survives in the Royal Collection.

Handel became more intimate with Burlington's circle of artists after *Teseo*. His next opera *Silla*, dated in the libretto June 2, 1713, is dedicated

3.3 Joseph Goupy, *Belisarius Receiving Charity* (1747) after Luciano Borzone (Royal Collection Trust / © HM Queen Elizabeth II 2012 [OM 565])

to the French ambassador, Louis Marie d'Aumont de Rochebaron, and may have been commissioned by Burlington in d'Aumont's honor. By 1714 Handel was probably living in Burlington House: *Amadigi*, which premiered in May 1715, includes in the libretto a dedicatory address to Burlington, stating that "this Opera more immediately claims Your Protection, as it is compos'd in Your own Family [household]." Like the earlier *Teseo*, its libretto was based on a French source.

The coincidence of Burlington's patronage of Handel with increased French connections in Handel's operas suggests a political position. Queen Anne had successfully negotiated peace with France, and the sudden shift of Handel's librettos to French sources in *Teseo* and *Amadigi* and his composition of an opera dedicated to the French ambassador in *Silla* illustrate how artistic work could potentially serve a specific alliance. The French interest, however, was not wholly supportive of Britain's aims. It opposed the Hanoverian Protestant succession and promoted instead the Stuart bloodline to the throne. Louis XIV had recognized James II's son as the true British king in 1701 (James II having died), and, despite the Utrecht peace agreement of 1713 having obliged France to recognize the Hanoverians and cease harboring the Stuart claimant, the French remained sympathetic to James's claim to the throne, and the Jacobites maintained their political center in Paris. At least some of the London populace, not surprisingly, saw the French ambassador as a representative of "James III." A contemporary witness described "the Rabble" greeting the ambassador with a cry of "No Papist, No Pretender" ("Pretender" being the name given to "James III" by supporters of the Protestant succession). Burlington himself may have supported James's claims.[26] Certainly some of those associated with his patronage circle did: following the Jacobite uprising in 1715, Pope, a Catholic, who was openly accused of Jacobitism, fled London, as did Jonathan Swift; Lord Oxford was arrested and sent to the Tower. Among Handel's contacts, the Granvilles, too, were supporters not just of Queen Anne but of a Stuart succession. Following George I's accession in 1714, Mary Delany's father was imprisoned briefly, and the family barely managed to flee London for Gloucestershire. Lansdowne (George Granville), a leader of the Jacobite Party, was in 1715 charged with high treason and sent to the Tower, where he spent eighteen months; in 1720, he fled to Paris and became a leader of the party in exile there.

It would be a mistake to consider Handel a political innocent, but it is impossible to know the extent of his knowledge or awareness. In the libretto of *Silla*, Handel was still (for the last time) identified as Master of Music at the Hanoverian court, yet one of the ways the story of the opera can be read is as a scurrilous attack on his employer, Georg Ludwig. The elector had divorced his wife, Sophia Dorothea, in 1694, and placed her under house arrest in Ahlden Castle (where she died thirty-two years later); it was well known that he had mistresses, and anti-Hanoverian propaganda suggested that he kept his two Turkish servants "for abominable uses," an accusation of homosexuality.[27] Similarly, the Roman emperor Silla, as described in Handel's libretto, "divorced many wives without cause" and "led a dissolute and lascivious life." The historical Silla had both male and female lovers, and in Handel's opera the mute character of Scabro, *"Favorito di* Silla," may indicate a homosexual attendant (the name itself implying licentious and indecent [scabrous] behavior). Even more important to the political moment, however, the opera opens with Silla entering Rome by force and, not content with the title he has, declaring himself "Perpetual Dictator," a reference perhaps, from the Jacobite point of view, to the elector "imposing" himself on England and declaring himself king as a result of the planned Protestant succession.[28] Even if those who chose the libretto understood the story in this way, however, it was only one of multiple possible interpretations. The factionalism of the period encouraged artistic works that allowed audience members on both sides to read them their way and authors to deny readings that could be deemed treasonous. If questioned on the meaning of *Silla*, for example, one could always say that the dictator represented James III, who would impose Catholicism on British Protestants and that his resignation of the crown pointed to the success and security of the Hanoverian succession.

Silla was produced on June 2, at about the same time Handel received notice of his dismissal—Kreyenberg's first letter to the elector about the firing is dated June 5. Handel's Hanoverian position had probably played a role in the decision to choose him as composer for this opera, just as it had when he was asked to write the music to celebrate Queen Anne's peace. In the case of the Utrecht Te Deum, his participation falsely associated Hanover with the peace process; in the case of the opera it might simply have been a delicious (or malicious) joke, having the Hanoverian Master of Music engaged in what was potentially an anti-Hanoverian story. Perhaps it was all in a day's work for an eighteenth-century composer to accept whatever commissions came his way. If, however, Handel was continuing to tell the Hanoverian envoys "all he knows," a condition Kreyenberg stated he had negotiated with the composer, then his employment by Jacobite sympathizers could have been a benefit to Hanover in terms of information, regardless of what texts he was given to set. In any case, Handel could not have been oblivious to political innuendo. One cannot help wondering what role he played, and what role he saw himself playing, in the three-cornered political struggle between Anne Stuart of England, Georg Ludwig of Hanover, and James Edward Stuart, the "Old Pretender" in France, when in 1712 and 1713 he was working simultaneously under the patronage of the queen, the elector, and Lord Burlington.

Whatever the political maneuverings swirling around him, Handel may have assumed, given the outcome of Kreyenberg's negotiations following his dismissal, that his career would be secure after the accession of George I. At first, this seemed to be the case. His music was performed at the church services in the Chapel Royal at St. James's Palace following the arrival of the royal family in 1714, the king continued the pension of £200 given him by Anne, and his operas were successfully holding the stage. Handel's level of activity both at court and for the public, however, quickly waned. In the second half of the 1710s opera productions were significantly curtailed, partly because of political uncertainty over the future of the government following the Jacobite uprising in 1715, and no new operas were commissioned from Handel between 1716 and 1720. Further, any notion that he would be taken up by the new king as the primary composer at court was quickly quashed. In Anne's court, it had been at least in part for political reasons that Handel had at different times supplanted the Master of the Queen's Music and the Composer to the Chapel Royal. George I also needed to consider political circumstance. Whereas Anne had found it expedient to employ the composer of the Hanoverian court, George I, as a foreign ruler, found it necessary to limit the number of Germans in his service. Although he welcomed Handel's music in the opening days of his reign, the king then turned away from his former employee to the English composer William Croft, official Composer to the Chapel Royal. Handel was not asked to compose again for the Chapel Royal for eight years.[29] On July 17, 1717, however, a lavish party was hosted by George I on the River Thames, and Handel was asked to supply the music.[30]

According to the traditional account, the performance of Handel's *Water Music* was arranged in an effort to repair the relationship between

Handel and George I soon after the latter's arrival in England (suppos-
edly because Handel had overstayed his leave in London).[31] Given our
knowledge of Handel's formal dismissal by the elector and the secret
arrangement for his continued diplomatic service, such a construction
of the historical situation can no longer be sustained. Handel actively
participated in services honoring the newly arrived king, and, moreover, the king quickly saw to the continuation of Handel's royal pension.
Further, the occasion on which the *Water Music* was played occurred in
1717, three years after the king's arrival. It may be that Handel preferred
to tell the story of the *Water Music* this way rather than speak openly of
the role he had played as informant to the Hanoverian court. Nevertheless, the elimination of the king's arrival as a possible date for the *Water
Music* does not necessarily exclude the reason typically given for its
composition as a means of reconciling the king to Handel. Baron Kielmansegg, who repeatedly appears at critical junctures in Handel's relationship to George I, oversaw the musical arrangements for the water
party. Perhaps he commissioned Handel's music specifically to restore
the composer's good relations with the king after a misunderstanding
about his loyalty. Given the political situation in 1717, such a concern
could have arisen on account of Handel's continued association with
suspected Jacobites who were part of Burlington's circle. Given the timing, it may also have resulted from the growing breach between the king
and his son, the prince of Wales.

Letters written from Hanover when Handel was first employed in
1710 emphasize the enthusiasm of Prince George and Princess Caroline,
rather than the elector, for Handel's music. Once George I mounted the
throne, the tension that had existed between him, as heir to the throne,
and Queen Anne, shifted down a generation to the new monarch and
heir. In Britain, the first public manifestation of this tension appeared
in spring 1717, when a break occurred between the king's men and an
opposition party headed by the prince. Possibly, during the years when
he was not commissioned to write for the court, Handel had begun
once again to associate closely with the prince and princess, leaving an
impression that he had aligned himself with their party. If something

like this occurred, then Kielmansegg may have commissioned Handel to compose the music for a planned water party in order to bring Handel's music again within earshot of the king. Two days after the event, *The Daily Courant* reported on "the finest Symphonies, compos'd express for this Occasion, by Mr Handel; which his Majesty liked so well, that he caus'd it to be plaid over three times in going and returning." Any rapprochement that may have occurred between the king and Handel, however, seems to have been only of the moment. No commissions were forthcoming from the court.

Meanwhile, and perhaps as a direct result of the instability created by the Jacobite uprising, a number of Burlington's circle, including Gay and Pope, as well as Handel's friends Dr. Arbuthnot and John Hughes, can be found outside London in 1717 at the estate of James Brydges, Earl of Carnarvon (created Duke of Chandos in 1719) at Cannons, near Edgware. Handel's presence there can be documented from August 1717. Although Chandos himself was never officially accused of being a traitor to the crown, he assisted Lord Bolingbroke, who afterward became secretary of state to the Pretender in Paris, in his flight from England early in 1715. Bolingbroke's approach to the Hanoverian agent in 1713 about Handel composing the Utrecht Te Deum and Jubilate, in a move that was sure to anger and embarrass the elector, suggests that even before the succession he had found ways to express his antipathy to the Hanoverian succession. In the aftermath of his successful escape from prosecution, a parliamentary commission created to identify collaborators prominently lists his friend Chandos by all three of his names: Brydges, Carnarvon, and Chandos.[32]

The anthems Handel wrote in Cannons, commonly called the Chandos Anthems, were written for the earl in 1717 and 1718 (before he became duke of Chandos). Handel also composed his first English oratorio, *Esther*, and the pastoral masque *Acis and Galatea* at Cannons in 1718, the texts of these pieces having been prepared collaboratively by Pope, Gay, Arbuthnot, and Hughes. *Esther* tells the Old Testament story of the deliverance of the Jewish community in Persia from a sentence of death. As presented in the libretto, Haman, the evil minister of King Ahasuerus, threatens to annihilate the Jews in Persia. Esther, the wife of the king, is, unknown to the king and his minister, of the Jewish faith. She bravely reveals her identity, whereupon the king acknowledges the loyalty of the Jewish population, honors Esther's cousin and guardian Mordecai for having previously saved his life, and punishes his minister Haman with death. The mythological story of *Acis and Galatea* tells of the death of Acis at the hands of his rival in love, the monster Polyphemus. Both of these dramatic texts can be read at face value, but they also, like *Silla*, offer the flexibility of multiple, allusive readings.[33] The *Esther* story could relate to Pope's situation as a Catholic and suspected Jacobite, and suggest, by analogy to the situation of the Jews in Persia, that Catholics, and perhaps even Jacobites, should as true patriots be spared condemnation. The story of *Acis and Galatea* could be understood politically as George I and James III competing for the hand of Britain (Galatea). Characteristically, given the plasticity of such readings, the question of whether the monster represented the Hanoverian or the Stuart would have been left open to the audience to determine, whatever the opinions of the artists or patron might have been.

During the years 1717 and 1718, when Handel provided music for Chandos and, through the auspices of Baron Kielmansegg, composed the *Water Music* for the king, Goupy moved in exactly the same circles. "Sometime before 1717," according to the artist, he was employed by Baron Kielmansegg to make copies of the seven tapestry designs ("cartoons") depicting events from the New Testament by the Renaissance artist Raphael, which were owned by the royal family and displayed in a special gallery at Hampton Court Palace.[34] After Kielmansegg's death in late 1717, Chandos bought the copies from Kielmansegg's widow and further commissioned from Goupy, as an eighth piece to the set, a copy of a New Testament painting by the seventeenth-century artist Poussin. In an age before photoduplication, artists could make a good living by providing first-class copies of work by earlier artists, and Goupy's work was especially prized. He reported receiving £220 for the seven Raphael copies he made for Kielmansegg, and Kielmansegg's widow did even better in selling them to Chandos for fifty guineas each (£357).[35]

In some respects there is a loose parallel between the practice of making copies of artistic masterworks and the creation of opera in this period. That is, composers typically provided new settings of librettos that had been previously set to music by other composers (as was the case for all of Handel's London operas except *Rinaldo* and *Silla*). The libretto for *Esther* is based on a play by the seventeenth-century French playwright Jean Racine, just as Goupy's paintings for Chandos were based on Raphael and Poussin. In all these cases, then, the duke affirmed his connoisseurship by associating himself with great works by renowned artists of the past through the mediation of younger, contemporary artists. If Handel's dramatic works for Chandos were presented in staged versions, as some commentators suggest, then Goupy, since he was already working for the duke and was probably experienced in set design, may have provided whatever painted backdrops were needed. If so, he most likely based these, like his paintings, on previous artistic masterpieces.

Goupy is known to have made copies of at least two paintings on the subject of *Acis and Galatea*, even though both probably postdate the Cannons performance: A "Galatea after [Annibale] Carracci" appears in the posthumous auction catalogue of Goupy's work,[36] and the *Triumph of Galatea, with Acis Transformed into a Spring* by Luca Giordano, from Burlington's collection, was copied by Goupy for Edward Harley (who had succeeded to the title of second earl of Oxford in 1724) in 1726.[37] It is impossible to gauge how many finished copies Goupy painted of either work, as he frequently produced multiple copies of a single painting (at different prices): Goupy charged Harley £31 10s. for his copy of Giordano's *Galatea* (as we learn from the bill dated March 26, 1726) and some years later for a copy of the same work charged his patron John Hedges £42.[38] The paintings by Goupy of scenes related to Handel's dramatic works often followed the productions, and may have been made as an archival record. Although they do not prove that he was involved in the creation of the original set designs, especially given that his specialty was in making copies of others' work, they are nevertheless suggestive of his participation. Further examples include Goupy's paintings of *Mutius*

3.4 Letter (1728) of Joseph Goupy to Cox Macro (© The British Library Board [Add. MS. 32556, f. 170ʳ])

Scaevola, relating to the opera of 1721 (for which Handel contributed the third act), and his miniatures of *Angelica and Medoro*, relating to Handel's *Orlando* of 1733.

Goupy stated that by 1719 he was easily able to earn £600 annually. This was a princely sum; by comparison, a building craftsman in 1750 might have expected to earn about £26 a year.[39] Contemporary documents attest to the breadth of Goupy's patronage at this time, not only from Kielmansegg, Chandos, and Oxford but also from the dukes of Devonshire and Rutland, Lord Cowper, and "severall persons of Rank & Quality." Goupy's employment by Kielmansegg for George I included "severall pictures," as well as "small pictures on Snuff Boxes." Dr. Cox Macro, a patron and correspondent of Goupy, stated that "George I had so great an esteem for him that when he came to Court, he sent him frequently Dishes from his own Table & ordered he should be served with the same Wine he used to drink of."[40]

The historian John Hawkins, writing at the end of the eighteenth century, placed Handel at this time in exactly the same circle of patrons:

> For some years after his arrival in England his time was divided between study and practice, that is to say, in composing for the opera, and in conducting concerts at the duke of Rutland's, the earl of Burlington's, and the houses of others of the nobility who were patrons of music, and his friends. There were also frequent concerts for the royal family at the queen's library in the Green-Park, in which the princess royal, the duke of Rutland, lord Cowper, and other persons of distinction performed; of these Handel had the direction.[41]

With his patronage from Burlington, Kielmansegg, Chandos, and others, as well as his £200 pension from the Royal Treasury, Handel would have been equally well off financially, and he used some of these earnings to support his mother in Halle. In a letter to his brother-in-law, written in February of 1719 (in French), Handel expressed "astonishment" that a letter of exchange (in effect, a bank transfer) that he had sent to a "merchant at Magdeburg" had not yet been honored. Despite the financial opportunities offered by private patronage, however, steady employment was not, and had never been, Handel's goal. His focus now was fixed on establishing himself in London as an opera composer. In the same letter to his brother-in-law, he explained that he had been detained in London "by affairs of the greatest moment, on which (I venture to say) all my fortunes depend."[42] The "affairs" resulted in the founding of an academy for the performance of Italian opera in London.

By royal charter dated July 27, 1719, George I formally established the Royal Academy of Music for a period of twenty-one years, granting it an annual subsidy of £1,000 for five years. Both Lord Burlington and the duke of Chandos subscribed £1,000, as did the earl of Manchester, whom Handel had met in Venice. Handel's friend Dr. Arbuthnot, and the Hanoverian resident, Kreyenberg, each committed £200. The duke of Rutland was a subscriber. At the time of its founding, the academy's board of directors numbered fourteen, including Heidegger, Arbuthnot, and Burlington. Already in mid-May, Handel had been ordered to travel to the Continent to hire singers, and in November, he was appointed "Master of the Orchester with a Sallary." The composers Attilio Ariosti (1666–1729) and Giovanni Bononcini (1670–1747) were approached to write operas for the academy.[43] Although Handel himself is never mentioned in this capacity, he, Bononcini, and Ariosti became the three resident composers.

Unlike most of the operas Handel had previously set for London, the "Academy Operas" eschewed epic poetry and spectacular effects. They focused instead on stories from history, often dealing with issues of succession that had particular relevance to the current political situation in Britain. *Floridante*, the second opera Handel wrote for the academy, provides an example. Based on a preexistent libretto and rewritten for the academy by the Italian poet and librettist Paolo Rolli, it had a good first run in 1721 and was revived by Handel in 1722, 1727, and 1733. In the original libretto on which Rolli's text is based, the setting is Norway; the rightful king and his family have been murdered, and the usurping tyrant has raised the late king's only surviving descendant as his own younger daughter.[44] The general of the tyrant's army, a Swedish prince, having been promised this daughter in marriage, has arrived in Norway following a military victory over France in expectation that the promise will be fulfilled. Instead, he receives orders to resign his post and leave the country. The king then summons his so-called younger daughter, reveals her true ancestry, and declares his own lustful desire for her. She rejects him as a murderous usurper. In the end, the tyrant is conquered.

When the daughter of the murdered king is declared queen of Norway, she raises her beloved Swedish prince to the position of king.

For a London audience this plot was perilously relevant. The Hanoverian succession continued to be opposed by the Jacobites. In 1717 there had been great concern about the king of Sweden having "projected to Land in England from Gottenberg with ten thousand men and to declare for the Pretender."[45] A libretto that dealt with succession, rightful heirs, usurpers, foreign princes, French opposition, and Swedish military strength might have been considered, in 1721, to border on sedition. Indeed, the plot line had already been "captured," as it were, for the Jacobites three years earlier. As some of those who supported the use of this text for London must have known, a setting of the same story had in 1718 been dedicated to James Stuart in Italy, thus rather openly associating George I with the usurping Norwegian king who is overthrown with the assistance of the Swedish general.[46] The choice of Handel, rather than one of his Italian colleagues, to compose a setting of this text in 1721 was perhaps a deliberate attempt by some within the Royal Academy of Music to paint the German composer, once again, on the anti-Hanoverian side. It is, of course, impossible to know what Handel thought when he was handed the libretto. He may have realized its potentially Jacobite slant, but he may have thought, or been persuaded, that having as the true heir a daughter who marries a foreign prince and invites him to rule jointly with her not only deflected any analogy from the Pretender but paralleled closely the rule of Mary Stuart, the elder daughter of James II, and her husband, the Dutch William of Orange, as joint monarchs at the Glorious Revolution in 1688, the antecedent for the Hanoverian succession.

The volatile political situation in London and the habit of London audiences to read political meaning into stage productions meant that there did not need to be an allegory in which individual characters represented specific living persons for a libretto to have political resonance: it sufficed for the libretto to contain situations analogous to current political events. And whether or not the authors intended an analogy, the audience was free to discover one. Thus, a plot set in such a geographically proximate country as Norway that included an ongoing war against France, raised enough concern for a decision to be taken to transplant the entire story away from Europe altogether. Opera-goers who attended the performances discovered that the action was now located in the Middle East. The usurping king became Persian (Iranian); his general came from Thrace (Turkey); and the conquered country (Tyre) lay along what is today the Lebanese-Syrian border.

Despite this global shift (pre-dating by more than 130 years the shift of Verdi's *Un ballo in maschera* from Sweden to Boston as a result of the Neapolitan censors' concern about a plot dealing with political assassination), there were those in the audience who saw (or were advised of) the anti-Hanoverian political analogy, and they mounted a factional demonstration during a performance. Dr. William Stratford, canon of Christ Church, Oxford, described the event (rather carefully and obliquely) in a letter of December 19, 1721, to Edward Harley (son of Lord Oxford, a known Jacobite who had been imprisoned in the Tower in 1715):

> Some things have happened at a new opera which have given
> great offence. It is called *Floridante*. There happens to be a right
> heir in it, that is imprisoned. At last the right heir is delivered
> and the chains put on the oppressor. At this last circumstance,
> there happened to be a very great and unseasonable clapping, in
> the presence of great ones. You will hear more when you come to
> town.[47]

In the opera, the usurper strives to absorb his change of station after he is shackled. "Che veggio? Che sento?" he sings (What do I see? What do I hear?). The instrumental introduction seems to depict him struggling in sporadic bursts against his chains, his loss of power vividly depicted by the fragmentation of the opening vocal line, and his different reactions, ranging from despair to anger, signaled with abrupt shifts of tempo. Stratford's letter suggests that at least some Jacobite sympathizers in the audience saw George I in this musical portrait, cheering the possibility of his being reduced to such a state once James was restored to the throne. Clearly the precaution of moving the action from Norway to Persia had not eliminated analogies to the current political situation for an audience both politically aware and active. In fact, the political plots of most of Handel's operas at the Royal Academy of Music in the 1720s place them squarely in the center of current political debates.

That politics invaded operatic texts was hardly surprising, given contemporary tensions. Indeed, the establishment of the Royal Academy of Music by royal charter meant that the directors were required to take the standard oaths of allegiance to the Hanoverian government, necessitating the oath-taker first to acquire a certificate of conformity by taking communion in the Church of England. There were three mandatory oaths: allegiance (to the reigning monarch), supremacy (of the monarch over any claims of the pope), and abjuration (of the Stuart claim to the throne). John Percival, who joined the board of directors of the academy in 1720, recorded his conformity in his summary of the year at the end of his 1720 letter-book, writing that on April 24:

> I qualified my Self for Directorship of the Royall Accademy of Musick, by takeing the Oathes this day at Guildhall before the Ld Mayor & Sr Wm Thomson Recorder, & then delivred into Court my Certificate of haveing taken the Sacrament at St James Church Westminster.[48]

At the time of *Floridante*'s premiere, the so-called Atterbury Plot to mount an invasion on behalf of the Stuarts was already in play, and the choice of this opera may be more closely tied to it than previously thought. That is, it may be that some of the directors (Burlington is one possibility) perjured themselves by hiding their Jacobite sympathies and taking the oaths dishonestly.[49] The plot was uncovered in April 1722, only a few months after *Floridante*'s premiere. Following the uproar the exposure created, the librettist Paolo Rolli and the composer Giovanni Bononcini, both Italian Catholic members of the creative staff who could have had an impact on content, left the academy, perhaps under pressure, but the performing musicians and set designers were not affected.

Goupy, although also a Catholic, definitely worked for the academy as a set designer some years after the Atterbury Plot, and he may have been employed from the outset. The directors had estimated in the first season the "scenes & Cloaths" would cost £1,000, but no designer was named. Goupy was well known to many of the directors, and he seems an obvious choice. As evidenced by his painting of *Mutius Scaevola*, he might have been involved in the production of *Muzio Scevola* (1721), an opera in which each act was written by a different composer. George Vertue, a contemporary engraver, art historian, and influential diarist of art and artists in his lifetime, places Goupy at the academy shortly afterward, recording that in 1724 "Mr P. Tillemans & Mr Jos. Goupee both jointly imploy'd to paint a Sett of Scenes for the Opera house in the Haymarket. Which were *much* approv'd of." The king's commission of Goupy to repair Andrea Mantegna's *The Triumphs of Caesar*, a set of paintings at Hampton Court, in 1725 could therefore be related to his contribution to Handel's opera *Giulio Cesare* (1724). In 1727, Goupy was specifically named as the set designer in the libretto of Handel's *Riccardo primo*:

La Musica è del Sig. Giorgio Fedrico Handel.
Le nuove Scene sono del Sig. Giuseppe Goupy.

In fact, *Riccardo primo* represents a sea-change. On June 11, 1727, George I died unexpectedly while abroad, bringing his son George II to the throne. George II and Queen Caroline were Handel's age, and from the time of his first employment in Hanover, Handel seems to have had a naturally close relationship with them. The new king chose Handel to write the anthems for his coronation service on October 11 at Westminster Abbey. This was something of an aberration, given that the English composer Maurice Greene had just been appointed organist and composer of the Chapel Royal in August 1727, but throughout his reign George II chose Handel to compose the music for all significant royal events. In his annotated copy of Mainwaring's biography, George III wrote of Greene that his grandfather George II had "forbad him composing the Anthems at his Coronation . . . and ordered that G. F. Hendel should not only have that great honour but except the 1st. choose his own words."[50] The music historian Charles Burney stated that Handel, upon being given words "by the bishops, for the anthems . . . took offence" and responded, "I have read my Bible very well, and shall chuse for myself."[51] If the initiative for Handel choosing his own texts truly came from the composer himself, then the king's ratification of this independence in addition to his preference of Handel above his appointed composer of the Chapel Royal speaks to the special relationship that continued between George II and Handel throughout the remainder of their lives. And with regard to the coronation, the king's confidence in Handel was not misplaced. The four Coronation Anthems are stunning compositions, at least one of them, "Zadok the Priest," having been sung at every British coronation since.

Riccardo primo, lavishly dedicated to George II only one month after his coronation, was a joint effort of Handel and Goupy. Since about 1706, when they both sought artistic enrichment in Italy, their professional journeys had overlapped in terms of the number of patrons they shared, including Cardinal Ottoboni, Lords Burlington and Cowper, Baron Kielmansegg, the dukes of Chandos and Rutland, and George I. The establishment of the Royal Academy of Music in London was a joint effort by many of those same patrons, and the double attribution to Handel and Goupy in the libretto of *Riccardo* marks the culmination of this period in which both men sought patronage and financial security. In another sense, however, it marks a fork in the road after which their career paths separated.

Although both had sought and received patronage in the same circles, and to a lesser extent continued to do so (both were later patronized, for example, by Henry Furnese, a subscriber to the Opera), Handel had somehow parlayed his employment and dismissal by the elector of Hanover into a substantial royal pension.[52] If Handel's success in obtaining a court position that allowed for entrepreneurial independence was the result of training passed on by his father and half-brother, it was a family legacy of great value. As a result, Handel did not need to seek service with a sole patron. He benefited as well from the umbrella patronage of and employment by the Royal Academy of Music. This also had its pitfalls. He could have been fired from the company, but then he would still have had his pension, which was indeed the case when the opera company failed in 1728: his income from the Royal Treasury gave him the time to regroup and start up a new company. Goupy, without such a pension, needed a more standard situation. After working for a broad patronage circle in the 1710s and early 1720s, he found steady employment with John Hedges, later treasurer to Frederick, Prince of Wales. When Hedges died in 1737, however, Goupy was left without the remuneration due him. Although he was able to move directly into the service of the prince, perhaps a path Hedges had prepared, Goupy lost both his patron and his income after Frederick died unexpectedly in 1751. He fell into poverty and died nearly destitute.

Handel and Goupy traveled in Italy during the same years, started their careers in London at the same time, and worked in the same patronage circles for many years, but, as a result of divergent circumstances, established their careers on different financial bases. Handel's pension allowed him to be more entrepreneurial as he faced repeated professional crises, and even to reject patronage. Goupy's patronage brought him increasing fame and wealth, but his financial security was totally dependent on the whims and, as it turned out, the lives of his patrons. A pension was not, of course, a guarantee of success, nor was patronage destined to failure, as many contrary examples could attest. Nevertheless, while Goupy remained in the closed arena of private patronage, Handel, protected by his pension, moved into London's burgeoning mercantile economy. His operas, bought and produced by the directors of the Royal Academy of Music, were transformed into performances and sold to subscribers and single ticket buyers. His professional success, therefore, depended not on pleasing a single patron but on a much wider, though still largely aristocratic, public.

4.1 Portrait of Handel attributed to Balthasar Denner, oil on canvas, feigned oval, 1726–1728 (© National Portrait Gallery, London)

FOUR

Commerce and Trade

1711–1730
Rinaldo *to end of Royal Academy*

IN EIGHTEENTH-CENTURY BRITAIN, the idea of the "East" was as much cultural as geographical, consisting of the Ottoman Empire (which included a good swath of North Africa), the Persian and Mughal Empires, and also Polish and Russian territories. Imaginatively, the East embodied an exotic Other, simultaneously alluring and dangerous. Commercially, it was the locus of natural and man-made products that could be sold in Britain and a potential market for British materials and merchandise. The prominence of the Middle East and Far East in Handel's operas and the depictions of Eastern seaports and cities in his art collection speak to the importance of the Orient in contemporary artistic and commercial thought, affecting financial investment, education, literature, and art, as well as popular tastes in decoration and design. While the choice of *Rinaldo* as the subject for his very first London opera demonstrates the fascination with the exotic, Handel's later Eastern operas for the Royal Academy of Music, including *Tamerlano* and *Riccardo primo*, can be closely tied to the commercial interests of the British East India Company.

From the moment he arrived in London, and regardless of any diplomatic assignments he may have undertaken, Handel pursued the

COMMERCE AND TRADE: *Timeline*

1711

February 24
premiere of *Rinaldo* (set in
Jerusalem), Handel's first opera
for London
June
Handel returns to Hanover
midsummer
Handel receives 1,000 taler, his
first year of Hanoverian salary
September 10
establishment of the South Sea
Company

1712

midsummer
Handel receives his second year
of Hanoverian salary
early autumn
Handel returns to London

1713

by May
Handel receives £186 7s. 11d.
for his work at the Queen's
Theatre (leaving more than that
outstanding)
June
Handel fired from his Hanove-
rian position

opportunity to compose an opera for the public stage. As we have seen,
he quickly connected with the impresario Johann Heidegger and sought
official backing from the Lord Chamberlain through his secretary, John
Stanley. He also must have taken advice on the most desirable subject
for an opera. In part, the success of *Rinaldo* resulted from the opportunities it offered for spectacle, its magical elements being closely modeled on *The British Enchanters* by George Granville, Lord Lansdowne.
Lansdowne's work also provided a model in its adaptation of an epic
tale of knight-errantry. Whereas *The British Enchanters* was based
on the Renaissance epic of *Amadis de Gaula* (but filtered through the
seventeenth-century French opera of *Amadis* by Jean-Baptiste Lully, a
source Handel would later use directly in his opera *Amadigi*), Handel's
Rinaldo was adapted from Torquato Tasso's epic, *Gerusalemme liberata*.
The decision to use the Rinaldo story was made by Aaron Hill, manager
of the Queen's Theatre. As he explained in the preface to the libretto:

1714

midsummer
Handel receives £100, first
half-year payment of pension
from Queen Anne
August 1
Queen Anne dies; the elector of
Hanover becomes King
George I

1715

ships sailing out of Ostend in the
Austrian Netherlands
begin to compete with the British East India Company
for trade
autumn (?)
establishment of Thomas
Weston's Academy in
Greenwich
midsummer
Handel receives £200, first
full-year payment of British
pension continued by George I
September–October (?)
Handel purchases £500 in South
Sea stock
October 10
Handel receives the half year of
salary in arrears from Hanover

1716

March 13 and June 29
Handel authorizes his South Sea
dividends to be paid to a third
party

I could not chuse a finer Subject than the celebrated Story of
Rinaldo and *Armida,* which has furnish'd OPERA'S for every
Stage and Tongue in *Europe.* I have, however, us'd a Poet's
Privilege, and vary'd from the Scheme of *Tasso,* as was necessary
for the better forming a Theatrical Representation.

After Hill wrote the drama, the Italian poet Giacomo Rossi "fill[ed] up
the Model" in the proper shape of an Italian opera. Hill then added an
English version of Rossi's verses.

The locus of the story in the Middle East provided a framework for
the spectacle, but it also offered an opportunity to capitalize on the growing imaginative interest in the East that was being fed by the journals of
English travelers and merchants and by the popularity of such Oriental
tales as *One Thousand and One Nights.* Hill himself had traveled widely
in the Levant, and his journey had taken him, among other places, to

Commerce and Trade *continued*

←———

1718
Handel's *Esther* (set in Persia)
performed at Cannons

1719
February
formation of the Royal Acad-
emy of Music
spring
Handel sells his South Sea stock
by this time
June (?)
Handel leaves for the Continent
to hire singers for the Royal
Academy
November 30
Handel appointed by the
academy as "Master of the
Orchester with a Sallary"

1720
April 27
Handel's *Radamisto* (set in
Armenia) premieres at the Royal
Academy
summer (?)
James Hunter enrolled at
Weston's Academy with his
cousin Charles Masters
September
collapse of South Sea stock after
its peak in August

Jerusalem, the setting of the opera. In 1709 Hill published a travel narrative of the countries he visited: *A Full and Just Account of the Present State
of the Ottoman Empire in all its Branches: with the Government, and Policy,
Religion, Customs, and Way of Living of the Turks, in General. Faithfully
related from a Serious Observation, taken in many years Travels thro' those
Countries.* The book offered, as Hill explained, lest the lengthy title was
not sufficient, a description of "The Present State of Æthiopia, Egypt,
the Three Arabia's, Palestine, and the Whole Ottoman Empire."

Hill's personal knowledge of Jerusalem gave him a solid geographical basis on which to build the opening scene of the opera depicting the
Christian assault on the city walls, while his historical and religious judg-
ments, which led him to grieve that the "Lands *of old,* possess'd by the
religious *Patrons of GODS Holy Doctrine,* should now be own'd by the
Defiling outcasts of Humanity, by Swarms of *Infidels,*" lent impetus and
support to the battle he depicted between the Christians and the Saracens. Donning the mantle of a modern-day Herodotus, he filled the *Full
and Just Account* with the stories and tales he heard on his journey as well
as firsthand observations. He allowed himself fantastical images of "dried
dead bodies . . . whisk'd like paper" and blown upon the unsuspecting

1721
December 9
Handel's *Floridante* (set in
Persia) premieres at the Royal
Academy
December 16 (?)
Weston's students perform the
play of *Tamerlane* (Nicholas
Rowe?)

1722
spring (?)
Weston's students repeat their
performance of *Tamerlane*
before the Lords of the Admiralty
December
formal establishment of the
Ostend East India Company
(Austria)

1724
February 20
Handel's *Giulio Cesare*
(set in Egypt) premieres
at the Royal Academy
October 31
Handel's *Tamerlano* (set
in Turkey) premieres at
the Royal Academy

traveler in a sand storm, and wrote of ghosts, hobgoblins, and apparitions that appear and disappear in the desert, leading the unsuspecting astray.

Hill's reported supernatural experiences served as background to the opera's fantastical scenes. Act I, scene vii, of *Rinaldo* contains the follow-ing stage direction:

They have drawn their Swords, and are making at each other;
when a black Cloud descends, all fill'd with dreadful Monsters
spitting Fire and Smoke on every side. The Cloud covers
ALMIRENA and ARMIDA, and carries 'em up swiftly into the Air,
leaving in their Place, two frightful Furies, who having grinn'd at,
and mock'd RINALDO, sink down, and disappear.

The event leaves Rinaldo in amazement and he "stands immove-able with his Eyes fix'd on the Ground." In his account of "Arabia *the* Desart," Hill previewed this theatrical scene. He described how "Christian Strangers . . . are sometimes miserably overtaken by the danger of a *Storm* . . . lifting Men and Camels from the *Desart*, or at least so fills the Air with Clouds of Sand, driv'n up and down by unre-

Commerce and Trade continued

1725
Spain agrees to support Austrian trade

1726
March 12
Handel's *Scipione* (set in Spain) premieres at the Royal Academy
May 5
Handel's *Alessandro* (set in India) premieres at the Royal Academy
August 12
Henry Lannoy Hunter, brother to James, apprenticed to the Levant Company in Aleppo

1727–1729
Anglo-Spanish War; siege of Gibraltar begins (February 1727)

sisted *Whirlwinds,* that the Wretched *Traveller,* quite blinded with their Fury, stands, *unknowing what to do."* And he asked the reader to try to imagine himself in this position, directly requesting the empathy he hoped to elicit from his theater audience with the staged depiction of Rinaldo's inaction and astonishment.

> Imagine, Reader, what a miserable State you wou'd believe
> your self reduc'd to, were you left alone, amidst the wild, and
> unfrequented *Sands* of these unmeasur'd *Desarts: Nothing*
> near you, nor within the reach of the most Sanguine Hope, but
> dreadful *Serpents,* unknown *Monsters,* and a thousand barbarous
> Enemies to *Nature* and *Humanity.*

Although Hill's personal experience of the East lay behind details of the opera's scenario, the underlying theme of the opera was one that Hill shared broadly with a wide spectrum of British society: a strong belief in the superiority of Western morality over Eastern treachery. Rinaldo is a fictional Christian hero in service to the historical figure of Godfrey of Bouillon (c. 1060–1100), whose tomb Hill had visited in Jerusalem, copying out its epitaph.[1] He travels to the East, where he faces disorienting apparitions and armed infidels. His successful conquest of Jerusalem

1727

May–June
Ostend East India Company officially
suspends trade; siege of Gibraltar halted
June 11
George I dies
October 11
Coronation of George II
November 11
Riccardo primo (set in Cyprus) pre-
mieres at the Royal Academy with sets
by Joseph Goupy

1728

February 17
Handel's *Siroe* (set in Persia) pre-
mieres at the Royal Academy
April 30
Handel's *Tolomeo* (set in Cyprus)
premieres at the Royal Academy
June 1
Royal Academy closes

leads to the conversion of the sorceress Armida, as well as Argantes, the Saracen king of Jerusalem, to Christianity. When Armida sings, "Conquer'd by you, we wou'd embrace Your Faith," the ending rings with the victory of the Christians over the Arabian infidels, rationality over magic, and participatory government over despotism. These blatant oppositions find little resonance in Handel's score. Distinctive musical Orientalisms, such as insistently repeated rhythms, distinctive orchestration, and pentatonic or other Eastern scale patterns, which appear in later compositions ranging from the Turkish dances of Mozart's *Abduction from the Seraglio* to the full-blown exoticism of Rimsky-Korsakov's *Scheherezade*, had not yet coalesced into mannerism. Nevertheless, at critical junctures in the drama Handel found a variety of ways to distinguish between Eastern and Western characters by manipulating the European musical system in which he worked, and at times he approached the later "exotic" style.

Handel's musical setting of *Rinaldo* most clearly delineates the West from the East when the military forces meet for the climactic battle. In the libretto, the entrances of the two armies seem balanced: first "the Pagan Trumpets sound a March, and the Army is seen to pass the Gate, and in military Order descend the Mountain," and then "the Christian Trumpets sound, and the Army in Military Pomp and Order, marches

Commerce and Trade *continued*

←——→

1729
December 2
Handel and the impresario
Johann Heidegger resume opera
productions at King's Theatre

1731
February 2
Handel's *Poro* (set in India)
premieres at King's Theatre
March 16
Ostend East India Company
officially abolished as part of the
Treaty of Vienna with Austria

1732
February 1
Henry Lannoy Hunter in
imbroglio in Aleppo, leading to
extensive correspondence on the
nature of Eastern rulers

over the Stage." Handel created differentiation by disregarding the parallelisms of these directions. When the Saracen forces come forward with Argantes at their head, their march has a jingling, almost toy-soldier quality generated by a rather banal melody that turns upon itself in short rhythmic values and seems to go nowhere. The Christian march, by contrast, depicts power and dignity, making use of longer note values and expanded phrasing, advancing with a sweep of melody that emphasizes the forward thrust in upward-octave runs and leaps. The West is also signaled with the instrumental brilliance of four trumpets and drums, while the East, in direct opposition to the stage direction, is consigned to the relative poverty of strings. In one recent recording, the addition of "Turkish" percussion instruments (bass drum, triangle, and cymbals) to the Saracen march brings out the similarity between Handel's conception of Orientalism and later janissary marches.[2] More subtly, the two groups are differentiated by key area, with the Pagans in B-flat major and the Christians in D major. This was not an arbitrary distinction: given that the German word "Kreuz" denotes both "cross" and "sharp" (the musical symbol for which is a double cross), the harmonic distinction between sharp and flat keys had special religious significance in Germanic music.[3] Throughout his career, Handel tended to identify religious adversaries with the flat side of the tonal spectrum and the righteous Christians with the sharp side.[4]

In Handel's lifetime, the standard tuning system gave more individuality to the various keys than now (the rise of equal temperament having smoothed out the differences), and the harmonic variations that resulted from the tuning allowed different keys to project distinctly different moods, although there wasn't total agreement on what these were in each case. Handel's friend Johann Mattheson, to take one example, described D major as warlike and rousing (although he allowed that if a flute were used instead of a trumpet the key could be delicate). He saw B-flat major, by contrast (the key Handel used for the Pagans), as "somewhat modest" and incorporating both the "magnificent and dainty." In *Rinaldo*, therefore, the sharp and flat keys of the opposing military marches suggest a religious meaning (with the Christians in a sharp key and the Saracens in flats), while the specific keys and differences in instrumentation emphasize the superior might of the Western forces. Handel's musical settings of the two marches in *Rinaldo* thus rise to the level of the text in depicting the West's victory over the Eastern forces of Armida and Argante in terms of both religion and military strength.

To a significant extent, Britons' sense of religious and military superiority over the East depended on and grew out of their increasing domination of international commerce. Toward the end of the sixteenth century, the English had established multiple companies for the development of Eastern trade: the Muscovy Company for trade to Russia and the Baltics in 1551, the Levant Company for trade to Turkey and Palestine in 1581, and the East India Company for trade to the East Indies in 1600. Formed on the basis of joint stock, whereby a group of private investors would provide start-up and operating costs in hopes of a large return on their investment, the companies were granted exclusive royal charters for trade, and often for colonization as well. Investors could make vast financial gains, but they also faced the risk of unlimited personal liability for all losses and debts should the venture fail. The circle of those who could hazard such an investment was, therefore, small. However, the employment base necessary for the regular operations and maintenance of these companies was huge—including a full hierarchy of traders who bought and sold the merchandise, seamen who moved the people and the goods, and accountants and clerks who oversaw the voluminous record-keeping and correspondence. Those who were willing to invest their own human capital in learning the trade sometimes reaped as much reward as the financial investors. As a result, England's international trading companies became primary employers at home and abroad for enterprising young men of quality who lacked the promise of hereditary entitlements typically granted to first sons. The families of two of Handel's legatees illustrate the importance of trade to different levels of society.

In 1747, Elizabeth Palmer (née Peacock) married Ralph Palmer, the third of that name in as many generations (see Palmer-Peacock-Verney in the Dramatis Personæ and the Palmer family chart, Image 6.4). Many years before, in 1680, a sister of Ralph's father, an Elizabeth Palmer by birth, married John Verney (1640–1717) when she was sixteen. The marriage produced four children, and despite Elizabeth Verney's death in 1686 (at the age of twenty-two), the Palmer and Verney families remained close. Born a second son, John Verney had been raised with the knowledge that he would have to become financially independent. The practice of primogeniture, or the passing of entire estates from first son to first son in order to keep them intact, meant that younger sons, if not independent, became a drain on the family fortunes. The typical path for younger sons was either the life of a courtier, if the family wielded enough influence to secure a placement, or a career in the military, the church, or the law. Although Verney's father had determined that his younger son should pursue law, John himself begged to be allowed to pursue trade, and in 1659 his father sent him first to a school where he could learn accounting and then, paying £400 and signing a £1,000 bond, apprenticed him for seven years to a Levant Company merchant. In 1662, John sailed to Aleppo and in 1668, at the end of his apprenticeship, was granted the liberty to trade on his own account. He returned to England in 1674 with a fortune of £6,000 and entered into the import-export business, trading English cloth for Levantine silks and other products.[5] As it turned out, the unexpected death of his elder brother meant that John inherited his father's title and estates, and it was his commercial success that saved the fortunes of the family.

Verney's early career path contains surprising similarities to Handel's, despite the difference in the social status of their families, and illustrates the parallels between the careers of musician and merchant trader. Like Verney, Handel was a second son. His older half-brother had already followed their father's profession of barber-surgeon, perhaps at the specific directive of the elder Handel, who, like the elder Verney, determined that his younger son should then follow "the study of the Civil Law." The boy's evident interest in music, therefore, was not encouraged. Just as there was some concern in the seventeenth century that by turning merchant a gentleman's son lost status, Handel's father thought that music as a profession "had little dignity."[6] Ultimately, however, he was persuaded to hire a tutor in music for the boy, paralleling the accession of Verney's father to his son's wishes to learn mathematics and accounting. If Handel's father had lived, perhaps he, like the elder Verney, might have funded some kind of apprenticeship, but as it was, he died shortly before Handel's twelfth birthday.

James Hunter, born into a family of merchant traders and one of the two men named by historian John Hawkins as an intimate friend of Handel, was also a younger son. His father, who died when James was three, directed in his will that his eldest son be sent as an apprentice to Aleppo. Thus, in 1726, the firstborn, Henry Lannoy Hunter, was duly apprenticed to the merchant trader Henry March at a cost of £1,400, and sent to work for the Levant Company in Aleppo. The will left open the question of whether the younger sons should also be apprenticed, but the high cost, given the lack of a specific directive in the will, may have discouraged consideration of the idea.[7] Coming from such a powerful lineage of merchants and silk dyers, however, all of the sons were probably educated with the possibility of an apprenticeship or, at the least, a livelihood in trade in mind. In 1720, Hunter's uncle Sir Harcourt Master, one of the directors of the South Sea Company, sent his youngest son to Thomas Weston's Academy in Greenwich, a school known for its training of seamen and merchants, and it seems likely that the family would have chosen to send the orphaned Hunter boys there as well.[8] Like John Verney some sixty years earlier, they needed to attend a school where they would learn accounting and other subjects directly related to trade.

Weston, Assistant Astronomer Royal and an expert in navigation, established his school around 1715, specifically emphasizing the skills needed for a trader, accountant, clerk, or seaman, and his students included sons of naval officers, international traders, and even the landed aristocracy. In 1728, an advertisement for the school listed Weston's curriculum as including "Writing, Arithmetick, Merchants Accompts, or the Italian Method of Book-Keeping," the last item referring to the widespread business practice of double-entry accounting that showed debits and credits in different accounts and thus necessitated the entry of each transaction twice. Other subjects included "Foreign Exchanges, the Mathematicks (in English, Latin or French)," as well as "Short-hand," which would have been useful for merchants or ship captains who needed to keep records or diaries, and "Drawing, Fencing, Musick and Dancing." Although the four last could be said to serve the purpose of enhancing the social status of the graduates, drawing was essential for technical purposes and good swordsmanship critical for self-defense. Weston also taught multiple languages: English (reading, writing, and speaking to enhance leadership skills and social status), Latin, Greek, and Hebrew (for ancient texts), French (the international language of the day), Italian (important in the Middle East, where Italians had preceded the English in trade and often served as dragomen—that is, interpreters—for the Levant Company), and both High Dutch and Spanish (to be able to deal with Britain's main trading competitors in the East). Finally, Weston also provided "Lectures of Geometry, Geography and Astronomy three Days a Week." Such an education would have stood the Hunter boys in good stead for any career in trade.

Weston geared his textbooks directly to issues of commerce. In his *A New and Compendious Treatise of Arithmetick, in whole Numbers and Fractions, Vulgar and Decimal . . . With a Large and Copious Appendix Containing several useful Tables of Monies, Weights, and Measures . . .* (second edition, 1736), an entire section, from which the following problem is taken, is devoted to financial partnerships:[9]

Two Merchants, A and B, commence Partners, A having £240 in Trade for 12 Months, and B having £240 in Trade for 14 Months;

and they gain clearly £125 9s. How must this Gain be divided
between them?
Answer: A's Part is £57 18s. and B's £67 11s.

Hunter entered into just such a partnership for trade to North Amer-
ica and the West Indies when he set up in business in the late 1720s,
and he must have needed to resolve problems like this on a regular basis:
how to divide profits between himself, his partner, and the various ship
captains with whom they dealt. Indeed, in 1738 Hunter and his partner
were forced to sue the captain of the *Neptune* for their share of the proceeds from its voyage to Philadelphia and Jamaica.[10]

A second text by Weston, *A Copy-Book Written for the Use of the
Young-Gentlemen at the Academy in Greenwich* (1726), offered instruc-
tion in writing and drawing. Drawing was crucial as an aid to scientific study and to all sorts of documentation useful to the trader, from
botanical drawings of plants to map-making. Weston himself was a fine
draftsman. John Flamsteed, the Astronomer Royal, praised Weston particularly for his precise drawings of the constellations, and it was on such
detailed astronomical charts that navigation depended. Without the
mechanical and digital methods of reproduction available today, meticulously accurate drawing provided the only way to communicate many
types of information, including the discoveries that resulted as scientific
knowledge and geographical exploration expanded what was known
about the earth and the sky.

Penmanship was also critical. Whether one was going into business
for oneself or looking for employment with one of the large joint-stock
companies, orderly record keeping was essential.[11] Not only was the need
for writers tremendous, but scribal work, especially at the East India
Company, increasingly provided an entrée into higher-level positions.
One of Hunter's nephews, for example, started out his career in 1766 as a
"writer" for the British East India Company at Bencoolen (now Bengkulu,
Indonesia). Hunter himself had recourse to scribal skills after he and his
business partner were declared bankrupt in 1741, when for a few years he
transcribed music in Handel's scriptorium under the direction of his pri-

4.2 Handwriting samples from Thomas Weston, *A Copy-Book Written for the Use of the Young-Gentlemen at the Academy in Greenwich*, c. 1726 (National Art Library 86.T.127; © Victoria and Albert Museum, London)

mary copyist, John Christopher Smith. Hunter's handwriting in his will and in these manuscripts bears a striking resemblance to the pedagogic examples provided in Weston's *A Copy-Book* and represents a style otherwise unfamiliar among the broad circle of Handel's friends.

In addition to practical studies in mathematics, writing, drawing, and languages, Weston taught skills that would be essential to a good position in society, such as music and dancing. Perhaps Hunter honed his musical skills through Weston's training. It may also have been through Weston that Hunter was introduced to the theater in 1721. In that year, "the ingenious Mr. Weston of Greenwich, having lately erected a Theatre for the Use and Diversion of the young Gentlemen under his Tuition, the Play of Tamerlane was last Week performed there, with vast Applause."[12]

Since one mission of Weston's Academy was to "put out [the successful students] as Apprentices to Masters of Ships and Substantial Commanders, for better improvements of their talents, and becoming Able

In the Name of God, Amen — I James Hunter
of the Parish of Saint Mary Stratford Bow in the County
of Middlesex Scarlet Dyer do this Nineteenth day of
July in the Year four Lord One thousand seven hundred
and fifty one make my Last Will and Testament in
Manner and form following —

    I will that all Estates whatsoever and wheresoever
that I dye seized or possessed of, Interested in, or Intituled
unto, I give, devise, and bequeath unto ~~my Wife Catherine~~ mr Edward Cooke
~~her~~ his Heirs Executors or administrators, I do hereby nominate
Constitute and appoint ~~my~~ the said ~~Wife Executrix~~ Edward Cooke Executor of this my
Will and I also appoint and desire my Worthy Friend Mr.
John Ellicott of Hackney to join with ~~her~~ him as Executor of
this my Will and to accept of a Ring of the Value of five
Guineas for his Trouble, and I hereby revoke all former
Wills by me at any time heretofore made, and this is my
last Will and Testament, In Witness whereof I have
hereunto set my Hand the Day and year first above
written ——————————————— James Hunter

    N.B. The abovenamed Edward Cooke who I appoint
    Executor is Brother to my deceased Wife —
             July 1757 — James Hunter

4.3 James Hunter's will in his own hand (1751, amended 1757), first page (The National Archives, Kew, ref. PROB 10/2217)

Seamen and good Artists," the ties of the Academy to the Royal Navy were strong.[13] Therefore, it is not surprising to find that in 1722 the "Scholars of Mr. Weston" repeated their school performance of "Tamerlane" before the Lords of the Admiralty. This play could have been any one of three English plays about the Asian emperor Timur: Christopher Marlowe's *Tamburlaine* (1587), Charles Saunders's *Tamerlane the Great* (1681), or Nicholas Rowe's *Tamerlane* (1701). Rowe's is the most likely, as it had remained popular, enjoying repeated performances on the London stage. Any of the three, with their portrayal of Eastern despotism and treachery would have helped to inculcate the British views of East and West in boys who were being trained for service in the Royal Navy or the East India Company. In 1724, Handel took up the story in his opera *Tamerlano* for the Royal Academy of Music.

At the beginning of the eighteenth century, as stated earlier, the opportunities for significant financial returns from investment in international trade were limited. Men such as John Verney and Henry Lannoy Hunter, whose families could afford the apprenticeship fees, might make fortunes as traders, but others suffered failure, and death lurked on the seas, onboard ship, and in the close atmosphere of the trading posts. Venture capitalists who could afford to underwrite the establishment of a joint-stock company were few, and those who benefited were fewer: the legal acceptance of unlimited liability for any and all debts should the company fail meant that such backers not only risked but sometimes lost far more than their initial investment. The prospect of investing without enduring the risk of physical danger or financial loss well beyond the initial investment only became widely available to arm-chair investors when various joint-stock companies began buying up large chunks of the British national debt and making it available in small units for resale (what in the United States is referred to as bonds, and in Britain as stock).

Years of war in Europe, including the War of Spanish Succession, had left the British government with an accumulated debt of over £13 million. When the Bank of England was established in 1694 as a joint-stock company it used its capital to buy £1.2 million of the debt, in effect loaning the government that amount in return for regular interest payments. The financial success of this model led the East India Company to follow suit in 1708, when it transformed its entire capital reserve of £3.2 million into government debt. Then, in 1711, the South Sea Company was established as a joint-stock company with the goal of absorbing the remaining £9 million of government debt.

Although superficially another international trading business like the East India Company, the South Sea Company had no capital reserves other than the initial investments made by its joint-stock owners. Despite the risk that investment in joint-stock entailed, individuals holding bonds were encouraged to trade their interest-bearing financial instruments for shares ("stock" in American terminology) in this newly formed and unproven company. Further, in return for its commitment to manage the national debt, the South Sea Company acquired government permission to increase its capital by selling shares directly. The market buildup was such that the company had thousands of shareholders by 1715. One of these was Handel.

The "buzz" about South Sea stock was terrific, and as more and more people clamored to buy, the price rose, and the resultant bubble served to confirm the value of the investment. By 1720 the price had risen from the nominal value of £100 per share to over £1,000 before confidence waned, the bubble burst, and the price of stock fell back to £126 before the South Sea books were closed in December. The crash left countless investors, many of whom had bought on credit, financially ruined.

George Granville, Lord Lansdowne, living in exile in France and a leader of the Jacobite cause, was one of the big losers; having borrowed money in order to invest in South Sea stock, he lost £10,000 when the bubble burst, significantly worsening his already difficult financial situation. He was, however, able to look beyond his personal problems to see the opening the financial crisis might offer for a spontaneous revolution against the government. He composed a memorandum that was published in the name of "James III," expressing the Pretender's sympathy for the widespread suffering caused by the crash and his intention, once restored to the throne, to provide a better government for the people he loved.[14] In an era of such political instability, the crash of stock prices affected not only individual investors but the security of the government itself.

The investor-directors of the South Sea Company, including James

Hunter's uncle Sir Harcourt Master, had taken on unlimited liability in expectation of huge returns, and for a while they reaped great rewards. Now the broad extent of the losses and the desire of the government to find scapegoats for the crisis led Parliament to hold the directors of the South Sea Company strictly and personally liable. The House of Lords required each director to submit a detailed list of all his financial transactions, as well as an inventory of his personal possessions. Judged according to Parliament's assessment of their individual culpability, many directors were compelled to forfeit most of their gross worth, requiring the liquidation of their property, including houses, land, and furnishings. This led, in at least one case, to suicide, but in almost all cases to financial ruin. The ruling of the House of Lords against Master left him with capital amounting to only £5,000. According to the inventory he submitted, his gross worth had been £70,760, which included income from his farms and estates and all the furnishings of his houses on Tower Hill, London, and at Greenwich. With the ruling of Parliament, the future of every member of Master's family changed irrevocably.

The lack of suitable dowries for Master's daughters who survived into adulthood explains, at least in part, why only one married. Master's second son, Charles, who had been sent to Weston's Academy with the seeming expectation that he would rise through the Levant or East India Company, appears never to have secured a place. A sequence of family wills illustrates the continuing impact of the parliamentary decree over years. Charles, who died in 1741, wrote only a few sentences, leaving his entire estate to Mssrs. Clutterbuck and Thurmond "in trust for the payment of my Debts" and the residue to his "Mothers [stepmother and mother-in-law] and Sisters equally."[15] Master himself, four years later, left "all of the Estate . . . which I am or may be possessed of or any ways entituled to, to my Two Daughters Joanna and Dorcas Master, which I do not do because I love and Esteem them more than my other Children but because I think after what I have to leave them they will not be so well provided for as the others are."[16] As late as 1752, ongoing concern for the impoverishment of Master's daughters was such that a maiden aunt singled them out with significant bequests of 3 percent annuities: £400 to Elizabeth, Joanna, and also to Mary, the one married daughter, and £500 to Dorcas.[17]

Handel's income during the first half of the 1710s cannot be detailed with precision, but enough evidence exists to provide a good sense of it. His annual salary from Hanover was 1,000 taler (about £225), and he received this amount at midsummer in both 1711 and 1712 (minus a mysterious small deduction in 1712). He lost that income stream when he was dismissed from this position in 1713, but George I made sure he received the 500 taler in arrears from that half year of Hanoverian employment in October 1715.[18] In December 1713 Handel officially entered the service of Queen Anne with a pension of £200, receiving his first half payment of £100 in midsummer of 1714 and his first full payment in 1715.[19] Meanwhile, the operas he presented on the London stage between 1711 and 1715 brought him significant income as well. Although the theater manager of the Queen's Theatre absconded in January 1713 with the proceeds of that season to date, leaving only £162 19s. to be divided between Handel, Heidegger, and the singers "in proportion to their Sev[era]ll contracts," the financial recovery of the theater over the course of the remaining season must have been good, although not complete. By May, Handel had been paid £186 7s. 11d., but was still owed £243 12s. 1d.[20]

Handel's name does not appear on the subscription list of shareholders in the South Sea Company published in 1714, but two signed orders dated March 13 and June 29, 1716, authorizing the dividends on his South Sea stock to be paid to a delegated third party, survive. To receive the quarterly dividend, Handel would have had to have invested at least three months prior, and if Handel made the effort to collect his first dividend in person, this pushes back the time for his purchase of South Sea stock to September 1715, a likely moment financially as it follows the summer receipt of his full £200 pension for the first time and at least one further payment of £50 from the opera.[21] Although it is difficult to make a direct comparison between the purchasing power of a British pound in Handel's lifetime and our own, it helps to know that between 1700 and 1750 the annual income of about 85 percent of the population of Great Britain was £50 or less.[22] Handel's annual pension of £200 already made him well-off, and the additional payments from the opera clearly left him with discretionary income for investment. With money in his pocket, Handel would naturally have been attracted to the financial opportunity that was the talk of London. Indeed, the 1714 subscription list shows that at least one person close to Handel had already made the leap: Dr. Arbuthnot had invested £500. Subscription lists from 1720 show that Heidegger had invested £1,000. Handel invested £500.

In contrast to the directors and most of the investors, Handel appears to have been one of the lucky few. The year he invested in the South Sea Company, 1715, the stock reached its lowest price on October 26 at £88 (daily stock prices were published in various newspapers). If he bought at this low, it was a very good investment: the cost of £500 of stock at £88 per share (that is, below the nominal price of £100) would have been £440. As Handel's name appears thereafter on none of the surviving subscription lists compiled for 1720, it suggests that he sold out before the crash. If so, the timing of the sale of his stock may have related less to a keen investment sense than to the establishment of the Royal Academy of Music. In the unofficial capacity of music director, he was ordered abroad to hire singers "as you shall judge fit to perform on the English stage."[23] The warrant with his instructions was dated May 14, 1719. Although it is not known exactly when Handel departed for the Continent, and it could have been even before the warrant was issued, there can be no doubt that if he sold his stock beforehand, he made a profit. At the end of June, for example, South Sea stock was at £117, which, if Handel sold at that time, would have resulted in a selling price of £585. Assuming a purchase price of £440, this would have amounted to a profit of £145 (worth about £30,000 today).

When the Royal Academy of Music was established in 1719 at the height of the South Sea bubble, it was founded on the same joint-stock principle as the major trading companies, the Bank of England, and the South Sea Company. Like those companies, the academy attracted directors who hoped for financial gain from their investment. However naïve the expectation may have been to earn money from producing opera, the original "Proposall for carrying on Operas by a Company and a Joynt Stock" (1719) optimistically offered a prospect of a 25 percent profit. The shared joint-stock basis and the hope of gaining revenue from the production of opera indicate, at least in the minds of the directors (many of whom also had vested interests in the Levant and East India Companies), the relationship of the academy to trade: both involved the purchase of exotic foreign goods that were marketed to the English public.

On November 30, 1719, the German-born Handel was appointed "Master of the Orchester with a Sallary," and, over the course of the academy's nine seasons, served along with the Italians Giovanni Bononcini and Attilio Ariosti as one of the composers. During this time, he had at his disposal an international company, including some of the greatest opera singers of Europe: Margarita Durastante, with whom Handel had worked in Rome and Venice; the great castrato Senesino; the Venetian castrato Matteo Berselli; the Venetian soprano Caterina Galerati; and the Florentine soprano Maria Maddalena Salvai. British participation in the artistic side of the opera company was rare, but one exception was the English singer Anastasia Robinson; originally a soprano when she first sang for Handel in 1713, she took on important contralto roles for the academy between 1721 and 1724. The orchestra of about thirty was made up of eminent musicians from Italy, France, and Britain. The librettists and stage designers were mostly from Italy, but also from France and Germany. As history illustrates, operatic success can never be guaranteed, but the directors of the academy ardently sought to import it at great expense.

The librettos, too, were imported. Unlike *Rinaldo*, operas presented by the academy did not have new texts, but were based on Italian librettos chosen from a large, preexisting pool and adapted or rewritten by the academy's Italian librettists, Nicola Haym and Paolo Rolli. Also unlike *Rinaldo*, the academy's operas eschewed the fantastic and emphasized instead the importance of the political, allowing for tension to arise between known historical or epic narratives and what seem to be pointed analogies to current political situations. That is, with the establishment in 1719 of the Royal Academy of Music, the use of magic and spectacular machinery in opera was largely abandoned in favor of librettos based on classical and medieval history that focused on issues of royal succession and dynastic relationships. In respect to its magical elements, therefore, *Rinaldo* stands apart from the later academy operas, but it remains closely connected to many, such as *Tamerlano*, which in their Eastern settings and depictions of conflict between East and West illustrate the multifaceted fascination of London society with the Orient and international trade.

During the nine years the academy produced opera (1720–1728), two-thirds of the librettos were set in the East. In its last four seasons, the proportion rose to four-fifths; that is, twelve of the fifteen new operas presented had settings in Eastern locales, including Persia in Ariosti's *Dario* (1725) and Handel's *Siroe* (1728); Turkey in Handel's *Tamerlano* (1724) and Ariosti's *Lucio Vero* (1727); India in Handel's *Alessandro* (1726); and China in Ariosti's *Teuzzone* (1727). This high percentage of Eastern settings is striking, given that two-thirds of the existing pool of Italian librettos from which the academy chose its operas were based on Western, principally Roman, themes, while only one-third had Persian or other Eastern settings.[24] Among the operas for the Royal Academy of Music, this proportion is reversed. Of Handel's fourteen academy operas, nine have Eastern settings. Although Roman operas had the advantage in the opening years of the academy, as one would expect from the larger proportion of such librettos among the available pool, Eastern venues began to dominate with the 1723–1724 season. This global shift in the settings of librettos chosen during the second half of the academy coincides with a period of crisis for the East India Company.

The financial stability of the East India Company was critical to the government financially and politically. Its role as a major guarantor for a large portion of the national debt increased in importance following the bursting of the South Sea bubble, but on an even more essential level, the company played a crucial role in Britain's military and political strength. Its ships, in conjunction with the British Navy, helped to hold off challenges to Britain's dominion over the seas, and its growing number of trading settlements in the East expanded Britain's dominion over land. Although it may have seemed, after an internal schism in the company was mended in 1709, that the global position of the British East India Company was secure, British supremacy in the Orient was seriously threatened in 1715 when competing ships began operating out of Ostend in the Austrian Netherlands. At first the sailings were sporadic, but as early as

1716 the East India Company presented a petition to George I protesting the "interlopers of Ostend."[25] In addition to the commercial threat it presented, the Ostend initiative of 1715 was tied to the Jacobite uprisings of that year, representing a political attempt to undermine the financial security of the government. A few years later, the formal establishment of the Ostend East India Company by the Austrian government coincided with a thwarted Jacobite conspiracy (the Atterbury Plot of 1722).

At least fifteen ships sailed from Ostend between 1718 and 1722, and Parliament quickly reacted. In 1719, a statute (5 Geo. I c. 21) was passed "for the better securing the lawful Trade of his Majesty's Subjects to and from the East Indies." It imposed stiff penalties for any British subject who independently or on commission from any foreign prince traded to the East Indies, and gave the East India Company the right to seize such persons and send or bring them to England to be tried in a court of law. On June 24, 1721, in light of continued sailing from Ostend, a second statute (7 Geo. I c. 21) was passed that greatly strengthened the penalties and forfeitures for such actions.[26] After the Ostend East India Company was officially established in 1722, the British East India Company was forced to reduce its dividend.

The global situation worsened in 1725, when Spain, which supported the Jacobites, agreed to back the Austrian trade. Austria, in return, promised to help Spain recover the Iberian peninsula of Gibraltar, a vital military gateway to the Mediterranean that the British had captured during the War of Spanish Succession and that Spain had ceded to Britain, along with the island of Minorca, in the Treaty of Utrecht. As a major naval power, Spain presented a serious threat to Britain's sea passage to the East, and when the king addressed Parliament in 1726, he acknowledged "the negociations and engagements entered into by some foreign powers, which seem to have laid the foundation of new troubles and disturbances in Europe, and to threaten my subjects with the loss of several of the most advantageous branches of their trade."[27] The relation of the Ostend company to the Jacobite threat and their Catholic allies was made clear in a pamphlet the same year: "I shall only add, that if *this* Company be not destroy'd, *ours must* be ruin'd: . . . *our* Commerce, and

Maritime Power must dwindle and decay, the House of *Austria* become Mistress of Navigation . . . and then, the *Liberties* of *Europe*, and the *Protestant* Religion will soon be destroy'd."[28] Although the company ceased operations in 1727, it was not finally shut down until 1731.

The Ostend crisis, although national in scope, also had a personal side for investors, including many of the directors of the Royal Academy of Music, especially in the aftermath of losses sustained as a result of the collapse of South Sea stock. Sir John Eyles (academy director 1726–1727) had been an East India Company director (1710–1714, 1717–1720) and was made sub-governor of the South Sea Company (1721–1733) after its crash of 1720. His brother Sir Joseph Eyles (academy director 1727–1728) was heavily involved in trade with Turkey and responsible for proposing the rate of remittances required by the forces in Minorca and Gibraltar. And James Brydges, marquis of Carnarvon (academy director 1726–1727), had a direct connection with the Orient through his father, the duke of Chandos, who not only was an original investor in the academy but since 1718 had been the governor of the Levant Company.

The importance of Eastern trade nationally, and the number of directors of the opera who were also directors of (or heavily invested in) the East India or Levant Companies or Members of Parliament, suggests that the use of librettos with Eastern settings may have had value as a lobbying or marketing tool to keep the image of the East in front of those who might assist them politically. On January 25, 1727, in response to the king's message to Parliament, the House of Commons voted a resolution—strongly supported, as the parliamentary record shows, by Sir William Yonge, who was Lord of the Treasury and also a director of the academy (1726–1727)—to expand the military and commit nearly £900,000 to increase the land forces at Gibraltar and Minorca. Some months later, the Austrian emperor agreed under pressure to suspend operations of the Ostend East India Company. As a result, both Britain's authority in the East and the directors' personal investments were preserved.

Not surprisingly, given the directors' interests, the number of operas set in Eastern locales during the life of the Royal Academy of Music closely followed the trajectory of the Ostend crisis. In its early years, only two of Handel's five operas have Oriental settings: *Radamisto* (1720) takes place in the Armenian kingdom of Asia Minor, while the libretto of *Floridante* (1721), as described in Chapter 3, underwent a substantial geographical shift from Norway to Persia, a setting that connected the Jacobite leanings of the libretto to the Ostend Company sailings.[29] At the time of *Floridante*'s performance, the Ostend Company was successfully using commerce as a way to attack the Hanoverian government of Britain, manning its operation with Irish Jacobite mariners and merchants who were able to smuggle their Eastern goods into England and undermine the legal market.

During the last five years of the Academy, beginning in 1724, seven of Handel's nine operas were set in the East, and the importance of the East India Company was such that even those without Eastern settings could be read in light of the Ostend crisis—for example, *Scipione* (1726). Based on the victory of the Roman general Publius Cornelius Scipio over the Carthaginians in Spain, the libretto had previously been tied to allied interests in the War of Spanish Succession by connecting Scipio with the Habsburg claimant to the Spanish throne, known as "Charles III" by those who supported his cause: an opera based on the same history (but not the same libretto) had been performed for Charles in Barcelona in 1710. At the time of Handel's opera, however, the closest reference was Britain's contest with Spain to retain possession of Gibraltar. In 1726, the text of the final chorus of *Scipione*, stating that Spain should be proud to be conquered by such a virtuous man, would have pointed directly to the current military situation and to George I as Scipio.

The vast majority of the academy operas set in the East depict the superiority of the West in terms of moral behavior and military might. That is, just as Weston thought it appropriate to introduce the concept of Western supremacy over Eastern despotism and tyranny to schoolboys for educational purposes by having them act out the story of Timur, the producers of opera in London considered it commercially advantageous to place this same story, which depicts the confrontation of the cruel Tatar emperor Tamerlane and the proud Bajazet, emperor of the Turks, in front of their aristocratic audience in the opera *Tamerlano* (1724). Only the

Grecian prince Andronico, the leading man of the opera who represents the West, stands apart from explosive anger and tyrannical behavior. The same opposition applies in *Giulio Cesare* (1724), in which the Roman hero overcomes the "bloody tyrant" Ptolemy, king of Egypt. In *Alessandro* (1726), Alexander the Great, having completed his conquest of northern India, achieves an enlightened, personal victory over his pride and romantic passion, and in *Riccardo primo* (1727), Richard the Lionheart conquers Cyprus and triumphs over the tyrannical governor Isaac Comnenus.

Handel's final two operas for the Royal Academy of Music, which follow Britain's victories against Austria for preeminence in the East Indian trade routes and against Spain for possession of Gibraltar, continue the use of Eastern settings, but shift away from a one-sided presentation of Western supremacy over the East. Instead, they attempt a more balanced depiction of Eastern rulers, showing honest princes as well as deceitful and haughty potentates. In *Siroe* (1728), Cosroe, king of Persia, slaughters the royal family of Cambaja and attempts to defraud his eldest son, the "valiant" Siroe, of the throne, but saved by him from death, acknowledges his wrongs and crowns Siroe king. In *Tolomeo* (1728), the rightful heir of Egypt has been deposed by his mother, lives in exile on the island of Cyprus, and suffers the wrath and fury of the "base tyrant" king Araspe (Cyprus suffers from tyrant kings to an unusual degree in Handel's operas), but is restored by the honesty and faithfulness of his brother. All six of the operas by Ariosti and Bononcini performed at the Royal Academy of Music during its last four years also had Eastern locales: *Artaserse* (1724), Susa, Persia; *Dario* (1725), Susa, Persia; *Elisa* (1726), Carthage; *Lucio Vero* (1727), Ephesus, Turkey; *Astianatte* (1727), Epirus (Albania/Greece); and *Teuzzone* (1727), China.

While the Eastern settings of these academy operas provided a metanarrative related to the Ostend crisis, the music contributed little to the invocation of the Orient in the imaginations of the audience. As seen in *Rinaldo*, Handel did not write in the "exotic" style that became so popular in the late eighteenth and early nineteenth centuries, and even the kind of musical confrontation between East and West found in the military marches of *Rinaldo* was rarely used later and not at all in the academy operas. Handel comes closest to replicating this kind of musical contrast in the choruses of his oratorios, where he sets up equally vivid distinctions between choruses for the ancient Israelites (understood as the ancestors of Protestant Britain) and idol-worshippers (who, for the British, could represent any non-Protestant form of worship ranging from a full spectrum of Eastern religions to Catholicism).

In the oratorio of *Esther* (1718), which Handel composed for private performance at Cannons, the libretto offered something of the same kind of confrontation found in *Rinaldo*: first, following the Persian minister Haman's announcement of his policy to eradicate the Jews, a chorus of Persians expresses its approval ("Shall we the God of Israel fear?"); and then, after an Israelite expresses the hope that Jewish persecution is at an end, a chorus of Israelites places its hope in God ("Shall we of servitude complain?").[30] Handel makes use of the parallel construction of the text to characterize the opposing groups, in effect basing both choruses on the same thematic material but transforming it. The haughtiness of the Persians, depicted in strong, off-beat accents and the fanatical iteration of a turning fugal theme on "nor age nor sex we'll spare," is transmuted for the Israelites into subdued reverence with interlinked cross-rhythms on the phrase "the heavy yoke and galling chain." A particularly strong example of "East-West" contrast also can be found in the later oratorio *Athalia* (1733). In the choruses for the worshippers of Baal, Handel emphasizes repetitive dance rhythms and simple melodies, while the choruses of the Levites (understood as "ancient" Westerners) are given more gravity, even when brief, by means of their intricate counterpoint and greater magnificence in the orchestral opulence of trumpets, horns, timpani, oboes, bassoons, and strings.

It was Handel's general practice to reserve the richer orchestral color for the West. The later musical tradition of reflecting the "luxuriant" East with rich orchestration and sinuous chromaticism, while depicting the "rational" West with more restrained orchestration and musical content, does, however, find a place in at least one of Handel's academy operas. In *Giulio Cesare* (1724), when Cleopatra arranges a pageant with the purpose of seducing Caesar, Handel captivates both the Roman emperor and the audience with an enchanting orchestration of muted violins, viola da gamba, theorbo, harps, and bassoons. More than twenty years later, in his setting of *Alexander Balus* (1748), adapted from the first book of Maccabees in the Apocrypha, he created a similarly magical sound for a different Cleopatra, daughter of an Egyptian king. Her aria "Hark, hark he strikes the golden lyre," with its accompaniment of flutes, harp, and mandolin, supported and enriched with violins, cellos divided into two parts, and pizzicato (plucked) basses, paints a clear picture of her Eastern allure. Such rich orchestrations are exceptions in Handel's depictions of the East. More often, as in *Rinaldo* and *Athalia*, he used orchestration to emphasize the splendor and power of the West rather than to depict the languor and sensuousness of the East.

One of the clearest examples of East-West depictions among the academy operas occurs in *Riccardo primo*, which Handel completed on May 16, 1727, at the peak of the Ostend crisis, while Spain was still laying siege to Gibraltar.[31] The work may originally have been destined for a premiere in June. As it happened, the opera house closed abruptly following a fracas between supporters of the rival prima donnas during an opera by Bononcini on June 6, and the death of George I on June 11 changed the political environment.[32] Exactly one month after the coronation of George II, which included the first performance of Handel's four Coronation Anthems, *Riccardo primo* opened on November 11. In the meantime, peace agreements with Austria had forced the suspension of operations of the Ostend Company, meaning that Britain could see its way clear to global supremacy in Eastern trade. *Riccardo primo*, heavily revised over the summer and early fall by the librettist Paolo Rolli to suit its new circumstances, celebrated these events.[33]

Rolli pays direct tribute to the new king in a dedicatory Italian sonnet directed to "the Sacred Royal Majesty of George II, King of *Great Britain, France, Ireland*, etc. Elector of the Holy Roman Empire, etc." The sonnet explains that the opera presents to George II his "warrior predecessor, Richard the Lionheart," who was "fast as an arrow in works of valor, / Bold, proud, but justly proud, / Great, loving, polite, sincere, / Quick to conquer and not slow to pardon." It goes on, however, to suggest that the king should not restrict himself to that forebear as a model, but rather look to himself, for he is a great king, who is "ready in arms" and "holds dominion over all the seas and many kingdoms." It concludes by stating that George has "honor and valor equal to this self-examination," and, like Jove, holds in his hand "the destinies not only of the Orient, but of the world."

While glorifying the new king, the sonnet also sets in play the cultural conflict at the heart of the drama. Richard I, presented as a symbol of Western monarchy, is quick to works of valor, quick to conquer, not slow to pardon, justly proud, and has the destiny of the Orient in his hands (whereas his successor George II has the destiny "not only" of the Orient but of the world). Opposed to him is Isacius, the tyrant of Cyprus, who, as described in the Argument printed in the libretto, is "puffed up with Pride" (as opposed to *justly* proud), "insolent and cruel." The princess of Navarre, Richard's betrothed, who is appropriately named Constantia in the libretto, arrives in the midst of a "strong and violent tempest," while Richard's ships struggle at sea. Orontes, Prince of Syria, who is at first a confederate of Isacius, changes allegiance to Richard when he experiences the valor of the one and the treachery of the other. Meanwhile Isacius forcibly woos Constantia, who vows that only Richard or death will have her (Act III, scene iv). The crisis comes to a head at the beginning of Act III as Richard gathers his men about him for an attack on the city walls. He calls for those who "on the Banks of the *Thames*, where Virtue, Liberty and Courage reigns," were "born to Acts of Justice, and of Honour," to follow him. He declares that the glory of their arms will shine in "the perfidious *East*" and subject "these savage Lands to Tameness." In the course of the opera, Richard, a brave and just Western monarch, converts Orontes, a Syrian prince, to Western honor, rescues untrammeled virtue from lust, and subdues the Eastern tyrant. Handel's musical setting of *Riccardo primo* brings the drama to life.

After the overture, the curtain opens on a raging storm, the roiling waters depicted with unusual violence by a concatenation of small motives: slicing octave leaps in eighth notes overlaid on thirty-second-note string whirrings, downward-running scales, and hammering repeated notes. Of particular import is the composed timpani part, to which Handel added detailed dynamic markings of "loud" and "soft" to paint the sound of the larger swells. Constantia's opening line of recitative and dialogue with her adviser, Berardus, breaks into the midst of this tumult and continues as the storm fades into the background. This opening depiction of Richard riding out a violent storm provides the fundamental image not only of the opera but also of Britain's place internationally, holding "dominion over all the seas." No other Handel opera begins in such a manner, but on hearing it nearly three centuries after it was written, Giuseppe Verdi's similarly striking depiction at the opening of his opera *Otello*, where the title character directs his ships safely to the island of Cyprus during a raging tempest while his wife watches anxiously from the shore, may come to mind.

Once the scene is set musically, Handel provides the characters with appropriate musical dress. As in *Rinaldo*, he showers the riches of orchestral variety on the Europeans: from the bass flute and sopranino recorder ("flauto piccolo") for Constantia to two trumpets and timpani for Richard's battle aria as he attacks the walls of the city, expanding to three trumpets after the victory is assured. When Orontes, Prince of Syria, transfers his allegiance from the tyrant Isacius to the British cause, his new mantle of "Valour, Justice, and fair Truth Triumphant" gains him two horns for his following aria ("Dell'onor di giuste imprese"). Previously, he, like Isacius, received only the most standard accompaniments. In addition, Handel gives the most elaborate music, in terms of technical difficulty and expansive structures, to the Europeans. The opening scenes of Act III offer a sequence of arias that permits a direct comparison of Handel's characterizations of Richard, Constantia, and Isacius.

In scene ii, Constantia has the briefest of arias, modeled by Handel out of recitative text, "Morte, vieni" (Come, death). Despite its miniature size, the aria maintains the "European" richness of orchestration and content. Set at a very slow tempo (*largo assai*), it combines strings in a pulsating, dotted pattern with an affecting melody for the muted sound of the bass flute in counterpoint with Constantia's vocal line. With its soft dynamic, gentle timbre, slow tempo, hesitant rhythms, and plangent melody, the aria is the aural embodiment of threatened virtue. In scene iv, following an aria for Isacius's daughter, the tyrant's own aria, "Nel mondo e nell'abisso" (In the world and in the abyss), blusters loudly in lines that turn and repeat but fail to develop a true forward drive. The repeated turning figures of this aria present a more sophisticated version of the static repetitions employed by later composers, and sometimes by Handel, to depict the East, and the orchestration is limited to strings and oboes. Then in scene v, Richard attacks the walls of the city, "Atterrato il muro cada" (Let the batter'd ramparts fall), in an aria that illustrates his vigor and strength by combining elaborate musical runs (demanding extraordinary breath control and vocal agility) with spectacular leaps and wide range (demanding great accuracy across an unusually large vocal tessitura). In the powerful orchestration, trumpets and timpani combine with oboes, bassoons, and strings to create a sense of overwhelming force.

The musical setting of the opera leaves no doubt that Richard is a hero, but it provides no aural pathway to an Oriental ambience. The responsibility for transporting the audience to the East would have fallen primarily on the stage sets, and the visual requirements of these operas were often significant. In *Riccardo primo*, not only was it necessary to provide an Eastern setting, in this case the near-East of Cyprus, but in addition, individual scenes demanded such spectacles as Richard's ships approaching a rocky coast on a "tempestuous sea," his encampment on "a pavilion" near the "rivers of Limissus," and his storming of the city walls at the head of his soldiers. In the only case of its kind in all of Handel's operas, the libretto specifically names the artist responsible for providing these scenes: "Le nuove Scene sono del Sig. Giuseppe Goupy."

Unfortunately, no drawings of Goupy's theatrical sets survive, but once again it is possible to turn to his work outside the theater to catch a glimpse of what he might have created. As noted in Chapter 3, Goupy's repair in 1725 of *The Triumphs of Caesar*, a set of paintings by Mantegna at Hampton Court, suggest his prior participation in the set design of Handel's opera *Giulio Cesare* (1724), and his copies of paintings depicting the myth of Galatea may indicate that he contributed backdrops to the performance of Handel's *Acis and Galatea* at the Cannons residence of the duke of Chandos. During the years Goupy was traveling in Italy, he executed a set of four paintings that depict panoramic views of the Port of Valletta, at Malta, and these could have provided a model for his

4.4   Antoine Benoist, *A View of the City of Malta, on the Side of the Jesuits Garden, or of the Island of Marsa*, engraving after Joseph Goupy, one of a set of four views, 1740s (The British Museum, #1953,0214.00; © The Trustees of the British Museum)

depiction of the coast of Limassol at Cyprus. Later engravings of these paintings, which state that the originals were "drawn on ye spot," were published in England and became very popular at a time when images of the East were increasingly collected by a broad spectrum of society.

Because such images provided a means of sustaining and increasing interest in Eastern geography and trade, the directors of the East India Company, some of whom were also directors of the Royal Academy of Music, encouraged their circulation. In 1732, the company commissioned their own set of *Six Sea Pieces* by Samuel Scott and George Lambert, another London scene painter, depicting the important settlements in the East Indies and on the route to them: the island of Saint Helena, the Cape of Good Hope, Bombay (now Mumbai), Tellicherry (Thalassery), Fort St. George at Madras (Chennai), and Fort William at Calcutta. Like Goupy's Malta paintings, these were engraved for wide circulation. Handel owned both sets, as the inventory of his art collection taken after his death indicates. It has been assumed that friendship with the artists was the reason he chose to acquire these Eastern views, "since there is no known personal association Handel may have had with any of these places."[34] However, the vistas were closely related to his creative work and to his financial interests. The ubiquity of Oriental imagery in Handel's art collection, in his operas, and in London reflects British imaginative and commercial interests in the East.

As previously described, some of the most fantastic elements in *Rinaldo* derived from Aaron Hill's experiences as a traveler in the Middle East. In contrast, the tensions depicted between Western leaders and Eastern potentates reflected the experiences of the traders of the Levant and East India Companies. That is, the *depictions* of the East in operatic librettos match the *descriptions* of the East in Levant Company records. In reporting on an altercation between Henry Lannoy Hunter, James

4.5 Andrea Soldi, *Portrait of Henry Lannoy Hunter in Oriental Dress, Resting from Hunting, with a Manservant Holding Game,* c. 1733–1736 (Tate Britain T11977; © Tate, London 2012)

Hunter's oldest brother, and the native residents of Aleppo, which incident led to a serious breach between the Levant Company and the local government, the language used by the Levant merchants to describe the subsequent negotiations closely parallels the descriptions of Eastern rulers in Handel's operas. The company records provide a detailed and colorful narrative of the chain of events.[35]

Returning in 1732 from an excursion outside the gates of the great Khan al Gumruk, the residential area for European traders, Hunter had his progress impeded by local villagers. When he struck the man who grabbed the bridle of his horse, he was set upon by a great number of villagers throwing stones, and his servant was taken hostage. On arriving back at the Khan, he lodged a complaint with the British consul, who immediately dispatched a janissary (Turkish guard) to the seraglio where the servant had been taken. The *kya* (deputy pasha) released the servant, but ordered the consul to send his dragoman (interpreter) to him immediately. On his arrival, according to his deposition, the dragoman learned that the story Hunter had told was not complete: that Hunter was riding not on the wide public street, as required by the pasha, but on the narrow passage for pedestrians (which Hunter later admitted), and that he bumped into an old man and almost knocked him down. Only at that point (and not without reason) did a villager grab hold of the bridle of Hunter's horse. Further, it was reported that Hunter thrashed the villager, broke one of his teeth, tried to take him captive, and, when the other villagers approached, drew his pistol and waved it in the air as if he would fire on them (as Hunter also admitted). With a mob of five hundred villagers, as estimated by the dragoman, gathered outside the seraglio insisting on justice, the *kya* demanded that the British delegation provide reparation to the injured man and, as an apology for the imbroglio, a gift for the pasha. The British at first offered to give the pasha some cloth and a watch, but the *kya* scoffed that this was an appropriate gift only for a servant of the pasha. He demanded either a cash settlement of 2,500 Levant piastres (*£p*) (about £360) or that Hunter be turned over from the secular administration to the cadi (religious judge), which could have meant a penalty of death. Ultimately, the Levant Company paid £50 to the villager for his tooth, another £50 to be divided among his companions, another £395 to various officials and servants, and £1,500 to the pasha.

As a result of this "imbroil" and the large sum paid in reparation, the consul and the senior merchants of the British contingent in Aleppo appealed to the British ambassador to the Ottoman Empire in Constantinople. They begged for political assistance against the payments exacted from them in order to release members of the company from the threat of physical punishment, including death, which "the Kya insinuated might ensue, Should We remove from the Pasha's Judicature to that of the Caddy's." They could barely contain their outrage that the Aleppan ruling officials, by permitting "a Concoarse of people to demand Immediate Justice," had found "an Effectuall way for them to Extort what Value they please." They pointed out that refusing these demands, "how exorbitant Soever," resulted in an insistence upon "the Execution of the Strictest Justice," as happened in the "most unhappy Instance in the Death of the Dutch Dragoman." Because of the "Approved Avarice of these Ministers," the delegation worried, "We may with reason apprehend the Worst from the Proud Haughty disposition of Our present Pasha . . . , who is a profest enemy to all Franks [Europeans] and Christians in generall."

The text of this letter corresponds to the language found in many of Handel's Oriental operas. In *Riccardo primo*, the English are "born to acts of Justice," the East is "perfidious," and Richard I is called upon to subject "these savage Lands to Tameness." In *Giulio Cesare*, Ptolemy, the king of Egypt, is described as "licentious," "naturally cruel and void of Honour," treacherous, barbarous, and a violator of "the Sacred Laws of Hospitality." In the libretto of *Tamerlano*, the English translation emphasizes this kind of language even when it is lacking in the original Italian: when Tamerlano refers to Bajazet in Italian as "this Ottoman," the English translation expands it to "This Ottoman—This haughty Prisoner!" And when Andronicus says in Italian that his beloved has entered the throne room "of the Tartar," the English translation reads that she has gone "to the proud Tartar's Palace." The shared language of Handel's Oriental librettos and the records of the Levant and East India

Companies suggest how familiar the operatic depictions of East-West conflict could have seemed to contemporary audiences.

To modern ears, the repeated opposition of courageous and virtuous Western heroes and tyrannical Eastern despots in Handel's operas can seem little more than caricaturish stereotypes or territory too dangerous to enter, a circumstance that has led some modern stage directors to sur-realistic or ahistorical productions overlaid with sight gags and slapstick. Examples include a *Giulio Cesare* on a largely barren stage in front of a chipboard wall with a large stuffed crocodile and Caesar in cowboy boots, and a *Rinaldo* on a unit set with a giant eye and a descending harpsichord out of which pop helium balloons.[36] But if one pays attention to the plights of the individual characters and listens to Handel's musical settings, it is immediately clear how real and deep are the human interactions and the emotions in every case. It was one of Handel's greatest strengths to be able to capture the essence of joy, despair, anger, and heartbreak and to communicate those emotions to the hearts of his listeners. For Handel's contemporaries, the musical impact must have been particularly potent, as the operas, far from being simply ancient history or Oriental fantasy, had remarkable ties to the experiences and emotions of many who worked for the Levant or East India Companies or traveled in the East.

The Royal Academy of Music ran out of funding in 1728, and closed its doors, marking the end of joint-stock funding for opera. As Handel set about to reestablish opera on a more entrepreneurial basis, Goupy assisted him by initiating a dialogue with representatives of the Italian singing stars, and with the help of Heidegger the reorganized opera com-pany resumed performances at the end of 1729. Over the next dozen years, various disruptions and displacements called for continued flexibility on Handel's part, but he continued producing opera until 1741. Eastern locales maintained an important, but less dominating, role in his own choice of librettos: *Poro* (1731) is set in India, *Sosarme* (1732) in Turkey, *Giustino* (1737) in Constantinople (Istanbul), *Berenice* (1737) in Egypt, and *Serse* (1738) in Persia. Goupy may, for a while at least, have continued to collaborate in these productions as set designer. His miniature paint-ings of Angelica and Medoro, as mentioned in Chapter 3, suggest a possible connection to Handel's *Orlando* (1733), an opera that tells of the love of Angelica, Queen of Cathay (China), and the African prince Medoro.

By the late 1730s, however, concerns for the survival of the East India Company were long gone, and interest in the East was increasingly consumer-driven as Oriental objects and artifacts for the home became stylish for a broad spectrum of society. Chinese porcelain was an especially desired collectible, and japanning (using "japan" or lacquer to provide a hard black gloss) became extremely popular. Mary Delany (then the widow Pendarves) wrote on September 9, 1729: "Everybody is mad about japan work; I hope to be a dab at it by the time I see you."[37] And in her will she specifically left all her "Plate Japan and China of all sorts" to her beloved niece.[38] Goupy, in his will, left a japanning set to one of Handel's prima donnas.[39]

For the very wealthy, Oriental architecture became fashionable as well. One of the large projects undertaken by the prince of Wales was the development of the gardens at Kew, and in 1749 Goupy designed both the Chinese Arch and the House of Confucius for that landscape. As a former set designer, Goupy now had the opportunity to create theater on a scale he probably had never before envisioned, but even these works turned out to be ephemeral. Although Chinese, Indian, and Moorish structures continued to rise at Kew throughout the eighteenth century, Goupy's Chinese Arch was removed during his lifetime in 1757, and the House of Confucius was demolished in 1844.[40]

Perhaps it was James Hunter who benefited most from the commercial trade with the East. After his bankruptcy in the early 1740s, he was able in 1745 to buy a dye house in Old Ford, and as a scarlet dyer he sold deep-red broadcloth to the East India Company, becoming one of the most successful dyers listed in the company records. After traveling across oceans and around continents, Hunter's dyed goods from Old Ford were transmuted by trade into the Indian chintz, Indonesian spices, and Chinese porcelain and tea that the English so craved, moving along the very trade routes that the successful elimination of the Ostend East India Company in the 1720s had helped to preserve for Britain.

5.1 Portrait of Handel by Philippe Mercier, c. 1730 (Malmesbury Collection)

FIVE

Music at Home

1715–1730
Chamber music and keyboard works, private concerts, publications

HANDEL'S MUSIC WAS HEARD not just at ceremonial events in St. Paul's, Westminster Abbey, and St. James's, or at operatic performances in the Haymarket Theatre (known as either the Queen's Theatre or the King's Theatre, depending on the reigning monarch). Increasingly during his London years, Handel's keyboard music, chamber music, and chamber reductions of his orchestral pieces were heard in private. From music students (royal and otherwise) and individuals playing through scores, to musical soirees, gentlemen's concerts, and music clubs in taverns, the sound of Handel's music became for many a part of daily life.

When he first arrived in London, Handel initially would have stayed in lodgings; later, as in Italy, he sometimes resided in the houses of his patrons. In 1723, however, he made a decisive change by leasing a house that would become his home for the rest of his life. Over time, the house on Brook Street became a focal point for musical activity. Here, as well as in the homes of friends and neighbors, Handel played and sang his newest compositions for select company. In 1736, for example, Lord Shaftesbury wrote a glowing report to James Harris about the composer playing through his new score of *Alexander's Feast* "not yet transcrib'd from his own hand," adding that "Handel was in high spirits & I think never play'd & sung so well."[1] Handel also held rehearsals in his home to which friends were invited; Mary Delany wrote to her mother that the composer was

MUSIC AT HOME: *Timeline*

1704	1707	1710	1710–1714
(Hamburg) Handel tutors Cyril Wych, son of the British envoy; Elizabeth Mayne (née Batt) begins childhood collection of keyboard pieces	(Rome) Handel's trio sonata HWV 392 composed	*autumn* Handel arrives in London for the first time *December (?)* Handel plays Mary Delany's "little spinnet" at the house of her uncle, Sir John Stanley	Handel attends concerts at the house of Thomas Britton, charcoal dealer

like "a necromancer in the midst of his own enchantments" after she, her sister, and Anne Donnellan attended the first rehearsal of *Alcina* at Handel's house in 1735.[2] Such musical activities at Brook Street, while of a special cast on account of their professional nature, took place within a social context of lively music-making in private settings by accomplished amateurs.

We have seen that during Handel's first years in London he was a man in a hurry. By February 6, 1711, some of his music had been performed at court in honor of the Queen's birthday, and *Rinaldo*, his first opera for the London stage, premiered on February 24. Lying behind these headline events, however, is a different picture of the composer as a young musician attending every musical event in London to which he could gain entry. The historian John Hawkins wrote that Handel was a regular guest at the "weekly concerts at the houses of the duke of Rutland, the earls of Burlington and Essex, lord Percival, father of the later earl of Egmont, and others of the nobility" and attended concerts at the homes of well-to-do merchants.[3] These and other concerts with amateur performers, such as occurred at the Angel and Crown Tavern, demanded a ready supply of keyboard and chamber music. Unlike operas, oratorios, or ceremonial

1710s–1720s
Handel attends the weekly concerts at the houses of Lord Burlington and John Percival (later Lord Egmont), William Caslon (a typesetter), and Henry Needler (an accountant); John and Philip Percival constantly seeking out new music for their concerts at London music dealers Vaillant, Riboteau, and Walsh, and at Roger's in Amsterdam

1714
Mattheson's two-volume set of keyboard suites becomes available at Meare's music shop, and Handel immediately plays through it for friends at the Queen's Arms Tavern

c. 1714
Handel teaches George Monroe, a pageboy of the duke of Chandos

1715–1734
Elizabeth Legh collects thirty-nine volumes of Handel's music in manuscript; Handel tutors Legh in vocal and keyboard skills (?)

1716–1718
(Hamburg) Handel's *Brockes Passion* performed (?), overture used in Op. 3, no. 2; Handel composes anthems for the duke of Chandos

compositions, this music was not intended for large-scale, public performance, but meant primarily for private (and often amateur) performance at home, court, chapel, or tavern. These musical gatherings represent one of the principal ways in which Handel's music reached a wider public.[4]

Handel wrote most of his chamber music between about 1715 and 1730 with the English social milieu in view. He published his first collection of keyboard music in 1720 at the end of his first decade in London, and his first collection of trio sonatas appeared in 1730, at the end of his second. These compositions for one to four players provided the opportunity for music lovers and musicians to absorb Handel's style in an intimate setting, and, somewhat like the four-hand piano adaptations of symphonic repertoire in a later century, they frequently were modeled on movements from his larger stage works. In an era without any means to distribute musical sound by mechanical reproduction, arrangements of large-scale musical works for the home helped to familiarize a public with a composer's style and raise interest in specific pieces. An even closer parallel to the later practice are the volumes of published keyboard arrangements of operatic arias and overtures. The English firm of John Walsh (father and son) printed many such collections. *The 3d Book of the*

Music at Home continued

1719	1720	1722–1723
February 18 "new concerto" by Handel performed in Hickford's Great Room (Op. 3, no. 2?)	**November** Handel's first volume of keyboard suites published (Cluer); *The 3d Book of the Lady's Banquet, containing great Variety of the most pleasant and airy Lessons for the Harpsichord* (Walsh) advertised for sale, contains movements from *Rinaldo* and the *Water Music*	Handel appointed music master to the three older daughters of the prince of Wales; works closely with Princess Anne until her marriage in 1734

Lady's Banquet, containing great Variety of the most pleasant and airy Lessons for the Harpsichord (1720) contained movements from *Rinaldo* and the *Water Music,* and the *Six Overtures fitted to the Harpsicord or Spinnet* (1726) are all taken from Handel's operas. In the late 1730s, Walsh became Handel's dedicated publisher, having conducted business with Handel (and sometimes having published Handel's music without the composer's input) from the time of his arrival in London.[5]

Private or semipublic musical gatherings that featured performances of chamber and keyboard music were popular. Handel apparently found his way early on, for example, to the celebrated concerts of Thomas Britton, a dealer in small coal (charcoal). Britton was a remarkable character. While he continued to sell charcoal, crying his wares on the streets of London in a blue smock with a sack over his shoulder, he also held regular concerts that attracted a fashionable audience from 1678 to his death in 1714. He kept his store of charcoal on the ground floor of his house. The concerts took place in a long, narrow, low-ceilinged room above, "where a tall man [as Handel was] could but just stand upright."[6] One contemporary wrote in his diary in 1712 that these concerts were "the best in town, which for many years [Britton] has had weekly for his own entertainment, and of the gentry, &c., gratis, to which most foreigners of distinction for the fancy of it, occasionally went."[7]

Handel, on his arrival in London, would have been one of the for-

1723	1725	1726	1727
July	John Christopher	*Six Overtures fitted*	*January 25*
Handel moves into the	Smith Jr. begins	*to the Harpsicord*	Mary Delany and
house on Brook Street,	music study with	*or Spinnet* (Walsh)	Elizabeth Legh attend
where he lives for the	Handel	published, all from	rehearsal of Handel's
rest of his life		Handel's operas	opera *Admeto* at his
			house

eigners who fancied attending these concerts. According to Hawkins, he didn't simply attend, but participated as a performer, an image that fits well with Handel also having made his presence known through performances at public and private gatherings upon his arrival in Italy. In addition to providing an opportunity to hear some of the best and most professional hands in London and meet some of its most important music lovers, Britton's concerts offered the newly arrived composer an intriguing example of British entrepreneurial ability in a man who was able to combine a small-coal business with the presentation of public concerts that attracted the gentry and nobility.

Indeed, one can hardly imagine Handel missing Britton's concerts, and many of the regular performers and auditors became his later associates. Johann Christoph Pepusch, who came to London from Berlin in 1697, was a regular harpsichordist at the concerts and later wrote a trio sonata entitled *Smallcoal*.[8] It was here that Pepusch may first have met John Hughes, a poet and violinist whom Hawkins attested was one of the regular attendees. Hughes provided the texts for Pepusch's *Six English Cantatas*, published in 1710, and the two later collaborated on a number of English masques. Both men also played important roles in Handel's life. After returning to Hanover in the summer of 1711, when Handel determined to learn English, it was to Hughes that he applied for English text to set to music.[9] By 1717, Hughes, Pepusch, and Handel were

Music at Home continued

1730	*1731*	*1733*	*1734*
first collection of Handel's trio sonatas, Op. 2, published by Walsh (revised 1733)	*July* William Hogarth paints Anne Donnellan with the Wesley family engaged in a musical performance	second volume of Handel's keyboard suites published by Walsh	*April 3* Donnellan hosts a music party for her women friends at which everyone plays and sings *c. April 8* Delany hosts a music party during which Handel plays and all the ladies sing *December* first collection of Handel's concertos, Op. 3, advertised for sale by Walsh (published earlier in the year)

all actively engaged at the Cannons residence of the duke of Chandos, where Hughes contributed to the libretto of Handel's *Acis and Galatea*. Handel most likely met both Hughes and Pepusch at Britton's concerts.

In addition to his musical interests, Britton was also a collector of books and manuscripts. In 1694 he sold part of his collection, amounting to 1,000 items in a wide range of subjects, including, as stated in the sale catalogue, books on "divinity, history, physick and chimistry."[10] At his death, all of the remaining collection was sold. The auction catalogue of his music library, listed in Hawkins's *History*, indicates the type of music typically played at private and semipublic house concerts.[11] Older consort music by such seventeenth-century English composers as John Jenkins, Matthew Locke, and William Lawes was a staple, but more modern trio sonatas were played as well. A collected set of instrumental music by a single composer, lacking a title or recognizable text, was often identified by a "work number" or "opus" (abbreviated "Op."). The printed sets of trio sonatas in Britton's library included Corelli's Op. 4 (1694) and both Antonio Caldara's Op. 1 (1693) and Op. 2 (1699). Manuscript copies of music existed side by side with newly published music, but the manuscripts were often copied from prints. A manuscript copy in Britton's

1735
April 11
Delany and Donnellan attend the first rehearsal of Handel's *Alcina* at his house

1736
January 24
Handel plays and sings through the new score of *Alexander's Feast* at his house for Lord Shaftesbury
November
Delany studies the keyboard method of Joseph Kelway and is given Handel's suites to learn
December
Donnellan sings Handel's "Verdi prati" from the opera *Alcina* at a house concert in Dublin

1738
Handel composes two keyboard suites for Princess Louisa

c. 1738
Handel prepares a keyboard version of his cantata *Crudel tiranno amor* (for a student?)

1739
February 28
second collection of Handel's trio sonatas, Op. 5, published by Walsh

hand of Corelli's first set of trio sonatas, Op. 1, survives at the Bodleian Library, Oxford, inscribed "used at his Assembly for many years."[12]

Corelli and Caldara, whose sonatas were especially admired in England, had been active in Rome during Handel's sojourn there. Corelli was concertmaster (lead violinist) for the performance of Handel's two Italian oratorios: *Il trionfo del Tempo e del Disinganno* (1707) and *La resurrezione* (1708). As the story goes, the two came to loggerheads over the overture to *Il trionfo*, which, being in the French style, demanded "a fire and force" to which the Italian was unaccustomed. Handel became so "piqued at the tameness" of Corelli's playing that he snatched the instrument out of his hand" and played it himself, but he ultimately substituted an Italian symphony for the original overture.[13] There is no specific evidence of an interaction between Handel and Caldara, but both were in Rome in 1708, and both had major works performed during the Lenten-Easter season. Caldara's oratorio *Il martirio di Santa Caterina* was performed under Cardinal Ottoboni's patronage at the Palazzo della Cancelleria, and Handel's *La resurrezione* was heard at the Palazzo Bonelli under Ruspoli's patronage. It is likely that the two composers attended the performances of each other's music and became acquainted.

Music at Home continued

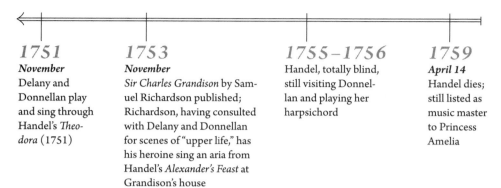

1751	1753	1755–1756	1759
November	*November*	Handel, totally blind,	*April 14*
Delany and	*Sir Charles Grandison* by Sam-	still visiting Donnel-	Handel dies;
Donnellan play	uel Richardson published;	lan and playing her	still listed as
and sing through	Richardson, having consulted	harpsichord	music master
Handel's *Theo-*	with Delany and Donnellan		to Princess
dora (1751)	for scenes of "upper life," has		Amelia
	his heroine sing an aria from		
	Handel's *Alexander's Feast* at		
	Grandison's house		

Artistic trends in Italy were followed in England as closely as possible, and we have seen how English aristocrats in Italy gathered not just music but also musicians to send back to London. When George Berkeley, the philosopher and later bishop of Cloyne in the protestant Church of Ireland, visited Rome in 1717, he made a point of writing John Percival (later the first earl of Egmont) in London about the musical performances he heard. He knew well that Percival would be interested—even though he himself was not—and wrote about the patronage circle of which Handel had been a part:

> I would say that I am a Judge of painting tho not of Musick.
> Cardinal Ottoboni has left off his entertainments, and Prince
> Ruspoli is the man who now gives musick every week to
> Strangers, where I am sure to fall a Sleep as constantly as I go.[14]

Handel's personal knowledge of such popular Italian composers as Corelli and Caldara would have been of great interest to all those attending any of the private music gatherings in England.

If one puzzles over how Handel might have recounted Italian anecdotes during his first year in London, before he had taken up the study of English, the realization is that, as in Italy, he would have spoken in French. Indeed, French would have retained its utility to him for years, as it was the primary language in the courts of both George I and II. John Percival indicates as much in describing a visit in 1724 to the prince and princess of Wales at Richmond: when the Anglican religion was attacked by various foreign ministers in the presence of the new primate of Ireland (the archbishop of Armagh), Hugh Boulter, and he remained silent, Percival could only conjecture, "Sure you must allow him to be Superlatively modest . . . But perhapps he dont understand French."[15] Handel, throughout his life in London, must have had frequent recourse not just to English and French, but also to German and Italian—German with the native-born members of the Hanoverian court, Italian with many of his musicians, French at court, and English in daily life—and despite any German accent he may have had, it is clear from his written German, French, and English that there can be no question about his fluency.

In contrast to spoken language, music was, if not universal, then pan-European. And even more than his stories (in whatever language he told them), the community of musical amateurs would have been eager to hear Handel's music. In 1710, Corelli was fifty-seven and Caldara thirty-nine. Handel was indebted to both and followed in their footsteps, but he was of a different generation. At the age of twenty-five, newly arrived from Italy, he represented the leading edge of modern music. We do not know precisely what music Handel might have offered for performance at Britton's concerts, but if he brought trio sonatas, the choice is limited. Only four of his trio sonatas can be placed before his arrival in London, and of these the Trio Sonata in F Major (now identified by its assigned number in the index of Handel's works—Händel-Werke-Verzeichnis—as HWV 392) has a particular youthful exuberance.[16] I like to think that Handel might have led with it in order to make an impression and set himself apart.

HWV 392, which survives only in manuscript, probably dates from 1707, when Handel was in Italy. It shares musical material with two sacred vocal works from the spring of that year, the solo cantata *Salve regina* and the choral *Dixit Dominus*, and it also borrows from Handel's first opera for Hamburg, *Almira* (1705). Even though Handel did not set out to publish his trio sonatas, the music circulated. By about 1730, Walsh was so

eager to produce a printed collection of the sonatas, for which he must
have seen there was a market, that he independently gathered the music
and published it as Handel's Op. 2, using another publisher's imprint. In
1733, he reissued the collection in his own name, making some corrections (perhaps under Handel's direction), and in 1739, he issued a second
collection of Handel's trio sonatas as Op. 5. Ultimately, much of HWV
392 appeared in print, but not intact. In a period when a composition
might be performed once, not published, and never heard again, it is not
surprising that composers often made use of earlier, dormant material in
the creation of new work. In the case of HWV 392, the trio sonata was
created in part from thematic material carved out of earlier vocal works,
but this turned out to be merely a temporary arrangement. Later, the
sonata was broken up and its movements reused in three different trio
sonatas.[17] Only with the publication of Op. 5 in 1739 was the musical
material of HWV 392, now spread over three separate works, "fixed."

Trio sonatas were most often written for two violins and cello
(although wind instruments could be used instead of strings), with a
keyboard instrument added to fill in the harmonies: sonatas *da chiesa*
(in the church style) emphasized serious and often contrapuntal writing and typically used organ, while sonatas *da camera* (in the chamber
style) incorporated more lighthearted material and used harpsichord.
HWV 392 is a sonata *da camera*, and its movements are infused with the
rhythms of dance. The second movement, Allegro (fast tempo), reflects
Handel's musical playfulness. The three string instruments engage in a
game of catch with a melody that starts off with a stretch of repeated notes
on one pitch, then veers off into a jazzy leaping motion, and finally accel-
erates further into fast-moving runs: one can imagine a group of children
taunting each other (*nyah, nyah*), then jumping and hopping around,
and finally running away. All three of these motives (or ideas) appear
and reappear among the three instruments, and things move along at a
jolly pace, when suddenly the music turns dark. Rather than following
the expected path, the music swerves away from what had seemed a safe
arrival and slides downward through a chromatic scale that provides
no clear harmonic footing. But just as quickly as this passage appears,

it disappears, and we are back in the game—yet something has irrevo-cably changed. The listener, caught off guard once, now knows that this young German composer writes music that doesn't quite mind its man-ners. Rather than setting up a theme and a rhythm and continuing along politely until the conclusion, Handel's music is remarkable for its inter-ruptions and dramatic juxtapositions. Anyone who has been thrilled by the unexpected exclamations of "wonderful, counselor!" in the middle of the chorus "For Unto Us a Child Is Born" in *Messiah*, or stunned by the sudden silences as Jephtha contemplates the death of his daughter in the oratorio *Jephtha*, knows this already. But for those listening to Handel's music for the first time, it must have been particularly power-ful, even shocking. For the first-time listener to the Allegro movement of Trio Sonata HWV 392, an increased attentiveness after the music unex-pectedly wanders into uncharted territory for a few measures pays off, for no sooner does Handel have all three instruments playing together once again at breakneck speed than the music cuts off sharply, as if a guillotine had fallen on it. After a long silence, the music returns to a style close to that of the earlier interruption, and it is with this passage, rather than the playful motives of the beginning, that the movement ends.

Britton was sixty-six in 1710, the year Handel arrived in London, and his taste, which tended toward chamber music and older styles, does not seem to have fully embraced more modern music. This was left to various concerts established after his death in 1714. John Wollaston, a painter best known today for his portrait of Britton, set up a series on Wednesday evenings, and another was founded at the Angel and Crown Tavern in Whitechapel.[18] Somewhat later, Handel may have participated at concerts hosted by William Caslon, an innovative developer of italic and roman typefaces. These were held first in Ironmonger Row in Old Street and then in "a large house in Chiswell-street." According to Haw-kins, Caslon's concerts consisted "mostly of Corelli's music, intermixed with the overtures of the old English and Italian operas . . . and the more modern ones of Mr. Handel."[19]

Henry Needler (1685–1760), an exact contemporary of Handel who had been one of the most important performers at Britton's concerts, also set up a concert series. He was by profession an accountant, and held various positions in the Excise Office, where, from 1724, he was accountant-general.[20] He was well known as a violinist, having studied with Daniel Purcell (1664–1717) and John Banister (1662–1736), professional composers and musicians who also performed at Britton's concerts; he was a member of the Academy of Ancient Music, of which Pepusch was a founding member, and from 1728 until his death the leader of that orchestra. Hawkins wrote that he "dwelt for the greatest part of his life in an old-fashioned house in Clement's-lane, behind St. Clement's church in the Strand, and was there frequently visited by Mr. Handel, and other [of] the most eminent masters of his time."[21] In a letter of 1729, Mary Delany told her sister of the beauty of Needler's playing: "I made Mrs. Taylor a visit this afternoon, where I met Mr. Neadler; he played two or three solos sweetly upon the violin: it soothed some of my melancholy thoughts, and I was sorry when he had done."[22]

As a violinist, Needler was an enthusiast for the music of Corelli, and reputedly introduced his concertos to England. Completed in 1711, these concertos were published posthumously, in 1714, as the composer's Op. 6 by Estienne Roger in Amsterdam. Walsh brought out his own edition in 1715. Both prints were available in London, but did not satisfy the growing eagerness for concertos that existed among Britain's amateur and aristocratic musicians. Capitalizing on this interest, Walsh published concerto arrangements of Corelli's trio sonatas in the 1720s, and in 1734 he brought out a set of six concertos by Handel, naming them Handel's Op. 3. As with his publication of Handel's Op. 2 trio sonatas, this was a publication hastily arranged. At least one of the concertos included was not by Handel at all, and some of the others may have been cobbled together by Walsh out of other works by the composer. Walsh issued a revised edition within the year, perhaps with Handel's assistance.

At least three of the concertos in the revised edition have sufficient pedigree in terms of early manuscript copies to verify Handel's authorship: Op. 3, nos. 2, 4, and 5.[23] All of them exemplify the reuse of music that otherwise would have lain unheard after its first performance. Op. 3, no. 2, derives from the original two-movement overture of the *Brockes Passion*, written for performance in about 1716 in Hamburg. Unlike the Passions of Bach that are based on the narrative story of Christ's Passion from the biblical accounts in the Gospels, the *St. Matthew Passion* and *St. John Passion*, Handel's Passion is based not directly on biblical text, but rather on a retelling by the poet Barthold Heinrich Brockes, from whom it takes its name. Many other composers besides Handel set this text, including Reinhard Keiser, the senior composer at Hamburg before Handel's arrival; Telemann, Handel's lifelong friend; and Mattheson, his friend from Hamburg.

Realizing that London audiences would never have the opportunity to hear his setting of the Germanic *Brockes Passion*, Handel found ways to reuse parts of it later, especially in the music he wrote immediately afterward at Cannons, including the Chandos Anthems and *Esther*. He turned the two instrumental movements of the *Brockes Passion* overture into the concerto Op. 3, no. 2, by adding a slow movement between them and two dance movements to follow. Although the resultant work was published only in 1734, it is probably the "new concerto" by Handel advertised in *The Daily Courant* on February 16, 1719 (at a time much closer to the composition of the Passion and the reuse of musical material from it), as one of the works to be performed at a concert in Mr. Hickford's Great Room in James Street near the King's Theatre. The newspaper announcement provides what information survives about this concert and illustrates Handel's cultivation, during his first decade in London, of the best British musicians, much as he had earlier fostered relationships with top-ranked professional musicians in Italy.

The concert was to be held on February 18 as part of a series established by Nicola Haym, the librettist of Handel's early London operas *Teseo* and *Amadigi*, whom Handel also may have met at Britton's concerts. As was typical of Haym's series, the concert at Mr. Hickford's Great Room included "Vocal and Instrumental Musick, by the best Hands"; in particular, the "new Concerto, Compos'd by Mr. Hendel," was "perform'd by Mr. Mathew Dubourg." This represents the first known interaction between the composer and the great violinist, who later would lead the orchestra in Dublin during Handel's visit when *Messiah* was premiered. Another of the performers listed in the announcement is the oboist Jean Christian Kytch, who first played with Handel in the orchestra of *Rinaldo*. He was also employed as a musician at the duke of Chandos's estate at Cannons while Handel was there, and remained important to the orchestral sound of Handel's operas through the late 1730s.

If Handel's Op. 3, no. 2, is actually the concerto to which the advertisement refers, then both Dubourg and Kytch would have been pleased with the prominence of the parts they were given. The first of five movements, a spirited Vivace, begins with highly profiled rhythmic figure in the orchestra consisting of a quick uptick to a note that then plunges down an octave. On each repetition, this motive moves a step higher, as if a giant figure is approaching step by step. After four steps the phrase begins again and is extended, now with the addition entwining filigree played by the two solo violins. The gravitas of the repeated falling octaves combined with the bustling figuration create a picture of a grand and regal entrance. The second movement joins murmuring cellos and pulsating strings in a velvety texture that dispenses with the plucked ping of the harpsichord. Against this lovely sound the solo oboe sustains a plaintive melody. After the third, fugal, movement for orchestra without solos, the fourth movement offers a distinct change from well-worked counterpoint with a lively minuet that alternates solo oboes and violins. The final movement's dancing gavotte is presented in three variants, the instrumental interest handed from oboes to cellos and basses and finally to violins. The overall compositional variety and orchestral color of this concerto, the different compositional origins of its movements notwithstanding, place it among Handel's great works.

Two other concertos in the revised Op. 3 set were also created out of works written at around the same time: Op. 3, no. 4, in part from one of the "Two New Symphonies" played at the performance of Handel's opera *Amadigi* on June 20, 1716, and Op. 3, no. 5, from the Chandos Anthems (1717–1718). All three of these Op. 3 concertos seem to have circulated in manuscript before Walsh published them in 1734 and were perhaps heard at the Caslon or Needler concerts, but manuscript copies survive only for no. 4 and no. 5. Both are in a volume dated 1727 from the private manuscript collection of Elizabeth Legh.

Legh was little more than twenty years old when she began collecting Handel's music in manuscript in 1715, and by the time of her death in 1734, her Handel collection contained thirty-nine volumes.[24] She is the only person known to have begun a comprehensive collection of Handel's music so early: other major collections were not begun before the late 1720s and most not until the late 1730s. Legh was an unlikely collector for a number of reasons. In contrast to the wealthy, male land-owner who was easily able to add luxury items to his library, Legh is the only woman to have initiated a manuscript collection during Handel's lifetime, she was unmarried, and as indicated in a draft contract drawn up by her father in 1709 when she was fifteen, had some sort of spinal deformity. The contract, if it was enacted, would have consigned her to the care of a woman who promised to work over the course of eighteen months to correct the problem to the extent that "in an even[ing] dress, without padding or other means to hide it, Elizabeth Legh shall in her cloaths appear strait an[d] even."[25] An ardent fan of Handel, Legh was acquainted with Mary Delany (then the widow Pendarves) who has provided us with a picture of Legh's attitude toward her father:

I dined yesterday at Lady Sunderland's, and in the afternoon came Miss Legh. She was in her good-humoured flights, and made us all laugh: she is very fond of me since I sent her word that I would never set my foot within her doors when I knew her father was at home, but would avoid him as I would *a toad*. She says I am a 'dear creature,' and she *loves me dearly.*[26]

Legh found great joy in music. She played the harpsichord and sang, and it is clear that she used her Handel manuscripts at the keyboard. The scores contain instances of unique transpositions of arias to a lower pitch, the addition of written-out ornamentation, and altered bass lines, all of which seem accommodations to Legh's own skills.[27] There is a wonderful anecdote that whenever she played the aria "Spera sì" from Handel's opera *Ottone* a pigeon flew down to the window from the dove-house "not far away." Legh marked this aria in her score "The Pidgeon Song."[28] One can assume she attended the performances of Handel's operas. She was close enough to the inner music circle around Handel to be present at the first rehearsal of his opera *Admeto*, which, if it followed the normal pattern, took place at the composer's house. She was so "transported with joy" by this experience that she was *"out of her senses."*[29]

Legh acquired her manuscripts of Handel's music from the composer's own scriptorium overseen by John Christopher Smith. Their source being so close to Handel lends these copies special authority today, as it also would have done during her life. It is unlikely, however, that her copies of Op. 3, nos. 4 and 5, provided the basis for performances of these concertos before they appeared later in Walsh's print. Not only is it difficult to imagine her lending out the scores, but also, as an unmarried woman without any family connection to the hosts, Legh would not have attended any of the gentlemen's consorts where the performances might have occurred.

The passion Legh exhibited in her decision to collect Handel's music in manuscript and in her private use of the scores for her own enjoyment was replicated among serious musical amateurs across the range of British society. The correspondence of John Percival and his brother Philip, both of whom were active in their musical communities and hosted regular concerts in their homes, illustrates the special importance placed on the acquisition of new music to perform.[30] Philip (Donnellan's stepfather) continually wrote from Dublin to inquire about new music, and John continually called in at London's leading music sellers: Francis Vaillant, Henry Riboteau, and John Walsh, each of whom served in turn as London agent for the Amsterdam firm of Roger.[31] Sometimes there was a specific request, as when John responded to Philip: "I have been at Vaillants and Welshes to get Manfredeni's Concerto's, but they neither have them nor know where to procure them. Perhaps I may learn from others."[32] On other occasions, there was only a plea for something new, as when Philip wrote in anticipation of his brother's visit to Ireland, "I shall be glad you cou'd bring over some new Concertos, Solos and Sonatas, for you must imagine a 6-Months Concert will wear our few very bare in that time."[33] When John traveled abroad, a special trip to Roger's establishment was de rigueur. Philip wrote, "When you are at Amsterdam you will probably enquire at Rogers, what New Musick he has and the rates. I gave direction to Ribeateaux [Riboteau] to Send for a great Cargo being duplicates of what I have, and I can know from you whether he charges too high a Rate."[34]

Printed music, however, was only part of the picture, for throughout this period, despite the growth of publishing, there remained music that could be acquired only in manuscript, like Handel's concertos before the appearance of Walsh's prints. Manuscripts could be purchased commercially, provided by a hired copyist, or written out oneself. Philip Percival, for example, wrote in 1715, "I will get the Cantatas writ out as Soon as possible but that which you take for Wilderers [Johann Hugo von Wilderer] . . . is by Sr Perti [Giacomo Antonio Perti] for none of Wilderers are for a Bass . . ."[35] Copying by hand was, of course, the only way to transmit newly written works, and Philip, like many amateur performers, also composed. In 1721 he sent his brother a copy of a concerto he had written for Henry Needler (presumably a concerto for violin, but it no longer survives). In response, Needler promised to send one of his own, but in the meantime offered a "Concerto in D# [D major]" by Francesco Geminiani and also informed the Percivals of "Some pieces lately printed in Holland" by Vivaldi, Giacomo Facco, and Evaristo Felice dall'Abaco.[36] Philip's response illustrates how hand-copied music and news about new publications passed between amateurs:

> I am obliged to Mr Needler for the Musick he promist: I had one
> of Geminiani which Mr Needler copy'd when I was in England &
> is in d#. if this be a new one I shall be glad to have it as also those
> of Vivaldi, & the others you mention'd, and the opera of Astartus
> [*Astarto* by Giovanni Bononcini, which had twenty-three
> performances at the Royal Academy of Music in the 1720–1721
> season, the most for any opera during the life of the Academy]
> when publish'd, and particularly Some of Mr Needlers own.[37]

The summer months, when both private concerts and the public season were in abeyance, offered a particularly good time for adding to one's stores of music by copying, as suggested by Philip's request to his brother in June 1714: "if at ye same time [the music is sent] you cou'd send me a good pen for drawing lines for Musick of a Moderate Wideness, I shou'd be very glad, my own being worn much, for I am still collecting & I hope you will have your share of pleasure one time or other, as well as my Self . . ."[38]

Although concerts at the houses of gentlemen musicians did not typically include much vocal music, Philip Percival's concert in Dublin was an exception. He wrote about performing cantatas by various composers, and even an oratorio for four voices by Bononcini,[39] which gives a sense of the vitality of vocal music performed at his concert: "We are next Wednesday at our Consort to perform ye little Serenata, you brought from Italy, *No, No, non ti credo*: Kit Usher performs Thirsis, his Sister Fillis, & Nancy Chloris; & were it not that our little Fraternity is near upon ye Dissolution for this season, we should have [a] store of Anthems & other pretty things, wch would much improve us as well as divert us."[40] In contrast, John Percival expressed his frustration at not being able to include as much vocal music in his concert: "We have adjourned our Concert [for the season] as you have done. I wish we had such vocal pieces performed in it as you have in yours, but our voices are so often out of the way, and have so little tast for any thing above a Cantata for two parts, and especially for the Church Stile that I have not near the pleasure with them as I had at our Concert in Dublin . . . "[41]

The complaints voiced by John Percival about not being able to program music in the sacred style at his home concerts point to the importance of the church as another venue for music composition and performance. The Percivals regularly corresponded about the music they heard at church and were active in suggesting singers to fill professional openings in the King's Choir in the Chapel Royal and the cathedrals in Dublin.[42] Handel, when he first arrived in London, attended church services in part to hear the music and meet other musicians, but one of his principal interests was the hope of gaining an opportunity to play the organ. Hawkins provided a vivid description:

> When Handel had no particular engagements, he frequently went in the afternoon to St. Paul's church, where Mr. Greene, though he was not then organist, was very assiduous in his civilities to him: By him he was introduced to, and made acquainted with the principal performers in the choir. The truth is, that Handel was very fond of St. Paul's organ, built by father Smith [no relation to John Christopher Smith], and which was then almost a new instrument; Brind was then the organist, and no very celebrated performer: The tone of the instrument delighted Handel; and a little intreaty was at any time sufficient to prevail upon him to touch it, but after he had ascended the organ-loft, it was with reluctance that he left it; and he has been known, after evening service, to play to an audience as great as ever filled the choir. After his performance was over it was his practice to adjourn with the principal persons of the choir to the Queen's Arms tavern in St. Paul's church-yard, where was a great room, with a harpsichord in it; and oftentimes an evening was there spent in music and musical conversation.[43]

On one such occasion in 1714, "Mr. Weely, a gentleman of the choir, came in and informed them that Mr. Mattheson's lessons [a term used in this period to refer to keyboard pieces, in this case by Handel's friend and colleague from Hamburg] were then to be had at Mr. Meares's shop; upon which Mr. Handel ordered them immediately to be sent for, and upon their being brought [a two-volume set of twelve keyboard suites], played them all over without rising from the instrument."[44]

Handel's own first set of keyboard lessons, or suites, was published "for the author" in 1720 by the English publisher John Cluer. Handel wrote in a prefatory note: "I have been obliged to publish Some of the following lessons because Surrepticious and incorrect copies of them had

got abroad." The reference seems to be to a pirated edition of his keyboard works that appeared sometime between 1719 and 1721, and Handel's response was either to the printed edition or to an awareness that
publication was pending. The volume appeared with the imprint of the
Amsterdam house of Roger, but was prepared by Walsh in London, most
likely while Handel was on the Continent hiring singers for the Royal
Academy of Music. Handel's reaction to this pirated edition typifies the
vigor with which he responded to the unauthorized use of his music and
to competition throughout his life. Not only did he immediately have the
suites published with his direct oversight, but he applied for and received
a Royal Privilege granting him a monopoly to publish his own work for
fourteen years. Although the specific source or sources used by Walsh
cannot be identified, manuscripts of Handel's keyboard works and keyboard arrangements of other works are known. Once again, an important early copy appears in Legh's collection, a manuscript of keyboard
music dated 1717–1718.[45] Here were works that both men and women
could enjoy and play in the privacy of their homes or at musical gatherings, and it is no wonder that publishers rushed them into print, whether
authorized or not. The ability to play the keyboard well was a standard to
which both sexes aspired.

The set of eight keyboard suites by Handel published in 1720 contains a wealth of musical invention, including improvisatory preludes,
fugues, formal dance movements, rollicking gigues (jigs), melting slow
movements, and virtuosic variations. The most famous of the variations
is the movement that concludes the Suite in E major (HWV 430). After
beginning with a simple presentation of a tune characterized by melodic
leaps, emphasizing the intervals of the third, fourth, and fifth, there follow five variations based on rhythmic diminutions—the method of pro-
gressively dividing a single note of a specified duration into quarter notes,
eighths, sixteenths, and so on, each reduction in note value squeezing
more notes into the same space of time. The original tune moves largely
in eighth notes (in other words, with eight notes equivalent in time to the
basic measure of one whole note). In the first variation, Handel shifts the
right hand into sixteenth notes, doubling the speed with which notes are

played, and in the second, he tries out this speed in the left hand. In the third and fourth variation, he follows the same pattern, now dividing the measure into twenty-four notes (eight groups of triplets). In the last variation he speeds up the notes still further, now sharing thirty-second notes between the two hands. The charmingly simple melody heard against an increasing whir of notes demanding ever more virtuosity from the player gives the movement a delightful and thrilling effect.

This popular movement is frequently titled "The Harmonious Blacksmith" because of a story devised after Handel's death that the composer took shelter from the rain in a blacksmith's shop and was inspired to the tune when he heard the striking of hammers upon the anvil. The story was granted so much credence that an effort was made to find "the" blacksmith. A candidate was chosen, one William Powell, and in 1868, more than a hundred years after Handel's death and long after the story had been discredited, the burying place of this parish clerk was marked with an elaborate gravestone identifying him as "The Harmonious Blacksmith." In another, somewhat simpler, version of the story, a music publisher in Bath, asked why he had so titled the movement, said that his father had been a blacksmith and that the melody was one of his favorite tunes, although it is unclear whether this is supposed to mean that Handel heard the tune and used it, or the blacksmith heard Handel's movement and liked it.

Despite the story's being ahistorical, one can easily envision the scenario in the music. The movement begins with the village blacksmith humming the tune as he arrives at his place of work or perhaps as he begins to strike the anvil. In the first variation, the "hammered," repeated note represents an intensification in the work, and the increasing speed of the diminutions depicts further escalation, finally resulting in a showering of sparks (thirty-second notes). Although fanciful, the story pleased generations of nineteenth- and twentieth-century keyboard students who studied this movement with their music teachers.

Learning music was essential at the upper levels of society. When Handel sought the acquaintance of Mary Delany's uncle Sir John Stanley in 1710, as related in Chapter 3, he "performed wonders" on the "little spinnet" (a small harpsichord) of the ten-year-old Delany, who declared her intention to learn to play just as well. Although she surely did not achieve that level, we know she kept working at it. As she wrote to her sister in 1736:

> My brother has *tied me down* at last to learn of Kellaway [Joseph Kelway] . . . and has made me a present of Handel's Book of Lessons. I don't find Kellaway's method difficult at all, and I believe a couple months' learning will be of use to me, at least 'twill make me practice.[46]

In 1739, Delany's sister, Anne Granville, judged the playing of Kelway "very little inferior to Handel."[47]

Delany frequently played at home and often accompanied her friend Anne Donnellan when she sang, but she was always hesitant about performing for company. Indeed, one of the difficulties for the presentation of vocal music at the gentlemen's concerts, as suggested in John Percival's comments about not being able to obtain enough good voices, was the cultural resistance to women performing in public.[48] Women of the upper and middle classes were taught to play keyboard and to sing, activities which showed off marriageable young women to advantage at private social gatherings. Beyond the age of courtship, however, women singers rarely performed outside their own homes, even when they had exceptional voices. Typically women did not take up any other instrument, and I know of no instance of a woman instrumentalist participating in any gentleman's consort.

In Philip Percival's Dublin concert, the singers were all family members. For example, the "Nancy" who sang the part of Chloris was his stepdaughter, Anne Donnellan, and his first cousins sang the roles of Thirsis and Fillis. In John Percival's diary, the only female amateur regularly mentioned as singing at his musical gatherings was his daughter Helena. After 1730, Donnellan regularly attended these concerts with her mother and stepfather, but there is never even any mention of her singing. In a diary entry of March 8, 1734, for example, John listed Donnellan as attending, but named the singers as his daughters Helena and Katherine (the latter of whom the year before had been married to Sir Thomas Hanmer, also in the audience), the professional opera singer Francesca Bertolli, and a "Mr. Mathies" (most likely the professional musician John-Nicola Matteis).[49]

Anne Donnellan was, nevertheless, widely acknowledged as a first-rate singer: Lord Orrery suggested that a man would likely throw himself at Donnellan's feet after hearing her sing Handel's "Verdi prati" from the opera *Alcina*.[50] Most often, however, she sang privately. In particular, Donnellan sang through Handel's scores with Delany at the keyboard. As late as 1751, Delany wrote to her sister, "I have got [Handel's] *Theodora*, and have great pleasure in thrumming over the sweet songs with Don[nellan], who sings every evening."[51]

Women represented a significant portion (if not the majority) of the end market for published song collections—purchased by them (or for them) for home consumption—and they frequently sang from them in their own homes and among other female company. Mary Delany wrote to her sister about such a party at Donnellan's house:

> Yesterday Lady Dysart, Lady Weymouth, Lady Cath. Hanmer, and your humble servant, met at Mrs. Donellan's, where we sang and played, and squabbled about music most extravagantly; I wish you had been there to have made up the chorus.[52]

William Hogarth depicted Anne Donnellan on the brink of song in his painting of the Wesley family. Wesley was Donnellan's cousin; born Richard Colley, he took the name Wesley in 1728 when he succeeded to the estates of his cousin Garrett Wesley. The painting of the family group illustrates a musical event about to occur.

Wesley tunes his violin, his older daughter sits at the harpsichord, Donnellan holds an open score as she prepares to sing, and the younger daughter strikes a pose with which to start her dance. All three musicians look intently at Mrs. Wesley, who seems to be giving the beat to begin.[53] Delany, an amateur painter who had studied with Goupy's uncle Lewis Goupy, was fortunate to watch Hogarth as he painted this work and

5.2 Anne Donnellan shown singing, in William Hogarth, *The Wesley Family*, 1731 (© Stratfield Saye Preservation Trust)

delighted when he offered her lessons: "Hogarth has promised to give me some instructions about drawing that will be of great use,—some rules of his own that he says will improve me more in a day than a year's learning in the common way." Not surprisingly, she heartily approved of Hogarth's portrait of the Wesley family.[54]

> I am grown passionately fond of Hogarth's painting, there is *more sense* in it than any I have seen. I believe I wrote you word that Mr. Wesley's family are drawn by him and Mrs. Donnellan [the woman standing] with them. I have had the pleasure of seeing him paint the greatest part of it; he has altered his manner of painting since you saw his pictures; he finishes more a good deal.

A year later, Delany described another musical moment with the Wesleys in Dublin when after dinner at a relative's house, the company "all adjourned to Mr. Wesley's, where I was placed at the harpsichord, and after jangling a little, Mr. Wesley took his fiddle and played to his daughters' dancing . . . We parted at half an hour after one [in the morning]."[55]

In addition to her singing, Donnellan, like most women of her class, would have had keyboard skills. In her will, she bequeathed her harpsichord to Miss Elizabeth Crosbie, the daughter of a cousin. Delany left her harpsichord and her own "written Musick Books" to her great-niece and godchild, Georgina Mary Ann Port. Among Handel's other friends, James Hunter not only had a double-keyed harpsichord made by Burkat Shudi, to whom he bequeathed it, but also, according to the auction of his belongings after his death, a fine violin and "sundry Sorts of Flutes," which he left to John Walsh.[56] Even the artist Goupy owned "Four Flutes

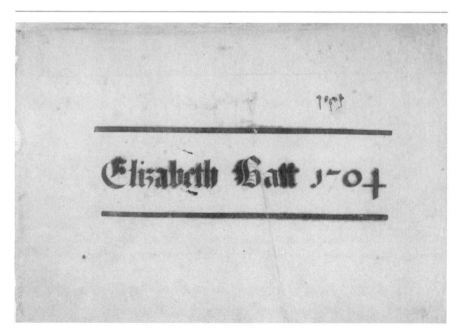

5.3   Elizabeth Batt keyboard book, 1704 (© The British Library Board [Add. MS. 52363])

5.4 Anonymous, miniature portrait of Elizabeth Mayne (courtesy private collection)

in a case," which he bequeathed to the son of William Lewis, an iron-monger on Fleet Street.

The childhood music book of Elizabeth Mayne, another fine musician among the group of friends considered here, survives in the British Library with her maiden name and date carefully lettered on the front page in Gothic print: Elizabeth Batt 1704. The date must represent the year the book was begun, when Elizabeth was nine, with additional pieces added over time, such as arias from the opera *Thomyris* (1707). Not surprisingly, the selections are largely by English composers: Purcell, Blow, Jeremiah Clarke, and William Croft. Some indication of the importance of music in the Batt household appears in bequests made by her father, Christopher Batt, who died in 1739, when Mayne had already been widowed for twelve years. He left Mayne "my House Organ and my Harpsicord made by Henricus Von Burgen," and to her daughter Elizabeth (his granddaughter), who was then fourteen, he left "my Harpsicord made by Cawton Aston."[57] According to family lore, when Mayne's son John married, his bride, Isabella Raymond, was Handel's student and was given a house organ by the composer as a wedding present. Given that the marriage took place two years after Handel's death, this account cannot be correct. However, such stories typically contain a kernel of truth, and it may be that Isabella was actually studying Handel's method with John Christopher Smith Jr.

Smith Jr. arrived in London at the age of eight in 1720 to join his father, who was overseeing Handel's scriptorium. He began studying with Handel by 1725.[58] His stepson later wrote of him:

> Under the tuition of Handel, Smith made so considerable a proficiency in music, that in the eighteenth year of his age, he commenced teacher, and instantly obtained, through his master's recommendation, and his own merit, so much employment, as to enable him to maintain himself without assistance from his father.[59]

In later years, Smith Jr. also took over the direction of oratorio performances from Handel once failing eyesight prevented the composer from continuing in that role. As Handel bequeathed his little house organ to Smith Sr., and the instrument does not appear in his will or his son's, it might be *just possible* that Smith Jr. gave the organ formerly in Handel's house to Isabella Mayne.[60]

Throughout much of his life, but never as a primary activity, Handel taught keyboard practice and composition. In Hamburg he tutored Cyril Wych, son of the British envoy. We hear nothing of Handel doing any teaching in Italy or Hanover. The earliest notice of Handel teaching in London comes through the duke of Chandos, who in 1724 wrote a letter of recommendation for a former page, George Monroe, saying that he had seen to his musical education about ten years previously by having him study with "Mr. Handell and Dr. Pepusch" and that he had thus become "a perfect master both for composition and performance on the organ & harpsichord."[61] Notations in her manuscripts suggest that Handel may have tutored Elizabeth Legh. By about 1722, Handel had been appointed music master to the three princesses, Anne, Amelia, and Caroline (aged respectively thirteen, eleven, and nine), daughters of the prince and princess of Wales, later George II and Queen Caroline, for which position he received £200 a year in addition to what had become by 1723 an annual pension of £400. Princess Anne was genuinely musical, and it was claimed many years later by the organist, composer, and theorist Jacob Wilhelm Lustig that in 1734, the year Anne married and moved away from London, Handel had declared: "Since I left your native Hamburg... nothing on earth could induce me to teach music, with one exception—Anne, the flower of princesses."[62]

The most active years of Handel's pedagogical activity in London fall more or less between the publication dates of his first set of lessons (1720) and his second (1733). In addition to these keyboard suites, there are a number of works from the period that could relate directly to his teaching. In particular there is a set of about ten cantatas in Handel's hand that he revised from earlier versions, mostly made in Italy, for pedagogic purposes. Two general characteristics are apparent in these revisions: first, all are written or transposed for soprano; and second, all have heavily figured basses. In the Baroque era, the harmonic component of the harpsichord part in ensemble music of any type was rarely written out. Rather, the composer provided a single-line, melodic bass, which the performer filled out harmonically guided by the other written parts and the occasional number (figure) indicating, when this might not otherwise be clear, what interval or intervals should be used above the bass. In the pedagogical cantatas, the bass figures are unusual both in the number per measure and in their harmonic completeness. That is, in this set of works, Handel generally indicated the exact chords (and not just the rare and unexpected musical interval) throughout. It is thought that he may have prepared the cantatas to use in teaching keyboard harmony to Princess Anne. In 1723, Anne's daily schedule lists practicing the harpsichord (or reading) between 4:00 and 5:00 in the afternoon, and after that playing music with Handel until 6:30.[63] As Anne was highly regarded not just for her keyboard skills but also as a singer, the transpositions of the "pedagogic" cantatas to soprano could indicate the range of her voice. In 1734, John, Lord Hervey referred to Handel as Anne's "singing master."[64]

Ornamented arias found among Elizabeth Legh's known manuscripts of Handel's music, and in other manuscripts more tentatively associated with her ownership, suggest that Handel may have been her "singing master" as well. Many are written or transposed for alto, indicating Legh's vocal range, but what is of particular interest is the added ornamentation. The group includes five arias from Handel's opera *Ottone* transposed down to the alto range, some with added ornamentation in Handel's hand; the arias "S'estinto è l'idol mio" and "Ch'io lasci mai" in Legh's manuscript of *Amadigi*, the first with added ornamentation and the second with an altered bass line; and "Deh! v'aprite," in Legh's manuscript of *Teseo*, transposed down and ornamented.[65] These unique versions have puzzled scholars. They were prepared in the 1710s or 1720s, close to the time of the original productions of the operas, but in many cases, the ornamentation, new bass lines, or added phrases make them incompatible with the orchestrated versions in the operas. All of these revisions and transcriptions were most likely prepared for amateurs— Handel's students or musical friends. Professional Italian singers would not have wanted or needed written-out ornamentation, especially not ornamentation that clashed with the orchestral parts intended for professional performance. Rather, these altered versions seem to be designed for private performance at home among friends or, alternatively, to teach Handel's vocal students how to ornament an existing part.[66]

An adaptation by Handel from the late 1730s of his orchestral cantata *Crudel tiranno amor* (1721) displays all of the same characteristics.[67] Like the cantatas possibly prepared for Princess Anne in the early 1720s, the work has been transposed up. It contains all the movements found in the original, but discrepancies in the bass lines, added ornamentation, and changes in the vocal part make this version, like the aria adaptations associated with Elizabeth Legh, incompatible with the orchestral score.[68] In this case, however, the bass line has not merely been fully figured to assist a beginning student, but rather a keyboard part has been largely written out (apparently for a player who did not have the ability to harmonize a bass from sight even if provided with the numbers indicating the intervals to be used). In particular, the recitatives are strikingly realized with big, multi-note chords in both hands. The frequent doubling of the bass line at the lower octave in the recitatives, and often at cadential (pausing) points in the arias as well, suggests that Handel was trying to re-create on the harpsichord the big sound of orchestral music by imitating the use of the double bass, which, by playing an octave below the other bass instruments, lends greater power to the music. In fact, his use of bass lines doubled at the lower octave in movements from his keyboard suites indicates that he frequently thought in terms of orchestral sound, even when not adapting a keyboard work from an orchestral score.

It is not known for whom Handel wrote the keyboard arrangement of *Crudel tiranno amor,* but the younger daughters of George II, Princesses Mary and Louisa, who were born about the time Handel first took up teaching their three older sisters, are possible candidates. Among the very small handful of keyboard works Handel is known to have written after 1720 are two suites from the same period as the adaptation of *Crudel tiranno amor* that are labeled in a contemporary manuscript "Lessons composed for the Princess Louisa."[69] Although Handel continued to receive payment as music master of the daughters of George II throughout his life, it is difficult to believe that Handel was still teaching any of the princesses much after the mid-1730s. In 1759, the year of his death, he is still listed among the "officers and Servants of the PRINCESS AMELIA" as *"Musick Master, G. F. Handell 200 l."* in *The Court and City Kalendar; or, Gentleman's Register, for the Year 1759*, but it seems highly improbable that he was still, or for many years previous had been, serving in this capacity.[70] Although Amelia never married, remained in London, and was by then the only one of the three older princesses still living, there is no evidence of her having much interest in music. In Philippe Mercier's painting of the four older children of George II, entitled *The Music Party*, Amelia is the only one not playing an instrument. While Prince Frederick plays the cello, Anne the harpsichord, and Caroline the mandora (a form of lute), Princess Amelia looks bored, with an open book in her lap. The annual salary of £200 that had been granted to Handel by George I for teaching his granddaughters continued long after it ceased being a fee for service.

The historical record is full of young women at the keyboard playing and singing. Not surprisingly, the image is replicated in contemporary fiction. Samuel Richardson, author of three of the most important epistolary novels of the eighteenth century, *Pamela* (1740), *Clarissa* (1748), and *Sir Charles Grandison* (1753), modeled his characters on the society he knew. All of Richardson's heroines are musical. Even Pamela, a beautiful servant girl, is able to entertain company with her keyboard skills on the spinet, as well as with her singing and dancing.[71] Clarissa, the daughter of a newly wealthy family, is more highly trained, and music is one of her few consolations. On one occasion, trying to "compose my angry passions at my Harpsichord," she doesn't just play, but composes a musical setting to a poem that fits her situation. Richardson included an engraved copy of the song in the book.[72] The actual composer is unknown, but the poem, unattributed in the novel but said to be by a lady, was written by Elizabeth Carter, a close friend of Delany and Donnellan. Nor was this the only connection to this circle of friends, who

5.5 Philippe Mercier, *The Music Party,* c. 1733, including Prince Frederick and Princesses Anne, Amelia, and Caroline (The Royal Collection © 2011 Her Majesty Queen Elizabeth II / The Bridgeman Art Library [ROC 399065])

were all partial to *Pamela* and *Clarissa*, corresponding with one another about their reactions. Donnellan wrote of the characters in *Clarissa*: "I have admired Clarissa, and wept with her. I have loved Miss Howe, and execrated Lovelace with her; and a little despised Mr. Hickman. I have shook with horror and resentment at Lovelace and all his crew. I have detested the whole Harlowe family. In short, I am thoroughly acquainted with them all, and have had every passion and affection raised in me by them."[73] Delany and Donnellan's circle counted Clarissa as one of their friends. Her life reflected their experiences, and even her will closely paralleled theirs when she bequeathed to her cousin "my harpsichord, my chamber-organ and all my music-books."[74]

By the time Richardson came to write *Sir Charles Grandison*, he had become friendly with Delany, her sister Anne Dewes, and Donnellan, and his correspondence shows that he solicited and used their advice.[75] He wrote to Donnellan in 1752: "I want much your assistance and Mrs. Delany's, in describing a scene or two in upper life."[76] She responded that he was "very humble in desiring help and scenes to be given [him]," but that if she was to help, she did not want "merely to be told of a scene between such and such, and the little incidents of the story," but needed to know "the passions, the scenery."[77] Given the example these women set for Richardson of "high and fashionable life" both in long visits and in letters, it is not surprising that the heroine of *Grandison*, Harriet Byron, not only plays and sings but is said specifically to be able to sing and play the fine airs of Handel. The depiction of musical evenings was modeled closely on the kind of social gatherings attended and hosted by Delany and Donnellan. In one such scene, Harriet is a guest at the house of Sir Charles. He asks one of his sisters to play "Shakespeare's Cuckow" ("When Daisies Pied," from *Love's Labour's Lost*) to raise his spirits, which she does "with so much spirit and humour, as delighted every body." Then his other sister "played one of [Domenico] Scarlatti's lessons," at which "for the swiftness of her fingers, and the elegancy of her manner, she could not be equalled." Finally the heroine is asked "to favour us with some of Handel's music," one of the guests saying that she had heard her "sing several songs out of the Pastoral [*Acis and Galatea*], and out of some of his finest oratorios." One of the sisters then produces the music to Handel's ode *Alexander's Feast*, which Grandison calls "the noblest composition that ever was produced by man." Although hesitant to sing something from that work out of context, Harriet plays and sings "Softly sweet, in Lydian measures," choosing it because it "not being set so full with accompanying symphonies, as most of Mr Handel's are, I performed with the more ease to myself, though I had never but once before played it over."[78]

Relaxed musical evenings at Delany's house must have been similar in geniality and range of music, but some, by comparison, were spectacular. In 1734, Delany described one in letters to her sister. First she enthusiastically laid out her plans for the party:

> Next week I shall have a very pretty party. Oh that you were to be here! The Percivals, Sir John Stanley, Bunny [her brother Bernard Granville], Lady Rich and her daughter, Mr. Hanmer, Lady Catherine [Hanmer], Mr. Handel, and Strada [his prima donna], and if my Lady S. will lend me her harpsichord, she shall be of the party.[79]

After the event, her joy was palpable, and her report must have occasioned at least a little jealousy in her sister and mother:

> I must tell you of a little entertainment of music I had last week; I never wished more heartily for you and my mother than on that occasion. I had Lady Rich and her daughter, Lady Cath. Hanmer and her husband, Mr. and Mrs. [Philip] Percival, Sir John Stanley and my brother, Mrs. Donellan, Strada and Mr. Coot. Lord Shaftesbury begged of Mr. Percival to bring him, and being a *profess'd friend* of Mr. Handel (who was here also) *was admitted*; I never was *so well* entertained at *an opera*! Mr. Handel was in the best humour in the world, and played lessons and accompanied Strada and all the ladies that sung from seven o' the clock till

eleven. I gave them tea and coffee, and about half an hour after
nine had a salver brought in of chocolate, mulled white wine and
biscuits. Everybody was easy and seemed pleased, Bunny staid
with me after the company was gone, eat a cold chick with me,
and we chatted till one o' the clock.[80]

Handel continued his social and musical visits with Delany and Donnellan throughout his life. Even well into the mid-1750s, after he had
become totally blind, Delany reported hearing him play at Donnellan's
house in Berkeley Square. In 1755, she wrote that she had "two musical entertainments offered me yesterday—a concert at Lady Cowper's,
and Mr. Handel at Mrs. Donnellan's."[81] And a year later she wrote that
having "promised Don. to call on her and meet Mr. Handel," she did so.
As she reported later to her sister, "He was not in spirits any more than
myself, but his playing is *always* delightful!"[82]

6.1 Miniature portrait of Mary Delany by Christian Friedrich Zincke in a "friendship box" containing four portraits, c. 1740: shown here Mary Delany (bottom) and Mary Howard, Lady Andover. The two portraits on the reverse (not shown) are of Margaret Cavendish, Duchess of Portland (the original owner of the friendship box), and Elizabeth Robinson Montagu (© private collection, National Portrait Gallery, London)

SIX

Marriage, Wealth, and Social Status

1728–1741
The "second" Academy to the last opera, Deidamia

WHEN A LACK OF FUNDING forced the Royal Academy of Music to close its doors in 1728, Handel faced a decision about his future. In the end, financially bolstered by his royal pension, he entered into a partnership with Heidegger, the impresario with whom he had been associated since his first arrival in London. The two men were granted the continued use of the King's Theatre as well as the costumes and sets of the academy. After a break of only eighteen months, Handel resumed the production of operas with the premiere of *Lotario* on December 2, 1729.

From the outset Handel and Heidegger faced an enormous task, their joint endeavor aiming to succeed where subscription and high-level patronage had failed in the Royal Academy of Music. Then in 1733 the difficulty was compounded with the establishment of a competing Italian opera company, the so-called Opera of the Nobility. Lord De La Warr wrote to the duke of Richmond, "there is a Spirit got up against the Dominion of Mr Handel, a subscription carry'd on, and Directors chosen, who have contracted with Senesino, and sent for Cuzzoni, and Farinelli . . . Porpora is also sent for."[1] Senesino, Handel's leading male singer since 1721, joined the new venture in June; Cuzzoni, a former leading lady for Handel during the Royal Academy period, returned to

MARRIAGE, WEALTH, AND SOCIAL STATUS: *Timeline*

1707	1709–1710	1715	1718
(Rome) Cardinal Pamphilj expresses his admiration for Handel and his music in two texts set by the composer: the oratorio *Il trionfo del Tempo e del Disinganno* and the cantata *Hendel, non può mia musa,* which compares Handel to Orpheus	(Venice) the relationship of Handel with the singer Vittoria Tarquini reported by the dowager duchess of Hanover and, later, recorded (obliquely) by the biographer Mainwaring in terms of Handel's cantata *Apollo e Dafne*	*May 25* Handel's opera *Amadigi* premieres, featuring "Pena tiranna," a lover's lament, a favorite aria of George III	*February 17* Mary Delany (née Granville, age seventeen) forced to marry Alexander Pendarves

sing for the Nobility in 1734. Nicola Porpora, an important Italian composer, arrived in 1733, and his most famous singing student, the great castrato Farinelli, in 1734. A city that had had difficulty supporting one opera company was unlikely to be able to support two, especially as the rival companies largely split the aristocratic patronage. When Handel's five-year tenure at the King's Theatre ended in July 1734, the Opera of the Nobility took over the lease and with it the annual £1,000 subsidy from the king that was tied to that venue. Forced to make other arrangements, Handel negotiated with the impresario John Rich for the use of the theater in Covent Garden, and in the autumn of 1734 began to produce his operas there in direct competition with the Opera of the Nobility.

During this critical period, Princess Anne had actively supported Handel, but her marriage in March 1734, to Willem IV (or, more commonly William), Prince of Orange-Nassau, would leave him without one of his greatest allies.[2] When she departed London for the Netherlands, John, Lord Hervey (vice-chamberlain and lord privy seal of the court of George II), reported (using third person) that "she had Handel and his operas so much at heart that even in these distressful moments she spoke as much upon his chapter as any other, and begged Lord Hervey to assist him with the utmost attention."[3]

Anne's wedding was politically important not only because it marked the marriage of the Princess Royal but also because the nuptials were the first in England of any Hanoverian heir. Preparations for the ceremony

1720	**1721**	**1722**	**1725**
April 24	*December 9*	*August 16*	*February 13*
Handel's opera	Handel's opera	marriage of Elizabeth	Handel's opera
Radamisto premieres,	*Floridante* premieres,	(née Batt) and John	*Rodelinda* premieres,
featuring "Ombra	featuring "Ah, mia	Mayne	featuring "Dove sei," a
cara," a husband's	cara," a favorite duet		husband's lament
lament	of Elizabeth Legh		*March 8*
			death of Delany's first
			husband, Alexander
			Pendarves

were extensive and elaborate, and the London papers reported that the composer to the Chapel Royal, Maurice Greene, had been commissioned to write an anthem for the occasion. Shortly after the text of his anthem was published, however, Greene was suddenly, and without explanation, replaced by Handel, who did not hold an official position at court as composer (his annual income of £600 from the Royal Treasury resulted in equal measure from the pension granted him by Queen Anne that was continued by George I, his appointment as music tutor to the young princesses, and a largely honorific court title). One can only suppose that Anne demanded the change. Handel also wrote a celebratory work in honor of the marriage, the serenata *Parnasso in festa*, which told of the festive gathering of the gods of Parnassus to celebrate the wedding of Peleus and Thetis. Both compositions drew heavily on music from Handel's oratorio *Athalia*, which had been performed in Oxford in the summer of 1733 but not yet heard in London. The reuse of music from the oratorio may have been in part to satisfy Anne's desire to hear it before her departure. A performance of the oratorio itself would not have been possible: Handel's Italian opera singers in London were not capable of managing the English text, and the story of *Athalia*, a usurping female tyrant, would have been highly inappropriate in the season of a Hanoverian wedding.[4]

   The biblical texts of Handel's anthem "This is the day which the Lord hath made," differ from those Greene had, or would have, set, and inasmuch as the selections are unusual, Handel may have played a significant

Marriage, Wealth, and Social Status continued

1726

March 12
Handel's opera *Scipione*
premieres, featuring
Berenice's "Scoglio d'im-
mota fronte," a woman's
defiance

1728

Anne Donnellan, who
never marries, refuses
the proposal of marriage
from George Berkeley,
later Bishop of Cloyne
June 1
closing of the Royal
Academy of Music
December 17
clandestine marriage of
Catherine and James
Hunter (age seventeen)

1729

December 2
Handel and
Heidegger
resume opera
production at the
King's Theatre
with the premiere
of Handel's
Lotario

1731

December 6
marriage of
Handel's niece
Johanna Friderica
to Johann Ernst
Floercke; Handel
sends expensive
wedding gifts

role in their choice. Whereas Greene had stuck with the conventional "Queen's psalm" ("My heart overflows with a goodly theme," Psalm 45), Handel, for what was apparently the first time in a royal wedding anthem, struck out into the "wisdom books" of Proverbs and Ecclesiastes.[5] Perhaps the newly chosen text represented something of Handel's personal regard for the woman he referred to as "the flower of princesses": "A good Wife is a good Portion . . . Strength and Honour are her Clothing . . . She opens her mouth with Wisdom, and in her Tongue is the Law of Kindness . . . Many Daughters have done virtuously, but thou excellest them all."

The serenata *Parnasso in festa* may, in contrast, have carried a more political message. In the text Handel set, the gods of Parnassus turn out to celebrate the wedding of Peleus and Thetis, but a look at the backstory reveals that the sea-goddess Thetis had only assented to marriage with the human Peleus after he had been taught how to subdue her by the sea-god Proteus. If this story was chosen specifically to reflect the marriage of Princess Anne to Prince Willem, then the libretto certainly had a Hanoverian slant. Anne's grandfather, George I, had first hoped for a marriage between Anne and her cousin Frederick, Prince of Prussia, later Frederick the Great, a match that would have enhanced the power and wealth of the family, but this plan did not succeed. After further efforts to negotiate a suitable marriage for her repeatedly failed, she is

1733

January 27
Handel's opera *Orlando* premieres at King's Theatre
July 10
Handel's oratorio *Athalia* premieres in Oxford
December 29
opening of the Opera of the Nobility in competition with Handel

1734

March 13
Handel's wedding serenata *Parnasso in festa* premieres
March 14
marriage of Princess Anne; performance of Handel's wedding anthem "This is the day"
July
Opera of the Nobility takes over the King's Theatre and Heidegger joins with them; Handel moves to Covent Garden in collaboration with the impresario John Rich

1735

April 16
Handel's opera *Alcina* premieres, featuring "Verdi prati," a favorite aria of Anne Donnellan

reported to have said when informed of the impending match with the prince of Orange, a hunchback who brought neither wealth nor power to the alliance, that she would marry the prospective groom "if it was a baboon." Her father, George II, responded, "Well, then, there is baboon enough for you."[6] When her fiancé arrived in London in November of 1733, Anne did not bother to meet him. Rather, she remained "in her own apartment at her harpsichord with some of the opera people."[7] The choice of subject for the serenata may have suggested this indifference on Anne's part and stressed that it was only with special dispensation from George II (the sea-god Proteus) that the lesser House of Orange (the mortal Peleus) was able to wed with the mighty House of Hanover (the goddess Thetis).

Parnasso in festa premiered on March 13, 1734, and Anne and Willem were married the next day in the chapel at St. James's Palace, at which service Handel's anthem "This is the day which the Lord hath made" was performed. The serenata was heard three more times, after which, on April 22, Anne left London to reside in the Netherlands. As a composition tailored to a specific occasion, *Parnasso in festa* would not have been frequently performed, and after the premiere of *Athalia* in London, in 1735, there would have been even less reason to hear it, but it seemed to have a special cachet at court and perhaps with Handel himself. It was revived

Marriage, Wealth, and Social Status continued

1736

April 27
marriage of Frederick, Prince of Wales; performance of Handel's wedding anthem "Sing unto God"
May 12
Handel's wedding opera *Atalanta* premieres

1737

May 14
Handel is reported to have suffered a "paralytick disorder"
June 14
closing of the Opera of the Nobility
June 25
end of Handel's season at Covent Garden
October 29
reorganized opera company opens at the King's Theatre with Handel as composer

1740

May 8
marriage of Princess Mary in London by proxy; Handel's anthem draws on selected movements from the anthems he had written for the Prince of Wales and for Princess Anne
November 22
Handel's opera *Imeneo* premieres (perhaps at one point to have been associated with the wedding of Princess Mary)

for two performances in 1737, for a single performance in 1740, and once more on Anne's seventh wedding anniversary on March 14, 1741.

The years after Anne's departure were difficult for Handel. The Opera of the Nobility continued its direct competition with him until 1737, and although he triumphed, he suffered physically and financially. His physical collapse in the spring of 1737, described in the papers as a "paralytick disorder," resulted in his traveling to Aix-la-Chapelle for treatment. Meanwhile his cash reserves dwindled to nothing. At the end of the opera season in 1732, Handel had deposited £2,400 into a cash account at the Bank of England. Over the six-year existence of this account, there were no further deposits, despite Handel's composition of such masterly operas as *Ariodante* (1734) and *Alcina* (1735), the publication of his Op. 3 concertos (1734), and the composition of both an anthem ("Sing unto God") and an opera (*Atalanta*) for the wedding of Frederick, Prince of Wales, in 1736. Yet Handel does not seem to have considered himself in desperate straits. During these years, even though he wasn't able to set aside any money at all, the £600 he continued to receive annually from the Royal Treasury kept him afloat personally and professionally.[8]

Handel's financial situation, which was dependent on how much of his income he needed to allocate for professional expenses to further his career, concerned only his own way of life. He never married. Unlike Prin-

1741

January 10
Deidamia premieres, Handel's
last Italian opera

February 10
final performance of *Deidamia*;
last performance of an Italian
opera produced by Handel

1743

June 9
marriage of Mary
and Patrick Delany

1747

February 23
marriage of Elizabeth and
Ralph Palmer

cess Anne and Prince Frederick—and more generally, the children of most aristocratic families—he was not required to wed, nor does it seem he wanted to. He was, however, a handsome young man and in his early years apparently attracted admirers of both sexes. Cardinal Benedetto Pamphilj referred to Handel's allure in his libretto for *Il trionfo del Tempo e del Disinganno* (1707), when he described the composer as "a graceful youth who awakens sweet delight with enticing tones" and placed him (and his music) in Pleasure's palace among the earthly temptations that must be renounced. In the cantata text *Hendel, non può mia musa*, the cardinal went so far as to suggest that his own sexual desire had been awakened by the composer, whom he described as a greater musician than Orpheus.[9] Handel also attracted the prima donna Vittoria Tarquini, a married woman who was also the mistress of Prince Ferdinando de' Medici of Tuscany. Given the prince's importance as a patron, a liaison between Handel and Vittoria probably would have been damaging to both of their careers, but Mainwaring claimed that Tarquini was willing to ignore the risk: the singer was "so little sensible . . . of her exalted situation, that she conceived a design of transferring her affections" to Handel, since to her "HANDEL seemed almost as great and majestic as APOLLO, and it was far from the lady's intention to be so cruel and obstinate as DAPHNE."[10] Writing in 1799, when the sanctification of Handel was already in full flower, William Coxe argued that "Handel was too prudent to encourage an attachment, which might have occasioned the ruin of both."[11] Whatever the true nature of their relationship, rumors flew. In 1710, when Handel arrived in Hanover, the elector's mother wrote to her daughter in Berlin:

> Here there is no news save that the Elector has taken into his service a kapellmeister named Handel, who plays the harpsichord marvellously to the enjoyment of the Electoral Prince and Princess [later George II and Queen Caroline]. He is a good-looking man and the talk is that he was the lover of Victoria.[12]

If Handel did have a relationship with Tarquini, it may have been the first in a sequence of such liaisons. An eighteenth-century copy of Mainwaring's biography annotated (perhaps) by George III contains the comment that Handel's "Amours were rather of short duration, always with[in] the pale of his own profession."[13] There is, however, no evidence for such "amours."

Coxe took pains to emphasize that Handel's not marrying "must not be attributed to any deficiency of personal attractions," but rather to the composer's independent disposition, "which feared degradation, and dreaded confinement." Although this explanation smacks somewhat of special pleading, Handel's resistance to restrictive commitments can be documented clearly in his professional life and could have influenced his personal life as well. It was, after all, an attitude inculcated in him as a boy. A dread of confinement, however, is only part of the picture. Handel's marital status was surely influenced as much or more by social convention, as Coxe implied with undocumented anecdotes about supposed female students of Handel who were "desirous of a matrimonial alliance." In one case, according to Coxe, the family absolutely forbade the marriage of their daughter with a "fiddler." In the other case, the marriage was dependent on Handel "renouncing his profession."[14]

In eighteenth-century England, marriage was a prime factor in social mobility and financial security. The well-to-do hoped to cement and increase their wealth and land holdings through advantageous matches, while the less-well-off sought to marry up. Personal choice was often forfeited or forbidden as families negotiated advantageous mergers. In such a market, Handel was not a prize marital candidate. He was a foreigner, without landed property (the prime measure of wealth), and despite his musical talent and annual pension, he was insecure financially. In the social structure of the period, musicians were often accorded servant status, a practice that had concerned his family when he was younger. Handel, following his family's guidance, held himself apart from such employment by never taking a position in Italy or England as a household musician. He also adopted the designation "esquire" shortly after his arrival in London, indicating that he considered himself a gentleman by birth. Although marrying down the social ladder would have been possible, Handel's strong self-image must have made that idea unthinkable (again, according to Coxe, he feared social "degradation"), and his lack of property and social status obstructed his marrying up.

All of Handel's close friends and legatees lived outside the boundaries of conventional marriage. Bernard Granville, Goupy, and Donnellan chose not to marry. Delany was forced into a hated marriage as a teenager. Widowed at the age of twenty-five, she lived the life of a single woman for eighteen years. When she considered a second marriage, to the cleric Dr. Patrick Delany, she met with strong family opposition even though she was then forty-three years old. "D.D.," as she called him, had neither appropriate fortune nor appropriate birth, and her decision to marry in spite of her family's disapproval caused a permanent strain in her relationship with her male relatives. James Hunter married unconventionally at the age of seventeen, and the Hunter family appears not to have fully acknowledged his wife, despite the marriage's lasting twenty-eight years until her death in 1757. Although Ralph Palmer married at the more appropriate age of thirty-five, his wife, Elizabeth (née Peacock), was the daughter of former servants, and the unequal match permanently altered his relationship with his extended aristocratic family. Elizabeth Mayne was the only one of this group of friends to have had children. She was also the only one to marry conventionally, at least in the superficial sense of having had it agreed upon by both families and a full marriage contract drawn up. It was hardly conventional, however, that her husband-to-be had murdered a prostitute in Exeter eleven years before the wedding.[15] As it turned out, Mayne was widowed after only four years and lived single until her death forty-four years later.

Marrying for love was unusual, and generally considered a wholly insufficient reason for marriage, but women, in particular, continued to desire and discuss the possibility. Elizabeth Robinson Montagu repeatedly turned to the subject in her letters to Donnellan, naming love and friendship as equally "necessary to be the Foundation of Marriage." She recognized, however, that she was "Laying Schemes fitter for the Virtuous Utopia then the present State of Great Brittain."[16] In Handel's operas, the frequent triumph of true love over obligation or tyranny, but also of duty over unregulated passion, anticipates the later importance of these emotional themes in the English novel. Operatic arias were published in collections, separated from the plot of the opera in which they first appeared, and often with newly written English texts. Many of these described the trials and realization of love or plumbed the depths of despair, and they found a ready market, the music reflecting the emotions and experiences of Handel's audience.

Most of Handel's operas, in addition to whatever political or financial messages they may have contained, revolve around courtship and end with a wedding. *Radamisto* (1720) and *Rodelinda* (1725) stand out by portraying strong marriages rather than courtship. In both works, the couples must overcome tremendous obstacles to their happiness, and the husbands, when separated from their wives, express their deep and abiding love. Radamisto, when he thinks his wife has died, does not cry or shout, but in the aria "Ombra cara" quietly pleads with her departed spirit to be happy and to wait for him: after he has taken revenge for her death, he will fly, ever faithful, to embrace her. The simple and sustained melody suggests that Radamisto is calm and controlled, but the constant waves of flowing eighth notes in the strings bespeak a flood of emotion into which the repeated appearance of a sliding chromatic descent gives voice to the pain not otherwise expressed. The intensity of the love he expresses is stronger than any raging at fate could possibly be. In *Rodelinda*, it is the husband, Bertarido who is thought dead, and when he returns in disguise to reclaim his kingdom from the usurping tyrant (an ever-popular theme in London during this period), he stumbles on his own supposed tomb. Contemplating death, his thoughts turn to his wife. "Dove sei," he sings. "Where are you, my dearest beloved? Come bring comfort to my soul." As with Radamisto's "Ombra cara," Bertarido's "Dove sei" is quiet and intense. The urgency of his love is depicted by his beginning the aria, so to speak, before it starts, the opening question, "Where are you?" plaintively wafted into space without accompaniment at the end of the recitative. Throughout the aria, the short phrases, the repeated emphasis on the word "vieni" (come to me), and the yearning expressed in the gentle extensions of the word "consolar" (console) depict the deep love a man might have for his wife. The couples in *Radamisto* and *Rodelinda* illustrated the ideal of a loving marriage strong enough to withstand the fiercest strokes of destiny.

More often, however, opera (and literature) focused on the obstacles facing young lovers on the path to a desired union. In both *Scipione* (1726) and *Floridante* (1721), a young woman (the principal heroine) faces the threat of a forced marriage after she has given her love to another. In *Scipione*, the conquering general Scipio not only desires Berenice but holds a legitimate claim over her as a prize of war. Her steadfast resistance to Scipio's approaches and constancy to her beloved drew from Handel one of his most powerful arias, "Scoglio d'immota fronte" (Like an unmoving rock). While strings, oboes, and bassoons rage around her, Berenice holds her ground, entering into the tempest with a thrilling phrase leaping upward through the notes of the most stable chord (the tonic) of the key, reaching a high A before falling back an octave. Her strength in the face of forces mounted against her probably exhilarated the audience, especially the women for whom such resistance was not socially feasible. In *Floridante*, young lovers declare they will remain faithful despite their forced separation. The build-up in the intensity of their emotions makes "Ah, mia cara" (Ah, my beloved) a very powerful duet. First, Floridante sings that leaving Elmira means going to his death, and Elmira responds that if he leaves she will die of grief. Then the two voices begin to join together, initially in short, almost fragmented, phrases, and finally entwining over a long period lovingly extended as the young lovers alternate in completing each other's phrases and resist separation. Elizabeth Legh, a woman whose spinal deformity largely eliminated her from the marriage market, wrote "O imortall" over the top of this duet in her score, indicating her appreciation of the music, but also suggesting the vicarious pleasure she took in participating in a kind of emotional experience closed to her in any other way.

In most of Handel's operas, the young lovers conquer adversity, but the pain of lost or unreciprocated love is never absent. In *Amadigi* (1715), Dardano, having realized that he has no chance of winning Oriana from Amadigi, sings of his anguish in "Pena tiranna," an aria that continued to be copied and anthologized to the end of the eighteenth century. The repeating bass emphasizes the sense of endless despair, and the plangent sound of the bassoon and oboe solos resounds with Dardano's distress. In 1784, George III asked Mary Delany to assist him in borrowing the score of this aria specifically from the rare collection of Handel manuscripts that her nephew John Dewes had inherited from her brother, identifying it by its English text, "Still I adore you, tho' you deny me."[17] More complex is the regret experienced by Ruggiero in *Alcina* (1735) when he is released from the magic spell placed on him by the sorceress Alcina and turns to follow his betrothed, Bradamante; rather than expressing joy at his reunion with her, he looks back at the magical island he realizes will be destroyed and mourns its loss. His aria "Verdi prati" (Verdant meadows) expresses with simple but deep poignancy the inherent difficulty of giving up youthful desire for adult respectability. As Ruggiero looks back, the beautiful, short-breathed phrases of his melody create an elegy to enchantment. An anonymous author wrote in the *Universal Spectator* shortly after the opera's initial run that "Alcina's Beauty, and Inconstancy proves the short Duration of all sublunary Enjoyments, which are lost as soon as attain'd." Although this is certainly true of *Orlando furioso*, the sixteenth-century epic poem by Ludovico Ariosto on which the libretto was based, Handel's music added to that moral the lingering attractiveness of such delights. Anne Donnellan received special compliments for her performances of this aria at private musicales.

The past twenty years have witnessed an extraordinary revival of Handel's operas on the stage, yet alongside this commercial success is a persistent complaint about their "convoluted plots." A quick search on the Internet offers a plethora of such statements touching on most of the operas, including all those just mentioned. *Radamisto* is described as having a plot that, "predictably, is convoluted and fairly incidental,"[18] while *Rodelinda* is seen as a "standard issue *opera seria*—[with] . . . arias linked by a plain recitative dramatizing a convoluted plot."[19] Listeners are cautioned that "the plot of *Amadigi di Gaula* is convoluted,"[20] and it is said that "to describe the plot of *Alcina* as convoluted would be the height of understatement."[21] This conviction is so strongly held that it is assumed to be unassailably true, and directors have felt free to turn the so-called complexities into comedy. No one experiencing the original productions, however, would have thought the plots difficult or convoluted. Not only would the audience members have recognized the frequent allusions to contemporary politics and international trade, but the themes of love and longing touched them personally. The marital experiences of Mary Delany, James Hunter, and Elizabeth Palmer, as well as the refusal of Anne Donnellan to marry, illustrate the kinds of situations that made the stories of obstructed ardor so relevant to Handel's audience.

Mary Delany's first marriage offers a particularly poignant example. Following the Hanoverian succession, her family faced difficult times, as noted in Chapter 3. Her father, Bernard Granville, was a younger son without an independent income and financially reliant on his elder brother, George Granville, Lord Lansdowne, the poet and dramatist whose popular dramatic opera *The British Enchanters* (1706) had influenced the construction of Handel's *Rinaldo* (1711). The Granville family, however, supported the Stuart restoration, and in 1715, Lansdowne was charged with high treason and imprisoned in the Tower of London. Bernard himself was briefly incarcerated, and to escape suspicion and reduce expenses, the family fled London for a more rural existence in Gloucestershire. After Lansdowne was released early in 1717 from the Tower, he made his residence at Longleat, the grand estate in Wiltshire to which he had gained a right by marriage. When he and his wife extended an invitation to the sixteen-year-old Mary Delany (then Granville) to come stay with them, the family accepted with alacrity. In the years before the Hanoverian succession, Delany had lived with her uncle Sir John Stanley and his wife in the hope that she would be advanced through their social connections, and now a new opportunity had opened up with another well-to-do aunt and uncle. Delany traveled to Longleat with her father.

Soon after their arrival, Lansdowne informed his brother of a necessary reduction in the income he could provide to him, and before Bernard Granville left Longleat, he explained to his seventeen-year-old daughter their family's financial indebtedness to her uncle. It was in this context, shortly after the departure of her father, that Lansdowne presented his niece with the prospect of marriage to Alexander Pendarves, a political crony from Cornwall who was nearly sixty. She found him repulsive. As she later wrote: "I thought him ugly and disagreeable; he was fat, much afflicted with gout, and often sat in a sullen mood, which I concluded was from the gloominess of his temper."[22] He was also an alcoholic. Lansdowne, however, saw the marriage as a way to secure Pendarves's interest in Parliament and at the same time, to lessen his financial obligations to his brother. Although Delany resisted the match, her uncle gave her little choice. Years later she described her visceral aversion to Pendarves and her uncle's equally strong demand for her compliance. "He took me by the hand, and after a very pathetic speech of his love and care of me, and of my father's unhappy circumstances, my own want of fortune, and the little prospect I had of being happy if I disobliged those friends that were desirous of serving me, he told me ... how despicable I should be if I could refuse him because he was not young and handsome."[23]

"How can I describe to you," she continued, "the cruel agitation of my mind!" But she submitted. After the marriage on February 17, 1718, the couple went off to Pendarves's estate in Cornwall, where she was separated from most of the friends and family who might have provided support and comfort. In the autumn of 1720, when Pendarves had business in London that necessitated his attendance, the couple moved into "a house in a very unpleasant part of the town (Rose Street, Hog Lane, Soho)."[24] Although she may have disliked her accommodation, being in London brought Delany back in touch with old friends and family, and attending the opera became one of her great pleasures.

In a letter of November 29, 1720, Delany (then Mrs. Pendarves) wrote enthusiastically of going to the opera to see Bononcini's *Astarto*, and although there is no specific mention of it in her surviving letters, it seems likely that she also saw Handel's *Floridante* a year later.[25] Described today not just as "convoluted" but "convoluted to the point of being indecipherable," *Floridante* was immediately relevant to contemporary political issues and to international trade, as has already been mentioned, and its depiction of personal issues relating to marriage is no less powerful.[26] For Delany, the opera, although set in Persia, would have seemed in all three of these ways a reflection of her own world.

The Jacobite interpretation of the usurping tyrant's overthrow in *Floridante* as an emblem for the desired removal of the Hanoverians and restoration of the Stuarts would certainly have resonated with Delany, given that her uncle Lansdowne was leading the Jacobite cause in Paris. The Oriental setting of the opera might not have had the same kind of personal resonance, but the romance and mystery of the East would surely have been attractive, with its flavor of the popular *One Thousand and One Nights*. In one scene, Elmira, the principal female character, awaits her beloved, the prince Floridante, for a secret nocturnal meeting in a walled garden. Her aria, "Notte cara" (Dear night), the slow tempo (Lento) and dense harmonies, with throbbing and overlapping strings, and a repeated downward fall of the melody, bespeak a dark, heavy, even oppressive atmosphere completely different in character from the English night pieces with trilling nightingales or rising moons that Handel would write later.[27] It is the closest Handel ever came to depicting the sultry night air of Persia.

Delany would have identified personally with Elmira, recognizing aspects of her own life in that character's experiences. The only surviving member of the true royal family, Elmira has been raised from infancy as a daughter of the usurping King Orontes. When Orontes reveals to Elmira her true lineage (making it clear that not only is he not her real father but also that he is the murderer of her family) and then declares his lustful desire and claims her in marriage, she rages at him, spitting out the first word of her aria, "Barbaro" (Barbarous man), without waiting for the orchestra to begin. She considers it a horror that she owes her life to him and calls him a monster. In the final aria of Act II, "Ma che vuoi più da me," she asks of fate, "What more do you want from me?" and wishes for death rather than marriage to her stepfather, the murderer of her family.

The parallels between Elmira's situation and Delany's forced marriage are striking. Although her uncle did not claim her for himself, he did so for a close friend and contemporary, and she was in a situation of knowing that her family owed their financial support to him. She later described her emotions in terms appropriate to an operatic plot:

> I acted as they wished me to do, and for fear of their reproaches, made myself miserable: my chief motive, I may say, was the fear of my father and mother suffering if I disobliged [my uncle] ... I considered ... that if I showed the least reluctance, my father and mother would never consent to the match, and that would inevitably expose them, as well as myself, to [my uncle's] resentment ... I was married with *great pomp*. Never was woe drest out in gayer colours, and when I was led to the altar, I wished from my soul I had been led, as Iphigenia was, to be sacrificed.[28]

Alexander Pendarves's death on March 8, 1725, released Delany from her seven-year nightmare, but the hoped-for financial reward failed to materialize. Since Pendarves failed to sign a will, the bulk of his estate went to his niece, Mary Pendarves Basset, and Delany received only her widow's jointure (one-third of the income from the property held by her deceased husband). Lord Lansdowne, in Paris with the Jacobites, secured a lawyer to make a claim on behalf of his niece, but he could no longer remember the terms that had been agreed on at Longleat, and his papers in England were not at his disposal.[29] After a while the case was turned over to Edward Stanley (no relation to Sir John Stanley) and only resolved years later. On August 15, 1734, Delany wrote to her sister:

> We came last night to town: ... I to sign and seal the agreement between Mrs. Basset and me, and then a fig for the law and the

lawyers! I shall cast them all off, and hope never more to have anything to say to them and their quirk and quibbles.[30]

In a decree registered in the Court of Chancery on December 8, 1729, Delany had been granted £370 "per annum half yearly for her life in full satisfaction of £400 per annum claimed by the said Mary Pendarves [Delany]."[31] This legal agreement gave Delany a bare sufficiency to maintain herself in the style that the status of her family demanded, and she wrote to her sister in March 1734 that her reduced income would cost her "pains and management to keep myself clear."[32] As her great-great niece, Lady Llanover, the editor of her correspondence, explained many years later, the death of Pendarves without a will left Delany "with an income of a few hundreds instead of many thousands a year," the level of support that had been anticipated as a result of the marriage.[33] Although it was a modest portion, Delany received the £370 per annum (in half-yearly or single payments) into her account at Goslings Bank until her death in 1788.[34] Image 6.2 shows her receipt of the full payment for 1766 on November 4 (and provides a good example of her signature).

Delany's concern about living as a widowed gentlewoman on an annual income of £370 sheds light on the inadequacy of Handel's royal pension of £600 as an annual income for an eligible bachelor, especially as he was sinking all he could of this funding into his commercial operatic ventures.[35] Written in 1734, the year Delany's legal case concerning her late husband's estate was resolved, Jacob Vanderlint's book entitled *Money answers all Things* laid out the cost of living for a gentleman with a family. His view was that "few Gentleman can subsist on *£500 per Annum,* as the Prices of Things now go ... including their Families, with Servants and all."[36] In 1737, when John Percival was negotiating a marriage for his only son, the mother of the prospective bride wrote to Lady Percival spurning Percival's offer of £1,500 per annum: "I am sorry I am oblig'd to make any Objections, to a person of his Character, becoming my relation, but £1500 p^r anum, canot with thee best management, permit their living answereable to their Quality, atended with Ease to themselves." In a subsequent letter, she remains concerned about the "present

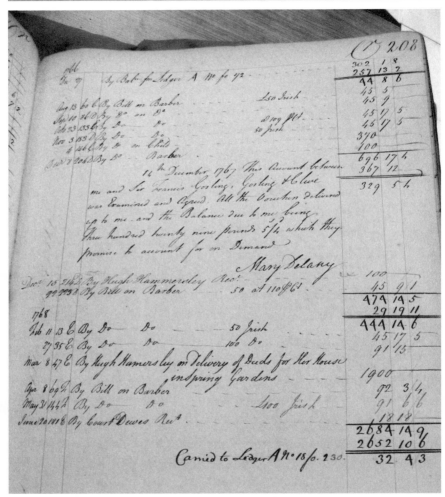

6.2 Delany's account at Goslings Bank from December 27, 1766, to June 20, 1768 (courtesy Barclays Group Archives, Manchester: ACC 130/39, p. 208)

Settlement, of £2,100 per anum."[37] Handel, although he aspired to and achieved a level of gentility, never approached the social rank of John Percival, Lord Egmont, but in 1737, he would not even have come close to Vanderlint's minimum of £500 per annum for a marriageable gentleman. At this time he had sold off all of his long-term investments, and the expendable cash in his account at the Bank of England had fallen to £200.

By 1739, even that was gone. Although 85 percent of the population of Great Britain earned £50 or less annually, Handel's income, quite aside from his foreign birth, profession, and lack of landed property, made him ineligible for marriage in the upper society in which he moved.

Despite her reduced income, Delany gained a level of social independence in widowhood that single women lacked. She abhorred the financial necessity of marriage for most women and remained opposed to it even after her happy marriage to Patrick Delany almost twenty years later. As late as 1759, she wrote to her sister wondering whether her niece Mary needed to marry at all and then defended her friend Donnellan's decision not to marry against the criticism of Donnellan's sister, Mrs. Clayton:

> I am quite of your mind about marrying; I should be very sorry to have Mary married before she was twenty, and yet if a very desirable match offers sooner, I don't know how it can be refused, if *she must* marry *at all?* A propos, we dined last Thursday at Mrs. C's., she was very lively. After dinner the discourse ran upon women living single: she said it was a foolish scheme, for *after forty* it was awkward because they *were insignificant*; and she spoke with great contempt of them. I was angry at the indignity, and said, but with great calmness, *"I wonder you should say so, for who makes better a figure, or lives more comfortably than your sister Donnellan, whose drawing-room is constantly filled with the best company, and whose conversation is much sought after?"* It would have diverted you to have seen how blank she looked. "Oh! but," she added, "they grow jealous and suspicious."——"Not at all," said I, *"unless they were inclined to it when young."*[38]

As Delany's letter suggests, Donnellan was snubbed by her family for not marrying, especially since a match appropriate to wealth and station had presented itself. As Elizabeth Robinson Montagu reported, Donnellan turned down a proposal of marriage from George Berkeley, later bishop of Cloyne, a close associate of the Percivals. She wrote that Donnellan's "reasons for refusing him I know not, friends were consenting,

circumstances equal, her opinion captivated, but perhaps aversion to
the cares of a married life, and apprehensions from some particularities
in his temper hinder'd the match."[39] Berkeley was looking for a wife in
1728, in advance of traveling to Rhode Island to begin work on his project of setting up a college on the island of Bermuda to train Protestant
clergy and convert the native populations. Maybe the prospect of leaving England for the colonies did not appeal to Donnellan. On August 1,
1728, Berkeley married Anne Forster, thereby substituting one Anne for
another and the daughter of the former Chief Justice of the Common
Pleas of Dublin (Forster) for the daughter of the former Chief Baron of
the Irish Exchequer (Donnellan). Berkeley described his wife's future in
a letter of September 3, 1728, to John Percival.

> Too morrow we sail down the River[.] M[r] James and M[r] Dalton
> go with me. So doth my Wife, a daughter of the late Chief Justice
> Forster whom I married since I saw your Lordship. I chose her for
> the qualities of her mind and her unaffected inclination to Books.
> She goes with great Chearfullness to live a plain farmers life, and
> wear Stuff of her own Spinning. Accordingly I have presented her
> with a Spinning Wheel and for her encouragement have assured her
> that from hence forward there shall never be one yard of Silk bought
> for the use of my Self her self or any of our family. Her Fortune was
> Two Thousand pounds originally but travelling and Exchange have
> reduced it to less than Fifteen hundred English Money.[40]

Whether or not Donnellan's refusal to live "a plain farmers life"
required the rocklike strength portrayed by Berenice when she refuses
the advances of Scipio in Handel's *Scipione*, the subsequent actions of
her family probably did necessitate at least strength of mind. A number
of her closest relatives took the (unsympathetic, but not illogical) view
that her refusal to make a suitable marriage, and thereby to contribute to
the family wealth, disqualified her from any family benefits. When Donnellan's brother Christopher, who died in 1751, challenged this position
by making her the chief beneficiary of his will, the surviving family rose

6.3 Miniature portrait of Anne Donnellan by Rupert Barber (fl. 1736–1772), 1752 (© National Museums Northern Ireland, Collection Ulster Museum, Belfast: BELUM. U1889)

up to prevent her from receiving the legacy. A small error in the wording of the will allowed Nehemiah Donnellan, her older brother and head of the family since their father's death, to claim most of the estate. Delany estimated Donnellan's loss at £1,500.[41] When Donnellan's mother died six months later, leaving her unmarried daughter a legacy that included her house in St. George Hanover Square, this too was overturned, so that Donnellan received only a few hundred pounds and some books.[42] Delany expressed her irritation about Donnellan's treatment to her sister: "Mrs. D's great offence is that her mother has left her all she could, and her younger brother did the same (though she will not enjoy the latter); the whole would not have amounted to £6000, and the other brother's estate is better than two thousand pounds a year, and the sister is in *vast* circumstances. How strange and how worthless are such enviers!"[43] Donnellan was left with a total bequest from her mother of £1,000, and with the investments she made in various annuities and East India stock, she received an annual income in dividends of about £160.[44]

Just as women who chose not to marry could be ostracized from the family and their wishes ignored, so those who married beneath them could suffer the same fate for putting their own desires above the maintenance or improvement of family status and wealth, the exchange of which could make winners of both parties. That is, in making marriages for their children, straitened landowners often sought wealth to cover their large expenses, and wealthy merchants sought social status. Daughters were expected to accept marriages that, if possible, added to the prestige, if not the wealth and land holdings, of their birth families, while also bringing benefits to their husband's families. At the very least, daughters who married, as in Delany's case, freed their birth families from the responsibility of supporting them. Although men did not suffer from family censure as much as women for the failure to make an advantageous match, younger sons were vulnerable. Primogeniture, or inheritance by the firstborn son, ensured that a family's wealth would be consolidated and not dissipated by sharing among siblings. Younger sons were, however, expected to marry strategically, both for themselves and for the family, and to enter professions that would provide them with an income, such as ministry or the military. By marrying well and entering a profession, younger sons, like daughters, could relieve the family of their support and potentially add to the family's status.

James Hunter, a particular friend of Handel, married without family consent at the age of seventeen. He was the youngest of three sons, and his situation was complicated by the death of both of his parents by the time he was three. His father, John Hunter, the fourth born but the eldest son to survive to adulthood, had been the primary beneficiary in his generation of a distinguished Huguenot mercantile family that had emigrated from France more than one hundred years before. In John's will, he asked that his personal belongings, including furnishings, clothing, jewelry, books, and art, be divided among his three sons equally, "as

by the Custom of the City of London they are intituled unto," but that
the main body of the estate (his extensive stock holdings) be used to purchase land and real estate for his eldest son, Henry Lannoy, and to pass by
generation to the eldest male child.[45] John chose his next younger brother,
James Hunter, a barrister of Middle Temple, and Christopher Lethieul-
lier, an eminent colleague among the Huguenot silk dyers, as guardians
for his sons "untill their respective ages of one and Twenty Years."

John Hunter's will provided for his eldest son, Henry Lannoy, to be
sent to Aleppo as an apprentice, which, as we have seen in Chapter 4,
duly occurred. No specific provision was made for the younger sons,
John and James, but both seem to have wanted to follow in the family
tradition of mercantile trade. James's early marriage, four years before
the custody agreement set up by his father was scheduled to end, does
not seem so much a rebellion, if it is possible to read any intent into his
actions, as an attempt to gain independent, adult status. Unlike many
others, he did not run off to one of the disreputable marriage houses in
the environs of the Fleet Prison, where disgraced clergy or those who
pretended to be clergy enacted marriages for a fee without asking any
questions, but he went through the process of acquiring a marriage
license from the Master of Faculties of the Archbishop of Canterbury.[46]
A license allowed a marriage to go forward without the delay or publicity associated with the traditional reading of banns (an announcement
of the forthcoming marriage) for three successive weeks at the couple's
parish church. Unlike the reading of banns, the acquisition of a license
required a fee and a sworn testimony (allegation), usually made by the
groom, that there was no impediment to the marriage.

Hunter's procurement of a license suggests a desire to act properly in
adult society, but the underlying purpose must have been to accomplish
what otherwise would have been impossible. Marriage under the age of
twenty-one was not permitted by the church without a written statement
of approval by a parent or guardian. We can assume that such permission was or would have been withheld, as James Hunter lied in his sworn
allegation that he was "above twenty-one years." He asserted equally
that his proposed wife, Catherine Cooke, was also "above twenty-one

years," a statement that can be doubted. The license, dated December 17, 1728 (James's seventeenth birthday), stated that the planned marriage was to be solemnized at the parish church of St. Mary le Savoy. In the end, James and Catherine were married in the private chapel of Somerset House, probably before the end of the month. The couple remained married, apparently happily, for the rest of their lives. Over the years, however, the wedding cost Hunter material support and encouragement from his family, and it seems his wife was never fully welcomed by them. When she died in June 1757, the notice placed in the *London Evening Post* contained an undercurrent of Hunter's resentment in the pointed phrases "not unlamented" and "esteemed by all her Acquaintance":

> Friday last died at Bow, not unlamented, the Wife of Mr. James Hunter, Scarlet-Dyer. She was Virtuous, Good, and esteemed by all her Acquaintance.[47]

Elizabeth Palmer unquestionably had the experience of being rejected by the family of her spouse, Ralph Palmer. The Palmers were landed gentry going back generations, proud of their family heritage and of advantageous marriages made. In particular, Ralph Palmer's aunt Elizabeth, his father's sister, had enhanced the family's status with her marriage to Lord John Verney (the Aleppan trader we first encountered in Chapter 4) in 1680; he later was named first viscount Fermanagh. She bore him four children before her death six years later. Although Fermanagh remarried twice more, he had no further offspring. Because of the children, the ties between the Palmers and the Verneys remained strong, especially through Ralph Palmer's father, a barrister and an avid correspondent with some of the great names of his day, including the physician Sir Hans Sloane and the painter Jonathan Richardson. He was typically referred to in the Verney correspondence as Uncle Palmer. Like the Verney family, he would certainly have expected his own two sons, Ralph and Hamey (named after Baldwin Hamey, the esteemed seventeenth-century Flemish physician to whom the Palmers were also related by marriage), to carry on and enhance the family name. Fer-

managh's son, Ralph Verney, later first earl Verney, was godfather to the young Ralph Palmer, and since the earl's son, also Ralph Verney, was only two years younger than his godson, the two Ralphs were brought up side by side as equals (see the family chart, p. 176) and sent together to John Le Hunt's Grammar School in Brentford.[48]

When Palmer's father passed away in 1746, the Verneys were the only family left to the two Palmer sons. Neither young man was married at the time, and both would have been expected to make alliances appropriate to their blood relationship to the aristocracy. It came as a shock, therefore, that after taking up his inheritance by primogeniture, Ralph Palmer made a marriage that, although financially advantageous, was well beneath him socially. The first earl Verney (Palmer's godfather) recorded his intelligence about the Peacock family in a note dated February 11, 1747; it is written on the back of a letter whose subject, as he states, was about one of his tenants "not carrying on his Dung," which phrase resonates with the tone of Lord Verney's comments on Palmer's pending marriage.

Miss Peacocks father was first footman to S[r] John Forbes a merchant in y[e] city who made him afterward his Clerk as Merchant & justice of y[e] Peace s[d] Peacock married S[r] John Forbes's Cook of an ordinary Character by whom he had y[e] present Miss Peacock & one son a profligate who married & left one Daughter to whom he had given £500 y[e] estate of money & land of six thousand pounds value falling to her by her brother dying before he was 25 y[r] old. Miss Peacocks mother is quite deaf. y[e] above account was given me by Cap[n] Tench on Wednesday y[e] 11th Feb: 1746–7.[49]

Elizabeth Peacock's father had died on June 13, 1737.[50] As the first earl Verney had been informed, Peacock left his entire estate in trust for his only son, George, once he attained the age of twenty-five, or in the event he died before that time, to his daughter Elizabeth on her twenty-fifth birthday or marriage, whichever came first. He also took

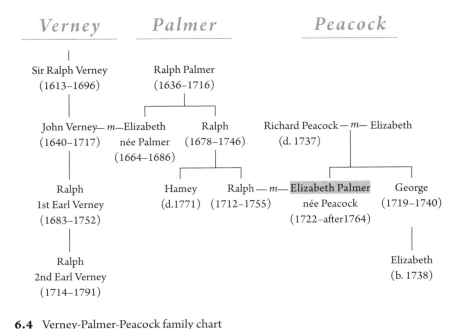

6.4 Verney-Palmer-Peacock family chart

care to "Strictly Charge and Command my said Daughter not to marry without the Advice and Consent of her Mother and of such of my said Executors and Trustees as shall be then living."[51] In July, less than a month after his father's death, George Peacock, then only nineteen years old, slipped off and married one Mary Deblois at Fleet Prison.[52] His disappearance forced the executors of his father's will to pay out of the estate for "Advertisements in Several News Papers & Coach hire & Expenses at Several Taverns & other Places Searching after the Defendant George Peacock when he absented himself from home."[53] In November of the same year, this "profligate" son, as Lord Verney describes him, contested his father's will in Chancery, claiming the whole estate on various grounds and denying the restriction on the estate to pay £50 per year to his mother.[54] In March 1738, a daughter of George Peacock was christened in the parish of St. John, Hackney. In February 1740 George Peacock himself died having "attained his age of one and Twenty Years but not having attained his Age of five and Twenty Years." Therefore, the full family inheritance passed to his sister, Elizabeth.[55]

Just as George Peacock had contracted a marriage on the heels of his father's death, so Ralph Palmer moved forward with preparations for his marriage to Elizabeth Peacock immediately following the death of his father, in February 1746. Having succeeded to his inheritance in March, he purchased a large double house in May—on Curzon Street in St. George Hanover Square (about ten blocks from Handel's house)—and immediately started improvements (as is clear in the financial records of the ironmonger Thomas Wagg).[56] In July, Elizabeth Peacock's mother took legal steps to separate her granddaughter from the Peacock estate (to which the infant might have had a claim as the child of the deceased son) by writing her own will. Making her daughter sole executrix, she bequeathed all of her "Personal Estate and Effects whatsoever and wheresoever" to her granddaughter Elizabeth Peacock, stating that this bequest "shall be in full of all claims and demands whatsoever which she may have or make for or out of any Part of the Estate or Effects of my late husband Richard Peacock deceased." She thus cleared the way for her daughter to inherit all of her father's real estate and stock holdings without impediment.[57] Early in the new year, events accelerated. On February 6, Elizabeth Peacock turned twenty-five, thereby coming into her father's estate; on February 11, Lord Verney described the low status of Elizabeth Peacock's family on the back of his correspondence; on February 20, Ralph Palmer secured a marriage license from the bishop of London; and on February 23, Ralph Palmer married Elizabeth Peacock.[58]

The meticulous preparation, legal and otherwise, undertaken by Palmer and his in-laws following the death of his father and in advance of his wedding illustrates that this was a carefully considered marriage. Despite her parents' low beginnings, Peacock's father had managed to acquire a substantial estate. It seems likely (there is no surviving marriage contract) that Peacock brought more wealth to the union than Palmer. The newspaper announcement of the wedding may have exaggerated her worth, but the sense of the marriage as financially advantageous is clear: "On Monday last Ralph Palmer, Esq., a Gentleman of good Estate, was married to Miss Peacock, a young Lady of 20,000£ Fortune."[59] The announcement emphasizes her wealth, but makes her lack of status clear by omission. Palmer's mother, in contrast, had been described in the notice of her death in 1746 as "daughter of Sir John Ernle, (Chancellor of the Exchequer in the Reigns of King Charles II, James II, and William III) by Elizabeth Lady Seymour, Relict of the Lord Seymour, and Mother of the Duke of Somerset."[60] Ralph and Elizabeth Palmer avoided marrying in a parish church, choosing instead the Mayfair Chapel (also known as St. George's Chapel or Mr. Keith's Chapel) in St. George Hanover Square. The chapel was built in 1730 for the purpose of performing marriage ceremonies without license, publication of banns, or permission of parents, but also served couples like Palmer and Peacock, who had recourse to it for reasons of privacy. Its practice ended with the Marriage Act of 1753, "an Act for the Better Preventing of Clandestine Marriage."

Ralph and Elizabeth Palmer lived on Curzon Street in Handel's neighborhood from 1747 until Ralph's death in 1755. The widowed Mrs. Palmer did not remain in this large residence, which combined the seventh and eighth house west of the Mayfair Chapel (off Chapel Street West), but instead leased it immediately to Count Karl Colloredo, imperial (Austrian) ambassador to Great Britain.[61] By the end of the year, the house was in the hands of the Verneys: Elizabeth Palmer first assigned the deed to Elizabeth Verney, sister of the first earl Verney, who then transferred in 1758 it to the second earl Verney, Palmer's childhood friend.[62] As Handel states in his will, Elizabeth Palmer resided (until 1757) on the corner of Park and Chapel (now Aldford) Streets before moving to Kensington.[63]

Palmer left his entire real and personal estate, including "plate Jewells Musical Instruments and Watches" to Elizabeth "to and for her Sole use and benefit during the Term of her natural Life," bequeathing them "after her decease" to his brother Hamey Palmer. While it was logical to leave the Palmer estates ultimately to his younger brother, since Ralph and Elizabeth had no children, there was less reason to do so with his personal property. One senses that his hand was forced, as it had been immediately after the marriage when the Palmer land holdings in Leicestershire were legally protected against Elizabeth being able to claim "any Dower or Widows Estate whatsoever in or out of the said Premises or an part thereof."[64] The Palmer and Verney families believed in "securing

6.5 Transfer form (June 30, 1761) signed by Elizabeth Palmer (courtesy of The Bank of England; AC28/781, transfer #6570, p. 253)

[the bride's] inheritance in default of issue," as Ralph Palmer's father had written to the first earl Verney at the time of his marriage, and the legal maneuverings to deny an inheritance to Elizabeth Palmer immediately following the wedding may have been for the purpose of achieving this end in lieu of a prenuptial contract.[65] Since Ralph Palmer died without issue, all of Peacock's wealth may have devolved directly to Ralph Palmer's brother and obliquely to the Verneys. Elizabeth Palmer's widow accounts at the Bank of England, continuing only until 1764 with no indication of her death, show that Hamey Palmer held power of attorney over all her transactions; Image 6.5 shows the only transfer form signed by her rather than by her brother-in-law.

Mary Delany, Anne Dewes (née Granville), Anne Donnellan, and Elizabeth Montagu (née Robinson) frequently wrote in their correspondence of what they saw as an inappropriate yoking of marriage to the financial gain of the husband. In one long letter, Delany wrote approvingly of a man who married for love, allowing his wife to pass on her marriage portion (dowry) to her youngest sister, and then rebuked another, who had left his unmarried daughter a handsome legacy with the proviso that she not marry the man to whom she was inclined. She concluded: "I have no notion of love and a knapsack, but I cannot think riches the only thing that ought to be considered in matrimony."[66] At times her anger boiled over:

> Would it were so, that I went ravaging and slaying all odious men, and that would go near to clear the world of that sort of animal; you know I never had a good opinion of them, and every day my *dislike strengthens*; some *few* I will except, but *very few*, they have so despicable an opinion of women, and treat them by their words and actions so ungenerously and inhumanly.[67]

In the exchange of status and wealth of the Palmer-Peacock marriage, Elizabeth Palmer came out the loser when her husband died. It seems she not only lost the large "bride's portion" she had brought to the marriage, but that after her husband's death, she also lost the status he had brought to her.

Years after her happy second marriage to Patrick Delany, Mary Delany still inveighed, in a letter to her sister, against the inequities and abuses of matrimonial customs:

> Why must women be *driven to the necessity* of marrying? a state that should always be a matter of *choice*! and if a young woman has not fortune sufficient to maintain her in the station she has been bred to, what can she do, but marry? and to avoid living either very obscurely or running into debt, she accepts of a match with no other view than that of interest. Has not *this* made matrimony an irksome prison to many, and prevented its being that happy union of hearts where mutual choice and mutual obligation make it the most perfect state of friendship?[68]

We do not know Handel's thoughts on the topic of marriage, but he clearly approved of the marriage in 1731 of his niece (and goddaughter) Johanna Friderica Michaelsen to Dr. Johann Ernst Floercke, a professor of law at the University of Halle. When Johanna's father (Handel's brother-in-law) wrote to request his approval for the marriage (Handel being Johanna's only living, blood relative on her mother's side), Handel responded (in French) with enthusiasm and expressed his pleasure by sending elegant gifts:

> As I now have no nearer relative than my dear niece and have always loved her particularly, you could not apprise me of more welcome news than that she is to marry a person of such distinguished character and attainments. Your agreement alone would have sufficed to place her on the pinnacle of happiness, so I take the request that you make for my approval as a further proof of your condescension. The sound upbringing which she owes to you will assure not only her own happiness but also afford you some consolation; and you will not doubt but that I shall add my voice thereto to the best of my ability.
>
> I have taken the liberty of sending the bridegroom as a small wedding-present a gold watch by Delharmes, with a gold chain, and two seal-rings, one of amethyst and the other of onyx. I trust you will approve my sending on the same occasion as a small wedding-present to the bride, my dear niece, a solitaire diamond ring; the stone weighs a little over 7 ½ grains, is of the first water and quite perfect.[69]

Handel seems to have accepted the conventions of marriage—not only with regard to his own situation but also for others. The women to whom he left gifts, Mrs. Palmer, Mrs. Mayne, and Mrs. Donnellan, were either widowed or single. He left no bequest for Mary Delany, perhaps because he felt it inappropriate, since by custom and law a married woman had no financial independence from her husband. However, it may also be that his close friendship with Delany's brother Bernard Granville, who had strongly opposed his sister's marriage, led Handel, like Delany's elder male relatives, to omit her from his bequests. Delany's residence in Ireland at the time of Handel's death could also have been a factor, as the friendship bequests made by Handel in the final days of his life are largely restricted to those who were living near him. Handel did, however, remember Granville in his will, even though, like his sister, he was not residing in London.

If Princess Anne's marriage caused Handel any regret, it was not on account of the match itself, but on the realization that it would lead to Anne's departure from London. The serenata he composed for the occasion, *Parnasso in festa*, is striking in its focus on the lingering sadness of love lost. Indeed, Act I is so occupied with the story of Apollo's loss of Daphne that, despite there being no role at all for Daphne, the entry in John Percival's diary for March 23, 1734, reads: "I went to the Opera House in the Haymarket to hear Hendel's *Serenata* composed in honour of the marriage, called 'Apollo and Daphnis.'"[70] Maybe Percival left after the first act, as the second is equally engaged with Orpheus's loss of Eurydice. Both stories elicit heartrending laments. In Act I, Clio, the muse of history, responds to Apollo's story of losing Daphne with the aria "Quanto breve," saying, "How fast do our enjoyments fly, / in the same moment they are born and die." Based on the beautiful air in *Athalia* where the righteous Josabeth expresses the concern she feels for her adopted son, "Faithful cares in vain extended," the aria has a gentle triplet rhythm, its 12/8 meter creating a sad, swaying motion while the harmony wanders through fragments of major and minor as through patches of sun and shade. In Act II, Orpheus expresses his own despair in the only accompanied recitative in the work, followed by his aria, "Ho perso il caro ben" (I have lost my dear love), based on the chorus in *Athalia* "O Lord, whom we adore." Again, the meter is 12/8, but here there is the heaviness of despair rather than the filaments of lost joy. Strong accents on each beat throb under the voice's sustained cries of desolation.

No author or model is known for the text of *Parnasso in festa*, and, given that the music is largely taken from *Athalia* and the words fitted to music already composed, Handel may have had a major role in its construction. At the least, it is intriguing that the two divinities of music whose losses are recounted, Apollo and Orpheus, are those who were adduced in references to supposed love interests Handel experienced in Italy: Pamphilj referred to him as Orpheus in the cantata *Hendel, non può mia musa,* and when Mainwaring represented Handel and Vittoria Tarquini as Apollo and Daphne, he seems to have drawn a connection to Handel's cantata *Apollo e Dafne.* If the deep expression of loss conveyed in *Parnasso in festa,* written as Handel contemplated Princess Anne's permanent departure from Britain, resulted from Handel's recollection of former loves, it would make the serenata something of a special case in his career.

Handel's operatic texts cannot be said to represent a personal record of his thoughts any more than they can offer a picture of his political views. He typically did not have a free choice of librettos and even in cases where he may have done, he probably would not have intended the audience to understand the music in this way. Rather, given the commercial necessity to compete successfully with his operatic and theatrical rivals, he would have wanted to attract listeners, much as earlier in his life he had satisfied patrons such as Prince Ruspoli, Queen Anne, and Lord Burlington by having his music resonate with their emotions and concerns. The lives of his friends illustrate how relevant his librettos could be to the audience for whom he composed. It is of particular interest, therefore, that the theme of love triumphant over adversity—be it human conflict, sorcery, madness, tyranny, or convention—which appears so frequently in Handel's early and middle operas, falls away at the end of his operatic career.

In 1737, when the attempt to sustain two separate and competing opera companies in London failed, Handel, following his recovery at the spa at Aix-la-Chapelle from a physical collapse, returned to the King's Theatre after his four years of exile at Covent Garden. As in 1729, he probably joined with Heidegger to oversee the company. By the end of the year, he had already finished his next opera, *Faramondo,* and *Serse* (Xerxes) was completed by early February 1738: the former premiered in January 1738, the latter in April. Heidegger then advertised a subscription for the following season, but this did not succeed, and Handel apparently carried on by himself producing oratorio and opera (probably all without full staging) at the King's Theatre. He then made arrangements to move to the theater at Lincoln Inn's Fields for 1739–1740, when, for the first time, he produced a season of all English works. He prepared his third and final wedding anthem, for the delayed nuptials of Princess Mary on May 8, 1740, which was celebrated in London by proxy, the absent groom represented by one of the brothers of the bride. Handel also may have kept an operatic work, similar to those he had written for Anne and Frederick, in reserve for this occasion. The possibility is suggested by his holding back the repeatedly revised score of *Imeneo*, a work that revolves around Hymen (Imeneo), the god of marriage. Perhaps the nature of the wedding by proxy precluded this type of public celebration; it may also have influenced Handel's anthem, which was not newly composed but pieced together from movements taken from the anthems for Princess Mary's older siblings. It would seem, however, that Handel waited until he was sure an opera would not be needed for Princess Mary's wedding before bringing *Imeneo* to the stage.

Meanwhile, a new company had been formed for the performance of Italian opera under the direction of Charles Sackville, Earl of Middlesex. The so-called Middlesex company opened its first full season, having made some trial runs in 1739 with varying success, at the Little Theatre in the Haymarket on January 22, 1740. Handel did not join with this endeavor; nevertheless, he did not leave Italian opera behind. In October and November of 1740, he revised and completed *Imeneo* and composed what would be his last opera, *Deidamia*. *Imeneo* premiered in the autumn of 1740, *Deidamia* in early 1741. These operas are exceptional in that authority figures do not relinquish their passions by dint of reason or clemency, and love does not conquer all. In Handel's earlier operas, the librettos typically dramatized moral lessons illustrating how the powerful should behave: tyrants who allowed vulgar desire to control their actions were generally brought to repentance or self-knowledge, and true love was crowned with marriage. Often the moral was stated clearly in the Argument provided at the beginning of the libretto, and in one case, Handel's first opera for Italy in 1707, later known as *Rodrigo*, this moral was the official title: *Vincer se stesso è la maggior vittoria* (To conquer oneself is the greatest victory).

In *Scipione* (1726), the Roman governor of Spain, Publio Cornelius Scipio, lays siege to New Carthage in North Africa and takes it by assault. He claims one of the women captives (Berenice) for himself, which is his right as conqueror. Yet after learning of her previous commitment to another, then (quoting the Argument) "as a Testimony of his signal Magnanimity, he immediately quitted his Pretensions, and generously restor'd her to him, as well as all the Treasure her Father had before offer'd for her Ransom." In making this gesture, Scipio speaks the words frequently associated in Handel's librettos with moral victory: "Now the fall'n Enemy has felt his Doom, / I'll try new Triumphs, *I'll myself o'ercome*, / And prove the bravest Conqu'ror at home" (emphasis added). In *Orlando* (1733), the eponymous hero-knight harbors an immoderate love for Angelica, but she shares a reciprocal love with Medoro, who in turn is loved by the shepherdess Dorinda. Orlando's passion drives him mad, and it is only with the assistance of his guiding spirit that his senses are restored. When he sees what havoc he has wrought in his madness he repents and gains self-knowledge, stating of himself (emphasis added):

> He quell'd Inchantments, and in Combat conquer'd,
> And often laid the fiercest Monsters low;
> *Now he's victorious o'er himself, and Love—*
> Angelica, be join'd to thy Medoro.

Once again, the Argument provided the moral: "a wise Man should be ever ready with his best Endeavours to re-conduct into the Right Way, those who have been misguided from it by the Illusion of their Passions."

In Handel's last two operas, a strikingly different ethos obtains. Men do not gain wisdom and conquer their passions so that the leading lady can be restored to her true love, whether husband or fiancé. Rather, the heroine is forced to relinquish love. In *Deidamia*, the hero Achilles, who shares a reciprocal love with Deidamia, hides in her court dressed as a woman in order to avoid being forced to part from her by those who seek his military assistance in the Trojan War. Ulysses traps him into revealing himself by offering to let the women choose from among an assortment of rich jewels and fabrics among which he has placed a shield, helmet, and sword. Achilles, of course, is more attracted to these than to the trinkets, and when Ulysses tells him of the Grecian troops going forth to defend the honor of Greece, he declares himself ready to fight and departs. Deidamia, desolate in the knowledge that Achilles goes to his death, as his fate has been long foretold, demands that the implements of war that have undone Achilles's disguise be removed from her sight. When Ulysses tries to comfort her, she chides him as the author of her pain. Her aria "M'hai resa infelice" follows directly on the recitative with no instrumental introduction, and the voice enters by itself with only the barest bass accompaniment. The slow tempo and the floating isolation of the voice in its highest register seem to indicate that time has stopped. "You have made me unhappy / that you might boast of it? / You will be able to say you oppressed / a faithful soul," sings Deidamia in a state of painful disbelief. She can only manage half a phrase at a time, and Handel creates the sense of her singing into a void by repeating her phrase at a lower register in the violins, the soulful echo emphasizing that there is no answer to her pain. Then suddenly, shaking off her paralysis, she turns to rage at Ulysses, praying that when he is next at sea horrible, driving tempests will overwhelm him in sight of his homeland. The music changes abruptly with hammering violins and rushing scales in the voice bringing the storm to life. But neither of these moods can be sustained as she is first overwhelmed again by grief and then once more torn by anger. By eschewing the normal "da capo" form (in which an ornamented repetition of the opening material returns at the end), a shape the text could easily accommodate, Handel clearly depicts that for Deidamia there will be no return, no closure.

The situation of Rosmene in *Imeneo* is even more stark. Sharing a reciprocal love with Tirinto, she is stalked by Imeneo. Like Achilles, Imeneo dresses as a woman in order to be near his love (the cross-dressing of the heroes in Handel's last two operas is another noteworthy difference from earlier work), but in this case it serves to disguise him from her. By this fraud, however, he happens to be on hand when she and her companions are captured by pirates and thus is able to save their lives. As a result, he claims Rosmene as his prize. If *Imeneo* were to follow the precedents set in Handel's earlier works, such as *Scipione* and *Orlando*, the hero, who in this case is the god of marriage, would recognize the faithful love of Rosmene and Tirinto, conquer his passion, and relinquish her to him. But this doesn't happen. Rather, Rosmene, pushed beyond endurance by the choice she is forced to make between the love she feels and the duty imposed on her by her country and her father figure, who (sounding very like Lord Lansdowne when his niece resisted his insistence that she marry Pendarves) calls her love "mere Perverseness," retreats into feigned madness in order to separate herself from what is being compelled. In setting this pretended nervous breakdown, "Ahi, che mancar mi sento!" (Ah, my senses desert me), Handel turned to his opera *Tamerlano* and the music he had written for the suicide scene of Bajazet, sultan of the Ottoman Empire, in which the sultan's increasingly weakened state is depicted by striking harmonies sinking slowly through adjacent, chromatic notes in an extraordinarily unusual manner. Whether Handel thereby meant to connect Rosmene's rejection of her lover Tirinto and dutiful acceptance of Imeneo with death is unknowable, but it does resonate with Mary Granville's image of herself as Iphigenia being led to the sacrificial altar when she resigned herself to marriage with Pendarves. In these late operas, Handel gave up the creation of romantic love stories and presented marriage as it more frequently existed among his audience: a social contract that preserved and defended wealth and status.

Handel's continued composition of Italian opera in a difficult and sometimes hostile environment for years after his large-scale English works were being well received has puzzled commentators. The answer to this conundrum may be that, like Rosmene in *Imeneo*, he was obligated. However, the commitment he made, unlike marriage, was not for life. When George I granted a royal charter for the establishment of the Royal Academy of Music, it was for a stated "Term of One and twenty Years." The Academy presented its first opera in April 1720, and Handel continued, it seems almost doggedly, to produce opera for twenty-one years thereafter, the performance of *Deidamia* on February 10, 1741, being his last. After that date, when he finally felt himself contractually free, no manner of persuasion ever convinced him to compose opera again.

JOSEPH GOUPY,

Engraved by R. Bean, from the Original Picture.

Pub. by C. Dyer, Compton Str. Soho.

7.1 Engraving of Joseph Goupy by Richard Bean, c. 1810–1817, possibly after Michael Dahl (© National Portrait Gallery, London: NPG D2795)

SEVEN

Ambition, Law, and Friendship

1738–1749
Saul, Samson, Belshazzar, Susanna, Solomon

WHEN HANDEL ARRIVED IN ENGLAND in 1710, one of his ambitions was to write opera for the London stage, and from *Rinaldo* (1711) to *Deidamia* (1741), he had done so—largely successfully. The last decade of this thirty-year period, however, was financially difficult. During the 1710s he had apparently made a profit in South Sea stock before the bubble burst and left many investors destitute, and he reinvested in South Sea annuities the first day in 1723 that the Bank of England offered them for sale. Year after year, he expended most of the capital in this annuities account over the course of the opera season, only able to replenish it after the season ended. Yet based on rising balances, his net profits rose continuously: £300 in 1725, £700 in 1726, £1,100 in 1728, and £1,250 in 1730. The account reached a high point of £2,400 in 1732, at which time Handel sold out and deposited the proceeds into a cash account. In the following years, Handel faced intense competition with the Opera of the Nobility, and when he suffered a "paralytic attack" in 1737, he became for a period physically incapacitated. In 1739, despite his annual pension of £600, his cash account bottomed out at zero.[1]

During this decade, Handel faced not only intense rivalry with a competing Italian opera company but also stiff opposition from proponents

AMBITION, LAW, AND FRIENDSHIP: *Timeline*

1732

February 23
Handel's *Esther* performed privately at the
Crown and Anchor Tavern
March 13
John Frederick Lampe and Thomas Arne begin
producing operas in English at the Little The-
ater in the Haymarket
May 2
Handel introduces *Esther* at the King's Theatre
(first London theater oratorio performance)
May 17
Lampe/Arne produce Handel's *Acis and Galatea*
June 10
Handel introduces *Acis and Galatea* at the
King's Theatre
June 22
Handel sells off all of his South Sea annuities
(£2,400) and opens a cash account

1733

June
Opera of the Nobility organized to rival Handel's
company
autumn
Joseph Goupy named drawing master to the
prince of Wales; moves his lodgings from the
house of Dorothy Chaveney to the apothecary
John Gowland
November 9
James Hunter sued by the Bank of England for
defaulting on a bill of exchange

of English opera. In March 1732, his compatriot John Frederick (Johann
Friedrich) Lampe and the English composer Thomas Arne began producing operas in English at the Little Theatre in the Haymarket. In December 1732, Aaron Hill, the man who had prepared the libretto of *Rinaldo*,
solicited Handel's interest in this endeavor, begging him "to deliver us
from our *Italian bondage*; and demonstrate, that *English* is soft enough for
Opera."[2] But even this plea from Hill was not enough to dislodge Handel
from his chosen path. While engaged in a direct struggle for supremacy in
the field of Italian opera with the Opera of the Nobility, he appears to have
had no interest in what was considered the lesser form of English opera. It
was only years later, after he had successfully established English oratorio
in London, that he turned to secular drama in English (but unstaged, in
the manner of his oratorios) with the composition of *Semele* (1744) and
Hercules (1745). In the first years of the 1730s, however, English oratorio
did not exist as a fixed form, and it was Princess Anne, apparently, who
gave Handel some of his earliest encouragement in the direction of producing oratorio in the public theaters. According to Charles Burney, it

1734

July
Opera of the Nobility takes
over the King's Theatre and
Heidegger joins with them;
Handel moves to Covent Gar-
den in collaboration with the
impresario John Rich
December
Opera of the Nobility performs
Handel's *Ottone* at the King's
Theatre

1736

Goupy appointed cabinet
(private) painter to the
prince of Wales
January
Goupy moves to house on
Savile Row
October 3
James Hunter sues for his
proceeds from the ship
Neptune

1737

June 20
Goupy's patron John
Hedges dies without making
any financial provision for
him

was she who in 1732 wanted to see Handel's *Esther*, written twelve years earlier for the duke of Chandos and performed privately at Cannons, fully acted on the London stage, but the bishop of London forbade the proposed use of the children of the Chapel Royal in the opera house.[3]

Because of the strong sense of impropriety attached to the public performance of biblical drama, Handel seems initially to have connected his public oratorio performances with such ceremonial compositions as the Coronation Anthems and the Birthday Ode for Queen Anne. He borrowed movements unchanged from both of these works in his revision (and expansion) of *Esther* (1732) and also in *Deborah* (1733), which followed directly on *Esther*'s success. John Percival wrote of the latter, "It was very magnificent, near a hundred performers."[4] Perhaps Handel thought that for the privilege of hearing such courtly magnificence he could double the prices of tickets for the opening night, but he suffered as a result, being compared in the press to Sir Robert Walpole, First Lord of the Treasury, who was trying to introduce a highly unpopular new excise tax at the same time. According to Lady Irwin it was again Princess Anne who thought the work

Ambition, Law, and Friendship continued

1739
January
Goupy sues the estate of Hedges in Common Law "in this present Hillary Term"
January 16
Handel's *Saul* premieres at the King's Theatre
February 1
Hedges's brother and heir countersues Goupy in Chancery
March 28
Handel withdraws his last £50 from the Bank of England; he holds no accounts for the next four years
April 4
Handel's *Israel in Egypt* premieres at the King's Theatre

1739–1744
Handel strongly opposed by Margaret Cecil, Lady Brown, and other "fine Italian ladeys"; Handel supported by Elizabeth Mayne "at the time of his persecution"

1740
July 15
Hedges v. Goupy case in Chancery settled out of court
by July 19
Handel and Goupy set off together for Germany

"had merit enough to deserve a guinea" (21s.) and who encouraged Handel to double the ticket price (from 10s. 6d.) for the premiere. Lady Irwin was not wholly convinced: "'tis excessive noisy, a vast number of instruments and voices, who all perform at a time, and is in music what I fancy [to be the sound of] a French ordinary [public house or tavern] in conversation."[5]

Handel followed *Deborah* with *Athalia* (1733), its libretto, like that of *Esther*, adapted from Jean Racine. Composed for the Publick Act (graduation ceremony) in Oxford, it was generally well received by the huge audience gathered, but not everyone approved. The published account of the "Oxford Act" reported complaints from those who believed that the Sheldonian Theatre had been "erected for other-guise Purposes, than to be prostituted to a Company of squeeking, bawling, out-landish Singsters, let the Agreement be what it would."[6] As we saw in Chapter 6, Handel reused a good deal of *Athalia* in his wedding anthem and sere-

1741

July 9
James Hunter and his partner declared bankrupt; around this time Hunter appears as a copyist in Handel's scriptorium (previously identified as "S7")
summer
Handel socializes (with Goupy?) at the house of Henry Furnese
autumn 1741–
autumn 1742
Handel travels to Dublin; *Messiah* premieres in Dublin, April 13, 1742

1743

February 18
Handel's *Samson* premieres at Covent Garden
March 23
first London performance of *Messiah* at Covent Garden
May 2
Handel opens a new account in South Sea annuities with a purchase of £1,500 of stock, his first account at the Bank of England after four years
June 9
marriage of Mary and Patrick Delany, disapproved-of by her family
July 28
John Christopher Smith writes of attempts by the prince of Wales and others to persuade Handel to compose an opera for the Middlesex company and of his plan to enlist Joseph Goupy to help
by autumn
Handel refuses to write a new opera for Middlesex
November 15
Middlesex company performs Handel's *Alessandro* under the name *Rossane*

nata for Princess Anne, giving her the opportunity to hear much of the music, if not the oratorio itself, before she left Britain with her husband.

Perhaps, then, it was Anne's departure that caused Handel temporarily to abandon biblical oratorios in English after 1733. Only with the new impetus of a libretto prepared by Charles Jennens did he resume their composition, producing *Saul* in January 1739. At the end of that year, following the earlier failure of both the Opera of the Nobility and the English opera company, Lord Middlesex took his first steps toward setting up yet another new Italian opera company in the Little Theatre at the Haymarket. Even though Handel wrote two more operas, he kept himself separate from this undertaking. By February 1741 he was done with opera. In the meantime, Jennens had prepared, as he called it, "another scripture collection" for Handel (which phrase identifies his first such "collection" as *Israel in Egypt*). As he wrote to a friend on July 10, 1741 (see Image 9.2):

Ambition, Law, and Friendship continued

1744

February 10
Handel's *Semele* premieres at Covent Garden
December
death of Sir John Stanley; Mary Delany receives a
token bequest in his will

1745

January 5
Handel's *Hercules* premieres at the King's Theatre
January 10
James Hunter, still in bankruptcy, buys a dye works
in Old Ford
January 17
Handel writes in the *Daily Advertiser* that he is
forced to cut short his season
January 25
Handel writes in the *Daily Advertiser* that the gener-
osity of his subscribers will permit him to continue
with a reduced season
March 27
Handel's *Belshazzar* premieres at the King's Theatre

c. 1745

Goupy paints his caricature of Handel as a hog

> I hope he will lay out his whole Genius & Skill upon it, that the
> Composition may excell all his former Compositions, as the
> Subject excells every other Subject. The Subject is Messiah.[7]

Jennens anticipated that *Messiah* would be performed the following season in London, but he was to be disappointed.

In October 1741, Handel left for Dublin, and *Messiah* was premiered
there. Some thought he had left London for good. In a letter to the *London Daily Post* at the end of Handel's season the previous April, one
"J.B." pleaded with those "Gentlemen who have taken Offence at any
Part of this great Man's Conduct . . . to take him back into Favour, and
relieve him from the cruel Persecution of those little vermin, who, taking advantage of their Displeasure, pull down his [play-] Bills as fast as
he has them pasted up; and use a thousand other little Arts to injure and
distress him." Doing anything less, he wrote, would be "an unpardon-
able Ingratitude . . . as this Oratorio of *Wednesday* next is his last for this
Season, and if Report be true, probably his last for ever in this Country."[8]

It seems, however, that Handel was once again, as he had been when

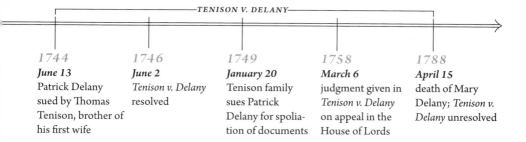

1744	1746	1749	1758	1788
June 13	**June 2**	**January 20**	**March 6**	**April 15**
Patrick Delany sued by Thomas Tenison, brother of his first wife	*Tenison v. Delany* resolved	Tenison family sues Patrick Delany for spoliation of documents	judgment given in *Tenison v. Delany* on appeal in the House of Lords	death of Mary Delany; *Tenison v. Delany* unresolved

he first visited London from Hanover in 1710–1711, on a short leash. Writing to Jennens in December 1741 of the success he had already achieved in Dublin, he commented that the Lord Lieutenant of Ireland "will easily obtain a longer Permission for me by His Majesty" in order for him to mount a second series of performances. Clearly his annual pension of £600 from the Royal Treasury came with some strings, something that may also explain his diligence in continuing to write opera for the full twenty-one years of the royal patent for the Royal Academy of Music. Freed of the latter obligation, he wrote further to Jennens that he had no need of information about operas in London, as news of them in Dublin "furnishes great Diversion and laughter," adding that he himself had heard the first opera presented by Lord Middlesex's company before leaving and that "it made me very merry all along my journey."[9]

Handel returned to London in the autumn of 1742 and set about preparing a season of English-language works. The announcement in March 1743 of a performance of *Messiah* raised a controversy about setting the name of the Lord to music and having sacred text sung in a playhouse by a "Set of People very *unfit* to *perform* so *solemn* a *Service*."[10] Not

Ambition, Law, and Friendship continued

1749

February 10
Handel's *Susanna* premieres at Covent Garden
March 17
Handel's *Solomon* premieres at Covent Garden

1752

December
Mary Delany receives nothing in
the will of her uncle Sir Anthony
Westcombe

long afterward, Handel had a relapse of the paralytic disorder he had
first experienced in 1737. Despite extraordinary pressure placed on him
at the same time to compose an opera for Middlesex's company, Handel
refused absolutely. He then proceeded to compose *Semele* (1744), which,
except that it was presented without staging like an oratorio, was an
English-language opera, and managed thereby to enrage all the Italian
opera people that he would compose an operatic work in English for his
own concert series but not a work for them. After the production of a
second "English opera," *Hercules* early in 1745, opposition to his performances forced Handel to announce the abandonment of his season in
a letter to the public printed in the *Daily Advertiser* (January 17, 1745):

> Having for a Series of Years received the greatest Obligations
> from the Nobility and Gentry of this Nation, I have always
> retained a deep Impression of their Goodness. As I perceived,
> that joining good Sense and significant Words to Musick, was
> the best Method of recommending this to an English Audience; I
> have directed my Studies that way, and endeavour'd to shew, that
> the English Language, which is so expressive of the sublimest
> Sentiments is the best adapted of any to the full and solemn
> Kind of Musick. I have the Mortification now to find, that my
> Labours to please are become ineffectual, when my Expences
> are considerably greater. To what Cause I must impute the loss
> of the publick Favour I am ignorant, but the Loss itself I shall
> always lament. In the mean time, I am assur'd that a Nation,
> whose Characteristick is Good Nature, would be affected with

the Ruin of any Man, which was owing to his Endeavours to entertain them. I am likewise persuaded, that I shall have the Forgiveness of those noble Persons, who have honour'd me with their Patronage, and their Subscription this Winter, if I beg their Permission to stop short, before my losses are too great to support, if I proceed no farther in my Undertaking; and if I intreat them to withdraw three Fourths of their Subscription, one Fourth Part only of my Proposal having been perform'd.[11]

The subscribers rallied and the season continued with a final collaboration between Handel and Jennens in the oratorio *Belshazzar*, a high point artistically, but not a success with the public. In the summer of 1745 Handel again fell ill and stayed so into the autumn.

Although the period from 1738 to 1745 was remarkably fertile for Handel in terms of his creativity, including not only *Saul; Israel in Egypt; Messiah; Belshazzar;* and *L'Allegro, il Penseroso ed il Moderato* (all having librettos by or associated with Jennens), but also *Samson, Semele,* and *Hercules,* a lack of public support and continued illness made these years the most difficult of his career. Once more, the accounts at the Bank of England tell the story. After four years without any money in the bank, Handel was able to open new accounts for both cash and stock in 1743. Although he opened an additional stock account in April of 1744, he was unable to make any deposits into either of them in 1745, and his continued professional difficulties meant that his cash account repeatedly dwindled to nothing. By May of 1745 it stood at zero and remained so until February of 1747. This was a financial turning point, however, after which Handel never again made a withdrawal of any significance from any of his accounts.[12]

Difficult as the years 1738 to 1745 were for Handel, they were equally challenging for many of his friends. James Hunter, who had married in 1728 without consulting with his family, was immediately faced with making a professional career on his own. He quickly ran into difficulties. In the course of his work as an international trader, he signed three separate bills of exchange totaling £435 with one Christopher Gottlob Schultze, a partner with a firm in Zittau, Germany. A bill of exchange worked something like a modern check in which the account holder (A) demands the bank (B) to pay a third party (C) on a specific date. The business of trade, given the built-in time delay between the acquisition of goods or materials and the accrued profit from the sale of those items or products, ran on credit, and bills of exchange functioned as a form of paper money. The critical link in such a transaction was B, in this case Hunter, who, like a bank in a bank draft, guaranteed the funds. During the stipulated delay before payment was due (sometimes of several years), the bill itself, on account of its guaranteed value, was negotiable. That is, as happened here, the payee (C) might sell the bill to a fourth party at a discount (that is, for less than the face value) in order to access the funds early, which party might in turn sell it to another, and so on.

On May 7, 1731, Schultze sold the bills he held on Hunter at a discount to the Bank of England and left the country.[13] At the due date, the Bank demanded payment from Hunter. When he refused, they could have pursued the previous holder of the bill, Schultze, except that he was out of the country and, thus, out of their reach. The Bank thus sued Hunter in the Court of Chancery.[14] Although the details of the transactions leading up to this point are unknown, one possible scenario would have Schultze delivering goods on credit or making a loan to A (unidentified in this case) and demanding payment by a specific date. "A" then drew a bill of exchange on Hunter (B), who owed him an equal or greater amount on credit or debt, to pay Schultze (C) by date certain (the bill of exchange allowing A to erase his current debt to Schultze with his past credit to Hunter without any exchange of hard currency). Schultze, who suddenly needed to leave England before this date, sold the bill at a discount, enabling him to receive funds immediately. The Bank of England, having bought the bill at a discount, stood to make a ready profit, depending on the security of Hunter (B), which the bank therefore investigated to its satisfaction. The default of Hunter (B) broke an essential trust within merchant and financial circles concerning the security of bills of exchange.

Having lied about his age on the sworn allegation of his marriage license, Hunter now used his real age to absolve himself of responsibility, for underage persons were not legally responsible for their actions. According to law, "the *Age* of Twenty-one is the full Age of Man or

Woman; which enables them to contract and manage for themselves, in Respect to their Estates, until which Time they cannot act with Security to those as deal with them; for their Acts are in most Cases either void, or voidable."[15] The bank did not accept Hunter's argument, insisting that he "for Several Years before his Accepting the said Bills of Exchange had considerable Dealings in the Business of a Merchant and hath had Severall Bills drawn upon and accepted by him which he punctually paid" and "did Act in the Business of a Merchant as if he was of full age." Hunter's response was that he could not "apprehend how he could Act otherwise if he acted at all in such Business." Hunter also claimed that he had been defrauded by Schultze, but in February 1734 the court found all of Hunter's answers insufficient.[16] So in November 1734, Hunter paid the bank "By Cash . . . in full."[17] Hunter's ability to pay the bank was directly the result of the final adjudication of his father's will in October 1734, and it is possible that his repeated, but insufficient, responses to the Chancery suit were simply a delaying tactic in expectation of this event.

The resolution of the will hung on the homecoming of Hunter's eldest brother, Henry Lannoy, from Aleppo, in December 1733. When he returned to London, he moved in with James, his youngest brother who was already an established London trader, at his residence in Billiter Square: in his personal account book, Henry Lannoy detailed payments to James for board, as well as for expenses such as a hogshead of port wine and coal for heating.[18] At the settling of their father's estate some months later, however, Henry Lannoy received by primogeniture £14,962 4s. 11½d., and his younger siblings signed statements accepting the settlement. This changed the financial relationship of the brothers. On the same day as the settlement, October 25, 1734, Henry Lannoy made a loan of £5,100 to James: £2,500 in 3½ percent South Sea bonds, £1,110 in 3½ percent India bonds, and, at 4 percent interest per year, £1,500 in cash. Hunter then paid off the bill of exchange, but even so, his finances remained unsettled. Using the stock loaned to him by his brother as collateral, he took out a £3,000 loan from the Bank of England the following year.[19]

In 1736, he and his business partner Loth Speck submitted a complaint in Chancery against one Whitlock Pryce for their portion of the proceeds from the ship *Neptune*, which had returned from Philadelphia and Jamaica.[20] This suit appears to have gone nowhere. In 1737, James was able to pay his brother two years of interest in full, but in 1739 he was only able to pay two-thirds of the total. By September 1740 he had paid back his £3,000 loan from the Bank of England in full, along with the total interest charges (at 4 percent annually) of £573 17s. 1d.[21] Perhaps his earlier run-in with the bank made this financial obligation a priority. Other bills, however, were not paid. On July 9, 1741, a "Commission of Bankrupt" was awarded against Hunter and Speck and announced in the *London Gazette*; all creditors were invited to attend the first hearing.[22] The bankruptcy reveals something of Hunter's lifestyle and ambition for gentleman status. The financial claims against him included more than £108 for wine, £85 for fish, £20 for meat, £30 for periwigs, £7 for fabric, £22 for tailoring, £24 for hats, £12 for books, and £3 for bookbinding.[23] In addition, the merchants John Gerald and Thomas Cooper sued for what must be a professionally accrued debt of £4,538 16s. 9d. James's middle brother, John, sued for £600, the value of linen bought for him, and also for a £600 bond; his brother Henry Lannoy sued for his outstanding debt.

In the eighteenth century, bankruptcy existed as an accusation made by a creditor (it was not a state one could declare for oneself), and strict criteria needed to be met. Hunter only qualified for bankruptcy because he was a trader (other professions were not eligible), he owed more than £100 to a single creditor, and he was judged to have committed an "act of bankruptcy," that is, an act intended to prevent collection. Those who did not meet these conditions became insolvent debtors, liable to imprisonment, and thereby cut off from the means of escaping their debts. In contrast, bankrupts who were able to come to an agreement with at least four-fifths of their creditors about an equitable distribution of their assets could be released from bankruptcy by means of a Certificate of Conformity. Although many bankrupts, like Hunter, were never awarded a certificate, bankruptcy allowed them to work and their creditors to receive "dividends."[24] In 1742, Hunter paid his creditors five shillings in the pound (that is, 25 percent of what was owed). Henry Lannoy Hunter records this payment in his personal account book on September 30, 1742: "James Hunter my Bro[the]r Assigner in Bankruptcy being

5[s.] in the £ as *p*[er] Book . . . £1017 1[s.] 5[d.]"—indicating that Hunter's outstanding debt to him amounted to £4,068 5s. 8d.[25]

Although Hunter never absolved his debts completely—all his possessions were auctioned after his death in 1757 and a final dividend paid to his creditors in 1761—he was able, following the initial adjudication of the bankruptcy, to purchase a dye house in Old Ford on the banks of the River Lea and to make his living selling dyed cloth to the East India Company for export. The deed was signed January 10, 1745.[26] One should not, however, think of Hunter as impoverished and single-handedly dying yards of cloth on the outskirts of London. Rather, as is clear from the fire-insurance records of the Hand-in-Hand Fire and Life Insurance Society, the purchase of the dye house was the purchase of a business. The London insurance companies, established after the London Fire of 1666, which had left Hunter's great-grandfather with severe financial losses, flourished in the late seventeenth and eighteenth centuries. These records show that Hunter's "dye house" was a collection of buildings, including: a brick residence of ten rooms with wainscoting, one marble fireplace, and five stone fireplaces; two separate dye houses; a mill house and stable; separate rooms for servants; a ripping room; a still house and cart house; barn, coach house, and stables.[27]

For both Handel and Hunter, the years leading up to 1745 were

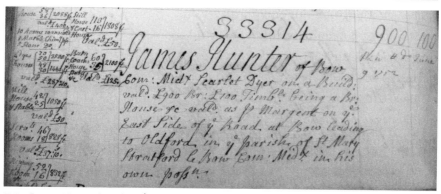

7.2 James Hunter's policy (1745, renewed 1752) with the Hand-in-Hand Fire and Life Insurance Society (London Metropolitan Archives, London: CLC/B/055/MS 08678/067, #33314, p. 286)

financially the most difficult of their lives, after which their situations eased. Hunter's troubles, though, did not dissipate, and it is during these years that one finds Hunter copying music in Handel's own scriptorium. It is not clear who was helping whom. Given the financial difficulties both men were experiencing, it may be either that Hunter was assisting Handel by providing a hand in the scriptorium, or that Handel had offered his friend an opportunity to earn some cash to tide him through his financial crisis. It also may be that Hunter was allowed to join the scriptorium simply to complete for himself the manuscript volumes of Handel's music in his own collection for which he could no longer afford to pay. Hunter's strong reputation as a music lover, and as an admirer of Handel's music in particular, outlived him. Sir John Hawkins identified him at the end of the eighteenth century not only as one of Handel's intimate friends but also as someone who aspired to a high level of discrimination in music and "at great expense had copies made for him of all the music of Handel that he could procure."[28] As late as 1858, Hunter's manuscript collection of Handel's music was still mentioned as one of only six made in Handel's lifetime.[29] Although it was long thought that Hunter's collection was broken up and lost, it now seems likely that the core of the Lennard Collection at the Fitzwilliam Museum (named for a nineteenth-century owner) preserves it.[30] One of the idiosyncrasies of this collection is that the initial period of acquisition ended abruptly in 1741, something that Hunter's bankruptcy explains.

Friendships such as that of Handel and Hunter may have been the only human relationships not governed during the first half of the eighteenth century by legal formalities or financial interest, and they were treasured for that reason. Elizabeth Robinson Montagu writing to Anne Donnellan thought friendship an essential basis to marriage, but noted its lack as "the Reason why matrimony is so seldom agreable even amongst People of Virtue & Goodness," for then "one is not sure of that gentle Treatment & Delicate Behaviour which makes Friendship Delightfull."[31] John Percival compared good friends to lovers (and not to marriage): "I confess I am pleased you should conceive as well as you can of me, friends resembling Lovers who desire to be esteem'd by the object they encline to."[32] One cannot assume, however, that friendships described as "intimate," such as Handel's with Hunter, or those openly loving and affectionate, such as Delany's with Donnellan, had a sexual component.[33] Neither can one rule it out. Sexual mores in eighteenth-century London were rather loose, notwithstanding a strict, if superficial, social code. Men openly visited prostitutes and kept mistresses, and homosexuality, despite being outlawed on penalty of death, flourished secretly—and sometimes openly. But it is well to remember that just as sex existed in London as a commodity without love, so too did intimate friendships without sex.[34]

Not surprisingly, perhaps, during the difficult period of 1738 to 1745, Handel seems to have been attracted to stories with a focus on friendship. His two great explorations of this topic appear in *Saul* (1739) and *Samson* (1743), and it is on these two oratorios that Hunter focused his scribal activity, copying the first forty-one pages of *Saul* for Bernard Granville's collection, as well as an independent full copy of *Samson*.[35] *Saul* opens with Israel celebrating the victory over the Philistines and Goliath. At first Saul heaps praise on David, the son of Jesse, who has slain Goliath, but when he senses that David has risen higher than himself in popular esteem, he commands his son Jonathan to kill him. Although the oratorio principally concerns the pride, greed, and envy that lead to Saul's downfall, the friendship of David and Jonathan is a recurrent and important thread.[36]

In the opening scenes, when David responds modestly to the praise of Saul and the crowd, Jonathan is quickly drawn to him: "Henceforth, thou noble youth," he exclaims, "accept my friendship, / And Jonathan and David are but one." His sister Merab, not so easily pleased, reminds Jonathan of David's poor fortune and low birth. But Jonathan responds in an aria: "Birth and fortune I despise! / From virtue let my friendship rise." Repetitions of the word "virtue" with pauses following each statement give emphasis to the basis of true friendship (specifically not birth or fortune), and long melodic extensions on the word "rise" suggest its scope. When Saul, filled with jealousy and rage, orders him to kill David, Jonathan is forced to weigh "filial piety" against "sacred friendship," and the latter wins. His aria "No, no, cruel father, no!" begins with his struggle to absorb the very idea of such an action, his halting voice interacting with melodic sighs in the violins, but it concludes with militaristic vigor:

"No, with my life I must defend / against the world my best, my dearest friend," he sings confidently, as violins now respond not with sighs but with a martial tattoo.

After both Saul and Jonathan die in the war against the Philistines, it becomes David's turn to express friendship's value. Toward the end of the expansive musical elegy on their deaths, David singles out Jonathan in his last words (which directly paraphrase 2 Samuel 1:26): "For thee, my brother Jonathan, / How great is my distress! / What language can my grief express? / Great was the pleasure I enjoy'd in thee, / And more than woman's love thy wond'rous love to me!"[37] Embraced by the powerful refrain of the choral community, "Oh fatal day! how low the mighty lie!" David's quiet lament depicts his personal pain, his single voice heard without further support than a "walking" bass line whose largely unbroken and even rhythm serves only to emphasize the sense of numbing isolation.

The belief that true friendship based on virtue transcends the love of women is further explored in *Samson*, which tells the story of the Israelite hero who has taken as his wife the Philistine woman Delilah ("Dalila" in Handel's libretto). Besotted with love, he reveals to her the secret of his strength, which lies in his hair, and she betrays him to his Philistine enemies. The oratorio opens after Samson's hair has been shorn in his sleep, and the former hero has been blinded and put in chains. Throughout the oratorio it is his friend Micah who stands by him as he is confronted in turn by his grieving father, the wheedling Dalila, and his boastful Philistine enemy Harapha. And it is Micah, after Dalila departs, who distinguishes male friendship from women's love. In *Saul*, Jonathan had given virtue as the basis of friendship, and now Micah describes women's love by its lack of that attribute, "It is not virtue, valour, wit, / Or comeliness of grace / That women's love can truly hit." Handel hammers home the first phrase ("It is not virtue, valour, wit") with circular melodic motion over a narrow range of three notes repeated over and over, emphasizing Micah's anger and derision. Later he puts this melody in the violins, against which Micah spits out the three attributes lacking in women's love, emphatically separating them so that the disdain becomes even more palpable. The chorus follows up this pronouncement with the trump card of "God's universal law to man" that "his life be ne'er dismay'd / By female usurpation sway'd" set as an exuberant fugue by Handel as if it were a "Hallelujah!"

Although drawing a direct line from a composer's work to his life is always hazardous, one is led to wonder whether Handel imagined himself as a man brought low by female arts. From the late 1730s, and after his return from Dublin, opposition to Handel was often described in terms of a single woman or a cabal of women. A poem thought to have been published in April 1739, *Advice to Mr. Handel: Which May Serve as an Epilogue to Israel in Egypt,* speaks of Handel's "foes" in the feminine singular, but plays out an allegory on the story of *Saul,* in which the female "fiend" takes on the character of the jealous king and Handel, the psalmist David.

> Reflect; true Merit always Envy rais'd,
> Who felt herself condemn'd, when That [Merit] was prais'd.
> In vain thou hop'st to charm with Sounds divine [like David the
>   harpist]
> The Fiend, who stops her Ears to Sounds like Thine [as did Saul];
> Deaf to the Charmer's Voice, tho' 'ere so wise:
> The more thy Art to sooth her Malice tries,
> The more her Javelin of Detraction flies [as Saul throws his jave-
>   lin at David]
> But flies in vain; her Javelin let her throw,
> Superior Merit still eludes the Blow [as David eludes Saul's javelin
>   and becomes king].[38]

The "Fiend" has been tentatively identified as Margaret Cecil, Lady Brown, an ardent supporter of the Middlesex opera in London from which Handel kept himself distant. Her opposition stepped up in the 1740s. The earl of Radnor wrote to James Harris on November 6, 1744, of various social events scheduled to conflict with Handel's performances, including that of "Lady Brown, who engaged every soul she knew at the play the same night . . . in short Lady Brown and such fine Italian ladeys, wil bear nothing but Italian singers, and composers."[39] Even Handel's close female friends saw the opposition to his work as driven by a cabal of ladies. Donnellan writes to Elizabeth Robinson in April 1740 about "the fine lady who admires and hates to excess; she doats on the dear little boy that dances, she detests Handel's Oratorios."[40] And Delany wrote in 1744 that "Semele has a strong party against it, viz. the fine ladies, petit maîtres, and *ignoramus's*."[41]

When Handel returned from Dublin in 1742, he had made his decision not to have anything more to do with Italian opera or with Middlesex's company. On arriving in London in September, he wrote to Jennens, punning on Middlesex's name: "The report that the Direction of the Opera next winter is committed to my Care, is groundless. The gentlemen who have undertaken to middle with Harmony can not agree, and are quite in a Confusion. Whether I shall do some thing in the Oratorio way (as several of my friends desire) I can not determine as yet."[42] By February 1743, he was advertising *Samson*, and at the end of the month, Horace Walpole, a director of the Middlesex company, could write, "Handel has set up an Oratorio against the Operas, and succeeds."[43] That is, Handel was seen, rightly or wrongly, not just as unwilling to cooperate with the opera company but also as setting up a competition directly against them.

John Christopher Smith, Handel's closest professional colleague and director of Handel's scriptorium, wrote to Lord Shaftesbury on July 28, 1743[44]:

> It seems that Mr. Handel promised my Lord Middlesex that if he would give him for two new operas 1000 guineas and his health would permit, He would compose for him next Season, after which He declined his promise and said He could—or would[—] do nothing for the Opera Directors . . .

Smith related that Lord Middlesex persisted, however, and made a new offer:

> He should have 1000 Guineas for two, or 500 Guineas for one new opera, and if his health would not permit Him to compose

any new one at all, and would only adjust some of His old operas, that He should have 100 Guineas for each . . .

There was also an explicit threat:

But in case Mr. Handel should refuse all these offers, that my Lord would have some of his old operas performed without Him and to let the Publick know in an advertisement what offers was made to Mr. Handel . . .

Given Handel's temperament, it may have been the threat that roused his anger, but for whatever reason, he now steadfastly refused to do anything. According to Smith, even an appeal from the prince of Wales fell on deaf ears. Handel had suffered a return of his paralytic disorder in early spring. His recovery was reported in the newspapers in April, but in May, Walpole still thought him incapacitated: "We are likely at last to have no Opera next year: Handel has had a palsy, and can't compose."[45] Either Handel suffered a relapse after his reported recovery or he had exaggerated the effects of the illness to escape the demand that he compose a new opera. The latter looks to be the case, as he seems to have had no difficulty composing the English music drama *Semele* in the month of June and the Dettingen Te Deum in July. In his letter to Lord Shaftesbury, Smith wrung his hands about this state of affairs:

But how the Quality will take it that He can compose for Himself and not for them when they offered Him more than ever He had in His life, I am not a judge and could only wish that I had not been employed in it either Directly or Indirectly . . .

In the midst of these failed negotiations due to Handel's intransigence, Smith hit upon the idea of calling on Goupy to make the case to the composer. Not only was the artist a well-known friend of Handel, but he was also in the employ of the prince of Wales. As an artist himself, he understood the requirements of patronage and knew the pitfalls, and like Handel, he had suffered a significant financial setback in the late 1730s, when in 1737 his employer, John Hedges, died without paying him for his work and without leaving him any bequest. Goupy sued Hedges's estate in the court of Common Law, and Hedges's brother and heir, Charles Hedges, countersued in the Court of Chancery. The court documents provide a chronicle of Goupy's life that is by turns entertaining and somewhat mysterious.[46]

In the 1710s and 1720s, the professional lives of Goupy and Handel had contained many parallels. The two shared many of the same patrons, including George I, Baron Kielmansegg, and the duke of Chandos. The Royal Academy of Music hired Handel to compose and Goupy to design sets for the opera. Within a year of Handel's moving into his house on Brook Street in 1723, Goupy moved into lodgings around the corner on Bond Street. Toward the end of the 1720s, however, Goupy gave up the broad-based patronage he had developed in exchange for what looked to be a sinecure: private patronage from John Hedges, a barrister and Member of Parliament. Goupy must have considered it a lucky stroke that in 1729, the year after the Royal Academy of Music closed its doors, Hedges was appointed treasurer to Frederick, Prince of Wales, opening up opportunities for him at court. By 1733, Goupy had been made drawing master to the prince (much as Handel had been named music master to the princesses ten years earlier). Thus, when Handel first fell into difficulties in the late 1720s, Goupy seemed to have landed securely on his feet, and he reached out to help his close friend. He served as a mediator (unsuccessfully) between Handel and his former librettist Paolo Rolli, and on July 4, 1730, the two men went together to the Bank of England to transfer £100 from Goupy's stock account to Handel's, but whether this amount was paid into Handel's account by Goupy or purchased by Handel from Goupy is unclear.

There is no documented record of Goupy and Handel working together in the 1730s as they did in the 1720s, although it has been thought that Goupy might have designed the set for Handel's *Atalanta* (1736), written in honor of the wedding of his patron, the prince of Wales. That the second earl of Oxford at his death in 1741 owned a miniature portrait by Goupy of Angelica and Medoro (young lovers in *Orlando furioso*) has also suggested that the artist may have played a role in the set design of Handel's opera *Orlando* (1733). Irrespective of these possibilities, Goupy's professional situation throughout most of the 1730s had been strong. It suffered a significant setback, however, in June 1737 with the death of Hedges.

Hedges's patronage had offered Goupy an extravagant lifestyle. As friends and servants later made abundantly clear in depositions supporting Goupy's legal suit against Hedges's estate, the artist spent a great deal of time with Hedges, both at his house in St. George Hanover Square and at his country house in Finchley. Hedges's servant testified to Goupy's regular attendance on his master (often staying at the Finchley house for "three or four days together"), to Hedges's frequent commands that he seek Goupy out, and to Hedges's discomfort when the artist couldn't be located. Goupy kept art supplies at both houses and did much of his work in those places. He also kept a fishing rod and tackle at Finchley, and had left a gold watch at one of the residences. Toward the end of 1733, Goupy moved a few doors down the street to new lodgings in the house of John Gowland, the apothecary on Bond Street who later attended Handel on his deathbed and received from the composer a bequest in his will. Since this move could not have been prompted for reasons of geography, it raises some questions about Goupy's relationship with his prior landlady, Dorothy Chaveney.

Like Goupy, Chaveney was probably of French heritage (she is often titled Madam rather than Mrs. in the Westminster rate books). The various alternative spellings of her name (Chaney, Chafney, and Chifney) suggest oral transmission, and just as Goupy's French name was probably Goupée (as it is sometimes spelled), Chaveney was probably Chavigny. Although she is described solely as Goupy's landlady, a different picture emerges with the understanding that the title of "Mrs." (like Madam) was honorific for adult women regardless of marriage and the realization that Chaveney was about ten years younger than Goupy and probably in her twenties when he moved into the house on Bond Street.

During the period Goupy lodged with Chaveney, he wrote to one of his patrons that "My Wife and Self joyn in our hearty Service to you & your Lady." As there is no record of Goupy ever marrying or any evidence that he was a married man, it seems that Goupy and Chaveney lived as man and wife during this period. When he moved to Gowland's house, she pressed him for the full rent of his period of residence (for which she had not charged him during his lodging). Goupy applied to Hedges for the money, and according to Hedges's brother, he paid out "the Sum of Two hundred pounds or some such Sum of Money for or on the Account of the said Goupy unto Mrs. Chaveny and to whom the said Goupy was at or about the time aforesaid considerably indebted." In other words, Hedges paid for Goupy's release from his relationship (of whatever type) with Chaveney.

Chaveney, however, was not willing to be so easily bought off. In 1736, probably in connection with his new appointment as Prince Frederick's personal painter (the actual title is "Cabinet Painter," in the sense of a cabinet being a private space), Goupy moved into his own house at 24 Savile Row. This elevation must have further aroused Chaveney's sense of injustice, for she succeeded in dictating a letter for Goupy to send to Hedges. The letter is remarkable from a number of points of view, not least of which is that it was written in a kind of code. Goupy wrote that when the "Coalman" had come he was "so unhappy as to have no Coal" for him; he therefore requested a loan from Hedges of £100. In the court documents, he acknowledged that the word "coal" in the letter meant "money." "Coalman" must therefore refer to some sort of creditor, suggesting that Goupy needed money to pay that person off. The letter having been composed by Chaveney, it seems likely that she was the creditor. The question is, for what was she demanding payment? The letter continues with what is perhaps its most remarkable sentence: "I am afraid you will think this is worse then the chance of getting the Itch of me, and I am more ashamed of this distemper then that I wish this desire of mine may not be troublesome to you." This sentence is not explained, but its aura of sexual innuendo is marked. It may be that Chaveney, because of her intimate association with Goupy, had information that would have been damaging to him and Hedges.

Lacking a detailed written record, such as that provided in the diary of Samuel Pepys, sexual activity remains behind closed doors.[47] However, William Bateman, the son of Hedges's half-sister, had openly acknowledged homosexual affairs and was separated from his wife on that account in 1738.[48] Mary Delany wrote casually to her sister in December of that year that Lord Bateman, as "you must know," has for "some times been famous for a male seraglio." Lord Hervey, Vice-Chamberlain and Lord Privy Seal at court from 1730 to 1743, was known to be bisexual. He married, sired children, and had affairs with women and men. It is thought he may have had an affair with the prince of Wales in the years 1730 to 1732.[49] If in 1737 Chaveney could have associated Hedges or Goupy (both of whom were employed by the prince), along with Bateman and perhaps the prince himself, with a homosexual circle, it would certainly explain the threatening undercurrent of the letter sent to Hedges.

Whatever the letter dictated by Chaveney meant, Hedges "so much resented [it] and was so Angry" on account of it that, according to his brother, "he would not for some time afterwards" condescend to see Goupy at all. He died about a year later on June 20, 1737, without settling his accounts with Goupy or leaving him anything in his will. Goupy sued, and Hedges's brother and legatee countersued. Having made its way through intricate legal channels, the case arrived at a summation on July 11, 1740, when both sides were asked to submit all "books, paper & writings in their Custody or power relating to the Matters in Question" and for these to be open to inspection by both sides. Goupy had attested that he had letters from Hedges that supported his claims, and their content must have persuaded Hedges's brother to drop his case. Four days after these materials were submitted to the court, Charles Hedges asked that his suit against Goupy be dismissed and that all papers delivered to the court be returned.

At no point in the many court documents is Handel's name mentioned, nor was Handel asked to make a deposition in support of Goupy, but the two artists remained in close contact during these years in the late 1730s that proved difficult for both of them. By the summer of 1740, Handel had overcome opposition from the Opera of the Nobility, and Goupy had probably received some payment from Hedges's estate and was gainfully employed at court by the prince of Wales. Together they kicked up their heels, dismaying some of Handel's supporters who worried about his health. As John Robartes, later Earl of Radnor, wrote to James Harris on July 19 (four days after the resolution of the case in Chancery): "Mr. Handel set out for Germany Thursday last in company with Goupée, therefore have little hopes of his *amendment*."[50] The next summer, Radnor fussed about the time Handel was spending with Henry Furnese in Gunnersbury. Furnese was one of Goupy's primary patrons (Goupy later sued his estate without success), and one can assume that the artist was present at the events Radnor mentions. He wrote in July that "Mr. Handel has dined with me but twice this summer but is mutch with Mr. Furnes in this neighbourhood," and again in August: "Mr. Handel instead of goeing to Scarborough to drink the waters, drinks wine with Mr. Furnes at Gunsbury and I fear eats too mutch of those things he ought to avoid. I would fain methinks preserve him for a few years longer."[51] Goupy kept for himself the painting he made of Gunnersbury House, not including it among the paintings he sold some years before his death. The portrait he painted of Handel for the prince of Wales, which no longer survives, was framed the following year and may also date from this period of conviviality.

It is no surprise, then, that in 1743, Smith chose Goupy as an emissary of the Middlesex opera company to Handel. Not only was he Handel's closest friend, but he also would have wanted to serve his patron, Prince Frederick, who specifically desired that Handel compose an opera for Middlesex's company. If he succeeded, he could also protect his friend from the threat of public censure contained in the final offer from Middlesex. It may be that Goupy was at least halfway successful, for Handel apparently granted the company use of his opera *Alessandro* (1726), and the Middlesex company revived this opera in the autumn of 1743 under the name of *Rossane*. Paolo Rolli, who had prepared Handel's libretto, revised it for Middlesex, and Giovanni Battista Lampugnani, the resident composer of the company, probably oversaw the musical alterations and substitutions. The addition of £100 of stock to Handel's South Sea annuities on May 4, 1743, may represent the payment from Middlesex for the use of this score (either directly paid as stock or purchased with his cash fee). As Smith related in his letter to Shaftesbury, Middlesex had offered Handel 100 guineas (£105) for permission to produce one of his old operas (if the composer was unable to provide a new one).

All then might have been fine, except that Handel immediately sat down and composed *Semele*, a full three-hour dramatic work set to an English opera libretto written by William Congreve about forty years earlier, at which time it had been composed by John Eccles but never performed. By any standard, Handel's *Semele* is a masterpiece of musical inspiration. It tells the story of the daughter of Cadmus, king of Thebes, who is on the point of marrying her fiancé, Athamas, when the ceremony is interrupted by Jupiter, who transports Semele to a private love nest, where, as she relates in an aria, she experiences "Endless pleasure, endless love." Juno, Jupiter's queen, is not pleased and enlists Somnus, the god of sleep, to her aid. She then plays on Semele's ambition and vanity, suggesting that if she demands Jupiter appear to her in his full raiment as a god, she will become immortal, while knowing full well that this will kill her. After her death, the chorus comments on her fall:

> Nature to each allots his proper sphere,
> But that forsaken we like meteors err;
> Toss'd through the void, by some rude shock we're broke,
> And all our boasted fire is lost in smoke.

A happy ending is achieved when Athamas agrees to marry Semele's sister, and Apollo appears with the announcement that "from Semele's ashes a phœnix shall rise, / The joy of the earth, and delight of the skies"—a reference to the birth of Bacchus, the god of wine.

The operatic libretto was adapted to the oratorio style with the addition of choruses, both dramatic and contemplative, that Handel set with his usual vigor. In addition, he delineated the individual characters in his musical setting with wit and pathos. Semele's "Endless pleasure," with its animated melodic extensions on "pleasure" and "enjoys," depicts her delighted ecstasy, while "O sleep, why dost thou leave me" captures the longing she experiences when Jupiter is absent—the expansion on the opening "O" a sensual combination of a long stretch and a sigh. In response, Jupiter (a tenor) sings "Where'er you walk," a hymn to love and one of the most beautiful arias Handel ever wrote. One of the most delightful moments of the drama occurs after Juno gives Semele a magic mirror and leads her to believe that she is already showing signs of "divine perfection" and "celestial beauty." As she gazes at her reflection, Semele sings, "Myself I shall adore, if I persist in gazing." On every repetition of the word "gazing" the musical setting is extended further and further, its small repetitions separated with breaks seeming to depict Semele's various poses and twists of the head as she gazes longer and longer with each iteration of the word.

Handel clearly lavished all of his considerable talents on *Semele*, and Smith expressed his concern about "how the Quality will take it that He can compose for Himself and not for them." *Rossane* opened the new season for the Middlesex opera at the King's Theatre on November 15, 1743, and *Semele* premiered at Covent Garden on February 10, 1744. Delany wrote of the former: "I was at the opera of Alexander, which under the disguise it suffered, was infinitely better than any Italian opera; but it vexed me to hear some favourite songs mangled."[52] She heard the rehearsal of *Semele* at Handel's house in January and described it as "a delightful piece of music, quite new and different from anything [Handel] has done."[53] And after the second performance she wrote: "Semele is charming; the more I hear it the better I like it, and as I am a subscriber I shall not fail one night."[54]

It seems fair to ask what Handel was up to. After refusing to write an opera for the new opera company, despite the generous financial offer of Lord Middlesex, stated desire of the prince of Wales, and urging of his best friend, he proceeded to write a secular dramatic work that with its lack of staging and added choruses was thinly disguised as an oratorio and performed during Lenten oratorio season. The subterfuge fooled no one. Jennens, who knew Congreve's libretto, described the work as "no oratorio but a baudy opera."[55] It is no wonder the opera people were angry. Delany wrote, "Semele has a strong party against it ... All the opera people are enraged at Handel."[56] She also reported, "I believe I wrote my brother word that Mr. Handel and the Prince had quarreled, which I am sorry for. Handel says the *Prince* is quite out of *his* good graces!" She added, however, "there was no disturbance at the play-house" as Handel's detractors had not been "so very absurd as to declare, in a public manner, their disapprobation of such a composer."[57]

Not surprisingly, Goupy also was angry. If he thought he had resolved the impasse when Handel agreed, as can be assumed, to let Middlesex perform an adaptation of his opera *Alessandro*, he must have felt personally affronted when Handel immediately composed an operatic oratorio for himself and quarreled with the prince. His response took the form of his art, a scathing caricature of Handel with the face of a hog surrounded by rich foodstuffs and noisy instruments. As he plays the organ, he tramples underfoot a banner that reads: PENSION BENEFIT NOBILITY FRIENDSHIP. The image depicts an avaricious and self-indulgent glutton who has snubbed offers of financial support, goodwill, the desire of the nobility, and the hand of friendship. After the death of both artists, it was reported that Goupy had claimed the "caricature entertained [the prince] and his Wife exceedingly."[58] Handel was not amused, especially, one must assume, after Goupy made an etching of the caricature and circulated it. It is not clear exactly when Goupy painted this image or made the etching, but the content of the drawing suggests 1745.

Handel's continued lack of cooperation was probably one reason for the departure of Middlesex's company from the King's Theatre in June 1744. Handel thereupon took it back for the 1744–1745 season, producing *Semele* again in December and premiering a new secular drama, *Hercules*, in January, following which a lack of public support led him to announce the abandonment of his season. What is particularly revealing about his published statement in the *Daily Advertiser* is his claim to have directed his efforts to prove that the English language was fully suitable to musical setting, which suggests that after years of fighting off competition from adherents of English opera while he composed Italian opera, he had now deliberately taken up the mantle of English against Italian opera with the composition of *Semele* and *Hercules*. Of course, this position pitted him directly against Middlesex's efforts, in whose cause his participation had been actively enlisted. There has to be some disingenuousness in Handel's statement that he was "ignorant" of the reason for the loss of "publick Favour."

It is impossible to know if Handel's choice of stories in setting *Semele* and *Hercules* had any particular meaning, but the opera people could easily have interpreted them as attacks. If the foolish ambitions of Semele

7.3 Joseph Goupy, *The True Representation and Character,* c. 1745, caricature of Handel; etching based on original Goupy painting (Gerald Coke Handel Collection, Foundling Museum, London / The Bridgeman Art Library [DEC 84584])

are associated with those of the Middlesex opera, then her fiery destruction at the approach of Jupiter in full array could point to the influence Handel's full compositional power had on the company. In *Hercules* (a work that will be more fully discussed in Chapter 10), the character of

Dejanira, Hercules's wife, whose passionate jealousy leads to his fiery destruction, might have been seen as a reference to the "fine ladies" who opposed Handel, just as the anonymous author of the "Advice to Mr. Handel," associated the female "fiend" opposed to Handel's "harmony" with the unreasonable jealousy of Saul. Perhaps the opera people, temporarily without a home or season, were pleased with Handel's announcement following the premiere of *Hercules* in January 1745 that he would be unable to continue his season. Although he resumed production after a few weeks on March 1, Elizabeth Carter, a supporter of the composer, reported that "Handel, once so crowded, plays to empty walls." She was, however, "unfashionable" enough to be "highly delighted" with the new oratorio *Belshazzar* (1745), Handel's first libretto from Charles Jennens since *Messiah,* and the last on which they would collaborate. She considered it "equal to any thing I ever heard."[59] Whether or not this oratorio pleased the opposition, it may be that it provided Goupy with the idea for his caricature.

Belshazzar is vain, self-indulgent, and dismissive of the advice of those who care for him. He is described before he appears by the bass Gobrias, a Babylonian formerly true to Belshazzar, but, having been personally betrayed by him, now joined with the enemy Persians:

Behold the monstrous human beast
Wallowing in excessive feast!
No more his maker's image found:
But, self-degraded to a swine,
He fixes grov'ling on the ground
His portion of the breath Divine.

Handel's setting emphasizes the degradation, the many repetitions and extensions of the word "wallowing" becoming one with the word's meaning to a humorous degree. One way of reading Goupy's caricature is as a visual reenactment of this dramatic moment, with Goupy as Gobrias and both the aria and the painting characterizing a former ally as despicable in similar terms. Indeed, in all versions of the image, Goupy also imagined Handel gazing into a mirror like Semele, as if it were the composer and not the Middlesex company who had overreached his "proper sphere" and was singing "Myself I shall adore." If the caricature entertained the prince and princess of Wales "exceedingly," it may have been because Handel was ridiculed by reference to his own brilliant, musical characterizations.

Handel, of course, was not without supporters. Anne Donnellan stood by him, as did Elizabeth Mayne, whose descendants have proudly written of her that "George Frederick Handel experienced the friendship of this lady at the time of his persecution."[60] After her marriage to the Rev. Dr. Patrick Delany in 1743, Mary Delany's freedom of independent action was somewhat lessened, but she and her husband also stood by Handel. She wrote in February 1744 of *Semele*, "Lady Cobham, Lady Westmoreland, and Lady Chesterfield never fail it."[61] In April 1744, she and her husband entertained her brother Granville, Donnellan, and Handel at her house on Clarges Street, and the composer played for them his new oratorio *Joseph and His Brethren*.[62] With the appointment of her husband as dean of Down, the couple then left for Ireland, where they arrived by June. Although the Delanys returned to London periodically, this shift in Mary Delany's center of activity permanently altered the easy relationship she had previously had with Handel. At no point, however, did it diminish her interest in or appreciation of his work, which she followed closely even from Ireland.

Patrick and Mary Delany had a rare marriage based on friendship. In all the trials they faced, from the opposition to their union by her family to a legal suit brought against Patrick Delany in 1748 by the family of his first wife, they were able to turn to each other as a friend as well as a spouse. In his written marriage proposal, Patrick Delany had placed friendship at the center of his desire as a widower to enter again into the marital state:

> I have lost a friend that was as my own soul, and nothing is more natural than to desire to supply that loss by the person in the world that friend most esteemed and honoured; and as I have been long persuaded that perfect friendship is nowhere to be found but in marriage, I wish to perfect mine in that state. I know it is late in life to think of engaging anew in that state, in the beginning of my 59th year. I am old, and I appear older than I am;

7.4 Signature and seal of Elizabeth Mayne on an indenture (1736) granting farmland in Teffont Evias to a tenant (courtesy private collection)

but thank God I am still in health, tho' not bettered by years, and however the vigour of life may be over, and with that the *vigour of vanity*, and the flutter of passion, I find myself not less fitted for all that is solid happiness in the wedded state—the tenderness of affection, and the faith of friendship.[63]

Because their marriage brought Mary Delany little if anything in terms of wealth or status, her brother vehemently opposed the union, and Mary Delany, like Anne Donnellan, was largely excluded from the wills of her close relatives. Despite having been her surrogate father, her uncle John Stanley, who died in December 1744, left Delany the same £100 he gave to her sister, with whom he was not close, and bequeathed his estate to her brother. Delany's sister, Anne, was so stunned that she queried the £100 gift to her, and she seems as well to have questioned the appropriateness of their brother receiving the whole estate. As she was wont to do, Delany insisted that the legacies were fitting and that their brother "deserved to be more distinguished" in the will, only saying of Sir John Stanley's behavior at the end of his life that it "grieves my heart."[64] Her pique finally manifested itself when her cousin William Monk, executor of her uncle's will, disallowed her the plates (or saucers) that went with the five covered bowls she was bequeathed because these were not specifically mentioned. In response, she offered to pay for the plates, "as the basons are no more complete without them than a flower without a stem," adding that if he has sent the frame belonging to the still-life she was bequeathed, "I am indebted to you for that, and desire to know what I must pay, for I don't find that was 'DEVISED' with the picture."[65]

Making matters worse financially, the family of Patrick Delany's late first wife, Margaret Tenison, filed a suit against him in 1744 with the purpose of recovering the fortune she had brought to the marriage (which following a childless marriage had devolved to her husband just as Elizabeth Peacock's fortune devolved to the Palmers), but shortly after that suit was resolved in 1746, the Tenisons initiated a further suit in 1749 charging Dr. Delany with deliberate spoliation of documents and deceit.[66] This case, which continued for a decade, swallowed up most of the dean's small income and left the Delanys with fewer resources. Then in 1752, Mary Delany received nothing in the will of her uncle Anthony Westcombe. He left a fortune to her brother Bernard, including a large home in Chelsea, and gifts to other members of the family, including her married sister, Anne Dewes.[67] Delany accepted her financial situation, writing to her sister in December about both Westcombe's will and her husband's legal problems. Of her uncle Westcombe, she wrote:

> As to his not leaving me a legacy I had no expectation of any: he has left his fortune to those I love as well as myself, and I am pleased with the disposition of it. I was much obliged to you for the copy of the will, one loves to know all particulars of a person so nearly related. I pray God that his last moments were enlightened; he had some good qualities, and he has had warnings most graciously allowed him for some years past.[68]

One week later, she added an update on her husband's legal situation with a further note on the Westcombe will:

> As to loss of fortune, I trust we can *very well bear it*, and should they take *all* that came from Mrs Tennison, we shall *still* have more left than a reasonable competency—the settling the accounts cannot take less than three or four years. . . . it is hard to restrain the passions and affections, when one sees innocence and true worth treated in the manner D. D. [Dr. Delany] has been, but he bears it all like a Xtian hero, and I hope his example has had some influence on me.
>
> Don't regret my having no token from Sir Antony Westcomb; he has done better, and shewed his gratitude to those friends who always obliged him . . . I feel myself lighter and better since in part we know what is likely to be our fortune; as to our way of living, we are rather more retired, invite no expensive company (in winter indeed we never did); our time used to be the spring for returning dinners, and that next year I hope will be employed in preparing for our English journey.[69]

After an appeal to the House of Lords, the case of *Tenison vs. Delany* was finally resolved in 1758 (although there was still another attempt to reopen it some years later). The decision required the doctor to pay £3,000, but his wife considered this "of trifling consequence," seeing that the "grand point" was gained in that the "Dean's character is cleared."[70]

Despite her regular absences from London, Delany and Handel remained friends. On a visit early in 1747, she interrupted a letter to her sister with the news of Handel calling on her unexpectedly: "Just as I came to this place, in came Mr. Handel, and he has prevented my adding any more."[71] Although the chronology disallows any direct connection to Delany's legal situation, it is striking that the only two of Handel's works to contain trial scenes, *Solomon* and *Susanna*, were composed in mid-1748 and premiered in early 1749. In both oratorios, false claims and accusations are uncovered, and truth and innocence vindicated.

The Delanys were not in London in February and March of 1749 when *Susanna* and *Solomon* premiered, but Delany would have gotten to know both works by playing them through after their publication. She always found solace in music, and especially in Handel's music. Given the public accusations against her husband, the depiction of falsehood unmasked must have resonated with her feelings.

The second act of *Solomon* focuses on the king's wisdom and leads naturally to a depiction of the well-known scene in which Solomon is asked to adjudicate in a case where two harlots claim to be the true mother of the same baby. After an attendant announces the presence of the two women, the First Harlot states that the other woman bore a son who died and now claims to be the mother of her own child. She then begins what seems to be an aria, "Words are weak to paint my fears." The Second Harlot, unable to stand this display of emotion, jumps up, as it were, to dispute the claim, singing over and over, "False is all her melting tale." Solomon then intervenes between them, singing, "Justice holds the lifted scale." In seeming spontaneity, and Handel's management of this effect is extremely deft, the aria becomes a trio, with each characterization sharply chiseled in the music: the hesitant dotted rhythms of the First Harlot in lyrically spun-out melody; the insistent nagging of the Second Harlot in hammered-out even notes; and the proclamation of Solomon about the scales of justice with its stately motion based, in a pun Handel must have enjoyed, on the stepwise motion of a musical scale. After the king rules to "Divide the Babe, thus each her part shall bear," the differing reactions of the two women are painted by Handel with great perception. The false mother welcomes the news with an aria that fairly dances a jig, "Thy sentence, great king, / Is prudent and wise," and includes a quick turning figure in the violins that curls like a contemptuous sneer. The musical effect is underscored by the final line: "For at least I shall tear / The lov'd infant from thee."

In contrast, the First Harlot can barely speak. The orchestral introduction to her aria, "Can I see my infant gor'd," a flowing, dotted-note pattern in the bass, later comes to represent her image of blood "gushing down his tender sides." Single strokes in the strings, frequently on dissonant harmonies, feel like repeated emotional blows. The vocal entrance, however, is totally unaccompanied, depicting her apparent loss of all

Granville

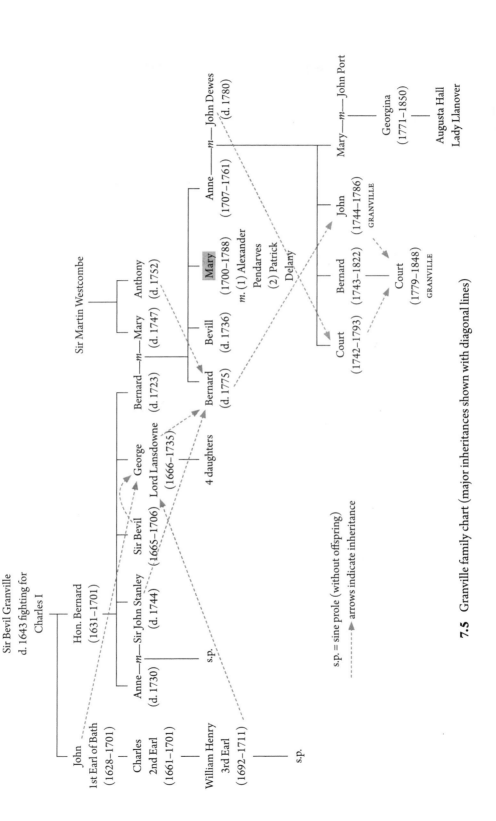

Sir Bevil Granville
d. 1643 fighting for
Charles I

Sir Martin Westcombe

John
1st Earl of Bath
(1628–1701)

Hon. Bernard
(1631–1701)

Charles
2nd Earl
(1661–1701)

Anne—*m*—Sir John Stanley
(d. 1730)   (d. 1744)

Sir Bevil
(1665–1706)

George
Lord Lansdowne
(1666–1735)

Bernard
(d. 1723)

Bernard—*m*—Mary
              (d. 1747)

Anthony
(d. 1752)

Anne————*m*— John Dewes
(1707–1761)   (d. 1780)

William Henry
3rd Earl
(1692–1711)

Bernard
(d. 1775)

Bevill
(d. 1736)

Mary
(1700–1788)
m. (1) Alexander
Pendarves
(2) Patrick
Delany

Mary—*m*—John Port

4 daughters

Court
(1742–1793)

Bernard
(1743–1822)

John
(1744–1786)
GRANVILLE

Georgina
(1771–1850)

Court
(1779–1848)
GRANVILLE

Augusta Hall
Lady Llanover

s.p.

s.p.

s.p. = sine prole (without offspring)

- - - ▶ arrows indicate inheritance

7.5 Granville family chart (major inheritances shown with diagonal lines) support. As she continues, the phrases repeatedly fragment and break off into silence. The use of silence embedded into the musical fabric becomes ever more searing, until she heartbreakingly resolves (Handel writes *"rissoluto"* in the score): "Rather be my hopes beguil'd [silence], / Take him all [silence], but spare my child." Handel was one of the first composers to use silence in this way to disrupt and impede the musical flow. The true mother's willingness to relinquish the child rather than see him harmed allows Solomon to discern the truth and dismiss the false petitioner: "Hence from my Sight," he sings, "nor urge a further Claim."

Susanna similarly faces a false charge. Interrupted at her bath by two Elders while her husband is away, she refuses their advances. When she threatens to reveal their actions, they falsely accuse her of adultery, knowing that their status in society will give their story weight. Indeed, the third act begins with Susanna being found guilty and condemned to die. The young prophet Daniel (who also plays a role in *Belshazzar* when he successfully reads the writing on the wall) intercedes, separates the Elders, and by interrogating them individually proves their story false. "Vain is deceit," he declares, "when justice holds the scale."

Susanna's response to the false accusation elicits one of Handel's most passionate arias, "If guiltless blood be your intent, / I here resign it all." Spitting out the words syllable by syllable, Susanna begins the aria with no introduction and merely a few notes in the bass as accompaniment, effectively interrupting the falsehoods being spun by the Elders. In small, downward-moving phrases, each followed by a large leap to a higher register, the melodic line finally sweeps upward on the word "resign." The first line thus passes through an unusually wide range, from the depths of innocent death on the word "blood" to heavenly resignation. "Fearless of death, as innocent," she continues, "I triumph in my fall," and Handel sets "fearless of death" on a single repeating note, making the emotional tone clear and insistent. The only melodic exuberance in the aria comes on the word "triumph." In the middle section of the aria, Susanna turns away from the Elders and prays: "And if to fate my days must run, / Oh righteous heav'n! thy will be done." Handel sets this as a simple and heartfelt hymn accompanied by strings. When the

Second Elder calls for her to be taken away, Susanna breaks out of her reverie and repeats the first section, "If guiltless blood."

Solomon and Susanna were both well attended at their first runs in 1749. Lady Shaftesbury wrote of the opening night of Susanna, "I think I never saw a fuller house," and Handel was able to make significant additions to his cash account after each performance.[72] He deposited £235 the day after the premiere of Susanna, £227 10s. 7d. after the second performance, and £115 after the third; and he deposited £300 after the premiere of Solomon. When the season was over, he used these and other deposits to buy an additional £1,100 of 4 percent annuities.[73] Neither oratorio, however, scored an unusual success: Solomon attained only three performances, and Susanna four. And neither was revived again until the spring of 1759, in the months before Handel's death. Although by then Handel was no longer conducting the performances himself, he still had control over them. It would be wonderful to know whether the depiction of virtue's triumph over false claims and accusations played a role in his decision to revive this pair of oratorios at that time, and it would be equally fascinating to have testaments from Handel's friends and legatees of the impact of these two works. Handel, Hunter, Goupy, and Delany had all faced public censure through lawsuits, bankruptcy, or societal opposition, and all might have seen themselves as overcoming undeserved defamation. Scars remained. Tensions had led to the loss of friendship between Handel and Goupy. Hunter was able to move forward with the purchase of the dye house in Old Ford, but he never fully escaped from bankruptcy. And the case of Tenison vs. Delany dragged on well into the late eighteenth century. As Handel composed Susanna and Solomon, as Hunter added these scores to his collection,[74] and as Delany played through these compositions at her harpsichord, each must have reflected in his or her own way on the place of justice, injustice, and virtue in their lives.

8.1 Marble statue of Handel by Louis-François Roubiliac, placed in Vauxhall Gardens in 1738 (© Victoria and Albert Museum, London [A.3&A-1965])

EIGHT

Making and Collecting

1738–1750

Roubiliac sculpture of Handel, Alexander's Feast,
concertos, collecting

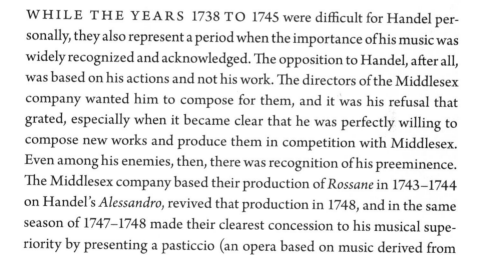

WHILE THE YEARS 1738 TO 1745 were difficult for Handel personally, they also represent a period when the importance of his music was widely recognized and acknowledged. The opposition to Handel, after all, was based on his actions and not his work. The directors of the Middlesex company wanted him to compose for them, and it was his refusal that grated, especially when it became clear that he was perfectly willing to compose new works and produce them in competition with Middlesex. Even among his enemies, then, there was recognition of his preeminence. The Middlesex company based their production of *Rossane* in 1743–1744 on Handel's *Alessandro,* revived that production in 1748, and in the same season of 1747–1748 made their clearest concession to his musical superiority by presenting a pasticcio (an opera based on music derived from various sources) entirely from Handel's operas—a fulfillment, perhaps, of Middlesex's threat in 1743 to produce Handel's music without his permission. The newspaper announcement of November 13, 1747, read:

Yesterday was Rehears'd, at the King's Theatre in the Haymarket, the Opera of LUCIUS VERUS: This Drama Consists of Airs,

MAKING AND COLLECTING: *Timeline*

1720

June 14
Handel receives a royal
patent for the publication
of his music for the term of
fourteen years

1735–1750

Charles Jennens, James Hunter,
Lord Shaftesbury, and Bernard
Granville acquire the core of
their major manuscript collections of Handel's music; James
Harris given Elizabeth Legh's
collection in 1741

1736

February 19
Handel's *Alexander's Feast,
or the Power of Music* premieres at Covent Garden

borrow'd entirely from Mr. Handel's favourite Operas: and so
may (probably) be justly styl'd the most exquisite Composition
of Harmony, ever offer'd to the Publick. . . . Mr. Handel is
acknowledged (universally) so great a Master of the Lyre;
that nothing urg'd in Favour of his Capital Performances, can
reasonably be considered as a Puff.[1]

A month later, on December 5, a new announcement offered an opportunity to those who had already attended the production to hear yet
more and different music by Handel:

Several Airs in the Opera of Lucius Verus, now performing at the
King's Theatre in the Haymarket will be chang'd for others; all
compos'd by Mr. Handel.[2]

Throughout his career, Handel's greatest competition frequently
came from his own music in the hands of others. The case of the Middlesex opera company was only the most recent example. In 1734, the

March 23

Handel's *Il trionfo del Tempo e della Verità* premieres at Covent Garden (a revision of *Il trionfo del Tempo e del Disinganno* from Rome, 1707)

March 8

full score of *Alexander's Feast* published by Walsh (with an engraved frontispiece of Handel by Jacobus Houbraken); Walsh pays Handel £105

April

Roubiliac's statue of Handel placed in Vauxhall Gardens; miniature painting of Handel by George Andreas Wolfgang (Royal Collection)

October 4

first set of organ concertos published as Op. 4 by Walsh

October 31

George II grants Handel a royal patent for a second fourteen-year term in the wording of which privilege Handel authorizes Walsh as his publisher

November 22

Handel's *Song for St. Cecilia's Day* premieres at Lincoln's Inn Fields Theatre

Opera of the Nobility had produced Handel's *Ottone*, and in 1732 the English opera company under the direction of Thomas Arne had performed Handel's *Acis and Galatea*. Handel's music also populated ballad opera, taking its place alongside traditional English song and recontextualized into new dramatic settings with English words.[3] Even *The Beggar's Opera* (1728), the first ballad opera, and the first operatic work in English to offer serious competition to Italian opera in London, used the famous march of the Christian army in *Rinaldo* for the chorus of highwaymen setting out on their nightly rounds, "Let us take the road."

In 1738, Jonathan Tyers placed a life-size statue of Handel in Vauxhall Gardens, the most important of the pleasure gardens in London, which, in the evenings from May to August, offered performances of music, displays of visual art, refreshments, and socializing in purpose-built structures (often with exotic themes), as well as attractive walkways and hidden arbors. Supper was served at nine o'clock, at which hour thousands of glass lamps were illuminated in the trees, creating a fantastical atmosphere. As the gardens were open to all who could pay the entrance fee of one shilling, they were host to an easy mixture of classes. Extremely

Making and Collecting continued

1740

April 21

Handel's Twelve Grand Concertos published as Op. 6 by Walsh "With His Majesty's Royal Licence and Protection"

1740s

Roubiliac markets a small "busto" of Handel for home ownership

1742

portrait of Handel by Goupy (now lost) framed for the prince of Wales

1746

Handel's library described as including a large collection of French and Italian music

popular with the fashionable elite, the gardens also had a reputation for moral license and for the ready availability of prostitutes, which was part of the attraction. For Tyers, the proprietor, it was critical to maintain a balance between freedom and propriety. Handel's statue by the French sculptor Louis-François Roubiliac offered a sense of culture and decorum while also appealing to a kind of national pride.[4]

The sculpture itself is remarkable. The composer is not presented in a formal pose, but casually in a dressing gown, with open shirt, no wig, and seated with his legs crossed, one slipper dangling, the other off. He holds a lyre on which he seems to be composing, while a naked putto (or infant) sits at his feet writing down the music. While the casual pose and attire are realistic, giving a sense of Handel as anyone's next-door neighbor, the lyre and the putto translate the human into the supernatural realm, associating Handel once again with the divinities of music: Apollo and Orpheus. Through his compositions, the auditors of his music were to be raised in stature as well. As announced in the *London Daily Post* (April 18, 1738):

> We are informed from very good Authority; that there is now
> near finished a Statue of the justly celebrated Mr. Handel,
> exquisitely done by the ingenious Mr. Raubillac . . . which is
> to be placed in a grand Nich, erected on Purpose in the great

1747

February

Ralph and Elizabeth Palmer, newly
married, move into their house on
Curzon Street; Ralph Palmer signs the
extraordinary antiquarian books in his
library, some of which are now in the
British Library, "Londini 1747"

1748

Thomas Hudson paints Handel's portrait;
Handel transports it to his family in Germany
in 1750 (?); mezzotint prints by Andrew Miller
and John Faber of Hudson's portrait of Handel
widely circulated

c.1748

Rupert Barber paints miniature portrait of
Handel in enamel for Anne Donnellan; she
bequeaths it to the British Museum (now lost)

Grove at Vaux-hall-Gardens, at the sole Expence of Mr. Tyers,
Undertaker of the Entertainment there; who in Consideration of
the real Merit of that inimitable Master, thought it proper, that
his Effigies should preside there, where his Harmony has so often
charm'd even the greatest Crouds into the profoundest Calm and
most decent Behaviour . . .[5]

The image became synonymous with the gardens and circulated
widely. It was sometimes used on the gold season ticket and often
engraved on publications of the songs sung at Vauxhall.[6] One of these,
"The Invitation to Mira, Requesting Her Company to VauxHall Garden," even mentions the role of Handel's music in its text: "Come, Mira,
Idol of ye Swains (So green ye Sprays, The Sky so fine) / To Bow'rs where
heav'n-born Flora reigns, & Handel warbles Airs Divine."

The years just preceding the installation of Handel's statue in Vauxhall Gardens had seen the composition and premiere of his *Alexander's
Feast, or the Power of Music* in 1736 and its immediate revival in 1737.
An oratorio-style work in English, its text is closely based on the ode by
John Dryden (Handel's composition is often called an ode as well) and
tells of the famous Greek musician Timotheus, whose music "could swell
the soul to rage, or kindle soft desire." Handel introduced this character

Making and Collecting continued

1750

January–March
Handel makes seven separate purchases of art at six separate art auctions

February 8
Handel and Bernard Granville both purchase art at the auction of Anthony Couzin, a former patron of Goupy; Handel buys a "Rembrandt" for £39 18s.

March 22–23
Handel and Christopher Batt both purchase art at the auction of dealers Gouyn and Major

1755

April 10–11
auction of Palmer's art collection, including Rembrandt's *Man in Oriental Costume,* now at the Metropolitan Museum, New York

1756

auction of the art collection of Elizabeth Mayne's brother, Christopher Batt, at which Charles Jennens is one of the purchasers; Charles Jennens commissions a portrait of Handel from Thomas Hudson

with a concerto for harp, which by its aural reference to the musician's lyre, gives the impression that Timotheus himself is playing. Then, in the course of the poem, Timotheus's music successively invokes "heav'nly joys," drunken pleasures, sadness, love, and military ardor. In his setting of these scenes, Handel, a modern Timotheus, painted each of these emotions for the audience. According to the mytho-historical story, the Greek musician's incitement of Alexander to military ardor and rage was so successful that it prompted the destruction of Persepolis; the reaction to Handel's setting, in contrast, was more positive. Dryden crowned the ode with the arrival of Saint Cecilia, patron saint of music, who moves the narrative out of the human sphere to the divine. Given that Cecilia's musical instrument is the "sacred organ," Handel was able to take on this role as both composer and performer, by inserting an organ concerto for himself at the climax of the work. A few years earlier, in 1733, when he was facing stiff competition, Handel had instituted the inclusion of organ concertos in his oratorio performances as an added attraction. With *Alexander's Feast*, the organ concerto, a genre invented by Handel and now closely tied to him in the minds of his audience, entered the drama itself.

The insertion of his own person into the drama by use of an organ concerto would have reminded Handel of his Roman oratorio *Il trionfo del Tempo e del Disinganno,* unperformed since 1707. In this work, set to a text by Cardinal Pamphilj, the character of Beauty (representing the human soul) must choose between the ephemeral joys offered by Pleasure and the eternal verities of Time and Truth. When Pleasure introduces Beauty to his palace of delights, he entrances her with art and music, the latter represented by an organ concerto performed by Handel. As the drama makes clear that this music is one of the luxuries that will need to be relinquished, it must have presented something of a hurdle to the young composer: the composition of music which is to be rejected in favor of higher spiritual values. What Handel wrote suggests that he carefully considered the problem. If the cardinal had imagined here a movement of stunning brilliance, to depict the difficulty of renunciation, Handel demurred. He instead provided music in Italianate style, but with excessive repetition and harmonic diversions that wander aimlessly and run into blind alleys. This, he seems to be saying, is music that you can reject in favor of mine. After Beauty chooses the righteous path, the oratorio ends with an achingly beautiful aria for her, "Tu del Ciel ministro eletto" (O thou, chosen minister of heaven), in which voice and oboe float above the barest chordal punctuation. The depth and simplicity of this ending movement hardly suggests giving up music; rather Handel invites the listener through his music to ascend to a higher plane.

In 1737, Handel decided to revise *Il trionfo.* To make the Roman oratorio suitable for his London audience, he changed the structure from two acts to three and added choruses and symphonies to mark these new divisions. More interestingly, he changed his relationship to the story. *Alexander's Feast* (1736) having given him the experience of placing an organ concerto for himself at the heavenly climax of a work, he used that work as a model. First, he shortened the concerto played in Pleasure's palace, thus reducing its impact, and replaced the organ solo with violin, removing himself from that awkward position. Then he added an organ concerto and concluding choral "Alleluia" at the end of the oratorio to follow Beauty's aria.[7] With this double stroke, he elevated himself from Pleasure's realm to the heavenly sphere.

In 1739, and for the third time, Handel yet again placed his person in

8.2   Engraving of Handel (1738) by Jacobus Houbraken, originally issued to subscribers of *Alexander's Feast* (The British Library, London / © British Library Board. All Rights Reserved / The Bridgeman Art Library [BL 71614])

spiritual realms at the end of an oratorio. In his setting of John Dryden's "A Song for St. Cecilia's Day" (Handel's work is often called *Ode for St. Cecilia's Day*), in which a succession of instruments are given their due, the laurel is reserved for Saint Cecilia's introduction of the organ to mankind. The organ, played by the composer, accompanies the final aria; "But oh! What art can teach, / What human voice can reach / The sacred organ's praise? / Notes inspiring holy love, / Notes that wing their heav'nly ways / To join the choirs above."

A subscription to the publication of the full score of *Alexander's Feast* in 1738 entitled the purchaser to an engraving that visually equates Handel with both Timotheus and Cecilia and draws a parallel to the statue of him by Roubiliac.[8] The composer's image, placed in an elaborate rococo frame, is placed at the top of the print and takes up about three-fifths of the page. Behind the frame to the left is a set of organ pipes (representing Cecilia's instrument) placed above a keyboard, which can be seen to the left at the bottom of the frame. Beneath Handel's portrait is a vignette of Timotheus "plac'd on high" as he performs for Alexander and "the lovely Thaïs" seated below. The depiction of Timotheus on a pedestal playing the lyre replicates Roubiliac's image of Handel, the image of the legendary Greek musician now modeled on Handel, rather than Handel on him.

The imaginary soundtrack for this image, although it encompasses all of Handel's music in a general way, consists most specifically of the "Timotheus" concerto from *Alexander's Feast* and, to a lesser extent, the organ concerto in that work and also the organ concerto with choral finale in *Il trionfo*. Like *Alexander's Feast* itself, these three concertos were published in 1738 by Walsh. They appeared as three of the six organ concertos grouped together in Handel's Op. 4: the harp concerto representing Timotheus, now adapted for chamber organ (Op. 4, no. 6), the St. Cecilia concerto for organ (Op. 4, no. 1), and, without its choral conclusion, the concerto used in *Il trionfo* (Op. 4, no. 4). The "Timotheus" concerto captures the image of the great musician playing for Alexander the Great. In the first movement, there is none of the interaction or exchange that one might expect in a concerto; rather the harp (or organ) plays most of the movement as an improvisatory solo. The orchestra is not only restricted to the muted sound of strings and recorders, but it also only appears briefly at four structural points (at the beginning, end, and two cadential moments in the middle) as supporting pillars to the form. If one associates the solo part with Timotheus's playing, then the orchestra becomes the pedestal on which he sits.

The "St. Cecilia" concerto, not surprisingly, sets a very different tone. It is at once more profound (first movement) and more celebratory (second movement). Handel, relying on his virtuosity and improvisatory skill, doesn't write out the organ part in full but provides only the barest harmonic outline in the first movement and in the third movement only ten skeletal measures with the notation "Organo ad libitum." Appropriately to the religious aspect of Saint Cecilia, the first movement has the feel of an organ voluntary, a kind of meditative introduction played at church services and often improvised, and the second movement, although joyful, partakes of the sacred contrapuntal (fugal) style. Indeed, both movements have embedded within them vaporous harbingers of music that later appear in *Messiah* (1742), the first movement presaging "I know that my Redeemer liveth" and the second, the "Amen" chorus that ends the work. This is not to suggest that Handel borrows in *Messiah* from the organ concerto of the *Alexander Feast* but rather that the two works share the same serious tone.

By the early 1740s, whether or not one liked the man or approved of his actions, it would have been difficult to avoid Handel's music or his image. If one attended Handel's own productions or those of his competitors, royal ceremonies (the coronation of George II, royal weddings, or the funeral of Queen Caroline) or national peace celebrations (Dettingen and Aix-la-Chapelle), the pleasure gardens or ballad opera, his music would play a role, if not dominate, while his image held center stage at Vauxhall and was duplicated on tickets and songs. During the eighteenth century, collecting became something of a mania: in addition to traditional bibliophiles and serious art collectors among the aristocracy, global exploration awakened a growing interest in the natural sciences and exotica among merchants and scholars, and people from all walks of life collected according to their means what might express

8.3 Gawen Hamilton, *A Conversation of Virtuosis ... at the Kings Arms* (a Club of Artists), 1735, including (left to right): George Vertue, Hans Hysing, Michael Dahl, William Thomas, James Gibbs, Joseph Goupy (standing center), Matthew Robinson, Charles Bridgeman, Bernard Baron, John Wootton, John Michael Rysbrack, Gawen Hamilton, and William Kent, oil on canvas (© National Portrait Gallery, London [NPG 1384])

their interests. Books and art of all types, coins and medals, scientific instruments, and natural artifacts ranging from rocks and shells to plant and animal specimens were avidly sought.[9] In the years between 1738 and 1745, Handel, too, became a valued collectible. His image circulated widely in engravings, paintings, and small sculpted busts, and his music appeared in the two most important luxury editions of his career. *Alexander's Feast*, which appeared in full score and complete in 1738, had 124 subscribers for 146 copies, and the Twelve Grand Concertos, Op. 6 (1740), attracted 100 subscribers for 122 copies. Among the subscribers were some of Handel's closest friends and associates.

Bernard Granville (Delany's brother), James Harris, Charles Jennens, and Lord Shaftesbury subscribed for both editions, as did James Hunter. All of these men also began, or acquired the core of, their manuscript collections of Handel's music in the same period. Jennens, who may have started collecting Handel manuscripts in the late 1720s, resolved in the early to mid-1740s to acquire a complete set of scores and parts of Handel's entire output; Hunter acquired the core of his collection (forty-nine volumes) between about 1736 and his bankruptcy in 1741; Shaftesbury's collection of sixty-nine volumes was gathered between about 1738 and 1750; Granville's set of thirty-eight volumes was mostly copied between 1740 and 1744; and Harris was given the manuscript collection of thirty-six volumes that had been owned by Elizabeth Legh in 1741.

Handel was, however, not just a collectible; he was also a collector. He amassed a significant library, and by the end of the 1740s was actively acquiring fine art with the advice of and in the company of his friends. Over the years, Handel had become familiar with many important collections, which offered him the opportunity to consider for himself various collecting options. Nicola Haym, musician, composer, and Handel's most important librettist from *Teseo* (1713) to *Tolomeo* (1728), was a significant collector of coins, antiquities, prints, and books.[10] After his death in 1729, his possessions were sold, and the auctioneer Christopher Cock listed most of the objects in a printed catalogue:

> A Catalogue of the Entire Collection of the Learned and
> Ingenious Antiquarian Mr. Nicola Haym (Deceas'd), consisting
> of his Cabinet of Compleat Series of Roman and Grecian Coins
> . . .; Several Antique small Statues and Busto's . . .; a very Choice
> Collection of Prints of the *Italian, French* and *Flemish* Masters . . .
> Some Pictures, his Instruments and Books of Musick, and many
> other Valuable Effects.[11]

Cock's separate catalogue for Haym's library contained 1,406 lots (each lot representing a single sale item, whether containing one or many individual pieces), which included not only works in divinity, philosophy, history, and philology, but also approximately 400 opera and oratorio librettos.[12]

Mary Delany, living on a very limited budget, collected shells, displayed them with care, and created rooms in "shellwork."[13] She wrote to her sister on June 30, 1734:

I have got a new madness, I am running wild after shells. This morning I have set my little collection of shells in nice order in my cabinet, and they look so beautiful, that I must by some means enlarge my stock...[14]

A few months later (April 12, 1735), she informed her mother that she hoped to be able to acquire the shell collection of a recently deceased collector, wondering if it would be sold at auction.[15] And in 1736 (September 2) she told Jonathan Swift that she had that summer "undertaken a work that has given me full employment, which is *making a grotto* in Sir John Stanley's garden at North End, and it is chiefly composed of shells I had from Ireland."[16]

The greatest eighteenth-century collectors opened their cabinets to visitors. Sir Hans Sloane's collection was one of the most important, consisting of books, prints, drawings, natural history, medals and coins, as well as shoes and shells. In June 1728, on the day before Anne Donnellan's sister was married, a party of about twelve, consisting of the prospective bride and groom, family and friends, "went to see Sʳ Hans Sloanes Cabinet of Curiosities" and "spent 4 or 5 hours there very agreeably."[17] When Handel visited in 1740 he is said to have outraged his host, who generally offered refreshments to his guests, by placing a buttered muffin on a rare book. Handel apparently thought Sloane's accusation was an attempt to blame his decision to give up providing tea for his guests on the "gormandizing German."[18] In 1753, Sloane bequeathed the collection to the nation in return for a payment of £20,000 to his heirs. Its more than 71,000 items formed the foundation of the British Museum in 1759.[19]

The creation of a great library was a time-honored goal for members of the upper classes, and any others with pretensions to social advancement. The library of Thomas Britton, the small-coal man who organized concerts in his upper room, contained not only music but a wide selection

of books in various fields and "also an extraordinary collection of manuscripts in Latin and English."[20] The first auction of his books, which
occurred in his lifetime, included 1,218 lots, many containing more than
one book. The posthumous auction of his collection contained 1,036
lots, of which Sir Hans Sloane was one of the most significant purchasers.[21] Britton, whose portrait by John Wollaston was part of Sloane's
collection given to the nation (but transferred in 1879 from the British
Museum to the National Portrait Gallery), was what then was called a
virtuoso, an amateur who collected with knowledge and discrimination.
John Percival was delighted to report from Paris his fifteen-year-old son's
initiation to this status: "He grows very fond of Antiques, and bought a
great many Glass Seals, Coppys of the French Kings Collection, which he
proposes to place in a Cabinet, this is the beginning of Virtuosoship."[22]

Handel's library, to the extent that it can be reconstructed, was that of
a professional musician. He carefully preserved his unique autographs,
carrying music he wrote in Italy and Hanover to London. None of these
scores would have been formally bound in his lifetime, which happened
only after they left his hands, but individual compositions may have had
their manuscript pages (estimated at 5,500 for the London works alone)
loosely stitched together. It is not known how he filed them, but his regular reuse of autograph material indicates that he had a system. The autographs now in the British Library are bound in ninety-seven volumes;
another fifteen are preserved at the Fitzwilliam Museum. Handel also
maintained the performance scores copied out from the autographs by
John Christopher Smith; these too he used regularly. They are mostly
preserved in the Hamburg State and University Library, Germany:
eighty-five scores in 123 volumes. Even though Handel did not have the
material bound in the way it now appears, the image of 235 volumes of
his own music in autograph and performance copies provides a sense of
the magnitude of this part of his library.[23]

In addition to this repository of his own works, Handel's library has
long been thought to have contained "a large quantity of printed and
manuscript music of other composers, unfortunately no longer individually traceable."[24] A memoir published in 1756 describes Handel's library

in about 1746. The anonymous Parisian author thought that the "rarest and most useful part for its possessor was a well-ordered manuscript collection of every opera performed in Italy," containing an account of each composer's life and work in the first volume for that set. He also claimed to have seen on Handel's bookshelves all the operas of Lully and Campra, presumably those that had been printed, as well as "Le Clair's symphonies" and all those musical and theoretical works of Rameau published before this time. It's difficult to know how much credence to give to this report. That Handel owned in manuscript "every opera performed in Italy" has to be an exaggeration, but one can imagine that to a French musician a large collection might easily have looked that way.[25]

To help offset the cost of special luxury publications or vanity prints, of text or music, advanced subscriptions were frequently sought. Surviving subscription lists included in published books and scores indicate that Handel subscribed to a small number of works, mostly by colleagues and associates, including works by authors with whom he had collaborated: John Gay, Aaron Hill, and James Miller. He may have subscribed to other works on account of the importance of the dedicatee, as in his subscription in 1733 to the poetic works of Horace (in Latin) dedicated to the prince of Wales. When Joseph Stanglini published of a new method of learning Italian in 1724, he apparently solicited subscribers from all those connected with Italian opera in London: among them, Handel, Bononcini, Senesino, and Heidegger (none of whom was likely to have needed the lessons). In terms of music publications, Handel subscribed to works by John Christopher Smith Jr., the son of his chief copyist and one of his most important students, and such contemporary composers as William Boyce (including his *Solomon* of 1743, pre-dating Handel's *Solomon* by six years) and Johann Galliard. He also subscribed to the first volume of keyboard suites published by one of his singers, Elizabeth Gambarini.[26]

That Handel must have had a large number of printed and manuscript scores of other composers is clear, if on no other evidence, from his custom of borrowing.[27] Inasmuch as his style is intrinsically based on improvisation and variation, it is not surprising that he often worked from given material. In essence, Handel's practice is similar to that of Renaissance composers working from a popular song or a snippet of Gregorian chant, or German Baroque composers who worked from a chorale melody, the latter being a style in which Handel was trained. There is a significant difference, however, in that the fragments and longer sections Handel used did not generally come from the public domain, as did chant, hymns, and folksongs, but from the work of other composers. Even this pattern had something of a history, but Handel's practice stands out. When Bach took a Vivaldi concerto and rewrote it, he kept the original intact, measure for measure, adding to it harmonic richness and contrapuntal motion. Handel proceeded differently, creating something new by taking a few measures here and there of a bass line or melody, in some cases from different pieces and composers. Even when he employed a longer section or movement, the way the material appears in context usually transforms it so that in the new composition it takes on a fresh shape and purpose. One might say that when Vivaldi presented Bach with the basic shape of an egg, Bach transformed it into a Fabergé egg, while Handel used given material like fragments of thread, weaving them into an opulent fabric.

Some of the scores that Handel probably owned, given his use of them over years, are operas by Reinhard Keiser that he heard in Hamburg, for some of which—possibly including *Octavia* (1705), *Nebucadnezar* (1704), and *Claudius* (1703)—he played in the orchestra. We know by anecdote that Handel made a point of procuring a copy of Mattheson's keyboard lessons immediately upon hearing that the publication was available (see Chapter 5); he may also have kept manuscript copies of Mattheson's operas *Porsenna* (1702) and *Cleopatra* (1704), which latter work Handel had accompanied at the keyboard. Because he is listed among the subscribers, we know that Handel owned a copy of Telemann's *Musique de Table* (published 1733); given his use of them, he probably owned as well the prints of Telemann's *Harmonischer Gottes-Dienst* (1726) and *Sonates sans basse* (1727).

Handel also brought music from Italy, but its extent is unknown. A manuscript copy of duets by Steffani in the British Library is signed "G. F. Hendel / Roma 1706."[28] As Steffani directly preceded Handel as music master in Hanover, Handel could have acquired more of Steffani's scores in that city. The manuscript of Bononcini's *Il Xerse* (1694) in the British Library may also have been Handel's: he certainly used the opera as a musical source for his own *Serse* (1738) and other works.[29] He probably owned or had access to a good number of scores printed in England, especially those issued by Walsh, who also published most of Handel's music. These would have included, given his compositional use of music from their scores, the opera of *Hamlet* (*Ambleto*), which was adapted for the English stage in 1712 from Francesco Gasparini's opera of 1705, and Giovanni Porta's *Numitore* (1720), which opened the Royal Academy of Music.

As with the musical scores, some literary works can be assumed to have been in Handel's library even without documentation. He certainly had librettos; we have seen that Handel collected librettos during his travels and often used them as the basis of his own operas (see Chapter 2). He would have had other texts as well. Foremost among them would have been at least two Bibles, one in German and the other the King James Version in English, as well as the Book of Common Prayer. Beyond the use Handel made of them personally, they would have been important to him professionally. At the time of the Coronation Anthems, he is quoted as having said about their texts: "I have read my Bible very well and shall chuse for myself."[30] As we have already seen, he also may have contributed to the selection of texts for Princess Anne's wedding anthem. He surely had recourse to the Bibles during his period of oratorio composition. In addition, Handel likely owned a number of the historical and literary works on which his operas were based, such as Tacitus's *Histories*, Tasso's *Gerusalemme liberata*, and Ariosto's *Orlando furioso*. Even his subscription to Horace's poems perhaps bore musical fruit, as he later composed a duet to an Italian translation of one of the poems.

Handel's library, while extensive, was still that of a working, professional musician; in contrast, the library of his neighbor Ralph Palmer was the work of a virtuoso collector. As is the case with Handel's library, however, there is no inventory. Our knowledge of Palmer's collection comes exclusively from books and manuscripts that have made their way into major repositories and still retain Palmer's Latin inscription. As he was the eldest son, he received on the death of his father a library whose core derived from his Flemish great-great-grandfather, Dr. Baldwin Hamey, having passed through generations of bibliophiles. Once he took up his inheritance, married Elizabeth Peacock, and moved into his residence on Curzon Street in Handel's neighborhood of St. George, Hanover Square, he seems to have inscribed each of these volumes "Bibliotheca Palmeriana / Londini 1747" and added a description in Latin of the book's contents. The treasures of the collection included the illuminated twelfth-century commentary by Hugh of Saint-Victor to "On the Heavenly Hierarchy" by Pseudo-Dionysius the Areopagite, now at the British Library, and thirteenth-century annals from Reading Abbey (providing a schedule of feasts), now at Worcester College, Oxford.[31] In all known cases, the ownership of these unique volumes passed to Palmer's cousin and boyhood playmate, the second earl Verney, probably by purchase.[32] At the posthumous sale of Palmer's extensive collection of fine art, Verney made a point of acquiring most of the very valuable items, as evidenced in a contemporary copy of the auction catalogue.

Auctions were a primary avenue for purchasing fine art, and the catalogues were generally published in advance, so that prospective buyers could plan ahead. The eighteenth-century art collector and agent Richard Houlditch (probably father and son successively) kept beautiful, handwritten transcriptions of catalogues of art sales in London from about 1711 to 1759. Because the Houlditches attended most of these, they were able in many cases to add both the name of the purchaser and the purchase price to individual works, thus creating an extraordinary record of the art market during the first half of the eighteenth century.[33] Mary Delany, who lacked the funds to be able to purchase paintings on the open market, used her artistic talent, which she had honed in lessons with Goupy's uncle Lewis Goupy and with Hogarth, to make amateur copies of fine art to display in her home, but she captured the competitive atmosphere of auctions where buyers or their agents competed to purchase specific pieces. In a letter to her brother Bernard, she describes the success (and failure) of her friend the duchess of Portland at the posthumous sale of the art collection of Sir Luke Schaub in 1758:

The Duchess of Portland has lost the "Dancing Children;" Sir
James Lowther bought it for £180 0 0—a dear bargain I think. Sir
Thomas Sebright the Sigismunda, at £404 : 5 : 0. Our friend was
not *quite disappointed*, for she got every lot she bid for of the first
day's sale except the Children . . .

You shall know the success of this day's sale. The Duchess bids
as far as £300 for "The Sleeping Child."

On Saturday night, she added:

Sir Richard Grosvenor bought the Guido at £328 [a reference
to *The Sleeping Child*], and was determined to bid as far as five
hundred pounds. *The Sigismunda* was sold to the Duke of Bedford
for £200 *before the sale*; only put into the sale and puffed up for
fear it should otherwise hurt the sale. For the Laughing Boy,
Vandyke, the Duchess gave £126; the View of Antwerp, £551 5s.;
the small picture, *Lot* 20, 3rd day's sale £23 2s.; the Raphael, £703
10s; *Lot* 15, 3rd day's sale, £43 4s. All the pictures sold for £7775
2s. 6d.[34]

Through the Houlditch volumes of auction catalogues, it is possible
to trace some of Handel's friends and associates as they pass through the
sale rooms. Palmer only appears posthumously in terms of the sale of his
collection, but Christopher Batt's purchases can be followed over years
until his collection too is auctioned after his death in 1756. Charles Jennens also plays a role in these volumes, as does Handel. Following these
art collectors through the auctions provides a better understanding of the
quality and value of the paintings they had in their houses and offers some
insight into Handel's motivation to build an art collection of his own.

In his will, Palmer left a life interest in the house and property on Curzon Street and all of its contents, specifically naming the library and art
collection, to his wife, Elizabeth, with explicit permission for her to sell it
all. If she chose not to sell, then on her death these possessions were to pass
to Palmer's brother. Newspaper advertisements shortly after Palmer's

death indicate that much, perhaps all, was sold or auctioned. Although one might imagine that Palmer would have added books to the great library he inherited, no known inscription bears a later date than 1747, the year he married and settled on Curzon Street. As his only appearance in the Houlditch volumes is the posthumous sale of his paintings, the situation with his art collection may be the same. Palmer's decision not to preserve these inherited collections within the family, but to allow them to be disbursed by sale with the proceeds going to his wife, must have exacerbated the negative reaction the family had to the marriage in the first place. Given the insistence of the Palmer and Verney families that a bride's dowry fall to the husband in lieu of children (see Chapter 6), however, it may be that granting his wife a life interest in his estate and permission through his will to sell the family heirlooms was the only way Palmer had of compensating her for this loss of fortune. Lord Verney's irritation at having to buy back family treasures to which he was entitled by descent (through his Palmer grandmother) can be witnessed in rough attempts to scrape off Palmer's inscription from the books that passed through his hands.

Ralph Palmer died on January 23, 1755, and by March 19, the auctioneer John Prestage was advertising a sale to be held on April 10 and 11 of "The genuine and intire Collection of fine Italian and other Pictures of RALPH PALMER, Esq." A later advertisement lists fifteen "capital Masters" included in the collection, identified as follows: Raphael, Titian, Correggio, Carracci, Caravaggio, Guido [Reni], Veronese, Tintoretto, Salvator Rosa, Luca Giordano, Poussin, Rubens, Vandyke, Rembrandt, and Claude Lorraine. Of the eight paintings bought by Lord Verney, seven were from this highlighted group of artists; the eighth was identified as Andrea del Sarto's famous copy of Raphael's portrait of Leo X with two cardinals (now at Museo di Capodimonte, Naples), but surely was not. Nevertheless, these eight paintings being among the works most sought after by collectors, they drew some of the highest prices. At £53 11s., the painting attributed to del Sarto was the most expensive, followed by Caravaggio's *Saint Andrew on the Cross* at £36 14s. and Poussin's *Moses Striking the Rock* at £32 11s. Verney was outbid on one item by Sir Paul Methuen, an important collector and patron of Goupy's work, who paid £28 17s. 6d. for Rembrandt's *A Turkish Bashaw.*

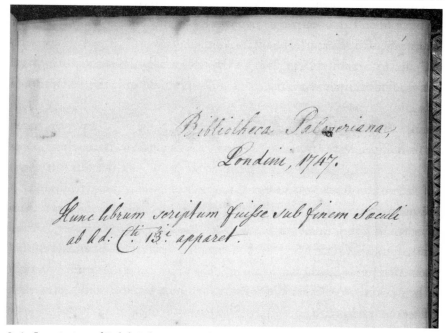

8.4 Inscription of Ralph Palmer in Hugh of Saint-Victor, *Commentary on Pseudo-Dionysius,* second or third quarter of the twelfth century, showing the attempt to scrape off "Bibliotheca Palmeriana" (© The British Library Board [Burney MS 308])

Misattributions, a common and continuing problem, as well as changing titles, make the identification of paintings listed in this and all other art auctions in the eighteenth century oftentimes problematic, but even without determining authenticity in all cases, Palmer's collection was clearly remarkable. The Rembrandt painting bought by Methuen (now in the Metropolitan Museum, New York) has gone through somewhat amusing name changes, in part one assumes for sociopolitical reasons: *A Turkish Bashaw* was changed first to *The Noble Slav* but is now titled *Man in Oriental Costume.*

The painting entitled *A Holy Family, an Angel Singing,* credited to Fra Bartolomeo in the sale of Palmer's collection, has now been attributed to Domenico Beccafumi, and is in the collection of the Princeton University Art Museum. Poussin painted at least three versions of *Moses Striking the Rock*; as neither of the two surviving originals belonged to Palmer, it seems likely, despite the attribution, that his painting was actually an unidentified copy.[35] Another Poussin listed in his collection, however, was authentic. *Titus Storming the Temple of Jerusalem,* was bought by Verney at the auction, but then lost from the late 1700s until 1995; now titled *The Destruction and Sack of the Temple,* it entered the collection of the Israel Museum in 1998.[36]

Christopher Batt (Elizabeth Mayne's brother) regularly purchased art at auction. As a result, the difference in price between what he paid for a painting and what that painting realized at the posthumous sale of his collection can be determined in a number of cases, providing a sense of the market over a number of years. There is no general trend in price up or down. Rather, the fluctuations relate directly to the perceived authenticity of the painting, which sometimes changed, and the perceived quality of the painter, which also varied. Paintings by some minor masters, such as Occhiali (Gaspar van Wittel), remained stable in value. However, with more highly esteemed artists, the prevalence and quality of painted copies, which fashion provided Goupy with his livelihood, often led to problems in attribution, as already seen in Palmer's collection. In at least two cases, Batt bought a work he thought original that was sold at his death as a copy. In these cases, the price fell dramatically: a landscape "by Berghem" (Nicolaes Berchem) that Batt bought in 1744 for £28 17s. 6d. was sold after his death as "in the style of Berghem" for £3 5s., and a work he bought in 1743 as by Borgognone (Jacques Courtois) for £11 6d. was sold as a copy by Tillemans, Goupy's colleague at the Royal Academy of Music, for £4 10s. In contrast, some prices soared, perhaps as much from bidding wars as from perceived value. As at the auction of Palmer's collection, many of the most expensive works were bought by family, in this case, Batt's nephew, John Mayne (son of Elizabeth Mayne).

Given that John Mayne was executor and heir of his uncle Christopher Batt, it is not clear why the collection was auctioned or, at least, why the paintings Mayne wished to retain were not held back. The sale of art collections was not common when an estate passed directly to an executor and heir, as is clear from the example of the Palmer family, whose collections passed through multiple generations. Nor did it happen in

8.5 Rembrandt van Rijn, *Man in Oriental Costume* (1632) owned by Ralph Palmer
(© The Metropolitan Museum of Art. Image Source: Art Resource, New York)

the Granville family: Bernard Granville inherited the estate and art collection of his uncle Westcombe; he bequeathed it to his nephew John
Dewes, who bequeathed it to his nephew Court Dewes, who sold the collection at auction only in 1844. It may be, however, that Batt's failure to
mention the art collection in his will meant that John Mayne had to go

through the process of buying the collection in order to lay legal claim to it (see Chapter 11).

At the auction of Batt's collection, John Mayne bought 19 of the 136 lots (most of which were single items) on offer. Although one might imagine that the proceeds from the 107 lots sold outside the family might easily have covered the price of Mayne's 19 purchases and still have provided a profit, this was not the case. Mayne was the only purchaser who spent more than £100 on a single painting, and he did so for four works: Claude Lorrain, *A Morning* (£170 2s.); Teniers, *A Large Landscape with a Farm House and Figures* (£168); Borgognone, *A Large Battle* (£159 12s.); and Gaspard Poussin (Dughet), *A Landscape with Figures* (£106 1s.). In all, Mayne spent £1,354 2s. 6d. to buy 19 of his uncle's paintings to which he seems to have had a right as heir. The remaining 107 lots brought in £1,319 9s. Not only was Mayne therefore out of pocket in terms of his own purchases, but he also suffered the additional loss of the majority of his uncle's art collection. It was, however, the price he had to pay to retain the best.

One of the biggest purchasers at the auction of Batt's collection other than Mayne was Handel's librettist Charles Jennens, who bought ten paintings in eight lots. Houlditch always gives the name as "Jennings," which was a common alternative spelling, but the identification of Jennens can be verified from the inventory of his collection published in 1766 in *The English Connoisseur*, an account of the collections "in the Palaces and Seats of the Nobility and Principal Gentry of England." The maintenance of such detailed catalogues illustrates the care with which collectors kept track of their acquisitions. Eight of the ten paintings acquired by Jennens in 1756 at the Batt auction appear consecutively toward the end of his inventory. These were, in the order listed: Monamy, *A Sea Piece*; Van Diest, *Two Landscapes*; Solimena, *An Emblematical Picture of Justice*; Sebastiano Conca, *Virgin and Child, and St. Francis with Angels*; Filippo Lauri, *St. Francis Asleep, an Angel Fidling*; Van de Velde, *A Storm*; and Keirincx, *Landscape*.[37] Jennens probably had disposed of the other two paintings, identified only as being of Italian provenance, before this inventory was published.

One fascinating aspect of an auction catalogue to which the names of purchasers have been added is the snapshot it can provide of a moment in time: looking at such a catalogue it may be possible to say "these people" were together in "this room" at this specific time. The Houlditch copies are particularly useful in this regard as a distinction is drawn between purchasers who were present and those who were represented by an agent. The Batt auction, as was typical, brought together politicians, merchant traders, members of the gentry and aristocracy, and artists: among them, Lords Harcourt and Egremont; William Beckford (West India sugar merchant, plantation owner, and father of William Beckford, collector, and author of the Gothic novel *Vathek*); John Mayne and Charles Jennens; Gerard Vandergucht, art dealer and engraver; and the young artist Joshua Reynolds. John Mayne's father-in-law, the Rev. Samuel Raymond of Belchamp Hall, was also present and bought two small paintings: *A Nativity* by "Old Palma" (Palma Vecchio) for £6 and *A Sketch of Women and Children* by Chardin for £2 19s. Houlditch was a buyer as well.

Handel was not present at the auction of the collections of either Batt or Palmer, as he had lost his eyesight completely by the mid-1750s. However, he must have known both of those collections, as well as those of Jennens and Mary Delany's brother Bernard Granville. Some time after 1745, when his financial situation had become secure, Handel's association with these collectors and their collections would have influenced his decision to begin attending art auctions. The Houlditch volumes record seven purchases by Handel at six different auctions in the first three months of 1750.[38]

On March 22 and 23, 1750, the sale of pictures "purchased abroad" by Charles Gouyn, a London jeweler and porcelain-maker, and Thomas Major, engraver, at Mr. Langford's in Covent Garden, attracted a cross section of London society.[39] The purchasers included Handel and his friend Christopher Batt; John Mayne's father-in law, Mr. Raymond; the great actor, playwright, and theater manager David Garrick; the art dealer Vandergucht; and the artist Thomas Hudson, who recently had completed a portrait of Handel. Batt bought the final item in the sale, clearly the pièce de résistance: Rubens, *The Crucifixion,* for the highest price paid at the auction, £79 16s. When John Mayne later acquired this painting at the auction of Batt's collection for £85 1s., it was more fully described as an "original Sketch for the Altar of yᵉ Great Ch. Att Antwerp" (for its subsequent history, see Chapter 11.)

At the same sale, Handel bought *A Landskip with Moses in the Bull-rushes,* the subject of an abandoned child linked to the composer's charitable interest in the Foundling Hospital in London (see Chapter 9). It was assigned to "Perocelle Senʳ" in the catalogue and long associated with Joseph Parrocel; the work is now attributed to his brother Louis.[40] At the sale of Lady Sunderland's estate, he bought two paintings: *A Landskip with a Bacchanalian* by "Prelemburck" (Poelenburgh) and *The Sacking of Troy* by Pietro da Cortona. The latter might have attracted Handel's attention, reminding him of the time he spent in Rome as a young man under the patronage of Cardinal Pamphilj, as the gallery vault of the Palazzo Pamphilj in the Piazza Navona was painted by Cortona with scenes from the life of Aeneas (but not including this scene). If the work entitled *The Siege of Troy* in the posthumous catalogue of Handel's collection is the same work, however, the attribution there is not to Cortona but to Poussin. Handel bought *A Conversation* by Watteau at the sale of the collection belonging to the artist Joseph van Aken, whom he may have known personally: Van Aken worked for Hudson as a drapery painter and may have assisted him in his portrait of the composer from 1748 (see Image 9.1). Hudson, serving as an agent for a number of purchasers, came away from the auction of van Aken's collection with more paintings than anyone else. At the auction of Mr. Humphrey Edwin's collection on March 16, only one week before the Gouyn and Major sale, Handel bought *A Small History* by (Annibale?) Carracci, but the only Carracci listed later in the sale of Handel's collection is *Venus and Cupid in an Oval,* which subject does not immediately suggest a "history"—unless the painting actually was a copy of, or otherwise related to, Annibale's *Venus and Anchises* (which includes Cupid) from the fresco cycle of *The Loves of the Gods* in the Palazzo Farnese in Rome. Because of the frequent difficulties with regard to titles and attributions, none of the specific paintings owned by Handel can be traced today, but his activity at the auctions gives a good sense of the seriousness and extent of his collecting.

The most important painting in Handel's collection, or at least the one he was most delighted by, was *A Large Landschape and Fig[ure]s*, attributed to Rembrandt, that he bought on February 8, 1750. He paid £39 18s., the highest price recorded for any of his purchases. Five days later, Shaftesbury wrote to James Harris about it:

> I have seen Handel several times since I came hither; and think I never saw him so cool and well. He is quite easy in his behaviour, and he has been pleasing himself in the purchase of several fine pictures; particularly a large Rembrant, which is indeed excellent. We have scarce talk'd at all about musical subjects, though enough to find his performances will go off incomparably.[41]

Handel purchased the painting at the sale of the collection of Anthony Couzin, a former patron of Goupy, and, indeed, a "Belisarius" by "Goupy"—actually a copy of a painting by Luciano Borzone and per-haps Goupy's most popular work—is listed in the sale directly above the Rembrandt bought by Handel; no purchaser is named (see below).

Bernard Granville purchased two works on the second day of Cou-zin's sale (February 9), and he and Handel probably attended both days together. Certainly Granville was something of an art adviser to Handel, particularly it would seem with reference to Rembrandt. In his will, Han-del bequeathed to Granville the Rembrandt he had purchased (described there more specifically as "Landskip, a view of the Rhine") as well as "another Landskip said to be done by the same hand" that Granville had made him "a present of some time ago." Jennens must also have been an adviser. Handel left Jennens in his will the "pictures [of] the old Mans head and the old Womans head done by [Balthasar] Denner." The Den-ner paintings bequeathed to Jennens in 1759 appear in the published cat-alogue of his collection nine pages further on than the group of works he bought at the auction of Batt's paintings three years earlier, suggesting that the inventory tracked accessions in chronological order. Therefore, although there is no record of who bought any of the paintings in Han-del's collection, the landscapes by Poussin immediately preceding the two paintings by Denner in Jennens's inventory could represent the two Poussin paintings in Handel's sale.

Only seven of the works in Handel's art collection can be traced through the acquisitions he made at auctions, and all of these occurred in 1750. That no purchases appear later can be easily attributed to Handel's failing eyesight, of which he began to complain at the beginning of 1751. In earlier years, when Handel's finances were neither as strong nor as secure, Handel probably collected by other means. One way would have been to acquire works, by purchase or gift, from artists in England. He owned works by Pellegrini, Marco and Sebastiano Ricci, Servandoni, Tillemans, and, of course, Goupy—all painters who were connected with opera in London in the 1710s or 1720s. These six artists account for fifteen of the sixty-seven lots on offer in the sale catalogue from the auction of his collection in 1760.[42] In addition, the painting of a sunset by John Wootton could come to him by or through Goupy, as the two painters were associates. Handel probably began his collection with prints, as these were less expensive than paintings. His sale catalogue lists eight sets of prints. Two of these sets are reproductions of art in Roman churches: Handel, like any modern tourist, probably acquired them when he was in Rome. One of the churches, Santa Maria del Popolo, was directly across the piazza from the church of Santa Maria di Montesanto, where much of Handel's Latin church music, commissioned by Cardinal Colonna, was heard at a grand service of Vespers for the annual celebration of the Carmelite order (see Image 2.3). Sets of landscapes or scenic views were likely of interest to Handel because of their similarity to operatic backdrops: two of these engraved sets were by Goupy. The six sea pieces by Samuel Scott and George Lambert, commissioned by the East India Company, speak additionally to Handel's interest in international trade.[43]

Goupy's original paintings were few, the only well-known examples being his caricatures, in particular that of Handel as a hog, and the four panoramic views of the Port of Valletta, Malta, from early in his career. These panoramic views were of sufficient interest to be later engraved and sold as prints, and Handel had a set in his collection. The "book of nudities" mentioned in Goupy's will and the apparently bawdy depictions of lewd poetry listed in the auction catalogue of works offered for sale by Goupy in 1765 (but held in reserve to be viewed on request) have not survived. Mostly Goupy earned his living making copies of Old Master paintings in private English collections, and these appear regularly in the Houlditch volumes. As already noted (see Chapter 3), he was commissioned by Baron Kielmansegg to make copies of the New Testament scenes in the Raphael cartoons then at Hampton Court (now at the Victoria and Albert Museum), and these copies were sold by Kielmansegg's widow after 1717 to the earl of Carnarvon (later duke of Chandos). Goupy made pastel copies of *Belisarius Receiving Charity*, a painting Lord Burlington purchased on his European tour of 1714–1715, for a number of patrons, including John Hedges, Lord Oxford, and Prince Frederick (see Image 3.3); Handel also owned a copy. He made a full set of copies for Prince Frederick of twelve paintings by Giordano telling the story of Cupid and Psyche, at that time owned by Sir Gregory Page and now in the Royal Collection.

Goupy's copies of works by Guido Reni were particularly admired. A poem of 1738, dedicated to Goupy and entitled "Guido's Ghost," depicts him making copies of Guido's work in the collection of Henry Furnese, at whose house in 1740 Handel is said to have eaten and drunk too much for his health (see Chapter 7). At the end of the poem, Guido himself gives Goupy permission to "Copy, whate'er my Skill brought forth," only regretting that he cannot claim Goupy's work for his own: "'Tis true it is not;—but I wish 'twere Mine." Goupy's copies of Guido include *Venus and the Graces, Liberality and Modesty, Apollo and Daphne,* and *Aurora.* Hedges owned copies of the first three; Prince Frederick all four. According to the engraver and antiquary George Vertue, whose notebook diaries provide a record of artistic activity in Great Britain during this period, the dressing room of the princess of Wales was adorned with "curious carvd frames and Glasses," "consisting mostly of several most valuable pictures [by Goupy] ... that he has copied and Imitated," which were all purchased "at once" by the prince.[44]

Goupy reached a wider audience, and enhanced his reputation, through prints.[45] Engraved sets, such as those produced by Goupy and his contemporary William Hogarth, were within reach of the upper-middle-class purchaser who probably could not afford to commission individual paintings, but still they would have been a luxury purchase. Only inexpensive single prints, often in pirated copies, enabled those to whom £50 represented two years' income (the average building craftsman earned about £26 a year) to aspire to connoisseurship.[46] Such piracy, however, resulted in significant losses for those who made their living by selling prints, and on February 5, 1735, a group of artists, including George Lambert (engravings of whose *Sea Pieces* were owned by Handel), Hogarth, and Goupy, signed a petition to Parliament for protection. The Engravers' Copyright Act, which prohibited unauthorized copies of engravings for fourteen years after their first publication, became law on June 24, 1735. Hogarth's famous series *A Rake's Progress* was published the next day, and the following year Goupy published a set of engravings after Marco Ricci. Even top collectors sought to acquire such prints.[47] Most of Goupy's engraved sets in the 1740s depict important works in noted private collections, such as those of the duke of Devonshire, Sir Robert Walpole, and Prince Frederick. These may have been commissioned directly by the collectors to publicize their powerful patronage and artistic discrimination.[48]

Among Goupy's lost works is a portrait of Handel for the prince of Wales; a record survives for the purchase of a frame made for it in 1742.[49] Portraits were an essential part of any great collection in order to claim a relationship, and thereby status, through ancestry or friendship or to demonstrate an affinity: Jacobites favored portraits of the Stuart monarchs, while Hanoverians displayed portraits of the Hanoverian family. Handel gave portraits of himself to close friends and family. One of the earliest is that attributed to Denner, the artist who painted the "Old Man's Head" and "Old Woman's Head" that Handel bequeathed to Jennens; it probably dates from the 1720s (see Image 4.1). Handel is thought to have given it to John Christopher Smith. Handel gave the superb portrait by Philippe Mercier from the 1730s, showing him in informal attire by the harpsichord, to Thomas Harris, in whose family it remains (see Image 5.1). The formal portrait by Thomas Hudson from the late 1740s, showing Handel in the fullness of his success, may have been taken by Handel to his family in Germany on his last trip to Europe in 1750 (see Image 9.1). A second portrait by Hudson, done in 1756, was commissioned by Jennens and shows the composer in old age and blind (see Image 10.1). Of course, Handel's friends and supporters also collected their own portraits of him. Anne Donnellan owned a miniature of Handel by Rupert Barber that she bequeathed to the British Museum; unfortunately, it is lost.[50] Sometimes supporters made their own images: the countess of Shaftesbury, for example, created her own portrait of Handel in pastel, based on the engraving that was included with the publication of *Alexander's Feast* in 1738.[51]

Of Handel's image in prints, Jacobus Houbraken's engraving for *Alexander's Feast* was the first of several produced over the next ten years. A miniature portrait from about 1738 by Georg Andreas Wolfgang (now in the Royal Collection) was later engraved in Berlin by his father, and a few years later in Paris, G. F. Schmidt engraved a version of Houbraken's print, probably for the French edition of Handel's Concerto Op. 4, no. 1, in 1741. In 1748, mezzotint prints by both Andrew Miller and John Faber based on the powerful portrait by Hudson became the most widely circulated image of the composer.[52]

Just as print copies of Handel's portraits saw wide circulation, so too did portrait busts of the composer by Roubiliac. Modeled in part on his statue for Vauxhall Gardens, these show the composer in informal attire with a soft hat rather than a wig (but the dressing robe he wears appears to be the same as that in the Mercier portrait). James Harris purchased some of these for himself and for friends and family (including Charles Jennens and the countess of Shaftesbury); his brother Thomas served as his eyes in London, going to Roubiliac's studio to look at the work.[53] The countess wrote to Harris on June 27, 1741:

> Thursday I recieved the busto of Hendal and am very thankfull to my cousin Thomas Harris for negociating this affair for me[.] I have dispos'd of it in a place of highest eminence in my room and please my self with thinking you will approve of it[.]

Roubiliac wrote on July 10, hoping for more business:

> I have reciev'd your obliging letter, and in answer I shall acquaint
> you that Mr Handel's busto shall be near ready to morrow, so I
> hope you will be pleased to send how to direct it. You know I have
> Mr Popes busto which I have likewise made after life. I have also
> Milton's and Newton's[,] so in case any of your friends should
> want you will be pleas'd to recommend them[;] but bustos being
> works by which there is little to be got but reputation[,] I desire
> you will let your friends know that my chief talent is marble
> works, such as monuments, chimneys, tables, all which I hope
> to do, to the satisfaction of those that will do me the honour to
> employe me.

For an artist who hoped to interest a collector in his work, as Roubiliac's letter makes clear, the other side of making was marketing, and like
the sculptor, Handel needed to sell the work he composed to make a
living. When the Royal Academy of Music planned for its opening in
spring 1720, Handel had been hired as the music director "with a Sallary," the amount unknown. For its first short season in 1720, the academy budgeted £200 for "operas"; for its first full season in 1720–1721,
£400. As there were two new operas in the opening spring season and
four the following year, it may be that the composers were paid £100 for
composing an opera. If so, then the fees, presumably lower, for revising
an opera must have come out of a different budget line (in spring 1720,
the English composer Thomas Roseingrave revised Domenico Scarlatti's *Narciso* for the academy, and in the autumn of 1720, Handel prepared
a heavily revised *Radamisto*, both of which works are unaccounted for in
the budget if all the funds allocated to "operas" were expended on new
work). The composing fee of £100 already seems little enough, given
that the two leading *singers* for 1720–1721 were budgeted for salaries
of £1,680 and £1,100.[54] In 1729, when the opera patrons discussed the
continuation of productions following the academy's closure in 1728,
Handel was granted £1,000 for the first year.[55] This was described as

covering the cost of operas whether by him or another, but it probably also included the musical direction, as the fees offered him by Middlesex in 1743 of 500 guineas (£525) for a new opera and 100 (£105) for a revised opera were said to be "more than ever He had in His life." Assuming a season typical to those that had been presented by the academy, Handel would have needed to budget about half of the £1,000 for the operas (given continuing payments of at least £100 for a new opera and somewhat less for a revised one); the other £500, if it represented his fee for music direction, may provide an indication of what Handel had formerly earned as "Master of the Orchester with a Sallary."

Once an opera was written and paid for by the company, the composer might be able to take the bulk of box-office receipts for a designated "benefit night," but otherwise the revenue stream from performance slowed considerably. Almost all of Handel's works for London were published, however—at least in abbreviated form—and for long periods Handel had a standing relationship with the firm of John Walsh. Surviving records show that the standard payment Handel received from Walsh for each opera was 25 guineas (£26 5s.). For a published oratorio, this fee dropped to 20 guineas (£21). An exception in many ways, the publication of *Alexander's Feast* included, for the first time in any of Handel's published work, the full orchestral score with all recitatives and choruses; it was sold by subscription, and the list of subscribers was headed by all seven of the children of George II. Although *Alexander's Feast* was shorter than his usual opera or oratorio, Walsh paid Handel four times the normal amount for an opera: 100 guineas (£105).[56] One reason for the much higher fee must have been that the availability of a complete, published score made performances possible without the composer's participation. That is, the quadrupled fee compensated in part for the loss of Handel's exclusive right to performance revenue.

Whether or not Handel received any percentage from sales of his published works, and there is no evidence that he did, he clearly wanted to prevent unauthorized publication of his compositions for at least three reasons: to protect his music from inaccurate editions, his name from false attributions, and his fee for the right to publish his music. So concerned was he about this that he applied for and received a royal patent granting him the sole rights to his music for fourteen years. The privilege, dated June 14, 1720, reads in part:

> Whereas *George Fredrick Handel*, of our City of *London*, Gent. hath humbly represented unto Us, That he hath with great Labour and Expence composed several Works, consisting of *Vocal and Instrumental MUSICK*, in Order to be Printed and Publish'd; and hath therefore besought Us to grant him Our Royal Priviledge and Licence for the sole Printing and Publishing thereof for the Term of Fourteen Years: We being willing to give all due Encouragement to Works of this Nature, are graciously pleased to condescend to his Request . . .[57]

In 1739, George II granted a second privilege to Handel's music, also for fourteen years. This time the privilege was granted to Walsh, as Handel "hath authorized and appointed *John Walsh* of the Parish of *St. Mary le Strand*, in Our said County of *Middlesex*, to print and publish the same."[58]

Complete scores of Handel's works were also created, however, in the great eighteenth-century sets of manuscript copies of Handel's works. These sets were prepared by the scriptorium run by John Christopher Smith, and must therefore have been overseen to some extent by the composer, but they were very limited in number. Those now identifiable include the sets commissioned by Elizabeth Legh (later passed on to James Harris), Jennens, Granville, Shaftesbury, Prince Frederick, and Hunter.[59] Further, the owners of these sets were conscious of a responsibility to protect Handel's intellectual property and Smith's commercial advantage.

The manuscript copies of complete scores of Handel's compositions released these works from the direct purview of Handel and Smith and allowed, as with the complete publication of *Alexander's Feast*, for performance under direction other than Handel's own. Thus when William Hayes of Oxford asked Shaftesbury if he could borrow his rare manuscript copy of Handel's oratorio *Joshua* in order to copy out parts for a performance in Oxford, Shaftesbury felt it necessary, first, to ask Handel for permission, as he thought "Mr Handel will not chuse to have it perform'd at Oxford," and second, to inquire of Smith, given that lending the score could undercut Smith's exclusive access to Handel's scores and the fees he received for copying them. When permission was granted, it was "done under a confidence of Dr Hayes's honour that he will not suffer any copy to be taken or to get about from his having been in possession of this score. For otherwise both Handel and Smyth (his copiest) will be injur'd." His only remaining concern was for the manuscript itself: "Pray desire too, care may be taken not to spoil the book. I mention this particular as a caution, because very often books and especially manuscripts, are much dirted by being thumbed about."[60]

Manuscript copies of Handel's works, and particularly those made under the direction of Smith at Handel's own scriptorium, had a value that printed works could not approach. James Harris gives a clear statement of this view in expressing his delight to Lord Radnor, his friend, for passing on Elizabeth Legh's set of Handel's manuscripts in 1740: "My own collection of Handel's music is cheifly of his printed works, which are most of them very incorrect, the older opera's more particularly. Tis this incorrectness which makes manuscript copies valuable even of those works which are already printed."[61] The accuracy of printed music, however, could reach high levels, depending on the quality of the publisher and the participation of the composer.

Just as William Hogarth published his engravings of *A Rake's Progress* immediately after the enactment of the Engravers' Copyright Act, Walsh and Handel planned a major publication to follow the granting of a royal patent to Walsh for the printing of Handel's music. The privilege was dated October 31, 1739. In the month previous, Handel had composed a set of twelve concertos at a furious pace; and Walsh announced a subscription for the publication "With His Majesty's Royal Licence and Protection[,] *Twelve Grand Concerto's ... Compos'd by* Mr. *Handel*" two days before the actual date on the patent. Handel clearly intended to perform all these concertos in the near future (and in some cases did so before the print appeared in 1740), but this was the only time he composed with the evident purpose of publication.

These concertos, Handel's Op. 6, are marvels of invention. In the tradition of the Italian concerto grosso by Corelli—the orchestration consists of a large ensemble juxtaposed with a solo trio of two violins and cello, and the structure adheres to no regular pattern—each one is fresh in form and style. Even the alternation of soloists and orchestra, a defining feature of the concerto, is not consistently present; rather, Handel often dispenses with the soloists and writes for full orchestra. The wealth of material in the more than sixty movements of the *Twelve Grand Concertos* is difficult to grasp from a brief overview. Overtures, instrumental arias, and minuets, as well as a polonaise, hornpipe, and musette, comprise only some of the styles found among them. Demonstrating their dazzling variety by contrasting the different types of movements is simple, but superficial. A fuller picture can be drawn by comparing Handel's diversity of approach in movements of the same formal category.

Most of the concertos include at least one fugal movement, but these vary so much one from another that they hardly seem to belong to the same genre. In the second movement of Concerto no. 6 in G Minor, the subject begins with a decisive downward chromatic motion, which sounds as if it might continue through the whole scale, but after only three notes, takes a large leap down and then hikes back up the chromatic scale to meet itself. Since Handel asks that each note be separately accented, the effect of the theme is not of slithering, as often the case with half-step motion, but rather of striding forward with conviction only to slip and fall, and then be forced to march back to where one started. In contrast, the fourth movement of Concerto no. 1 has a lively and ebullient fugue subject that outlines its G-major tonality simply, with sunny conviction. The thematic material suggests an uneventful progression, but just as the movement gathers itself together for a final iteration of the subject, Handel cuts off the music abruptly in midstatement. After this brutal and unexpected silencing, there is a pause before the instruments scurry timidly in on tiptoe to bring the movement quickly to a close. In the second movement of Concerto no. 7, Handel proves his wit and virtuosity by creating a fugue astonishingly based on the accelerating repetition of a single note: in the first measure the note is struck twice; in the second measure, four times; and in the third, eight. Only its concluding one-measure tail has any melodic motion at all. Nevertheless, Handel spins a high-spirited marvel, coupling bare rhythmic articulation and vitality with harmonic richness and depth. As a whole, the *Twelve Grand Concertos* resemble a Baroque landscape garden that one must wander through repeatedly to appreciate all the hidden structures and surprising vistas. Handel's contemporaries certainly enjoyed the exploration. After the first edition of 1740, Walsh published a second edition in 1741 and a third in 1746. The first Paris edition came in 1744; the second in 1751.

Handel received more remuneration for his music from composition and performance than from distribution, but it is striking how closely the reproduction of his scores parallels the hierarchical production and circulation of Goupy's art. In both cases, the most valuable were the individual copies made by hand (the manuscript copies of Handel's music, or Goupy's Old Master copies); next came the luxury publications of entire works (Handel's *Alexander's Feast*, the *Grand Concertos*, or Goupy's integrated sets of engravings), followed by printed collections (of songs from a single opera or oratorio or of paintings from a specific collection), and finally single prints (often unauthorized). Although for Handel performance drove distribution, it was the distribution, and not performance, that turned his image and his works into collectible items.

In the course of the 1740s, as Handel's reputation rose, the monumental manuscript collections as we know them were largely completed, and the engraving of Hudson's powerful portrait of Handel began to overtake the Houbraken image in the eyes of the public. When the *Fireworks Music*, composed for the Peace at Aix-la-Chapelle, was rehearsed in Vauxhall Gardens in 1749, the crowd in attendance was estimated at 10,000, and at the Bank of England Handel's accounts were not just healthy, but from 1743, his stock accounts uninterruptedly increased. As Handel became more secure financially, he became a collector as well as a collectible, developing a virtuoso collection of paintings and prints in addition to his professional library. By the end of the 1740s, he not only attended auctions with his virtuoso friends and colleagues but also bid for and acquired valuable works of art. The period was brief, however. All of his known purchases can be dated to the first three months of 1750. One year later, his eyesight had begun to fail, and blindness quickly put an end to both his collecting and his composing.

9.1 Portrait of Handel (1748–1749) by Thomas Hudson (Staats- und Universitäts-bibliothek, Hamburg, *Gemäldesammlung*: 11 [Hudson: Bildnis G. F. Händel])

NINE

Religion and Charity

1739–1750

A look back at Esther, *then* Israel in Egypt, Messiah,
Judas Maccabaeus, Theodora

HANDEL'S ART COLLECTION contained few religious works apart from the prints he brought from Italy. The lack of any images of the Virgin Mary, Joseph, or the saints, such as existed in Ralph Palmer's fine collection, would seem to suggest that the composer's Protestant upbringing had a stronger hold on him than his burgeoning interest in art. The same cannot be said for Mary Delany, who, being asked by her husband, the Rev. Patrick Delany, to take on the responsibility of decorating their new chapel at their home outside Dublin, made copies in oil of various religious paintings, including a Madonna and Child after Guido Reni and a Transfiguration attributed to Carlo Maratti.[1] The biblical images Handel did collect, such as Goupy's depiction of Hagar and Ishmael and Parrocel's *Moses in the Bullrushes,* point not so much to religion as to charitable works and dramatic scenarios. The Foundling Hospital in London for "the education and maintenance of exposed and deserted young children," established in 1741, counted Handel as a director from 1750, and fine paintings of Hagar and of Moses, both stories of children rescued from dire circumstance, were hung in the Court Room of the Hospital. In a more general sense, however, both of these Old Testament stories represent the kind of dramatic narrative that lies at the basis of Handel's entire collection: not only is sacred imagery lacking, but so is portraiture, an important part of most eighteenth-century

RELIGION AND CHARITY: *Timeline*

1689

May 24
Act of Toleration,
granting freedom
of worship to Protes-
tants not of the
Church of England
(1 Will & Mary c.
18)

1701

June
Act of Settlement
passed to ensure
Protestant succes-
sion

1711

December 20
Occasional Conformity Act,
forbidding Nonconforming
Protestants and Catholics
from qualifying them-
selves for public positions
by obtaining a sacrament
certificate in the Church of
England (10 Anne c. 6)

collections, and still-life, the favorite genre of Handel's Italian patron
Cardinal Pamphilj.[2] Like the historical paintings, character studies, and
landscapes in Handel's collection, the biblical stories point directly to
the stage and to Handel's creative imagination.

In eighteenth-century Britain, religious belief was not just a personal
matter but also an issue of great political significance. One cannot over-
estimate the importance of the Protestant religion and in particular the
Church of England to the history of this period. Although England had
separated officially from the Catholic Church in 1534 under Henry VIII,
the reality was harder to achieve and longer in coming. To speak only
of the quarter century immediately preceding Handel's first years in
London, the reversion to Catholicism of James II had led to the Glorious
Revolution of 1688, when Prince William of Orange, from the Protestant
Dutch Republic, invaded England at the invitation of members of Parliament and took up the throne jointly with his wife, Mary, the Protestant
daughter of James II.[3] After their deaths, Mary's sister, Anne, acceded.
Like her sister before her, however, she left no heirs, and therefore steps
had to be taken to secure the Protestant monarchy. The Act of Settlement
of 1701 ensured Protestant succession by skipping over more than fifty
Catholics in the line of succession and naming as heir to the throne the
dowager Electress Sophia of Hanover, "and the heirs of her body being
protestant."[4] The year following the Hanoverian succession to the throne

1714
August 1
death of Queen
Anne; Hanove-
rian succession

1717
May
prorogation (suspen-
sion) of the Ecclesias-
tical Convocations of
Canterbury and York
(governing bodies of
the Church of England),
making the British mon-
arch sole head of the
Church

1718
Handel composes
Esther based on a bib-
lical story of religious
tolerance

1719
January
Act for Strengthen-
ing the Protestant
Interest; the repeal
of the Occasional
Conformity Act (5
Geo 1 c. 4)

in 1714 witnessed the first major uprising of the Jacobites, those who supported James II's Catholic son, also named James, as the true king ("Jacobus" being the Latin form of James). The tension between Hanoverian
and Jacobite supporters continued at high pitch throughout Handel's life,
forming an important background to his compositions.

Handel's operas of the 1720s frequently had texts that related directly
to the issue of succession, and we have already seen in Chapter 3 how the
Jacobite interpretation of *Floridante* (1721) led to an apparent demonstration of support for the overthrow of the Hanoverian "usurper" and
the restoration of the Stuart line through James "III." Without doubt,
the Protestant monarchy faced hostile opposition, and concern for its
security over more than a century resulted in the establishment of various legal protections. Catholics were disenfranchised, disallowed from
studying at Oxford or Cambridge, and forbidden from owning land or
holding high office. Although many of these laws applied equally to all
recusants who did not conform to the Anglican communion, including
Protestants of other sects, in practice there was some differentiation.
Under William and Mary, the Act of Toleration (1689), had permitted
freedom of worship to Protestant nonconformists who took the oaths of
allegiance and supremacy and made the declaration against transubstan-
tiation, and, under George I, the law established by Queen Anne in 1711
forbidding "occasional conformity" was repealed in 1719, thus making it

Religion and Charity continued

1720

April 24
John Percival qualifies himself as a director of the Academy of Music by taking the Oaths of Allegiance, Supremacy, and Abjuration, after obtaining a Communion Certificate

1727

February 14
Handel takes the Oaths at the time of his naturalization as a British citizen

1731

February 25
first in an annual series of concerts of music by Handel to support the Sons of Clergy
April 6
Handel's *Rinaldo* revived; conversion of the sorceress Armida to Christianity at the end is deleted

possible for Protestant dissenters to obtain a sacrament certificate by taking communion in the Church of England and gain access thereby to the full range of freedoms and positions allowed to members of the Church.[5] Indeed, Latitudinarianism, a name given to the movement that rejected the enforcement of strict doctrinal and liturgical rules and entrusted the interpretation of Christ's teachings to the individual believer, gained in popularity during this period. Thus, despite all the laws supportive of a single, national religion, there was also a movement to ensure that the religious hierarchy was separated from control of the state: that is, to safeguard that no religious authority, neither the pope nor even the governing body of the English Church (Convocation), had authority over the reigning British monarch, who—although subject to the law of the land as defined by Parliament—was head of both church and state. In order to ensure this position, the government in 1717 prorogued (suspended) Convocation indefinitely; it did not resume its meetings until 1854.

That the Hanoverians had Latitudinarian views is not surprising, given their Lutheran background. They conformed, of course, to the Church of England (and official certificates of conformity were required, as we have seen, for all who served the king in any capacity—including the directors of the opera company); there was, however, a Lutheran chapel in the Palace of St. James. Handel, too, came from a Lutheran background, but prefatory to his becoming a naturalized British citi-

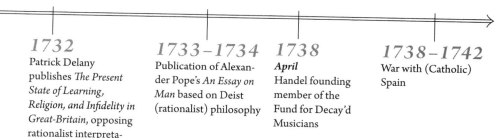

1732
Patrick Delany
publishes *The Present
State of Learning,
Religion, and Infidelity in
Great-Britain*, opposing
rationalist interpreta-
tions of the Bible

1733–1734
Publication of Alexan-
der Pope's *An Essay on
Man* based on Deist
(rationalist) philosophy

1738
April
Handel founding
member of the
Fund for Decay'd
Musicians

1738–1742
War with (Catholic)
Spain

zen in 1727, "George Frideric Handel took the Oaths of Allegiance and Supremacy, in order to his Naturalization," for which a formal certificate of Anglican conformity was required.[6]

Among Handel's friends, conformity coexisted within a wide range of Protestant belief. James Hunter came from a family of Huguenot (French Calvinist) refugees. Delany and Donnellan were both attracted to the Methodism movement within the Anglican Church during its early years (around 1740). Some years previous, between 1730 and 1734, Delany had even carried on a flirtatious correspondence with the move-ment's founder, John Wesley. Following the convention of the time, they used nicknames in their letters. Sometimes these names were based on abbreviations or general attributes of the person—such as Delany iden-tifying Donnellan as "Don" or, in reference to her voice, the nightin-gale Philomel (or Phil). Others were more pointed. Delany's name for her uncle Lansdowne was Alcander, a citizen of ancient Sparta whose shame and repentance following a terrible act led to his being forgiven; she named Mary Basset, her opponent in the lawsuit following the death of her first husband, Fulvia, an ambitious Roman matron. Delany's name for Wesley was Cyrus (the Great), King of Persia, considered the pat-tern for heroic and moral leadership, and he called her by her standard nickname, Aspasia, a beautiful Grecian woman renowned for her intelli-gence. She wrote to him, probably early in 1731:

Religion and Charity continued

1739
April 4
Handel's *Israel in Egypt* premieres; understood to depict by analogy the British people facing a "Popish Alliance" ranged against them; anti-Deist in its depiction of miracles and of God's intervention in the world (text probably by Jennens)

1740
August 1
Thomas Arne's *Alfred* includes "Rule Britannia!" (first performed privately for the prince of Wales)

1742
April 13
Handel's *Messiah* premiered in Dublin; anti-Deist in its depiction of miracles and prophecy fulfilled (text by Jennens)

Every Sunday evening, a gentleman in this town has a concert of music. I am invited there to-night, and design to go. I charge you, on the friendship you have professed for me, to tell me your sincere opinion about it, and all your objections. For, if I am in error by going, you ought to prevent my doing so again.

To which he responded: "Far be it from me to think that any circumstance of life shall ever give the enemy an advantage over Aspasia. He, who has overcome the world and its princes, shall give His angels charge over her to keep her in all her ways."[7]

Around 1750, Donnellan turned to Hutchinsonianism, an ultra-conservative response to modern scientific theory holding that all the secrets of the natural universe were contained in the Old Testament. Delany, noting that a number of her friends were "deep that way," wrote to her sister on February 22, 1752: "I am struck with their scheme, but don't know enough to talk on the subject. It is perfectly orthodox, and seems to promise perfect satisfaction in regard to the Holy Trinity . . ."[8]

Catholics naturally did not meet with similar tolerance, but even here there was some latitude. As Lord Chesterfield quipped to an English Jesuit: "It is to no purpose for you to aspire to the honour of martyrdom; fire and faggot [a reference to burnings at the stake] are quite out of vogue."[9] Goupy was Catholic, but this did not prevent him from being appointed to the inner circle of Prince Frederick's court as painter, artis-

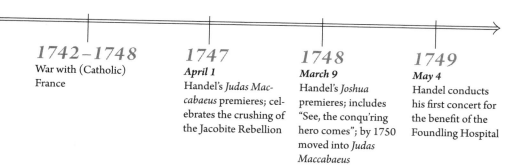

1742–1748
War with (Catholic)
France

1747
April 1
Handel's *Judas Mac-
cabaeus* premieres; cel-
ebrates the crushing of
the Jacobite Rebellion

1748
March 9
Handel's *Joshua*
premieres; includes
"See, the conqu'ring
hero comes"; by 1750
moved into *Judas
Maccabaeus*

1749
May 4
Handel conducts
his first concert for
the benefit of the
Foundling Hospital

tic adviser, and art teacher. Catholics were, however, required to register with the government, and were recorded in the Return of Papists, a
periodic nationwide census of Roman Catholics. The Return for 1767
lists a painter, aged seventy-eight, living in Kensington; this probably
was Goupy, who died there in 1769.

There was no one-to-one correspondence of Catholics with Jacobites
or of Protestants with supporters of the Hanoverian succession. Ardent
members of the Church of England, such as Charles Jennens, could reject
the Protestant succession on the grounds of the divine right of kings
(James Edward Stuart being king by birth and blood), and Catholics
could be loyal to the Protestant king. Only after the Papists Act of 1778,
however, were Catholics allowed to take the Oath of Allegiance (with a
waiver of the requirement for a Sacrament Certificate proving that the
oath-taker had previously taken communion in the Church of England).
Goupy would probably have taken the oath if he had been permitted.

During the 1710s, when Handel participated in the artistic circles
established by Lord Burlington at Burlington House and the duke of
Chandos at Cannons, he became a colleague of Alexander Pope, another
Catholic. In 1718, the poet, in collaboration with John Arbuthnot and
others, prepared a text for Handel based on the Old Testament story of
Queen Esther, which was, in effect, Handel's first English oratorio. It
may have been performed privately at Cannons in both 1718 and 1720
(the second time in a revised version); it then lay fallow for more than a

Religion and Charity continued

1750

March 16
Handel's *Theodora* premieres; a depiction of
Roman intolerance against the early Christians containing an argument for religious
freedom

May 1
Handel donates a chapel organ to the
Foundling Hospital and conducts a performance of *Messiah* at its inauguration, the
first in an annual series of *Messiah* performances at the hospital for its benefit

May 9
Handel made a governor of the Foundling Hospital

1752
(at latest)

Anne Donnellan attracted to Hutchinsonianism (opposing rationalist interpretations of
the Bible)

decade, after which a public performance in 1732 inaugurated the series
of biblical oratorios by Handel composed for London audiences.[10] The
story describes the deliverance of the Jewish people from oppression. In
the biblical narrative from the Book of Esther, the evil minister Haman
persuades King Ahasuerus of Persia to agree to the eradication of a population (the Jewish people, but not identified as such to the king) who
keep different laws from the king's other subjects. Unbeknownst to both
the king and his minister, the king's wife, Queen Esther, is Jewish. Supported and encouraged by her cousin and guardian Mordecai, the queen
braves the edict that condemns all who enter the king's presence without
his express command to death and enters the royal chamber to plead
for her people. Although fainting with fear, she is welcomed by the king
and invites him and his minister to dinner, where she reveals that both
she and Mordecai, who had once saved the king's life, are Jewish and
thus condemned by Haman's decree. Ahasuerus reverses the decree and
Haman is executed.

Given that English Protestants saw themselves as the true descendants of the ancient Hebrews, this text was frequently used in sermons
and dramatic works to illustrate the deliverance of the British people
from Catholic tyranny and was tied especially to celebrations of the Glorious Revolution of 1688 when, according to this analogy, Britain was

1754

January
the Foundling Hospital requests
proprietary rights to *Messiah*
and is denied by Handel

1767

August 3
a painter, aged seventy-eight
(Goupy?), recorded in
the Return of Papists in
Kensington

delivered from the threat of popery by the invasion of William III. This interpretation did not allow for a direct allegory between the characters of the story and specific individuals; rather, the text illustrated how the Protestant Church (Esther) had requested and received support from the state (Ahasuerus) against Catholic tyranny (Haman).[11] Of course, the text was not always interpreted this way, and it was a simple matter to see it in reverse, with Esther representing loyal English Catholics pleading with their Protestant king for tolerance. Among the many possible interpretations of the Esther story, this is one that could have resonated with Alexander Pope. One can almost see the oratorio as an argument for a Catholic relief act sixty years before the fact. No matter how one identified the persecuted minority in *Esther*, however, the story stressed the idea of religious freedom.

Handel's own interpretation of the *Esther* text is unknown, but he professed a strong belief in religious toleration and held firmly to his own beliefs in the face of opposing doctrines. When pressed in Italy to convert to Catholicism or, failing that, at least to be won over "to outward conformity," he replied that he was "resolved to die a member of that communion, whether true or false, in which he was born and bred."[12] According to Hawkins, Handel "entertained very serious notions" concerning religious toleration in England:

These he would frequently express in his remarks on the
constitution of the English government; and he would often
speak of it as one of the great felicities of his life that he was
settled in a country where no man suffers any molestation or
inconvenience on account of his religious principles.[13]

Although to modern eyes the extent of religious freedom in eighteenth-
century England might well be questionable, it was certainly far ahead
of other countries of Handel's acquaintance. Setting the story of *Esther*
gave Handel the opportunity to give musical expression to the idea of
religious toleration.

The emotional heart of *Esther* occurs when the queen enters the
throne room knowing there is an express decree forbidding anyone to
come into the king's presence without being summoned. Before she is
able to say a word, the king reacts in anger to the interruption and, reit-
erating the decree, states that the intruder must die. Recognizing his
queen, he instantly recants: "The law condemns, but love will spare." By
this time, however, Esther has swooned, and the king rushes to her side.
To this point the scene has developed very quickly in recitative. Now
time stands still as the king gently supports the fainting queen—or so
Handel's music implies (there are no stage directions). No one speaks as
pulsing repeated notes in the strings measure out the suspended action
while Esther's life hangs in the balance. After a few bars the notes offer
the smallest possible sense of movement. With the first violins moving
upward and bass downward, they open up a wedge out of which Esther's
weak voice finally emerges. Her vocal line twice falls from a high register
as she tries to gather her strength, the second time through a thicket of
unstable harmony, only succeeding on the third try to maintain a phrase
that sustains itself without collapsing. "Who calls my parting soul from
death?" she asks. Ahasuerus gently responds, and as the duet proceeds
the voices gradually begin to overlap and finally join together. The form
and shape of this movement follows no set plan and cannot be termed
either recitative or aria. Rather it seems to progress naturally, giving full
expression both to Esther's bravery in the face of her fear and to Ahasuerus's love and support.

The issue of tolerance for Catholics in Great Britain would have been easier to resolve if Catholicism could have been considered simply, as in Handel's formulation of his Lutheranism, as a "communion, whether true or false, in which [one] was born and bred." It was, however, much more: an opposing political force that threatened the sovereignty of the British Protestant nation. During the first half of the eighteenth century, Britain was continually at war with one or both of the Catholic nations of France and Spain: against both from 1702 to 1713, in either a declared war or hostilities with Spain in 1718, 1727, and 1738–1742, and at war with France from 1742 to 1748 (which years included the major Jacobite uprising on British soil in 1745) and from 1756 to 1763. Catholics were therefore seen by many as potential traitors. John Percival addressed this in a letter of November 24, 1723, to his Irish estate manager:

> I see there is a new Popish bill a framing: I think it would not be amiss if a clause were added to oblige the Parochial Clergy to return an account every year to their Diocessan, of the number of Papists & Protestants in their Several Parishes. The Bishops might be enacted to give the Same to the ArchBishops & they to the Lords in Parliamt by which means we Should be able to know our Strength, be more animated to Secure our Selves from any danger to us that may arrise from the number of Papists, & our zeal for reclayming those mistaken people encreased . . .[14]

In Handel's oratorios of the late 1730s and 1740s, the depiction of ancient Israelites helped to shape the unity and identity of the Protestant British nation during a period of near continual conflict by illustrating the perseverance and triumph of a community bound by a single true religion.

Handel's *Israel in Egypt* (1739) is the first oratorio that can be tied to a specific national event. The story tells of the exodus of the Israelites from captivity in Egypt. This may not immediately sound ripe as a metaphor for the situation of the British nation in 1739, but although the British population as a whole was not being held captive in a foreign land, British seamen had been taken prisoner in repeated skirmishes with Spanish vessels over the control of shipping routes. The issue for Britain was not just domination of the seas, but the liberty of the freeborn English-man from Catholic tyranny and oppression. As the politician William Pulteney asked during the parliamentary debates on whether to declare war on Spain (May 12, 1738):

> Have we not lived, Sir, to see the Spaniards insult us in the very
> Seas of which we call ourselves Masters? Have we not lived to
> see the Subjects of Britain made slaves by a People of whom they
> were once the Terror?[15]

Israel in Egypt was first performed on April 4, 1739, and war was offi-cially declared on October 23. When *Israel* was revived in 1740, a review of the oratorio that had appeared after its premiere was reprinted with an introduction that makes the connection between the work and the war direct. Given "the *supposal* of a *General Popish Alliance* against us," it stated, "it may be hoped, that what is therein said . . . [in the orato-rio] may, if attended to, help us forward in the right Way, to stand our Ground against *those* that have already, and as many more as shall here-after, think fit to declare against us."[16]

The text of *Israel in Egypt*, prepared for Handel probably by Charles Jennens, is, like Jennens's libretto of *Messiah*, a collage of passages from the Bible. In Part I, the Israelites mourn the death of their leader, Joseph. Part II depicts the rise of Moses, the plagues visited on Egypt, and the safe departure of the Israelites through the parting of the Red Sea. Part III celebrates the Israelites' freedom from captivity and the destruction of Pharaoh's army in the sea. It is this celebratory third part that can be tied to British objectives in the War with Spain: its cit-izens will be freed from captivity and the enemy sunk in the sea. The elimination of Spanish competition on British trade routes is espe-cially emphasized, with some statement occurring in fully half of the movements about the drowning of the enemy, including: "The Horse and his Rider has He thrown into the Sea"; "Pharoah's Chariots, and his Host, Hath he cast into the Sea"; "His chosen Captains also are drowned in the Red-Sea"; "The Depths have cover'd them, they sank into the Bottom as a Stone"; "Thou didst blow with the Wind; the Sea covered them, they sank as Lead in the mighty Waters." Handel treats these celebratory texts of Parts II and III with the power and force-fulness that forms such an important attribute of his music. George Bernard Shaw describes it perfectly:

> It was from Handel that I learned that style consists in force of assertion . . . When he tells you that when the Israelites went out of Egypt, "there was not one feeble person in all their tribes," it is utterly useless for you to plead that there must have been at least one case of influenza. Handel will not have it: "There was not one, not one feeble person in all their tribes," and the orchestra repeats it in curt, smashing chords that leave you speechless.[17]

This was not Handel's most inspired music, however, and it was left, iron-ically, for the Catholic composer Thomas Arne to capture the political moment in his English opera *Alfred* (1740), performed privately at first, based on the history of Alfred the Great, who in the ninth century had defended England against a Viking invasion. Arne's setting of "Rule, Bri-tannia!" is still sung today, and its origin at the time of the war with Spain clearly explains the otherwise odd-seeming reference to British slavery in the refrain: "Rule, Britannia! Rule the waves: Britons never will be slaves."

When Handel came to set the text of *Israel in Egypt*, it was the plagues that fired his imagination. When he first spoke of the work to Lady Knatchbull, James Harris's half-sister, early in December of 1738, he referred to it as "the ten plagues of Egypt," which Knatchbull confessed in a letter to Harris seemed to her an "odd subject." Handel told her spe-cifically that "the storm of thunder is to be bold and fine, & the thick silent darkness is to be express'd in a very particular piece of musick."[18] Indeed, the remarkable scenic depictions of the plagues create a dra-matic, musical trajectory of striking power. To depict the first plague, for example, which depicts the River Nile turning into blood, Handel expanded one of his keyboard fugues into full chorus; the angularity of its opening with large, sometimes dissonant, intervals perfectly depicts the sense of aversion in the text ("They loathed to drink of the River"); the successive notes seem not to want to touch but to jump as far away as possible not only from each other but also from the blood that flows in a viscous melodic descent throughout the setting.

Jennens combined three plagues in the next movement: the frogs, bovine pestilence, and human skin disease; but what caught Handel's imagination were the frogs. The only plague movement set for solo voice rather than chorus, it suggests that the king's minister himself is expressing his indignation: "Their Land brought forth Frogs," he sings, "yea, even in their King's Chambers." The frogs hop unimpeded in the violins before the voice enters, joined at the very end of the introduction by one giant frog in the bass. When the vocal line is extended on the first syllable of "chambers," the dotted rhythms make it sound as if the singer is repeatedly trying to catch the frogs without success. At the return of the opening textual phrase ("Their Land brought forth Frogs"), there is a pause in the voice as if to contemplate the situation, and then the singer, reaching a peak of exasperation, erupts with the single word "frogs!" in the upper range (an effect that works particularly well in the countertenor voice). But the frogs persist in the background even through the blotches and blains, and then take over once again in the orchestral conclusion. If one is tempted to giggle at the frogs, as I am, then the combination of flies, lice, and locusts in the next movement with violins whirring at thirty-two notes to a measure may bring forth a full-throated chortle. These seemingly humorous touches, however, make the effect of the succeeding plagues even starker.

The beginning of the hailstone chorus perfectly depicts the start of a major storm: big, single raindrops plop one after the other. Very quickly, these build into a storm of immense power, with thunder rumbling in the timpani and lightning running along the ground in the bass. The ferocity of this movement dissipates somewhat at the end, but even so there is no preparation for the thick darkness of the next. Starting with a single slow, throbbing note, Handel adds pitches one after another until a thick and opaque harmonic texture is created. The chorus quietly intones, "He sent a thick Darkness over all the land, even Darkness, which might be felt." As the orchestral pulsating increases into a kind of vibration (but still with thick, slowly moving harmonies), the fear becomes palpable. No longer willing to speak together, the chorus is reduced to frightened, whispery fragments of melody, first in one vocal range and then in another, and they never again cohere. The movement ends without a firm cadence in the voice. The sense of terrifying anticipation this creates is then released in the greatest horror of all: "He smote all the first-born of Egypt." From the hushed sounds of strings and dusky bassoon representing the thick darkness, one is catapulted into full orchestra with three trombones playing at full volume. The chorus spits out the text, and accented hammer strokes cutting through the texture at frequent and regular intervals depict the killing.

Handel's management of the succession of plagues is masterful. He must have known the tendency to laugh at the trials of one's enemies, and he captured that sentiment in the early movements only to shatter it. With the hailstones and thick darkness (the two movements he particularly mentioned to Lady Knatchbull) he eradicated aversion and amusement with power and fear, the whole trajectory leading to the dreadful slaughter of the firstborn children. In *Israel in Egypt,* Handel is more successful (and appears to be more comfortable) instilling pity and terror than depicting triumph at destruction.

Handel failed to achieve the kind of popular success with *Israel in Egypt* that Arne captured with *Alfred,* but he came close about a decade later in *Judas Maccabaeus,* the first libretto prepared for Handel by Thomas Morell.[19] The work, one of a number of political oratorios written by Handel in the mid-1740s, celebrated Prince William Augustus, Duke of Cumberland and second son of George II, for his success in crushing the Jacobite Rebellion of 1745. Prince Charles Edward Stuart, grandson of James II, had landed successfully from France in 1745 and raised a land army of Scotsmen with the purpose of restoring his father to the throne. Cumberland's victory at the Battle of Culloden in 1746, and the subsequent brutal "clearance" of the Highlands, put down the uprising and effectively ended any hope for a Stuart restoration. The story of *Judas Maccabaeus* (1747) tells of the Jewish community of Judea being forced to relinquish its religion and worship the Roman gods Jupiter and Bacchus. Judas leads the resistance against this decree and, by overcoming various setbacks, achieves victory for his people. The obvious (and at least superficially intended) allegorical interpretation was that Judas represented Cumberland, who had protected the British Protestant nation against Roman Catholic oppression. As with most librettos, however, an opposite construal is possible, allowing for the widest possible audience; that is, a Catholic could interpret the story as support for continued resistance against the oppression of a Protestant majority. Handel rises to the occasion of good, tub-thumping music and parts of the score achieved a high level of popularity, approaching Arne's "Rule, Britannia!" including the aria and chorus "Arm, arm, ye brave" and Judas's own aria, "Sound an alarm." Handel's real winner in this category, "See, the conqu'ring hero comes," comes from his next oratorio, *Joshua* (1748). By 1750, however, the movement was transferred into revivals of *Judas*, with which work it is now associated. Handel is reported to have said of it, "You will live to see it a greater favourite with the people than my other fine things."[20]

While Catholicism was widely viewed as a danger to the national polity, it was not feared as much as a religious threat to individual Protestant worshippers. That is, the worry was not that a single English Protestant could be persuaded to convert, but that a victorious Catholic force could, through an absolutist government, suppress Protestantism within the nation. Handel's British contemporaries felt that the most serious threat to an individual's Protestant belief lay not in Catholicism but in doubt fueled by scientific reason and freethinking. Deism, for example, held that God created the world in finished form as a clockwork universe that ran without intervention. Alexander Pope, who in the 1730s was moving away from Catholicism toward a more rationalist stance, expressed it in a subsequently much-repeated phrase in his poem *An Essay on Man* (1733–1734): "Whatever IS, is RIGHT." In both Deism and freethinking, the idea that God acted in the world through miracles was rejected, casting doubt on the veracity of the Bible and of traditional Church doctrine, the existence of the Holy Ghost, and the belief in Jesus as the Son of God and humanity's redeemer. Hutchinsonianism developed specifically to combat this point of view, and Delany's approval of it was partly based on its promising "perfect satisfaction in regard to the Holy Trinity."

In both private and public, literal and Deist interpretations of the Bible were hotly debated: John Percival's correspondence is threaded with this controversy. In 1729, he wrote to Bishop Richard Smalbroke to congratulate him on the first volume of *A Vindication of the Miracles of our Blessed Saviour*, refuting a recently published tract that argued for a figurative interpretation of the miracles attributed to Christ in the New Testament:

> You have treated the Subject Methodically and amply exposed
> that Writers insincerity; you have evinced the litteral Sense of our
> Saviours Miracles past reply, and shewn so much learning and
> Judicious application of it, So much Spirit and becoming zeal in
> defence of our Religion and the honour of its great author, that
> it is with impatience I wait for your Second Vol. which I promise
> my self will equal tho it cannot exceed the first, and must with
> the Blessing of God put an absolute Stop to this New Infedility,
> which Strikes at the Root of Christianity, and never enterd the
> minds of Jews Heathens or Turks.[21]

In 1731, George Berkeley (later bishop of Cloyne) complained to Percival from Rhode Island about the spread of freethinking from London to the colonies:

> What they foolishly call free thinking seems to me the principal
> Root or Source . . . of most other Evils in this Age, and as long as
> that Frenzy Subsists and spreads it is in vain to hope for any good
> either to the Mother Country or Colonies which always follow
> the fashions of Old England. I am credibly inform'd that great
> numbers of all Sorts of Blasphemous Books published in London
> are sent to Philadelphia New York and other places where they
> produce a plentifull Crop of Atheists and Infidels.[22]

Although open declarations of freethinking could be rebutted, Percival was especially concerned about adherents to the Church of England, priests in particular, who secretly harbored Deist thoughts. In 1722, he wrote of Lord Burlington's chaplain, Aaron Thompson: "These . . . are the Men who do more mischief to our Church than the most open Deists. For they like profest wolves are Shun'd having a mark by wch they'r known; but these are our very Sheperds, who instead of leading us to fair Springs, poison our Fountains."[23]

Dr. Patrick Delany entered the fray against rationalist, or nonliteral, interpretation of scripture in 1732 with his publication of *The Present State of Learning, Religion, and Infidelity in Great-Britain. Wherein the Causes of the Present Degeneracy of Taste, and Increase of Infidelity, Are Inquir'd into, and Accounted for.* Charles Jennens also strove against the rise of freethinking, expressing his views not in tracts or heavy tomes, but in the librettos he wrote for Handel.

Israel in Egypt, whatever its political message, contained a significant anti-Deist stance in its presentation of God's interventions on behalf of the enslaved Israelites: the plagues visited on the Egyptians and the parting of the Red Sea. For the rationalists these were events that could be explained by natural causes, but Jennens's libretto insists on them being divine miracles. *Messiah*, Jennens's next "scriptural collection" for Handel, also can be understood as an anti-Deist text.[24] The inclusion of Old Testament prophecy emphasizes the Virgin birth ("Behold, a Virgin shall conceive, and bear a Son") as well as Christ's miracles ("Then shall the Eyes of the Blind be open'd, and the Ears of the Deaf unstopped; then shall the lame Man leap as a Hart, and the Tongue of the Dumb shall sing"). And the presentation of the life of Christ largely through Old Testament texts, offers a "proof" of Christianity as the fulfillment of messianic prophecy. Jennens hoped that Handel would "lay out his whole Genius & Skill upon it" (see Image 9.2).[25]

Handel's score is indeed a magnificent achievement, a seeming miracle itself, composed and orchestrated as it was in only twenty-four days. *Messiah*'s global reach is nowhere more evident than in the popularity of the "Hallelujah Chorus," which may be the best-known piece of classical music ever written. The movement comes at the end of Part II in celebration of the ultimate victory of Christianity on Earth. Jennens's decision to precede this movement with texts of military victory suggests that, as in *Israel in Egypt*, the text of *Messiah* refers to the war with Spain, to contemporary concerns that France would join with Spain in Catholic opposition ("The Kings of the Earth Rise up"), and a belief that God's son would intervene and save his people (who were understood in gen-

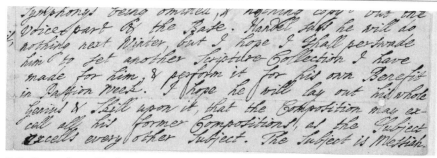

9.2 Letter from Charles Jennens to Edward Holdsworth (July 10, 1741) mentioning his libretto for *Messiah* for the first time (extract) (© Gerald Coke Handel Collection, The Foundling Museum, London)

eral to be Protestants, but more specifically, the Church of England) just as God protected the Israelites in Egypt ("Thou shalt break them [the enemies of the Church of England] with a Rod of Iron").

Would Handel have perceived the texts in such specific, political terms? It seems unlikely. He understood jubilation, however. The text of the "Hallelujah Chorus" contains three distinct textual statements in addition to the exclamation of "hallelujah." Between and in the midst of the chorus's exuberant iterations of hallelujahs, Handel gives sustained and highly differentiated musical profiles to these statements. He sets "For the Lord God Omnipotent reigneth" for full chorus and orchestra joined together in a single melodic line with no rhythmic or harmonic digressions. The musical monophony (the chorus singing a single line of music) depicts the monotheistic (one) God, and the word "omnipotent," leaping down and up an octave, encompasses the entire "universe" of a complete musical scale. After its first presentation for full chorus, the theme then appears in the lower voices and rises through the chorus finally to "reign" over outbursts of hallelujahs. To depict "The Kingdom of this World is become the Kingdom of our Lord and of his Christ," Handel sets the "Kingdom of this World" in reduced orchestration (strings only) and restricted range, reserving an explosion of light and sound (expanding into a high register and adding trumpets and drums) for the "Kingdom of our Lord and of his Christ." The juxtaposition is startling no matter how many times one hears it. Finally, he sets "and He

shall reign for ever and ever" as a round (or to use more official terminology, a canon), projecting Christ's reign into infinity with a form that
has no end. Handel brings the movement to a close with an acceleration
of hallelujahs driving into an anticipatory grand pause in all voices that
releases into a single, sustained HAL-LE-LU-JAH.

Jennens was not pleased that Handel chose to premiere this work
in Dublin rather than London, and he fueled some of his irritation into
criticism. When he heard the composer's *Samson*, whose text had been
prepared by Newburgh Hamilton from Milton, he, like a jealous sibling,
complained to Edward Holdsworth that Handel had not given his *Messiah* the attention he had given Hamilton's *Samson*. Whereas Jennens
deemed *Samson* "an exceeding fine Oratorio," *Messiah* disappointed him,
"being set in great hast." In fact, Handel had set the two works back to
back in *equal* "haste." After completing *Messiah* on September 14, 1741,
he was so little spent that he drafted the entire score of *Samson* by October 29. Jennens, however, seems to have been in no mood to be appeased
by facts. When Handel's paralytic disorder returned in 1743, Jennens
remained so splenetic that he took pleasure in the suggestion that his
complaints about *Messiah* had "contributed to the bringing of his last
illness upon him."[26] He insisted he would put no more scriptural words
into Handel's hands "to be thus abus'd," but by 1744 the two were once
again collaborating. *Belshazzar*, containing extensive quotation from
scripture, had its premiere in March 1745. In agreeing to work once more
with the composer, Jennens recognized, as he wrote to Holdsworth, that
Handel did not have the same aims as himself in "Religion & Morality"
(Jennens being an adherent to a "zealous, evangelizing Christianity" and
a non-Juror who refused to take the oaths of allegiance to the Hanoverian
monarchy on the principle of Divine Right). But Jennens added, "I must
take him as I find him, and make the best use I can of him."[27]

Jennens's notion of "using Handel" is intriguing and, given the quality and power of Handel's music, leads to a consideration of this idea as
a regular practice. One can imagine, for example, that the Catholic prelates in Italy, who were unable to persuade Handel to convert, nevertheless
fully recognized his talent when commissioning him to write music for
the annual feast of Our Lady of Mount Carmel celebrated in the church of

Santa Maria di Montesanto in Rome on July 16, 1707, but that is not necessarily the same as "using" him. In contrast, the choice of Handel in 1713
to set the Te Deum and Jubilate in celebration of the Peace of Utrecht that
England had negotiated unilaterally and against the expressed wishes of
his employer, Georg Ludwig, Elector of Hanover, has the feel of a distinct
political maneuver in which Handel was a pawn. Some of the librettos given
to Handel in the early years of the Royal Academy of Music that appear to
favor a Jacobite interpretation, like *Floridante* (1721), suggest something
similar. More ironic are those cases where Handel's music was deliberately used against him in the various competitive struggles he faced. The
English-opera adherents in 1732 produced his *Acis and Galatea*; the Opera
of the Nobility in 1734 produced his *Ottone*; and the so-called Middlesex company produced his *Alessandro* as *Rossane* in 1743. Although none
of these religious or political situations has the same flavor as Jennens saying that he would "make the best use I can of him" to advance his own
goals, they indicate a general sense that Handel's music was so compelling
that its force could be profitably harnessed. This was nowhere more true
than in the case of benefit and charity concerts, especially toward the end
of Handel's life, when his music was less under his own control.

Handel's personal association with organizational charity was
largely limited to three institutions: the Fund for Decay'd Musicians,
Sons of the Clergy, and the Foundling Hospital. He was a founding
member of the Fund for Decay'd Musicians (the predecessor of the
Royal Society of Musicians), which was established in 1738 to assist
families of musicians in need; in 1739 he was listed as one of the 228
members in its declaration of trust, and according to contemporary
newspaper accounts, he conducted the inaugural benefit concert on
behalf of the fund on March 20, 1739. The concert consisted of a performance of *Alexander's Feast* and a new organ concerto that he composed for the occasion. After this, the charity's concerts quickly fell into
a pattern, and although Handel's music was often highlighted, and he is
said to have been often in attendance, there is little evidence pointing
to his active musical involvement. In the final codicil of his will, made
only three days before he died, he bequeathed the fund £1,000.

The Sons of the Clergy, established in 1655 to support families of destitute and deceased clergy, began a series of annual benefit concerts in 1731. As with the concerts for the Fund for Decay'd Musicians, Handel's direct participation may have been minimal, but his music was omnipresent. The concerts regularly included performances of his Utrecht Te Deum and one or two Coronation Anthems, until 1746, when the Dettingen Te Deum replaced the earlier work.

The Foundling Hospital opened in London in 1739 for the "education and maintenance of exposed and deserted young children." Handel first became associated with the hospital in 1749, when he conducted a concert for its benefit consisting of selections from his music. Later that year, when asked to become a governor of the hospital (similar to joining a board of trustees), a position that required a donation of £50, Handel declined, saying that "he should Serve the Charity with more Pleasure in his Way, than being Member of the Corporation," a response that seems to indicate a preference for using his music for charitable ends rather than providing direct funding or taking an administrative role.[28] The following year, when he gave the hospital an organ for its chapel, he was, however, made a governor and the fee waived. The benefit performance he planned in 1750 of *Messiah*, to inaugurate the organ, proved to be the first of an annual series he himself conducted through 1753 and for the rest of his life authorized with his presence.

In early 1754, when it seemed that Handel's direct participation in the annual concerts might be ending, the hospital proposed a petition to Parliament that would give it proprietary rights to *Messiah*. The General Committee minutes of the hospital, in what appears to be an admirable understatement, report that this idea "did not seem agreeable to Mr. Handel for the present."[29] It may be that Handel, given his deteriorating eyesight, was concerned about losing "control" over his own music at a time when he was dependent on the performance of his work (including *Messiah*) for income.[30] Perhaps an attempt had been made to address this concern in the wording of the petition, which stated that in giving the hospital the rights to *Messiah*, Handel would nevertheless reserve "to himself the liberty . . . of performing the same for his own benefit during his life." If so, Handel was not appeased. Hawkins quoted him as exclaiming (with a heavy German accent): "For vat

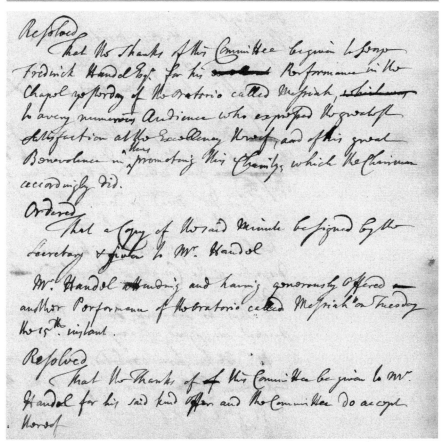

9.3 Resolution of the Foundling Hospital General Committee to thank Handel for benefit performances of *Messiah* in 1750 (© Coram / London Metropolitan Archives, London)

sal de Fondlings put mein oratorio in de Parlement? Te Teuffel! mein musick sal nat go to de Parlement."[31] In 1757, in the third codicil to his will, Handel bequeathed to the hospital a copy of the score and parts to *Messiah*, in effect granting it permission to continue the annual benefit performances indefinitely.

Although eighteenth-century English wills often used conventional language, there was no fixed format.[32] Often they began with a religious preamble that included an identification of the testator by parish and county, but there was no hard rule. In contrast, John Hedges (d. 1737), treasurer to the prince of Wales and patron of Joseph Goupy, left a will in rhymed doggerel, without either religious preamble or initial identification of himself, beginning: "This 5th day of May / Being Airy and Gay / To Hipp not enclin[e]d / But of Vigorous mind / And my Body in Health / Ile dispose of my Wealth."[33] Handel's will steers a middle course between these stylistic extremes that conveys the composer's strong sense of self and also, in some ways, reflects his musical practice: that is, Handel neither snubs convention nor is he subservient to it. He chooses enough standard wording at the outset to make clear his seriousness of purpose and then crafts a concise and authoritative statement of his testamentary wishes, by beginning "In the Name of God Amen," and then continuing that he "considering the Uncertainty of human Life doe make this my Will in manner following."[34] Throughout the will and its four codicils, he identifies himself by name only: "I George Frideric Handel," eschewing what would be the standard formula: I George Frideric Handel of Brook Street in the Parish of St George Hanover Square in the County of Middlesex, Esquire. One senses he considered his name identification enough; and apparently he also felt no need to make a declaration of his religious sentiments.

Many testators of this period, in addition to their major legacies, left small bequests for mourning clothes or mourning rings (a token to be worn in remembrance of the deceased) to a wider group of friends and relations. Elizabeth Mayne (d. 1769), one of Handel's own legatees, made a gift of "a Ring apiece of one Guinea value" to sixteen people, and John Gowland (d. 1776), the apothecary on Bond Street to whom Handel also left a bequest, left to "each of my Servants that shall be living with me at my decease the Sum of five Pounds for Mourning [clothes]."[35] Handel made no such gifts of remembrance, choosing to make only gifts of monetary significance, the smallest of which was £50. Nor did he, like testators who prepared their wills as death approached, give directions in his original will as to his burial. Nine years later and lying on his deathbed, he asked permission of the dean and chapter of Westminster to be buried in Westminster Abbey and left money for a monument, indicating his wish for posthumous recognition (see Chapter 11). But still, he gave no directions for a service. In not providing instructions for his funeral or determining forms of public mourning (rings and clothing) for his friends and servants, it would seem he wished to avoid dictating etiquette or patterns of behavior from the grave.

Also distinctly absent from Handel's will are bequests to charities that focused on behavioral modification through religious training, such as the Society for Promoting Christian Knowledge, which was responsible for setting up a network of charity schools throughout the country, the Society for the Propagation of the Gospel in Foreign Parts, or the Society for the Reformation of Manners, which aimed to suppress immorality by bringing offenders before the law. Despite the establishment of five major hospitals during his lifetime—Westminster (1719), Guy's (1721), St. George's (1733), London (1740; now the Royal London Hospital), and Middlesex (1745)—as well as a number of specialized facilities (like the London Lock Hospital, founded in 1746 for the treatment of vene-real disease), Handel also left nothing to dedicated medical institutions. Handel's philanthropy was distinctive in its focus on providing suste-nance to those in need and its rejection of impositions or directives of any kind. His financial and musical support went especially to children in need—to the families of clergy and of musicians, and to foundlings. In his lifetime, performances of his music supported various hospitals and the poor in debtors' prisons. Proselytizing religious and educational organizations find no place in either his charitable activities or his will.

Given that eighteenth-century Britain tied much of its sense of iden-tity to the Church of England and, in addition, saw itself ringed by Cath-olic states, proselytizing both within the country and internationally was widely embraced. John Percival actively supported the Society for Pro-moting Christian Knowledge and was particularly engaged in providing assistance to converts from Catholicism in England and in France. Wil-liam Conolly, Lord Justice of Ireland, thanked him for his contributions "for the Necessitous Starving Protestants in the North of Ireland."[36] He became involved with the project of translating the New Testament into Arabic "for the use of the Poor Christians in *Palestine* and other Oriental Countries, subject to the Jurisdiction of the Patriarchs of *Antioch, Syria,*

Jerusalem and *Alexandria*,"[37] which ran into difficulties when a "Man of Aleppo," who had been brought in as a translator, was found to be "a very Scandalous profligate fellow as to matters of Faith and Morals, and the Chief means by which he used to make himself agreeable to too many of our Countrymen in Italy was by laughing at, and turning the Christian Religion into redicule."[38]

Percival was also interested in spreading the gospel into the New World. He was integral to the success of James Edward Oglethorpe's plan for the establishment of the new American colony of Georgia (1732), but his interest in the colonies had first been sparked by George Berkeley's hope to establish a college on the island of Bermuda for the training of colonists and native Americans who would then return to their own communities as Anglican preachers and missionaries. As Berkeley (Anne Donnellan's former suitor) waited in Rhode Island for funding, his plan was derided in a delightful letter to Percival from William Byrd, a wealthy Virginia merchant who engaged in trade with the Native American peoples:

> When the Deans [Berkeley's] project was first communicated to
> me by your Lordship, I took the liberty to call it a very Romantick
> one. It sounds very well to convert the Indians, and to come
> to Bermudas, and meet them three fourths of the way for that
> Pious design but when he comes to put this Visionary Scheme
> in practice, he will find it no better than a Religious Frenzy. And
> I may venture to say so much to your Lordship, that the Dean
> is as much a Don Quixote in Zeal, as that Renow'd Knight was
> in Chivalry. Is it not a Wild Undertaking to build a Colledge
> in a Country where there is no Bread, nor any thing fit for
> the Sustenance of Man, but Onions and Cabbage. Indeed the
> Inhabitants are healthy but they owe this happiness to a Scarcity
> of every thing, which obliges them to a necessary temperance.
> Their Air is pure indeed, but it is made so, by a perpetual
> Succession of Storms and Hurricanes. Then when this Colledge
> is built, where will the Dean find Indians to be converted? There

are no Indians at Bermudas, nor within 200 leagues of it upon the Continent, and it will need the gift of Miracles to perswade them to leave their Country and venture themselves upon the great Ocean, on the temptation of being converted.[39]

Berkeley gave up this plan when it failed to receive the governmental support that had been promised, and returned in 1731 with his family to England.

Handel took no part in such schemes. His will and his expressed belief in religious freedom clearly demonstrate his resistance to organized efforts to convert individuals or whole groups. The very idea of forced conversion seems to have been anathema to him. *Rinaldo* (1711) offers the one case in Handel's dramatic works where such an event occurs. At the end of the opera, after the crusaders have won the climactic battle against the Saracens, the sorceress Armida declares to Goffredo, the Christian general, that having been conquered she will embrace his faith ("il vostro rito io piglio"). In his original version of 1711, Handel gave this moment the most perfunctory setting imaginable. When he came to revive the opera in 1731, he made many changes to the score, not all felicitous by any means, but among them was the complete elimination of the conversion and the substitution of a spectacular final exit for a decidedly unremorseful Armida and her lover Argante, leader of the Saracen forces, in a chariot drawn by flying dragons.

Handel's first English oratorio, *Esther*, had told a story of religious toleration. In his penultimate oratorio, *Theodora* (1750), which is unique among Handel's works in its presentation of a non-biblical religious story, he returned to this topic. The story concerns the early Christian community in Antioch who were ordered by the Roman governor, Flavius Julius Valens, to give up their religion and worship the goddesses Flora and Venus. Thomas Morell, the librettist, based the text on a long historical novel entitled *The Martyrdom of Theodora and of Didymus* (1687) by Robert Boyle, the famous seventeenth-century chemist. It seems improbable that Handel would have requested a libretto based on this source, but the topic itself must have appealed. According to

Morell, who is clearly a biased source, Handel considered this his favorite oratorio, or at least his favorite oratorio text.[40] It proved not to be a success with the public, however, which had come to expect big biblical histories with triumphant conclusions rather than an affecting narrative about ethical and moral choice that ends in martyrdom. Again according to Morell, Handel quipped, in a statement that should not be taken too seriously, "The Jews will not come to it (as to Judas [Maccabaeus]) because it is a Christian story; and the Ladies will not come, because it [is] a virtuous one."[41] It is, however, one of Handel's great masterpieces, as his close friends realized. Anne Dewes, Delany's sister, wrote to their brother Bernard Granville in the winter following its premiere: "Does Mr. Handel do anything new against next Lent? surely Theodora will have justice at last, if it was to be again performed, but the generality of the world have ears and *hear not*."[42]

Interpretations of *Theodora* vary, and as with Handel's other oratorios, the libretto can be read in multiple ways.[43] As the depiction of a government demanding conformity to a state religion could be considered analogous to Britain, the dissenting Christians could be understood, as some must have interpreted the minority Jewish community in Handel's *Esther*, as contemporary Catholics. Some who have agreed that the Roman state represents contemporary Britain argue instead that the text advocates for the Methodism movement within the established Church.[44] Neither reading, however, is likely to have occurred to Morell or to have been the general view. Despite the distinctive characteristics of *Theodora*, the Protestant audience most likely identified itself, as in Handel's biblical oratorios, with the minority community (in *Theodora* the dissenting early Christians and in *Esther* and *Israel in Egypt* the early Hebrews) and by analogy saw themselves throwing off the yoke (real or threatened) of Catholicism. Morell's earlier libretto for Handel, *Judas Maccabaeus* (1747), had a similar theme—an attempt to force the minority Jewish community in Judea to give up its religion and worship Jupiter—and that work openly celebrated the defeat of Catholic Jacobite forces in their effort to overthrow the Protestant government in Britain. In *Theodora*, Morell's reference to the pagan religion as *"Roman* rites" strongly implies a reading that equates mythology with Catholicism, Valens with the pope, and the dissenting Christians with the Protestant Church of England.

The oratorio opens as Valens proclaims a feast day in honor of the birthday of the emperor Diocletian and declares that all who refuse to join the sacred rites "Shall feel our Wrath, in Chastisement, or Death." Didymus, a Roman officer in love with the Christian Theodora, requests religious tolerance for those "whose scrup'lous Minds / Will not permit them . . . to bend the Knee / to Gods they know not," the specific wording echoing the Act of Toleration (1689) that offered "some Ease to scrupulous Consciences in the Exercise of Religion."[45] Valens responds, "Art thou a *Roman*, and yet dar'st defend / A Sect, rebellious to the Gods and *Rome*?" To which Didymus answers, "Many there are in *Antioch*, who disdain / An Idol-Offering, yet are Friends to *Cæsar*." The tyrant Valens insists, "It cannot be: They are not *Cæsar's* Friends, / Who own not *Cæsar's* Gods," and cuts off further discussion with the fearsome aria "Racks, Gibbets, Sword, and Fire, / Shall speak my vengeful Ire." In this initial scene the crux of the oratorio as an argument for religious tolerance has been set.

In the continuation of Part I, we are given a chance to get to know all the protagonists and to hear in the choruses the distinction between the roistering Romans and the prayerful Christians. Septimius, a Roman officer and friend of Didymus, suspects his friend is a Christian convert. He is sympathetic and declares, "I know thy Virtues, and ask not thy Faith." In his aria "Descend, kind Pity," he sings of the hope "That Liberty and Peace of Mind / May sweetly harmonize Mankind, / And bless the World below," but he believes that Valens must be obeyed: "We can only pity, whom we dare not spare." When Septimius announces Valens's decree to the Christians, Theodora states boldly that she is not afraid of death. Septimius only then discloses that Valens has not ordered her execution, should she fail to conform to the Roman rites, but rather that she be conveyed to a house of prostitution. "O worse than Death indeed," Theodora exclaims in recitative, "Lead me, ye Guards, / Lead me, or to the Rack, or to the Flames; / I'll thank your gracious Mercy!"

In her aria "Angels, ever bright, and fair, / Take, O take me to your Care," she pleads for death, but rather than striking a desperate or fearful tone at this harrowing moment, the aria radiates faith. In a major key, and sounding quietly transcendent, the aria begins with two violins descending one after another from a high F once and then again, suggesting that the angels, anticipating her call, have already started arriving to sustain her through this trial even before she voices her appeal to them. Although she is left to sing with only continuo support throughout most of the aria, the violins always answer, repeat, and affirm her pleas. In the last repetition of the text, they join together with her in sequence, and, finally, in the instrumental postlude, they provide a powerful sense of the angels lifting her soul into their care. Immediately, Theodora is led "trembling" away by the soldiers.

Part II sets the Romans and Theodora in sharp contrast, and the drama begins to move very quickly. First we see the Romans celebrating the feast with tributes to Flora, goddess of summer, and Venus, goddess of beauty ("Queen of Summer, Queen of Love"). This scene of revelry is juxtaposed with Theodora alone in her "place of confinement," and at first, as illustrated by the introductory symphony, her despair is too inarticulate for words. A repetition of four throbbing chords in the strings leads to a single, unaccompanied note for two flutes. Twice, the strings offer a different harmony, but the flutes continue to respond with the same single note. Only with difficulty and very slowly do the flutes gather to themselves a melody. Thereafter, Theodora gives voice to her despair ("With Darkness deep as is my Woe"), but envisioning eternal life, collects her thoughts. Her beautiful aria "O that I on Wings cou'd rise" shows her placing her faith in Heaven.

Didymus persuades Septimius to grant him admission to Theodora's cell. When she wakes and sees a man—the libretto specifically states that he appears with the visor of his helmet closed—she assumes he has come to assault her, but Didymus reveals himself and with some difficulty persuades her to take the opportunity to change clothes with him and flee. They sing a rapturous duet, "To thee, thou glorious Son of Worth, / To thee, whose Virtues suit thy Birth," in which they express their hope to meet again on Earth and their assurance that they will meet in heaven. The voices intertwine and interlock, first one and then the other singing phrases that converge on the same note. In extended passages, the overlapping voices move in and out of dissonant friction before arriving at a single pitch. In musical terminology this is called a chain of suspensions, and both words in their standard sense are appropriate to the setting. By illustrating the strong chains binding Theodora and Didymus and the painful suspense of this dramatic moment, the duet depicts the couple's powerful and bittersweet emotions at parting.

In Part III, when Theodora learns that Didymus has been condemned to die, she hurries to save him by presenting herself as a sacrifice. Didymus insists he is the one who should die. Septimius pleads for Valens to spare both of them, but Valens condemns them both: "Are ye then Judges for yourselves? / Not so our Laws are to be trifled with. / If Both plead guilty, 'tis but Equity, / That Both should suffer. / Ye Ministers of Justice, lead them hence, / I cannot, will not, bear such Insolence."

The oratorio ends with the Christians. Theodora's friend Irene announces that the couple's "Doom is past." For Handel no amount of religious zeal in the text can obscure the real human suffering brought on by intolerance, and he brings this point home in this final movement. The concluding chorus, "O Love divine," speaks of the transcendence of the young martyrs in somber rather than joyful tones.

When Morell asked Handel whether he considered the "Hallelujah Chorus" in *Messiah* his masterpiece, the composer reportedly responded, "No, I think the Chorus at the end of the 2^d part in Theodora far beyond it."[46] This chorus follows the duet of Didymus and Theodora after she agrees to his plan for her release from detention. The scene having shifted to the Christian community, Irene recognizes that, on account of their grief and worry for Theodora and Didymus, sleep's "kind Blessing is deny'd." She therefore calls the group together to pray "to *Him*, who rais'd, / And still can raise, the Dead to Life and Joy!" Making it absolutely clear that Irene (and Morell as well) did not intend this statement as a metaphor but as literal fact, the chorus then narrates the story from the Gospel According to Luke about Christ raising from the dead the son of the widow of Nain. The text offered to Handel, in its clear embrace of the existence of miracles and of God's continuing presence in the world, is an impassioned rebuttal of Deist thinking. Handel's personal beliefs are difficult to access, but his setting of the text as a series of dramatic scenes for chorus illustrates full engagement with the story.

The five-line text, which seems to me a rather unpromising narration of events, is divided by Handel into three sections:

(1) He saw the lovely Youth, Death's early Prey;
Alas! too early snatch'd away!
He heard his Mother's Funeral Cries:
(2) Rise, Youth, he said: The Youth begins to rise:
(3) Lowly the Matron bow'd, and bore away the Prize.

In the first part, Handel ignored the narrative quality of the opening lines and vividly depicted the funeral itself with a dead march in the somber key of B-flat minor. In the orchestral introduction, the bass descends chromatically against the rhythmic pattern of a pair of repeated notes in the upper strings, denoting heavy steps or perhaps the tolling of a funeral knell. The chorus picks up both motives and with the orchestra continues this solemn progression throughout the section.

In the brief middle section, he depicts the miracle with a shift into major that sweeps away the darkness with light (a technique Handel also used in painting the creation of light in *Samson*, "O first created beam"). Christ's command, "Rise, Youth, he said," follows the pattern of God's commands in both *Israel in Egypt* ("He spake the Word") and *Messiah* ("The Lord gave the Word"): with strict rhythmic conformity in all parts and either no accompaniment or instrumental bass only. Handel then, as he does typically in these cases, has the orchestra echo the choral setting as if to illustrate the words being sent into the cosmos. Immediately the downward motion of the funeral is transformed into rising scales in chorus and orchestra, exuberantly repeated six times as the youth awakens slowly from the dead. In nine short measures, the miracle is accomplished. The final section is a jubilant fugue with two themes: the first depicting the mother falling to her knees (sustained notes falling by leaps down an octave) and the second (quickened notes in a falling and rising motion) showing her as she lovingly lifts her son and guides him home. The long melodic extensions on the word "prize" emphasize the celebratory moment.

DURING THE FIRST HALF of the eighteenth century, religion in Britain had both a public and a private face. Within the general populace, it was an important factor in the creation of a national identity and understood as such. *Theodora*, like others of Handel's oratorios, including *Israel in Egypt* and *Judas Maccabaeus*, speaks to religion as it relates to specific aspects of state polity and the threat of external opposition from Catholic nations or Jacobite supporters of a Stuart restoration. Such external threats to the Church of England led to stringent legal measures to provide protection to the state, including both the exclusion of dissenters from social benefits and high office and also the requirement of formal oaths and certificates of conformity from those who would be included.

The threat to religion was not just external, however. Enlightenment thinking posed an equal or perhaps worse threat in its empiricist dismissal of miracles and prophecy. As opposed to external threats, there was no easy way to try to control the spread of rationalistic thought except by persuasion. Many of Handel's oratorio librettos also address this issue. *Israel in Egypt* (probably by Jennens) and *Messiah* (Jennens) are both based squarely on a belief in prophecy and miracles. More obvious examples are the stopping of the sun in *Joshua* (anonymous adaptor) and the writing on the wall in *Belshazzar* (Jennens). Morell's addition of the story of Christ resurrecting the son of the widow of Nain to the libretto of *Theodora* (it does not appear in the source text, Boyle's historical novel) is another example.

The oratorios, of course, were not limited to the topic of national religion, but spoke as well to issues of personal action and belief. The same period that instituted penal laws against dissenters also saw a growth in the Latitudinarian argument for acceptance of a variety of religious rites, especially within, but not limited to, the Protestant domain. The repeated topic of religious tolerance in the oratorios from *Esther* to *Theodora* reinforces anecdotal evidence that this was a matter of significant importance to Handel. This does not suggest, however, that he was in any way weak in his own belief, but rather that he opposed the imposition of belief by force or even, as his own case with the Italian prelates or his lack of support for evangelizing Christianity indicates, by proselytizing. In *Theodora*, Morell provided a particularly potent statement on religious freedom that echoes John Locke's *A Letter Concerning Toleration* (1689). In reference to Valens's decree that those who do not conform to the pagan rites face torture and death, Didymus speaks out to his friend:

> Ought we not to leave
> The free-born Mind of Man, still ever free?
> Since vain is the Attempt, to force Belief
> With the severest Instruments of Death.

Beyond any political or national messages the oratorio texts might contain, Handel's settings also display a deep sympathy for all victims, at the very least in the portrayal of their suffering. His depiction of the plagues in *Israel in Egypt* is dramatically constructed so as to emphasize fully the horror as their escalation in severity leads to the killing of the firstborn children of Egypt. When Samson brings down the temple of Dagon on himself and his foes, the crushing of the Philistines is set by Handel in a harrowing chorus, after which comes a formal but deeply moving elegy for Samson in a set of closely connected movements. Following this, the lively rejoicing of "Let the bright seraphim" and its attached chorus can feel unseemly, not just in terms of Samson's self-inflicted death but also the deaths of the Philistines. In fact, the oratorio originally ended with the requiem for Samson, and the joyful coda was added before the first performance, probably to satisfy audience expectations. Earlier, Handel had considered, but rejected, much to

Jennens's relief, adding a Hallelujah chorus to the end of *Saul*.[47] In *Theodora*, Morell planned for a cheerful and triumphant ending: either a long scene, ending in a celebratory chorus, during which Septimius describes the trials and deaths of the "matchless pair" as an inspiration to Christian conversion or, in lieu of that, a choral Hallelujah. Handel omitted all this. He clearly saw no victory in the martyrdom of Theodora and Didymus, and ended with the chorus that follows Irene's announcement of their deaths. Moreover, he overlaid that text, which speaks of "Love divine" as a source of "Fame, of Glory, and all Joy," not with "Streams . . . so bright" but with a solemn musical shroud. Perhaps Handel regretted all the vengeful triumphing at the end of *Israel in Egypt* and celebration at the end of *Samson* and by 1750 was secure enough to omit anything similar in *Theodora*.

The oratorios also illustrate the power of personal prayer as consolation and support. In *Susanna*, the title character is buoyed by prayer when she faces a false accusation that could result in her being condemned to death. Theodora, when condemned to a house of prostitution, sings: "When sunk in Anguish, and Despair, / To Heav'n I cried, Heav'n heard my Pray'r." Of course, prayers are not always answered according to the desires of the supplicant, and oratorio characters, like people in real life, sometimes rail against their fate. Nevertheless, the oratorios emphasize that strong spiritual belief, if maintained, could provide a bridge to acceptance and become a consolation in times of travail, illness, and death.

10.1 Portrait of Handel (1756) by Thomas Hudson (private collection / The Bridgeman Art Library [SSI 39982])

TEN

Sickness and Death

1737–1759
First "paralytic attack," a look back to Admeto, *then madness in* Saul *and* Hercules, *and* Jephtha *to* The Triumph of Time and Truth

ILLNESS WAS A CONSTANT in the lives of many during the first half of the eighteenth century. Digestive and respiratory disorders were prevalent, and painful gout stalked both Goupy and the well-to-do Philip Percival. The importance of antiseptic conditions had not yet been fully recognized, and contagion was rife. Contemporary medical practice—largely formulated on the idea of releasing bodily fluids that were thought to cause illness—must have done as much harm as good, involving as it did a combination of laxatives, purgatives, bleeding, blistering, and sweating. Descriptions of illnesses and potential remedies were a major topic of correspondence and, one must imagine, of conversation. In general, Handel seems to have had a very strong constitution, but from 1737 he suffered a series of what the newspapers called "paralytic attacks," which left him temporarily paralyzed and mentally confused. Like many of his contemporaries, he sought cures at English and Continental spas. Early in 1751 he began to suffer serious difficulties with his eyesight, and a year later he was reported to have become blind in one eye. By 1753, he was totally blind. He died six years later at the age of seventy-four.

The common illnesses that plagued the British and the kinds of treatments patients endured are described in detail in correspondence. Percival's friend George Berkeley wrote matter-of-factly to him from Trinity

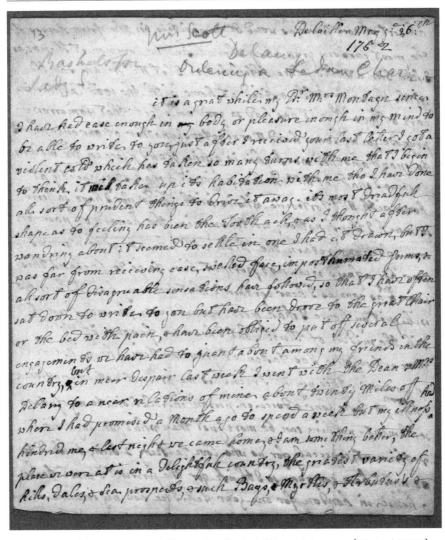

10.2   Letter from Anne Donnellan to Elizabeth Robinson Montagu (May 26, 1752) on having a tooth extracted for a cold (extract) (bMS Eng 1365 [50], Houghton Library, Harvard University, Cambridge, MA)

College Dublin about his treatment for colic, which involved "the loss of thirty-six ounces of blood with about a dozen purgings, and vomitings." One can easily imagine that these procedures made him forget about his abdominal pain, for he acknowledged that the remedy "reduced both it [the colic] and me to a very weak state."[1] Anne Donnellan wrote to Elizabeth Montagu from Delany's house outside Dublin about having had a violent cold that resisted "all sort of prudent things to drive it away." When it seemed to her as if the cold had settled in a tooth, she had it drawn, but this only led to infection and further discomfort (Image 10.2).

Some treatments were not just discomforting, but unequivocally poisonous. Mary Delany recommended that her nephew be given quicksilver (liquid mercury) for what had been diagnosed as worms. She provided the prescription: "A pound of quick-silver boiled in a gallon of water till half the water is consumed away to be constantly drank at his meals, or whenever he is dry." Delany's great-grand-niece, Lady Llanover, who edited her correspondence in 1861, added: "This prescription is worthy of the *bleedings* for *breathlessness,* as both appear well calculated to cure the disorder by killing the patient."[2] Other remedies sound like a cross between an old wives' tale and a magic charm. Delany assured her sister, for example, that "a spider put into a goose-quill, well sealed and secured, and hung about the child's neck as low as the pit of his stomach" would ease the symptoms of ague (a non-malarial fever), claiming *"Probatum est"* (it is proved).[3]

Treatments were often continued past any hope of remedy. Blistering, an application of hot plasters to the skin causing fluid to rise up to the blistering site, was suggested for almost any ill, and Delany was well aware that the painful procedure could be useless. She wrote of a dear friend suffering from childbed (puerperal) fever who died later the same day:

> She has not had since this day se'nnight [a week ago] three hours' sleep; her fever is very high, and she has been the greater part of that time delirious: she has had nine blisters, but to no purpose but to torment her, for they have injured her much![4]

Although it seems unlikely that Handel, before his first documented paralytic attack in 1737, could have escaped illness altogether, there is little evidence of any. We learn from newspaper reports that his singers intermittently fell ill, resulting either in their replacement or delayed

SICKNESS AND DEATH: *Timeline*

1724
publication of *An Essay of Health and Long Life* by Dr. George Cheyne; Handel may have been introduced to Cheyne's system after his first attack in 1737

1726
Annual Bills of Mortality give statistics on death in London; in this year the number of deaths was 28,418

1727
January 31
Handel's *Admeto* premieres at the King's Theatre; depicts the physical illness of King Admetus

performances. There are no such reports about Handel himself, but, despite his basic good health, he probably was unable to avoid the contagion of common respiratory and digestive disorders. Even without firsthand experience of illnesses and the treatments they occasioned, he would have been well aware of both. This was not, however, knowledge that he could transfer readily into his music. Although death haunted opera through murder and suicide, disease was not a welcome topic. It appeared in only one of Handel's operas, *Admeto* (composed in 1726; premiered in 1727), which tells of how the ailing King Admetus could be saved from death if another was willing to take his place. When no one else offers, his queen, Alcestis (Alceste in the libretto), sacrifices herself. Handel chose to open the opera in a remarkable way, he or his librettist radically altering their source libretto. Rather than having the entire overture played before a closed curtain, it was raised following the fugal, second section to reveal the dying and bedridden Admetus. Then instead of the typical closing minuet, Handel provided a ballet movement portraying the king's feverish vision of specters holding bloody daggers in their hands.

Deathbed scenes would have been familiar to most Londoners in the audience. Year after year, the Bills of Mortality covering the metropolitan area of London showed significantly more deaths than christenings. Without continual provincial and foreign immigration, the population of the city would have fallen. Instead, London's population rose from 400,000 in 1650 to 575,000 by 1700 and continued to expand

1733
January 27
Handel's *Orlando* premieres at King's
Theatre; depicts the madness of Orlando

1735
June 25
publication of Hogarth's *A Rake's Progress*;
depicts the inside of Bethlem (Bedlam)
Hospital
July 28
Handel mentions in a letter to Charles
Jennens his intention to visit the spa at
Tunbridge

throughout the eighteenth century, reaching 900,000 in the census of
1801.[5] This increase in population went hand in hand, however, with a
still faster rise in mortality, the poverty and crowding that resulted from
rapid growth fueling more disease. In 1700 the Bills of Mortality gave
the number of dead in central London at 19,443. By 1726, the year Handel wrote *Admeto*, it was 28,418.[6]

The bills listed the causes of death in two categories: disease and casu-
alties. The latter group, which included murder, drowning, suicide, and
execution, represented only a small fraction of the total deaths (one percent of the total in 1726). In contrast, the number of diseases listed in the
1720s reached seventy-five. A lack of knowledge about root causes meant
that many of those listed were more descriptive than diagnostic; the diseases listed in 1726, for example, included "bedridden" (3 deaths), "grief"
(18), "lethargy" (7), "rash" (5), and "suddenly" (111). The main "causes"
of death remained stable over years; in 1726, the largest categories were
"convulsion" (8,708), "fever" (4,666), "consumption" (3,764), and "aged"
(2,667). Handel's depiction of Admetus is consistent with the first two:
the king is racked with convulsions while suffering feverish visions.

As the curtain opens, the king is shown lying in his sickbed. The full
orchestra plays a pair of notes in a jerky short-long rhythm. After a brief
pause two more pairs are heard in quick succession. Then very quietly (Handel omits the oboes and marks the passage pianissimo) the strings describe
a weak falling-back in four descending notes. This alternation—of loud,
convulsive jolts followed by a subsidence—continues throughout the move-

Sickness and Death continued

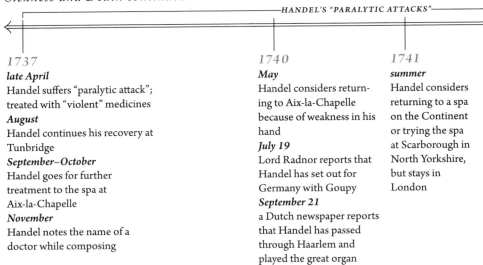

1737	*1740*	*1741*
late April Handel suffers "paralytic attack"; treated with "violent" medicines *August* Handel continues his recovery at Tunbridge *September–October* Handel goes for further treatment to the spa at Aix-la-Chapelle *November* Handel notes the name of a doctor while composing	*May* Handel considers return- ing to Aix-la-Chapelle because of weakness in his hand *July 19* Lord Radnor reports that Handel has set out for Germany with Goupy *September 21* a Dutch newspaper reports that Handel has passed through Haarlem and played the great organ	*summer* Handel considers returning to a spa on the Continent or trying the spa at Scarborough in North Yorkshire, but stays in London

ment, vividly depicting the king's seizures as a symptom of his fever and a reaction to his nightmare. In effect, the music provides the clearest possible stage direction to the singer. As the visions depart, Admetus rises in a feverish frenzy. In no condition to present a well-formed aria, he sings an agitated accompanied recitative whose only structure is to follow the emotional turns of the text. He calls out in confusion (*con stupore*) to the disappearing specters, but then recognizes more calmly and quietly (*adagio, e piano*) that his mind is disturbed. His agitation (*agitato*) quickly returns, however, and once again he calls out to the visions only to revert immediately to thoughts of his impending death. He hopes to die without losing his peace of mind, but the feverish specters reappear. This vacillation continues, reaching a climax when Admetus envisions the arrival of darkness, thunderbolts, and the rupture of the Earth. Completely exhausted, he prays quietly for death in a shortened song form.

Handel's depiction of this scene is so vivid and so realistic that one can easily imagine he was painting from life, but that assumption probably underestimates his imaginative ability and compositional skill. Whatever he may have witnessed before composing *Admeto* in 1726, he is not known to have been ill himself. The first possible hint of any ail-

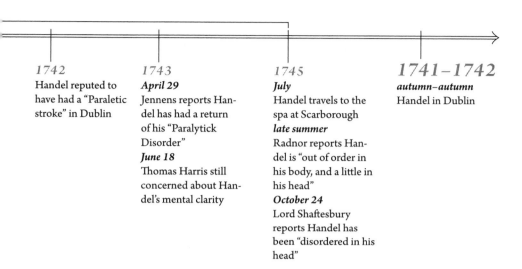

1742
Handel reputed to have had a "Paraletic stroke" in Dublin

1743
April 29
Jennens reports Handel has had a return of his "Paralytick Disorder"
June 18
Thomas Harris still concerned about Handel's mental clarity

1745
July
Handel travels to the spa at Scarborough
late summer
Radnor reports Handel is "out of order in his body, and a little in his head"
October 24
Lord Shaftesbury reports Handel has been "disordered in his head"

1741–1742
autumn–autumn
Handel in Dublin

ment comes in 1735, when he wrote to Jennens to thank him for "the oratorio" (which could refer to *Saul* or *Israel in Egypt,* or some other libretto he never set), saying that he had not yet had time to "read it with all the attention it deserves" but would do so once at Tunbridge.[7]

Tunbridge Wells was one of a number of spa towns in England and Europe whose mineral or thermal springs were thought to have restorative and therapeutic power. It is not known whether Handel first went to Tunbridge to seek a cure for specific physical symptoms or whether he found it a good place to rest and recuperate out of the city after a long opera season, but from at least 1735, Handel began with some regularity to spend a month during the summer at a spa. He was not alone. English and Continental spas were popular for rest cures and were prescribed for all imaginable illnesses. Anne Donnellan, the Percivals, and the Delanys, like Handel, could be found visiting a variety of them. Tunbridge, Bath, Scarborough, Cheltenham, and Islington were among the many English destinations, and trips were frequently made as well to Aix-la-Chapelle (Aachen) and Spa in the Ardennes near the Belgian border with Germany.

We first learn of serious ill health for Handel from Lord Shaftesbury, who wrote to James Harris on April 26, 1737, that he had been with the

Sickness and Death continued

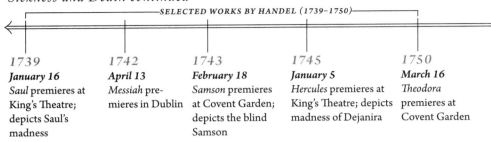

─SELECTED WORKS BY HANDEL (1739–1750)─

1739	1742	1743	1745	1750
January 16	*April 13*	*February 18*	*January 5*	*March 16*
Saul premieres at King's Theatre; depicts Saul's madness	Messiah premieres in Dublin	Samson premieres at Covent Garden; depicts the blind Samson	Hercules premieres at King's Theatre; depicts madness of Dejanira	Theodora premieres at Covent Garden

composer for "near an hour yesterday," and that although "he is in no danger upon the whole," it appeared likely that "he will loose a great part of his execution so as to prevent his ever playing any more concertos on the organ."[8] Shaftesbury identified the problem as a "rhumatick palsie" that affected Handel's right arm, "which was taken ill in a minute." He reported that Handel "is exceeding thankfull his disorder . . . did not attack him till he had done writing"—that is, composing for the season. In his next letter, only four days later, he was able to report: "Mr Handel is suprizingly mended[;] he has been on horseback twice."[9] Harris responded with concern to these letters and commented on the speed of Handel's recovery:

> It is certainly an evidence of great strength of constitution to be so soon getting rid of so great a shock. A weaker body would perhaps have hardly born the violence of medicines, which operate so quickly.[10]

Harris's reference to "the violence of medicines" suggests the sorts of treatment Handel received, which seem to have been of the common type. In the case of a maid whose treatment for rheumatic symptoms

1749

May 4
Handel conducts his first concert
for the benefit of the Foundling
Hospital
August
Handel travels to the spa at Bath

1750

June 1
Handel writes his will
early August
Handel leaves for Europe
August 21
a London newspaper reports on Handel being
overturned in a carriage and "terribly hurt"
September 8
Handel plays the organ for Princess Anne and
her husband in the Netherlands
December
Handel returns to London

was reported to Delany, this involved blistering, teeth extraction, strong potions, and "everything that cou'd be thought of," to no avail.[11] The good news, as Shaftesbury put it, was that in the composer's case, his "vast strength of constitution" was able "to bear all the rough remedies they have given him," so that he was likely to "recover again presently."[12] The more concerning, long-term issue was the extent to which Handel would follow through with the medical recommendations and alter his lifestyle. Shaftesbury wrote of Handel, "He submitts to discipline very patiently & I really believe will be orderly for the time to come that this unhappy seisure may possibly at last be the occasion of prolonging his life."[13]

For the moment Handel was "orderly" because of the paralysis or weakness in his right arm. As spring melted into summer and Handel thought about the impending autumn season, however, he must have become impatient with the pace of his recovery. He probably was encouraged to spend some time at a spa, and by mid-August he was in Tunbridge, where he met the literary scholar John Upton, a close friend of James Harris, and they "din[e]d together every day in the week."[14]

When neither submitting to the remedies of the London physicians nor taking the waters succeeded in restoring full function to Handel's right arm, the composer was at last persuaded to travel in September and

Sickness and Death continued

————————————————————————————————————HANDEL'S BLINDNESS——————————————

1751

February 13
Handel unable to continue the composition of *Jephtha* due to a "relaxation" in his left eye

March 14
report that Handel has lost the sight of one eye

June
Handel visits the spas in Bath and Cheltenham

August
Handel completes *Jephtha*; changes the last words of the text in the concluding chorus of Part I from "What God ordains is right" to Pope's "Whatever is, is right!" Handel consults with Samuel Sharp, surgeon; diagnosis of "incipient Gutta serena"; Sharp operates on Handel's eyes (?)

1752

January 9
Thomas Harris reports that Handel is blind in one eye and unlikely to be able to continue after the current season

February 26
Handel's *Jephtha* premieres at Covent Garden

August 17
newspaper report that Handel had been seized with a "Paralytick Disorder in the Head, which has deprived him of Sight"

November 3
Dr. William Bromfield operates on (couches) Handel's eyes without success

October to the thermal springs at Aix-la-Chapelle.[15] Biographer Mainwaring described a surprisingly rapid cure. Handel was said to have stayed "three times as long" in the hot waters as was normal and then after only a few hours to have played the organ in both "the principal church, as well as convent, . . . so much beyond any they had ever been used to" that the nuns took it for a miracle.[16] Knowing Handel's temperament, one imagines that his playing was less a miracle than a test he made after each treatment to see what amendment, if any, had occurred in his hand. A great recovery was reported in the *London Daily Post* in early November, and shortly thereafter Handel set about composing *Faramondo*, his next opera. He did not get further than an aria early in the first act, however, before he noted on the manuscript the name of a physician, Dr. Francis Philip Duval on Poland Street.[17] After the attack of 1737, Handel never fully recovered his health.

In May 1740, Thomas Harris reported to his brother James that Handel "having lately found a weakness in his hand" had determined to return to Aix-la-Chapelle.[18] Whether he did or not remains unknown. On July 19, Lord Radnor wrote to Harris that "Mr. Handel set out for Germany Thursday last," which sounds as if the composer

May 21
reported in correspondence
that Handel, unable to
conduct, wept during the aria
"Total eclipse" at a performance of *Samson*

August
Handel goes to Tunbridge with
Thomas Morell; Dr. John Tay-
lor operates on Handel's eyes
August 24
Taylor reports success, but this
turns out to be false

was headed either to Aix (Aachen) or Spa (Belgium), but then added
that since the composer was "in company with Goupée" he had little
hope of any improvement in Handel's condition.[19] On September 21,
a Dutch newspaper reported that Handel had passed through Haarlem and played the great Haarlem organ, but this leaves open all of
August for Handel and Goupy to have traveled first to a spa on the
way.[20] In July and August of 1740, Handel's friend Anne Donnellan
was in residence at Spa drinking the waters, and in August she made
a "bad day's journey" from Spa to Aix-la-Chapelle, which two resorts
were only thirty-four miles apart, to see the annual procession honoring the memory of Charlemagne.[21] Handel and Goupy could have
encountered her in either city.

In 1741, Handel considered returning to the Continent to drink the
waters at Spa or making the 192-mile journey within England to Scarborough in North Yorkshire, but took the easier course and stayed at
home. Again Radnor worried about the choice:

> Mr Handel instead of goeing to Scarborough to drink the waters,
> drinks wine with Mr Furnes at Gunsbury and I fear eats too

Sickness and Death continued

1755

December 4
Delany reports hearing Handel play the harpsichord at Donnellan's house

1756

March 27
Thomas Harris reports on Handel's playing on the organ "as good as ever" during the oratorio season

May 29
George Harris records in his diary that Handel played fortepiano at Jennens's house

December 12
Delany again reports hearing Handel play at Donnellan's house

mutch of those things he ought to avoid. I would fain methinks preserve him for a few years longer.[22]

Although Handel returned to the Continent in 1750, and may have visited Aix-la-Chapelle or Spa, his known spa visits after 1740 are all to English locales. In 1745 he went to Scarborough, in 1749 to Bath, in 1751 to Bath and Cheltenham, and in 1758, with his librettist Morell, he was back in Tunbridge. The newspapers reported in 1759, shortly before his death, that he was planning to go to Bath.

The thermal springs at Bath made this spa the most popular in Great Britain. Great efficacy was attributed to the waters, and so many visitors from the highest social strata made Bath a destination that it acquired its own social season, customs, and etiquette. Not all, however, thought the regimen of bathing in and drinking the waters, coupled with a strenuous social schedule, a likely cure. Philip Percival wrote to his brother John from Bath in 1718:

My Wife fancys she finds Some benefit by it, but for my Self I must own I drink because I am advised so to do but whether I am to expect to find a Sensible advantage by it or no time must shew, I hope faith is not necessary to go along with the waters to

1757
February 8
Shaftesbury reports Handel is composing
March 11
Handel's *The Triumph of Time and Truth* premieres at Covent Garden

1758
November 21
Thomas Harris reports that Handel has made "a considerable part of a new oratorio"

1759
April 6
Handel present for *Messiah*, the final performance of the oratorio season
April 7
newspaper report that Handel is planning to travel to Bath
April 14
Handel dies at home

render them effectually Serviceable for if so I doubt as to my own particular I should be little ye better . . . , so that altogether you may believe me when as I said before I wish it were over as you have heretofore said on a hunting occasion.[23]

And he expressed his sympathy when John was marooned in Bath for his wife's colic while the Royal Academy of Music was opening in London: "It is unlucky at all times to be indisposed, but more So when either business or good entertainments are Stirring, which is the case I hear at this time for the famous Bononcini I find is come over, & the Operas very fine . . ."[24] It was a few years later that John Percival first met Dr. George Cheyne, a Bath physician, under whose care he placed his wife: "My Wife is here under the direction of Dr Cheyne a very able Phisitian who I think has hit her disorder, & what he prescribes has already had good effect, but so obstinate a cholick as hers will require Some months Stay, & probably her return hither in the Summer Season."[25]

Cheyne became famous for arguing that proper diet and exercise could serve as both a preventative and a cure.[26] Sounding astonishingly modern, he urged "the great advantage of spare and simple diet," advising his patients to eat more vegetables and less meat, in particular less red meat, to drink more water, and to avoid wine and spirits.[27] He expected his patients "to deal in no other *Cookery*, but *Roasting* and *Boiling*," and considered sufficient rest and proper exercise "necessary to health." He warned that "eating late or full suppers frustrates the ends of sleep," and saw exercise as a means of preserving a good flow of blood, supple joints, and strong fibers (muscles). A particular concern of his was the danger of obesity, a continuing problem in his own life, which he considered a serious health threat not just for adults but also for children. He bemoaned the abuse of coffee, black tea, and chocolate, recommending "the simplicity of green tea," considered tobacco "pernicious and destructive" to many constitutions, and described snuff as *"good for nothing* at all." Cheyne promised no quick cures and described it a "folly" to expect one for a chronic disease. A firm believer in the premise that "'tis easier to *preserve* Health than to *recover* it, and to *prevent* Diseases than to *cure* them," he urged patients to take their health into their own hands and considered it a moral (and Christian) obligation to do so.

The doctors who treated Handel at the time of his first attack are not known. Shaftesbury mentioned a "Parry" who seems to have acted in a medical capacity, but he has not been further identified; nor is it known whether Duval, whose name Handel wrote on the composing score of *Faramondo* after visiting Aix-la-Chapelle in 1737, was someone he actually saw.[28] There is no record of his consulting Cheyne, but it seems a good possibility. Handel's friend Dr. Arbuthnot had consulted Cheyne for his own ailments in the 1720s, and in later years Arbuthnot probably recommended him to Alexander Pope and John Gay, Arbuthnot's literary collaborators on Handel's *Acis and Galatea*; both became Cheyne's patients. By the late 1730s, the number of people in the composer's circle who trusted his method suggests that Handel may have tried it as well. It is difficult, however, to imagine the composer a happy convert to Cheyne's dietary scheme.

One thing that can be said with certainty about Handel's physical condition is that his corpulence increased with age. This is readily documented in his portraits, and his gormandizing was so notable that it is mentioned repeatedly in contemporary documents by both critics and supporters—the one group describing him as a glutton, the other worrying about the impact that overeating had on his health. For example, at about the same time that Goupy's caricature put into visual form the image of Handel as a hog, George Harris wrote to his brother James:

> I saw your old acquaintance, Signr Handel, a few days agoe, in appearance very well, airing him self on foot in the park: I am told, that he would probably recover his health again, were he not so much of the epicure, that he cannot forbear going back to his former luxurious way of living, which will in the end certainly prove fatal to him.[29]

It is difficult to diagnose Handel's illness from his symptoms. Most likely his recurrent bouts of joint pain and palsy or paralysis were caused by nerve damage that led to weakness or numbness in the limbs (peripheral neuropathy). The possible causes of peripheral neuropathy are many. Handel's attacks are sometimes described as rheumatic, and the underlying problem may have been rheumatoid arthritis, an autoimmune disease. Even more likely, however, they resulted from a combination of lead poisoning (saturnine gout) and repetitive stress injuries. Lead would have entered his diet most directly as a result of his fondness for port: Handel wrote a note to himself on a manuscript from the 1720s about "12 gallons Port" and "12 Bottles french" with a reference to Duke Street (a largely commercial area off Piccadilly directly across from Burlington House, where such wines could be purchased).[30] Fortified wines from Portugal, such as port, were heavily contaminated from the lead-lined pipes used in the distillation process. The speed with which Handel repeatedly appears to have recovered also suggests lead poisoning or repetitive stress as a factor in his illnesses, as opposed to, say, a series of small strokes. At the spas, he would have given up drinking fortified wines and been largely separated from continual access to keyboard instruments. In all probability, Handel's recurrent "attacks" resulted from no single cause, but rather from a combination of contributing factors.[31]

Handel's experience of mental disorder affecting both his thinking and his speech at the time of his paralytic attacks complicates a retrospective diagnosis, although the conjunction is consistent with lead poisoning. In addition, physical illness accompanied by temporary paralysis could easily have affected his emotional state and resulted in the reported episodes of mental instability, but the cause and effect could also have run the other way. Cheyne recognized mental health as a factor in physical well-being. He identified psychological disorders as either "chronical" or "acute" and believed that the *"Chronical Passions, like Chronical Diseases, wear out, waste and destroy the Nervous System gradually."*[32] He added, however, that "some of these Passions, such as *Love, Grief* and *Pride,* when very intense and long indulg'd, terminate even in *Madness."*[33] He considered the acute passions, like acute diseases, more immediately "destructive than *chronical"* and, therefore, "more dangerous to *Health."*[34] No mention was made of any mental confusion at the time of Handel's first attack, but in later instances it always played a part. In April of 1743, Jennens wrote that Handel "has had a return of his Paralytick Disorder, which affects his Head & Speech."[35] And in June, Thomas Harris was still concerned that Handel's "head does not seem so clear as I could wish it to be."[36] In the summer of 1745, Radnor wrote to Harris that Handel was "much out of order in his body, and a little in his head."[37] In October, Shaftesbury reported that the composer had been "a good deal disordered in his head."[38] These bouts of mental confusion, which always occurred simultaneously with physical paralysis, and are only reported between the years 1737 and 1745 (from the age of fifty-two to sixty), do not suggest any significant, underlying psychological illness.

Handel's reported "attacks" all occurred at particularly stressful moments in his career: in 1737, at the climax of the tense competition between Handel and the Opera of the Nobility; in 1741 in Dublin, when Handel was in the process of reconsidering his career; in 1743, when he refused to write for the Middlesex opera company and angered the aristocracy; and in 1745, when he suffered so much from audience resistance that he was forced temporarily to cancel his season.[39] These coincidences would seem to suggest that his attacks were related to stress.

Even assuming a chronic, physical disorder underlying his symptoms, it may be that the condition only flared into an acute phase, including mental confusion and speech impairment, at such moments.

The concurrence of mental confusion with physical disease was commonplace. Benjamin Martyn, Lord Shaftesbury's amanuensis, wrote in 1738 about himself that he had had "such violent fits of the Head Ach, that I have sometimes almost lost my Eye Sight, and pretty often I am afraid my Understanding."[40] In 1739, John Percival included a note in his diary about his brother, Philip Percival, Donnellan's stepfather:

> I visited brother Percival, my sister, his wife and Mrs. Donellan, who arrived in London from Ireland the 31 of last month in order to go to the Bath for his health, and get a sound fit of the gout, which wanting, he often has of late been seized with short absences of memory and sense, so as to fall suddenly to the ground.[41]

Eighteenth-century medical practitioners were therefore careful in their diagnoses to differentiate insanity and illness. In the surviving casebook (1766) of John Monro, a leading "mad-doctor," this distinction is a prime concern. He wrote of one case that since the patient recently had "some remains of fever upon her I think it better to await the event of that before I sh^d pronounce her mad."[42] He was also careful to determine whether an apparent fit of madness was due to some other cause, such as drunkenness.[43]

Monro's casebook also provides a record of a consultation made by Handel's friend Goupy about a Mrs. Walker, described as his servant. The doctor was somewhat doubtful of the diagnosis. At the time of the examination, Mrs. Walker was already confined in a madhouse run by Peter Inskip in Little Chelsea. Monro described her as "mad enough" to be committed to Bethlem Hospital in Moorfields, London, but "at the same time [she] seem'd to me to have many symptoms attending her complaint that were paralytic." That is, like Handel, she may simply have been suffering mental confusion due to an underlying physical ill-

10.3 William Hogarth, "Scene in Bedlam," from *The Rake's Progress* (1735), plate 8 (private collection / The Bridgeman Art Library [XJF 397618])

ness. Nevertheless, Monro noted as the outcome of the consultation and examination: "brought to the hospital."[44]

Bethlem, or Bedlam as it was generally called, was the central asylum for the insane in London. For the confined, it would rarely have seemed a sanctuary: patients often were neglected, and those considered dangerous were chained. Rather, the hospital served as a means of incarcerating the mentally ill and as a form of entertainment for the curious: for a fee one was allowed into the wards to gape at the inmates, some of whom engaged in what were considered amusing behaviors. William Hogarth depicted this in his painting series *A Rake's Progress* (engraved and published in 1735). Tom Rakewell, the son and heir of a rich merchant, loses his fortune; he is imprisoned for debt and, then, having lost his wits, incarcerated for madness. Hogarth portrayed him at Bedlam unclothed and chained to the floor. Surrounded by fellow patients, including one man who thinks he is the pope, another who thinks he is king, and a musician playing a violin with a stick, he is attended by his true love, Sarah Young. In the background, two well-dressed aristocratic ladies take in the show.

Despite the greater cost of home care, friends and family often tried desperately to prevent the institutionalization of loved ones suffering madness. Goupy, when he came to write his will in 1769, struggled to provide support for a spinster who has "lived with me many years and is now so unhappy as to be deprived of her reason."[45] Identifying this woman as Sarah Wright, he arranged to leave "all my real and personal Estate of what nature or kindsoever or whersoever" to Wright's sister to cover costs. The background to this story was published by one "W" in a letter to the *St. James's Chronicle* seven years after Goupy's death:

> As Goupee had kept a Mistress in his Youth, who became mad, and could not bear to see in his old Age the Object of his Love and Pleasures confined in Bedlam, he took her to his own House, where the Expence of Attendance, &c. was so great, that he lived and died in very indigent Circumstances.[46]

The identification of the woman Goupy assisted as his mistress was, however, angrily rebutted shortly afterward by one "A.P.," who insisted rather that she was his housekeeper, who had only begun living with Goupy in 1759 (when the painter was seventy), a version of the story that more closely matches the case records of Dr. Monro.

Most likely, the Mrs. Walker in Monro's records is the same woman as Mrs. Wright named in Goupy's will. As "W" stated, the painter "could not bear" seeing her "confined in Bedlam" and therefore used all of his financial resources to keep her at home. (The other possibility—that in the last three years of his life Goupy was dealing with two separate madwomen—seems unlikely.) As the name in the will has to have been correct for the will to have legal force, the only question is the identity of Mrs. Walker in Monro's casebook. If "W" was correct that Sarah Wright was Goupy's mistress, it would seem that the artist disguised both his true relationship to her and her name when he consulted with Monro in order to protect her condition from rumormongers. This might have been particularly necessary if she was a known person in her own right. A singer by the name of Mrs. Wright appeared initially in 1728 in Handel's *Admeto,* sang the title role in *Athalia* in Oxford in 1733, and later performed at Lincoln's Inn Fields, but abruptly withdrew from the stage in 1750. If this soprano was the same person as the Sarah Wright of Goupy's will, then the continuation of her sad story may be inferred from surviving documents. In 1765, a Mrs. Wright appears briefly as a dresser at Covent Garden, perhaps the former actress-singer attempting to earn a little income by returning to an environment she knew. The employment did not last. Goupy's surprising decision to sell his art collection in the same year may have been the direct result of Wright's not being able to earn any money of her own and needing significant care. By 1766, when Goupy consulted Monro, his "housekeeper" was confined in a neighborhood madhouse. She was moved to Bedlam for a period, but brought home again by the artist. In his will, Goupy then made all the provision he could to continue to keep Wright out of the hospital and in the care of her sister.

Unlike physical illness, depictions of which are rare in opera, depictions of mental instability are not uncommon. Indeed, one might posit that opera and mental disorder go hand in hand. In Handel's works there are three particularly vivid portrayals of insanity, and these depict the three chronic passions that, according to Cheyne, can "terminate in madness": love, pride, and grief. The crusader knight Orlando loses his mind for love; King Saul's overweening pride and vainglory drive him to jealousy and madness; and Hercules's wife, Dejanira, becomes insane with guilt and grief when she realizes her jealousy has been the cause of his death. The depictions of madness in *Saul* and *Hercules* are discussed below.

In a baroque opera, normalcy was represented by the alternation of recitative and aria. Typically the recitative, which carried the dialogue and action, had a very simple accompaniment in order to keep the text moving. Arias, and the few duets and ensembles, which responded to and reflected on the action, were elaborately extended and accompanied in a variety of ways. The majority of these were in da capo ("from the top") form, where the long opening section returned with improvised ornamentation after a briefer and sometimes contrasting middle section. Handel's oratorios had a more flexible shape, but nevertheless adhered in general to the design principles of opera. The breaking of the typical pattern normally indicated a disturbance in the story or the character.

The abrupt discontinuation of an aria in midcourse always signaled a quick and severe dramatic event. Handel's cantata *Apollo e Dafne* tells of the god falling in love with the nymph and, after failing to win her by persuasion, vowing to take her by force. In Handel's setting, the final pursuit is depicted in an aria for Apollo. In the first part of this seeming da capo, he encourages himself, singing "Mie piante correte" (Feet, run after her; arms, grasp her!). In the middle section he senses success, "I touch her, I embrace her, I hold her, I seize her," but, suddenly, she is transformed into a laurel tree, and he loses her. The aria dissolves in the middle of a line, and the forward motion of the chase is dramatically halted as the music sinks first into accompanied recitative and then into simple recitative. Apollo stands dumbfounded. The breaking of the form not only paints a disruption in the psychological drama but also provides a clear musical depiction of the physical action. A technique obviously suited to high drama, it was also used by Handel in witty ways. In *Semele*, Juno and her messenger Iris attempt to awaken Somnus, the god of sleep. He struggles through the first section of his aria, "Leave me, loathsome light"; in the course of the middle section, he sinks ever lower into his bass register, and then, silence. The goddesses, knowing the form, wait a second or two for him to repeat the opening section and close the aria, but quickly realize that he has fallen back asleep and left the aria hanging. "Dull god!" exclaims Iris.

In *Saul*, the disruption of Saul's aria "A serpent in my bosom warmed" indicates an acute mental breakdown. The oratorio opens with the Israelites offering a song of thanksgiving for David's dispatch of Goliath and their victory over the Philistines. When David is shown into the king's presence, Saul welcomes him as a son, bestowing his elder daughter on him in marriage. A chorus of women, later joined by the men, praise both

Saul and David, singing that the king has slain "thousands," and David, "ten thousands." Saul resents this comparison, and is driven crazy by the insistent repetition of these lines, which are set to a four-measure jingle and accompanied by an instrument Handel had specially built for the effect: a small carillon using a regular keyboard to strike bells. Charles Jennens, the librettist of *Saul*, after seeing the instrument in Handel's house, wrote to a cousin (September 19, 1738):

> I found yesterday in his room a very queer Instrument which He calls Carillon (Anglice a bell) and says some call it a Tubalcain, I suppose because it is both in the make and tone like a set of Hammers striking upon Anvils. 'Tis play'd upon with Keys like a Harpsichord, and with this Cyclopean Instrument he designs to make poor Saul stark mad.[47]

Handel augments the effect of the chorus not just by its instrumentation and repetition but also by the careful depiction of the jubilant crowd as it moves from a distance into the king's presence. At first one hears the music as if at a distance, played on carillon and violins with the organ joining in on the melody line. Saul's younger daughter points out to her father (and also to the oratorio audience who are not seeing this acted out) the "daughters of the land" who are coming "In joyful Dance, with Instruments of Musick, / Come to congratulate your Victory."[48] As they come nearer the jingle gets louder. Handel reinforces the instrumental ensemble with oboes and viola, and one is now able to hear the women's chorus in three parts. As he absorbs the words, Saul exclaims, "What do I hear? Am I then sunk so low, / To have this upstart Boy preferr'd before me?" But this is not the end of it. Now the whole is played yet again reinforced by trumpets, trombones, and timpani, with tenors and basses added to the chorus. The extended layout of this scene is one of Handel's contributions to the libretto. It not only depicts the arrival of the women dancing and singing, but the increasing size and volume of the celebratory chorus also match Saul's rising anger.[49]

After Saul abruptly exits, his children refer to his rage as an "old disease" and urge David to take his harp, "and as thou oft hast done, / From the King's Breast expel the raging Fiend, / And soothe his tortur'd Soul with Sounds Divine." When Saul reenters, still "Rack'd with Infernal Pains," David sings for him "O Lord, whose Mercies numberless"; this is set with a harplike accompaniment for strings and followed by a symphony for harp. Given Handel's recent depiction of the power of music in *Alexander's Feast*, the full score of which was published the same year as *Saul*'s composition in 1738, it is noteworthy that David's singing and playing for Saul, as opposed to that of Timotheus and his harp for Alexander, has no effect. Instead, Saul launches into a furious and now fully developed rage aria in clear da capo form aimed directly at David, "A Serpent, in my Bosom warm'd." The opening section completed, Saul drives into the middle section (beginning "Ambitious Boy!"), but he hasn't the self-control to continue using words. He hurls his javelin at David, depicted by Handel with a rushing downward scale, and the aria abruptly ends without any sense of closure. It is with this break that Saul's madness is made manifest.

The treatment of mental breakdown in *Hercules* (1745) differs from that in *Saul* in that it contains a lengthy mad scene.[50] Dejanira, Hercules's wife, is disturbed from the outset and looking for reasons to worry about her marriage. First she fears for Hercules's safety and laments his absence, but after he returns safely, she falsely accuses him of having an affair with the captive princess Iole and angrily berates him. Her changes in emotion, vividly depicted by Handel, demonstrate her instability, and her subsequent actions confirm it. Hoping to restore the love she thinks she has lost, she remembers a magic robe given to her by the centaur Nessus as he was dying. Apparently she has forgotten the circumstances of this gift: Hercules had mortally wounded the centaur with a poisoned arrow when he attempted to abduct Dejanira. It stretches credulity that his bloodstained robe would, as the dying Nessus then told Dejanira, serve in the future to revive the "expiring Flame of Love." Ignoring the ill omens surrounding it, she sends the robe to her husband as a "Pledge of Reconcilement." Of course, it is poisoned.

Too late Dejanira learns that "These impious Hands have sent my injur'd Lord / Untimely to the Shades." "Let me be mad," she exclaims, hoping to escape her grief and guilt in insanity. For her subsequent aria, Handel's librettist, Thomas Broughton, provided a rather tidy text with a recitative followed by an eight-line air (aria) separable into two equal sections for a da capo. Handel ignored the potentially normative divisions between recitative and aria and between the two sections of the aria, providing instead a continuous and highly dramatic mad scene. Dejanira begins by frantically crying out, "Where shall I fly? Where hide this guilty Head?" Handel depicts her distress in broken vocal phrases, the space between them filled by the strings playing repeated notes in an agitated rhythm. Her mood then swings wildly, as Handel's performance markings clearly indicate: *adagio* (slow), *furioso, concitato* (agitated), *lento e piano* (slow and soft), *concitato, lento,* and *concitato.* As she imagines the Furies approaching to avenge Hercules's death, she calls out: "See! see! they come—*Alecto* with her Snakes, / *Megæra* fell, and black *Tisiphone!*" If Handel had adhered to the typical structure, these would have been the last lines of the recitative, and the aria, "See the dreadful sisters rise!" would have followed. In his first draft, he adopted this plan, giving the recitative a clear close (cadence) and setting the aria off with an orchestral introduction (ritornello). On revision, he eliminated both formal markers, obscuring the demarcation between the recitative and aria.[51] The obliteration of the most basic unit of baroque opera, the recitative-aria pairing, abetted by the violent shifts in emotion and disregard of da capo form (as in *Saul*), gives this setting special power as a depiction of madness.

Handel wrote *Hercules* in the summer of 1744, and a year later he had another paralytic attack. Shaftesbury wrote in October 1745, "Poor Handel looks something better, [and] I hope he will entirely recover in due time," adding, as already noted, that the composer had been "a good deal disordered in his head."[52] After this date, however, there were no further reports of any mental disturbances. Indeed, from 1745 to 1750 there were repeated comments about Handel's good health. Perhaps success was a curative, for in these five years all prior difficulties with competition, managerial demands, and audience resistance faded away. The political oratorios relating to the Jacobite Rebellion of 1745—*Occasional Oratorio* (1746), *Judas Maccabaeus* (1747), and *Joshua* (1748)—undoubtedly buoyed Handel's popularity with the public and probably helped him to decline any new requests from operatic circles. Having risen above the various forms of operatic competition thrown at him between 1733 and 1745—from the Opera of the Nobility, to the English opera adherents, to the Middlesex opera company—Handel made the decision in 1747 to rely solely on single-ticket sales, gave up offering subscriptions, and thereafter experienced the most lucrative years of his career. At the end of each season, he was able to make a substantive stock purchase out of clear profit: £1,000 in April 1747, £1,500 in March 1748, £2,000 in April 1749, and £1,100 in April 1750. From 1747, Handel's stock accounts only grew.[53]

Handel's health, newfound success, and financial security laid the groundwork for the remarkable year of 1749.[54] The oratorio season was one of the strongest he had ever produced, with premieres of *Susanna* and *Solomon*, as well as revivals of *Hercules*, *Samson*, and *Messiah*. After the close of the season, he added to his public success with *Music for the Royal Fireworks*, an orchestral suite written in celebration of the Peace of Aix-la-Chapelle that ended the War of Austrian Succession. It was heard first at a rehearsal in Vauxhall Gardens before a crowd estimated at about 10,000, and then at Green Park on April 27. Less than two weeks later, Handel offered his first benefit concert for the Foundling Hospital, which paved the way for the annual *Messiah* performances in support of the hospital that were inaugurated in 1750.

Perhaps these accumulated successes, together with the prospect of his sixty-fifth birthday on February 23, 1750, led Handel to put his affairs in order. In the month before his birthday, he consolidated his investments, amounting to £7,700, into a single account. In February, he made significant additions to his art collection, buying a number of works at auction. His oratorio season, which generally was defined by the period of Lent before Easter, ran from March 2 to April 12 and included the premiere of *Theodora*. Like previous seasons, it earned him a tidy profit that he was able to invest. Then on June 1, 1750, Handel wrote his will. His first provision, which was generous, went to his servant Peter LeBlond. Then he focused on his closest colleague and closest friend, leaving significant bequests, respectively, to John Christopher Smith and James Hunter. He concluded the will with gifts to family members in Germany. In early August, he made a few transfers at the Bank of England, and immediately thereafter set out for the Continent. On August 21, the *General Advertiser* reported: "Mr. Handel, who went to Germany to visit his Friends some Time since, and between the Hague and Haarlem had the Misfortune to be overturned, by which he was terribly hurt, is now out of Danger."[55] The type and extent of Handel's injuries are unknown, but in September he played the organ for Princess Anne and her husband the prince of Orange at Deventer in the Netherlands.

Handel returned to London in December and, to all outward appearances, continued his chain of successes. The 1751 season saw the premiere of *The Choice of Hercules* (a work that was tied to a revival of *Alexander's Feast* and completely different from the oratorio *Hercules*), and 1752 saw the premiere of *Jephtha*. Both seasons continued the string of spring stock purchases: £1,350 in March 1751, and £2,000 in May 1752. But in fact, everything had changed. While composing *Jephtha* in January and February 1751, Handel had been forced to put down his pen. He wrote a note into the score in German: "reached this point on Wednesday, 13 February, unable to continue due to a weakening in my left eye." Ten days later, on his sixty-sixth birthday, he added, also in German: "Saturday, the 23rd of this month, somewhat better, able to go on."[56] A report of Handel's visual difficulties must have spread, for one correspondent wrote as early as March 1751, "noble Handel hath lost an eye, but I have the Rapture to say St. Cecilia makes no complain of any Defect in his fingers."[57] In June he traveled to Bath with a Mr. Smith—perhaps his friend and neighbor James Smyth, the perfumer, rather than John Christopher Smith, father or son—and then carried on north to Cheltenham Wells. Back in London, he finished the composition of *Jephtha* over the summer. Some time after this, his deteriorating eyesight forced him to seek medical attention, and he consulted the surgeon Samuel Sharp at Guy's Hospital. With this new condition, Handel moved out of the care of physicians and into the hands of surgeons.

Sharp was an esteemed surgeon. In 1739 he had published *A Treatise on the Operations of Surgery*, and in 1750 he followed it with *A Critical Enquiry into the Present State of Surgery*, which reached four editions in London and saw translations into many languages. In general, surgeries were performed in the home of the patient, who often would refuse permission for any family members to be present during the operation. Without a full understanding of either antiseptic conditions or the importance of sterilizing surgical equipment, and with no anesthetic to control pain or antibiotics to fight infection, surgery was hardly a panacea, but in many cases it was the only hope for relief or even survival.

To give an example illustrative of contemporary surgical knowledge totally unrelated to Handel's medical needs, Sharp worried that mastectomies were not performed as frequently as they should be. He complained that "there are some Surgeons so disheartned by the ill success of this Operation, that they decry it in every Case, and even recommend a certain Death to their Patients, rather than a Trial." He fully realized, however, that the particular situation of each patient must be taken into account. Experience had shown him that success was more often achieved in cases where the tumor had come on slowly than "when it has increased very fast, and with acute Pain." He also acknowledged that when the tumor was "attended with Knots in the Arm-pit, no service can be done by Amputation unless the Knots be taken away."[58] Eighteenth-century mastectomies could, however, be successful. Elizabeth Montagu's mother (Mrs. Robinson) provides an example. Having, in 1744, discovered a swelling in her breast, she consulted with the surgeon William Cheselden, Sharp's teacher and mentor, who determined "that it was a cancer, but that not sticking to the ribs, it may be taken out without danger." Montagu called on her women friends for support, writing of her mother, "They assure us there is no danger of her Life, but it is terrible to think of the pain she must undergo."[59] Mrs. Robinson survived the surgery and was nursed by her daughters and their friend Anne Donnellan.

By consulting Sharp, Handel was seeking help from one of the top-rated surgeons in England. Hawkins wrote at the end of the century that the first diagnosis Handel received in 1751 was that the weakness in his eye was "an incipient Gutta serena," or the beginning of a permanent blindness caused by a disease of the optic nerve or some other systemic disorder without any such visible cause as an inflammation or cataract. Handel, therefore, was "prepared to expect a total privation of the sense of seeing, yet with hopes that it might prove only temporary, and that by the help of manual operation he might be restored to sight," but when the loss of sight was confirmed, he "readily submitted to the hand of Mr. Samuel Sharp, of Guy's hospital."[60]

From Hawkins's history, it is impossible to know whether Sharp made or agreed with the diagnosis of a "gutta serena," but a report on Handel's blindness in the *General Advertiser* (August 17, 1752) points to this judgment as the generally accepted one:

> We hear that George-Frederick Handel, Esq; the celebrated
> Composer of Musick was seized a few Days ago with a Paralytick
> Disorder in the Head, which has deprived him of Sight.

If, however, as seems the case from Hawkins's report, Sharp operated on Handel (and clearly he was a proponent of surgery), then he must have changed or expanded the diagnosis to include cataracts, as the purpose of eye surgery was specifically to correct that problem. In his publications, Sharp discussed two different ways of proceeding. The most common was called couching: the clouded lens was pushed out of the way of the line of vision by striking a needle through the eye to the lens and depressing the cataract. In order to treat the "succeeding Inflammation," Sharp strongly advised against powders that "leave a gritty substance in the Eye, which must be pernicious," but found "Bleeding, and other gentle Evacuations . . . absolutely necessary."[61] Sharp also described a more complicated procedure he had learned from Cheselden that involved cutting the iris to make an artificial pupil, but he cautioned that specifically in cases of a "Paralytick Disorder" the situation is "so often complicated . . . that the Success is very precarious."[62] Whatever Sharp did or did not attempt, Handel's eyesight was not restored.

In 1752, Handel's season went on as normal. It included the premiere of *Jephtha*, and in May, Handel added £2,000 to his stock portfolio. In the autumn, he consulted another well-known surgeon, Dr. William Bromfield, founder of the London Lock Hospital and surgeon to Frederick, Prince of Wales. On November 3, 1752, Bromfield couched Handel, and it was at first thought that the composer had "found some benefit" in the operation.[63] After this surgery, if the signs had been positive, Handel would have been fitted with a pair of thick convex glasses to compensate for the loss of the eyes' own lens, but no such image or description has come down to us. Perhaps the hopeful signs were too soon dissipated, for by early 1753, it was clear that no permanent improvement had been achieved. Handel was given to expect, as reported by Hawkins, that "freedom from pain in the visual organs was all that he had to hope, for the remainder of his days."[64]

The season of 1753 went ahead without any new works. The orchestra must have been led by John Christopher Smith Jr., as the countess of Shaftesbury wrote of her sadness at seeing Handel "sitting by, not playing on the harpsichord."[65] However, the composer continued to be able to play solo pieces on the keyboard and to improvise. Thomas Harris reported two different occasions during the season when Handel played the organ: at the first, he "played a concerto, & a long voluntary with a fugue, in which we all thought he did full as well as usual," and at the second, he played "full as well in invention, execution & all other respects as ever was heard."[66] As Shaftesbury commented on April 3, "Handel's playing is beyond what even *he* ever did."[67]

As the realization struck home of the permanence of Handel's blindness, his earlier depiction of the blind Samson took on totemic significance. The image of the great hero Samson reduced to pitiable incapacity by blindness had long been associated with the great English poet John Milton, who having gone blind in the 1650s published his *Samson Agonistes* in 1671. It was this text that Newburgh Hamilton adapted for Handel's *Samson* (1743). The musical setting of Samson's heartfelt cry in the first act of the oratorio now spoke with more than double force. "Total Eclipse!" Samson sings to a line that drops heavily into the depths. The words "no Sun" and "no Moon" elicit the same stretching, upward leap, as if trying to reach up to the light, but all collapses downward on "All dark amidst the Blaze of Noon!" Mary Delany wrote to her sister from Dublin, "Poor Handel! how feelingly must he recollect '*total eclipse.*'"[68] *Samson*, one of Handel's greatest works, was revived in every season from 1752 to 1755, and as Delany intuited from her long friendship with him, Handel was deeply affected by this passage. A friend wrote to James Harris's wife about a performance in 1753:

> You ask'd me about poor Handel. I paid my *devoir* to him at the oratorio, and cou'd have cry'd at the sight of him. He is fallen away, pale, feeble, old, blind, in short everything that cou'd most affect one . . . I was told, at the Total Eclipse in Samson, he cry'd like an infant. Thank God I did not see it.[69]

One almost hopes this is an exaggeration, but there is no doubt, from repeated reports, that Handel was sorely afflicted. Hawkins wrote, "His spirits forsook him; and that fortitude which had supported him under afflictions of another kind, deserted him in this."[70]

Although it would hardly be surprising if in the early years of his blindness Handel felt great distress, that emotion was neither constant nor permanent. From 1756 to 1758, James Harris repeatedly received reports of the composer's good health: "Handel is better than he has been for some years"; "I see Handel frequently who is in good health"; "Your old friend Handel looks plump, & large, & fat."[71] In March 1756, Thomas Harris reported of the oratorio season that Handel's playing on the organ was "as good as ever."[72] Moreover there were positive reports of his playing in private. At the end of 1755, Delany heard Handel play Donnellan's new Kirkman harpsichord at her home in Berkeley Square, and a year later she reported on another such visit to Donnellan's that Handel's playing was delightful.[73] In May we hear about him playing Jennens's fortepiano for the second time: he had first done so in 1740.[74] The portrait of Handel commissioned by Jennens in 1756 shows a stout, elderly man, distinguished in appearance, hardly pale and feeble. He sits with an erect posture and exudes a sense of strength despite his blindness (Image 10.1).

In the last years of his life, Handel's physician was Dr. John Belch-ier, an eminent surgeon and a colleague of Dr. Sharp at Guy's Hospital. A friend of Alexander Pope, Belchier had tried unsuccessfully, years before, to persuade the composer to make a setting of Pope's "Ode for Music."[75] If Sharp recommended his colleague to Handel in the mid-1750s when he himself was affected by ill health, Handel, already having known Belchier from previous years, would have found him a comfortable choice. In the summer of 1758, Handel traveled once more to Tunbridge in the company of Thomas Morell, librettist of *Theodora* and *Jephtha*. He may have gone specifically on the recommendation of Belchier in order to consult the flamboyant Dr. John Taylor, who had adopted the title "Chevalier." Although Taylor's extravagant self-promotion has led to charges that he was a charlatan, he, like both Sharp and Belchier, trained with Cheselden. Once again Handel was couched, and despite the self-laudatory poem Taylor published in the *London Chronicle* (August 24, 1758) about having restored Handel's sight, the procedure, as Thomas Harris wrote to his brother, was not "of any real service" to the composer.[76] Indeed, one wonders about the wisdom of performing yet another operation on a seventy-three-year-old man, which with all the attendant bleedings and purgings could hardly have added to his well-being. Eight years earlier the chevalier had similarly couched Johann Sebastian Bach in Leipzig without success, and the postoperative treatment Bach suffered is thought to have hastened his death.[77]

When illness or events of life moved beyond the agency of human intervention, nothing remained to the terminally ill and their friends but the practice of patience, resignation, and piety. In his correspondence, Percival repeatedly tied these attributes to final illnesses and to death. After the decease of his brother-in-law, he wrote to a friend: "Time can reconcile men to bear the greatest losses with Patience and Resignation but has not always Power to make us insensible and forget-full."[78] On the same occasion, he heard from another brother-in-law: "I hope from your habitual Piety and resignation to the will of God, that you your self will ... bear up under these great Calamitys."[79] And of the death of his sister-in-law he wrote: "'Tis over, and never Woman left the World with more Piety, Resignation, and detachment from Earthly things."[80]

The bare facts of Handel's life do not suggest that resignation was a prominent feature of his last years. Even though he no longer could conduct from the harpsichord, he continued planning for each oratorio season. He played the organ at his concerts at least until 1756, and reports of his playing privately on harpsichord and piano continue through the end of 1756. Shaftesbury wrote in 1757 not only that Handel's "memory is strengthened of late to an astonishing degree," but also that he had been composing.[81] His trip to the spa at Tunbridge in the summer of 1758 and his submission there to yet another surgery strongly suggest that he had not given up hope of an improvement or cure of his blindness. Thomas Harris wrote of repeated visits by the composer to his rooms in Lincoln's Inn Fields; he reported on November 21, 1758: "Handel was with me yesterday: he says he has workd hard, and has made a considerable part of a new oratorio."[82] Handel attended the oratorio season in 1759, which ended with a performance of *Messiah* on April 6, and the next day, the *Whitehall Evening-Post* reported that Handel "proposed setting out for Bath, to try the Benefit of the Waters."[83] Handel was, however, too ill to travel.

If Handel's continuing activity, including his presence at the final concert of his oratorio season in 1759 only eight days before his death, suggest a man who refused to accept his weakened condition and failed to think with piety on his "detachment from Earthly things," his last works offer a different picture—not by any means in a lessening of inspiration but rather in a more personal message intensely drawn. *Jephtha* is the oratorio he was composing in January 1751 when he was forced to recognize, if he hadn't previously, that his eyesight was failing. The story tells of Jephtha's vow to God that if he is successful in battle then what or whoever first greets him on his return "Shall be for ever thine, or fall a Sacrifice."[84] He arrives home triumphant, and it is his beautiful daughter, Iphis, his only child, who runs out to meet him. When family members learn of his vow, each one is thrown into emotional crisis. His wife, Storgé, cries out immediately, "First perish Thou; and perish all the

World!" and in her following aria, "Let other Creatures die," her rage pre-empts the orchestra as she launches into song without any instrumental introduction. Her passion only begins to subside as she describes her daughter, "So fair, so chaste, so good," leading to a silence that is all the more powerful for the aria's explosive beginning.

Iphis reacts to the news that she will be a sacrificial victim with stoic humility, praying, "accept it, Heav'n, / A grateful Victim, and thy Bless-ings still / Pour on my Country, Friends, and dearest Father!" Her aria "Happy they!" (referring to her country, friends, and father) begins with short phrases as she struggles to maintain composure: "Happy they! [silence] This vital Breath [silence] / With content [silence] I shall resign [silence]." The effect is heartbreaking.

In contrast, Jephtha cannot manage an aria, but rather pours out his anguish in one of Handel's most wrenching accompanied recitatives, "Deeper and deeper still." He argues with himself about whether the vow must be carried through, concluding: "it must be so." The silence that follows allows this resolution to settle on his own ears (and those of the audience); it also forms the boundary between Jephtha's internal debate in the first part of the recitative and the frenzied second section (concitato) where, as a father contemplating the sacrifice of a daughter by his own hand, he suffers "a thousand Pangs" that lash him "into Mad-ness." There follows a very slow (largo) section where Jephtha, trying to absorb the fact, simply repeats, "Horrid Thought!" leading to more silence. Finally, as he focuses on the image of his daughter, his voice trails off ("I can no more"). The silences express what cannot be said.[85]

It was while writing the chorus that follows this recitative and closes the second act that failing sight forced Handel to break off composing. He had divided the long text into four parts:

(1) How dark, O Lord, are thy Decrees!
All hid from mortal Sight!
(2) All our Joys to Sorrow turning,
And our Triumphs into Mourning,
As the Night succeeds the Day.

(3) No certain Bliss,
No solid Peace,
We Mortals know
On Earth below.
(4) Yet on this Maxim still obey:
What God ordains, is right.

The first section, comprising the first two lines, begins in a very slow tempo (largo) with the orchestra playing a repeated long-short rhythm that remains unrelenting throughout. Against this, the choral voices enter one at a time with the cry, "How dark!" What Handel felt while composing this text as his eyesight failed can only be imagined. It was at the end of this section that he was forced to stop.

Coming back to the score ten days later, on February 23, he completed the chorus. In the second section, the tempo is somewhat faster (larghetto), but the voices are separated one from another, and many of the musical lines end abruptly without a sense of continuation or closure; the third section is an elaborate choral fugue, the shorter note values and brief ornamental melodic extensions depicting evanescence, and the maxim of the last section provides a strong sense of finality. Handel set the phrase "What God ordains" without instrumental accompaniment, using a single melodic line that spells out an unstable harmony (dominant seventh chord) and demands resolution. This is followed by a pause for the voices during which the orchestra extends the dissonant chord with a unison arpeggio (playing the notes of the chord one at a time going up and down), almost making the phrase into a question and increasing the sense of anticipation. The answer, "is right!" arrives in two cadential chords hammered out by full chorus and orchestra. In the course of the movement, Handel drives home the point harmonically: each time the setting returns he ends it in a different key, and harmonically each one "is right." Handel finished the chorus on February 27, and did not return to *Jephtha* until June, when he began Act III.

There is more to the story of this chorus, however. At a late point in the compositional process, Handel went through the score and changed the original words of the maxim to "Whatever is, is right!" the Deist sentiment coming from Pope's *An Essay on Man*. Was this Handel's reaction to his failing eyesight? Is it an angry turning away from a God who would visit blindness upon a creative artist to a belief in a more impersonal clockwork universe? It is tempting to think so, as we know Handel was at his most despairing at the beginning of his blindness, and the musical setting of the maxim almost seems to confirm it. Further, although one might be tempted to argue that the setting is uniquely appropriate to its text, Handel in fact borrowed it from Theodora's aria "Fond, flatt'ring World, adieu!" He must have done so deliberately. *Theodora* immediately preceded *Jephtha* in composition and had been premiered only the previous season. Handel's linking of Theodora's resignation to Pope's fatalistic text paints a painful picture of deep personal anguish.

If Handel's last two works, *Theodora* and *Jephtha*, written, respectively, when the composer was sixty-four and sixty-six, seem reflective of a close spiritual relationship to God and personal, it must be remembered that Handel didn't write the texts. That does not mean, however, that he was not involved in the choice of subject or in the actual wording. Throughout his career, he turned down texts he chose not to set: a libretto by Mary Delany based on Milton's *Paradise Lost* and Pope's "Ode for Music" as suggested by Belchier are two examples. *Theodora* and *Jephtha* have important themes in common that would have resonated with Handel as he coped with his blindness. Both depict the necessity of acceptance. "His Will be done," says Didymus to Theodora. "It must be so," says Jephtha as he contemplates his vow. If, however, Handel even briefly harbored fatalistic, Deist views, both oratorios also offered him the hope of God's intervention through prayer, and the appeals that Theodora and Jephtha make to angels elicited from him two arias of aching beauty: "Angels, ever bright, and fair, / Take, O take me to your Care" for Theodora, and "Waft her, Angels, through the skies" for Jephtha. In both *Theodora* and *Jephtha*, innocence is protected from evil, if not from death: Theodora is rescued from the fate of forced prostitution and dies in God's care, and Iphis is spared death at the hands of her father when an angel explains that Jephtha's vow does not require that she be sacrificed but rather that she dedicate her life to God in "Pure, angelic, Virgin-state" (a judgment, however, that sacrificed any possibility of progeny to Jephtha and his wife and brought death to their line of descent). Morell's report long after Handel's death that in his last years the composer considered the chorus at the end of Act II in *Theodora*, "He saw the lovely Youth," far superior to the "Hallelujah Chorus" must, despite the obvious opportunity for bias on Morell's part or generosity on Handel's, be afforded some credence. Completely contrary to the tenets of Deism, it gives powerful expression to the miracle of resurrection.[86]

Handel's last collaboration with Morell was a revival of the composer's first oratorio, *Il trionfo del Tempo e del Disinganno*, written in Rome in 1707, which had already been revised and expanded in 1737 and 1739 as *Il trionfo del Tempo e della Verità*.[87] It describes the journey of a human soul (Beauty) toward transcendence and truth. In 1757, the oratorio, now titled *The Triumph of Time and Truth*, was further expanded with airs and choruses from throughout Handel's career, and Morell was given the responsibility of fitting English words to the previously composed music.[88] John Christopher Smith Jr., who worked closely with Handel and had taken over the direction of the oratorios, was involved in the preparation of the revision, but given all the reports of Handel's good health and greatly improved memory in 1757, one can assume that the composer took the lead in the collaboration. His decision, at the end of his life, to return to this particular work deserves consideration.

Handel's first revision of *Il trionfo* in 1737 and 1739 had appeared as one of a set of compositions involving a narrative or dramatic progression to heavenly realms. In each of these works—*Alexander's Feast* (1736), *Il trionfo* (1737 and 1739), and *Ode for St. Cecilia's Day* (1739)—Handel had marked the arrival at this higher spiritual plane with a concerto or an aria that included a virtuoso organ part for him to play (as discussed in Chapter 8). Revivals of both *Alexander's Feast* and *Ode for St. Cecilia* in 1755 might, therefore, explain Handel's renewed interest in *Il trionfo* at this time, but those works had remained in repertoire since their premieres and neither was overhauled as was *Il trionfo*. In a sense, there was no obvious reason for Handel to have turned back to this early work. Throughout the 1750s, Handel's great English oratorios were being regularly performed, and it can hardly be the case that Handel thought the expansion of an earlier work with a mélange of movements adapted from prior compositions would stand up to such oratorios as *Israel in Egypt, Judas Maccabaeus, Belshazzar, Jephtha,* and *Messiah.*

Certainly, history has been unkind to *The Triumph of Time and Truth,* largely dismissing it as being of little musical value. Its importance to Handel may, however, have been otherwise, and the only credible reason for him to have made the effort he did is that he found particular meaning in the text. On the one hand, the libretto offered a personal story of the human soul overcoming obstacles on the path to truth and grace; on the other, it suggested a professional statement that time would reveal the artistic truth of his work—a similar gesture to that made by Gian Lorenzo Bernini in the sculpture he left his family of *Truth Unveiled by Time.*[89] Bernini died in 1680, and in 1713 his son Domenico Bernini wrote of the popularity of the sculpture in his biography of his father: "The beauty of this work brought many great popes to see it, and even more often Queen Christina of Sweden and all the princes living in Rome; in fact there is not a sovereign or other (noble) who for devotion or affairs came to the city, that as soon as they arrived did not ask after the *Truth* of Bernini and come to his house to admire it as a thing, unique in this world."[90] It seems likely that when Handel was in Rome in 1707 and 1708 he would have heard the story and seen the work. Forty years later, as he came face-to-face with his own death, the composer may have made a connection between Bernini's sculpture and his own *Triumph of Time and Truth.* While in the original version of the oratorio in 1707 the twenty-two-year-old Handel was placed in Pleasure's palace as a luxury to be renounced by the soul (Beauty), and in the first revisions of 1737 and 1739 the fifty-two-year-old virtuoso placed himself on the ramparts of heaven to greet Beauty's arrival at the end of the oratorio, in *The Triumph of Time and Truth* of 1757, the seventy-two-year-old composer seems to have identified himself implicitly with the role of Beauty, with a soul reflecting on life's journey.

With this possibility in mind, certain of the changes take on special meaning. The subject of illness plays a new role, and, in the last act, Beauty renounces her former ways with the realization that she will otherwise have no comfort in sickness. Her aria is followed by the inclusion of one of the choruses from the Foundling Hospital Anthem (1749), "Comfort them, O Lord, when they are sick. / Make Thou their Bed in Sickness. / Keep them alive; let them be blessed upon the Earth." It is also striking that Beauty's path is obstructed not only by Pleasure, but also by Deceit, a new character. Although this addition offers a new symmetry, pitting Time and Counsel (formerly Undeceiver) against Pleasure and Deceit, it also highlights the difference between Deceit and Pleasure. Whereas the new arias for Deceit urge Beauty to ignore Time and think only in the moment, it is Pleasure, a seducer, who offers her the delights to enjoy. Importantly, neither Handel nor his music appears in Pleasure's palace in any guise; instead there are hunting horns (the horn flourish being perhaps the only wholly new music in the score) and an invitation to celebrate the hunt with Flora. Beauty's rejection of Pleasure thus resonates with Theodora's rejection of the worship of Flora demanded by the Roman governor Valens. When Counsel warns Beauty that "Vain [are] the Delights of Age or Youth, / Without the Sanction and Applause of *Truth*," she finds it difficult "To leave this Scene for Immortality." Only after dismissing Deceit, can Beauty take her "last Adieu" of Pleasure and, like Theodora after taking her adieu of the "Fond, flatt'ring World," turn her eyes toward heaven.

Although the translation from the Italian libretto may be Morell's, and the parallels with—or borrowings from—his text of *Theodora* are striking, it was Handel who made the decision to revive this work one more time, and it is just possible that he now heard in the words of Beauty's final aria his own "last Adieu" to the stage.

Guardian Angels, O, protect me,
And in Virtue's Path direct me,
    While resign'd to Heav'n above.
Let no more this World deceive me,

Nor vain idle Passions grieve me,
    Strong in Faith, in Hope, in Love.

The text suggests that Handel had accepted the prospect of death. No longer needing to trade with or vainly seek approval from the purveyors of Pleasure and Deceit, as he had been urged to do at a number of points in his career, the seventy-two-year-old, blind Handel could imagine a future in which his music would be given "the Sanction and Applause of *Truth.*" Two years later, on April 14, 1759, he died in his own bed, having made peace with his friends and, according to James Smyth, who was with him nearly to the end, "in perfect charity with all the world."

GEORGE FREDERICK HANDEL Esq.
born February XXIII. MDCLXXXIV.
died April XIV. MDCCLIX.   L.F.Roubiliac inv! et sc!

11.1 Marble monument of Handel by Louis-François Roubiliac, 1759, Westminster Abbey, London (© The Dean and Chapter of Westminster)

ELEVEN

Wills and Legacies

HANDEL'S LEGACY TO POSTERITY was his music. He took the first step toward its preservation by bequeathing all his music books—his own work and that of others—to his amanuensis, John Christopher Smith Sr., in his original will of 1750. At Smith's death in 1763 the collection passed to his son and namesake, John Christopher Smith Jr., who some years afterward gave Handel's autographs to George III in gratitude for having been granted a life pension. As William Coxe, Smith Jr.'s stepson, put it: "In the fullness of his heartfelt acknowledgment, [Smith] presented to the King the rich legacy which Handel had left him, of all his manuscript music, in score."[1] The autographs were thereafter kept as part of the Royal Music Library, until 1911, when King George V deposited the collection in the British Museum on permanent loan. In 1957, Queen Elizabeth II presented the Music Library to the Trustees of the British Museum as a gift.[2] Handel's will itself did not assure the preservation of his manuscripts in a single collection, but his gift to Smith started the series of actions that ultimately guaranteed it.

Handel's friends, also at times unwittingly, left a significant though lesser imprint on posterity. In some cases, their wills provided a testament to their hope that something they had shaped in life would be preserved or that a lasting legacy might be created in death. In other cases, an action they took in life turned out to ensure the preservation of artwork that might otherwise have been lost. The story of Handel and his friends would not be complete without following each of them

WILLS AND LEGACIES: *Timeline*

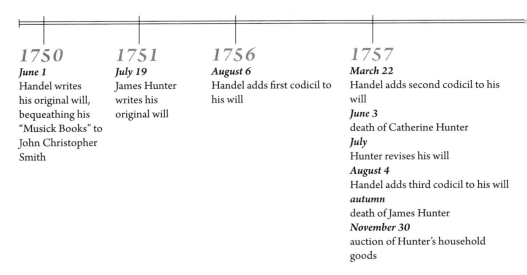

1750
June 1
Handel writes
his original will,
bequeathing his
"Musick Books" to
John Christopher
Smith

1751
July 19
James Hunter
writes his
original will

1756
August 6
Handel adds first codicil to
his will

1757
March 22
Handel adds second codicil to his
will
June 3
death of Catherine Hunter
July
Hunter revises his will
August 4
Handel adds third codicil to his will
autumn
death of James Hunter
November 30
auction of Hunter's household
goods

to their deaths and witnessing how their lives and legacies continued
to interact.

After Handel wrote his will in 1750, he left it alone for years, only
returning to it when he needed to make alterations due to the deaths of
previously named legatees. In the first codicil, of 1756, he adjusted for
the deaths of two German relatives and made contingency plans in case
of the death of another, but he also took the opportunity to augment the
bequests to two of the people who had been closest to him, especially
in his blindness: his primary manservant Peter LeBlond and Smith Sr.
These generous bequests were only possible because the annual oratorio series had continued to generate a significant profit for Handel even
after he ceased composing new works. Perhaps in acknowledgment of
this source of income, he also added bequests to two of his oratorio
librettists: Newburgh Hamilton and Thomas Morell. Finally, he named
George Amyand, a London merchant and Member of Parliament, coexecutor to serve jointly with his German niece Johanna Floercke, a decision that probably was recommended to him to facilitate the execution
of the will.[3]

In March 1757, Handel needed to add another codicil, on the death

1758
June
Hunter's dyeing equipment
sold at auction

1759
April 11
Handel adds fourth and final
codicil to his will
April 14
death of George Frideric Handel
June 26
Hunter's dye house sold

1761
April 14
final "dividend" offered to
Hunter's creditors

of his servant LeBlond. He transferred his bequest to LeBlond's nephew, John Duburk, who had replaced him, and added a much smaller bequest to his next underservant Thomas Bramwell. In his original will and in successive codicils, Handel generally recognized and rewarded the assistance of his servants before any other considerations; as his dependence on them increased in his last years, so did his acknowledgment of their service. In August 1757, Handel again returned to his will on the death of another German relative, which necessitated further adjustments. He also identified recipients for some of his largest and most valuable possessions, again focusing on people who had been essential to the success of his oratorios. To John Rich, the manager of the theaters at Lincoln's Inn Fields and Covent Garden, where many of his oratorios were performed, he left the "great" organ he had originally purchased in 1745 for the King's Theatre, but which was now situated in Covent Garden, and to Charles Jennens and Bernard Granville, both of whom must have advised him on his art collection, he left paintings. (Two other friends who shared their enthusiasm for collecting art, Christopher Batt and Ralph Palmer, had predeceased him.) Finally, he left "a fair copy of the Score and all the parts of my Oratorio called *The Messiah* to the Found-

Wills and Legacies continued

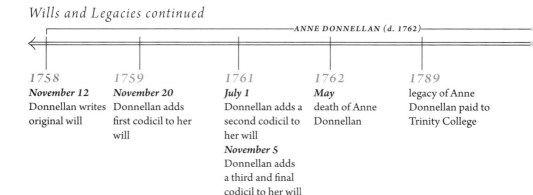

<table>
<tr><td>1758</td><td>1759</td><td>1761</td><td>1762</td><td>1789</td></tr>
</table>

ANNE DONNELLAN (d. 1762)

1758	1759	1761	1762	1789
November 12 Donnellan writes original will	*November 20* Donnellan adds first codicil to her will	*July 1* Donnellan adds a second codicil to her will *November 5* Donnellan adds a third and final codicil to her will	*May* death of Anne Donnellan	legacy of Anne Donnellan paid to Trinity College

ling Hospital," in a way compensating them for his earlier refusal to allow them the rights to the work through Parliament.

The final codicil to Handel's will resulted from the composer's own failing health rather than the deaths of any of his legatees. This last codicil was written on April 11, 1759, five days after he had attended *Messiah*, the final performance of the oratorio season, and three days before his death. As in his original will and earlier codicils, the order of the bequests reflects Handel's personal circumstances, but now differently. Whereas in the previous documents Handel had moved geographically from those nearest him to those farthest away, starting in all cases with the servants who had care of his day-to-day physical needs, then to his closest friends and professional colleagues, and finally to his German relatives, in this final codicil, the order is somewhat altered, now moving outward from his immediate, personal circumstances to the recognition of social and professional ties.

With the experience of having had his career curtailed by illness and ultimately cut off by blindness, Handel made the first bequest in this final codicil to "the Governours or Trustees of the Society for the Support of decayed Musicians and their Families one Thousand pounds to be disposed of in the most beneficiall manner for the objects of that Charity." He then increased his gift to his London executor, Amyand, and added bequests to the lawyers, his friend Thomas Harris and acquaintance John Hetherington, who had assisted him in the codicils and perhaps with the

1794	1763	1764	1768
February 22	*January*	*June 18*	*December 30*
establishment of the Donnellan Lecture at Trinity College (ongoing)	death of John Christopher Smith; Handel's "Musick Books" pass to his son, John Christopher Smith Jr.	Elizabeth Palmer's account at the Bank of England closed; last historical record	death of Elizabeth Mayne *May 6* death of Patrick Delany

original will as well. Handel's next gift, to James Smyth, the perfumer of Bond Street, identifies a person who must have helped Handel intimately in his last years. He was a close neighbor and probably served Handel in a professional capacity, especially in the final years.

11.2 Original signboard (1728) for the business of James Smyth, perfumer, who worked "at the sign of the civet cat" (courtesy private collection / photograph Pete Tripp)

Wills and Legacies continued

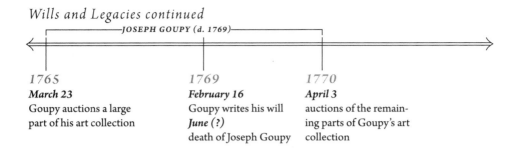

1765	1769	1770
March 23	**February 16**	**April 3**
Goupy auctions a large part of his art collection	Goupy writes his will	auctions of the remaining parts of Goupy's art collection
	June (?)	
	death of Joseph Goupy	

Smyth is the last person known to have been with Handel before his death, a situation Bernard Granville seems to have anticipated in his request to Smyth that he write him with the news when Handel died. Handel's next gift was to the violinist Matthew Dubourg, who led the orchestra in Dublin at the premiere of *Messiah* in 1742 and in Covent Garden, London, during the 1743 oratorio season: Dubourg was the only musician singled out by Handel in his will, and his more permanent return to London in 1752 to take up the position as leader of the King's Band suggests that he and Handel may have become close personal friends in the last years of the composer's life.

Continuing the series of bequests to those who had directly assisted him in the previous two years, personally, professionally, or medically, Handel increased the gift to his underservant Thomas Bramwell, surely in gratitude for additional caregiving necessitated by his blindness and physical condition. He then turned to Benjamin Martyn, an amanuensis of Lord Shaftesbury and a member of the Harris-Shaftesbury circle. Like the perfumer Smyth, Martyn lived around the corner on Bond Street; he was close to the composer by at least 1745, when Shaftesbury wrote of Handel to James Harris that on "most days he calls on Mr. Martyn."[4] In later years, he seems to have assisted Handel with the management of the oratorio seasons: Thomas Harris wrote to his brother in 1757 that he would send to Mr. Martyn "to know Handel's scheme of performances."[5] Handel next remembered his medical caregivers, giving bequests to the surgeon John Belchier and the apothecary John Gowland. Belchier was the doctor who took over from Sharp in the mid-1750s (see Chapter 10); Gowland, like Smyth and Martyn, lived on Bond Street (where he rented rooms to Goupy in the 1730s) and so was a close neighbor as well. Smyth reported in his letter to Granville that on the day before his death, Handel "desired to see nobody but the Doctor and Apothecary and myself."[6] Finally, Handel made sure that his original bequest of his "Clothes and Linen" to his late servant LeBlond was transferred to the nephew Duburk ("all my wearing apparel").

Having thus dealt with all his closest legal and medical advisers, as well as close professional associates and manservants, Handel turned to his own burial, a typical item in eighteenth-century English wills. However, unlike most will writers, he did not ask to be buried at his parish church, St. George Hanover Square, but requested permission of the "Dean and Chapter of Westminster to be buried in Westminster Abbey." He also left up to £600 for a monument. The permission granted, the provision for a monument resulted in a grand sculpture by Roubiliac: Handel stands in front of an organ with the score of *Messiah* (apparently resting on a table, on and under which lie an assortment of modern instruments) lying open before him to "I know that my redeemer liveth." Hovering above him an angel-like figure, identified by early commentators as David, plays the harp, and it seems almost as if the composer is transfixed by hearing the sound of his own music emanating from (or welcoming him to) heaven.[7] Handel made no mention in his will of who should create the monument, but Roubiliac was the obvious candidate for the job: his sculpture of Handel for Vauxhall Gardens in 1738 had become an iconic image, and he was famous for dramatic funerary monuments. He appears to have been immediately commissioned. A death mask of the composer taken by the sculptor, now lost, is said to have formed the basis for the likeness of the face. Handel thus became the alpha and omega of Roubiliac's career in London: the statue of the composer for Vauxhall Gardens established his reputation, and the Handel monument was his last work.

In many ways, Handel's request to the dean and chapter of Westminster and his setting aside funds for a monument would seem to be a natural conclusion to this final codicil, but there is a striking continuation. Other than various female relatives in Germany, including his niece Johanna,

Wills and Legacies continued

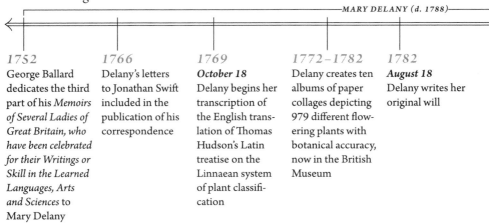

MARY DELANY (d. 1788)

1752
George Ballard
dedicates the third
part of his *Memoirs
of Several Ladies of
Great Britain, who
have been celebrated
for their Writings or
Skill in the Learned
Languages, Arts
and Sciences* to
Mary Delany

1766
Delany's letters
to Jonathan Swift
included in the
publication of his
correspondence

1769
October 18
Delany begins her
transcription of
the English trans-
lation of Thomas
Hudson's Latin
treatise on the
Linnaean system
of plant classifi-
cation

1772–1782
Delany creates ten
albums of paper
collages depicting
979 different flow-
ering plants with
botanical accuracy,
now in the British
Museum

1782
August 18
Delany writes her
original will

whom he named co-executor and residuary legatee, Handel had not mentioned women in the previous will documents. Suddenly this changes,
with a £100 legacy to "Mrs Palmer of Chelsea Widow of Mr Palmer formerly of Chappel Street." This bequest to a woman apparently led him to
think for the first time of his two maidservants. They are not named, and
their concern would have been with household matters rather than his
person; Handel left to each of them a year's wages beyond what was owed
to them. The reason for Handel's bequest to Mrs. Palmer is not known.
There is no correspondence or other documentary evidence identifying
her as a social friend, as there is for Delany and Donnellan, and Handel's unlikely juxtaposition of her bequest with those given to his maidservants suggests that he may have thought of her as needy. Given her
rejection by the Palmer and Verney families at the time of her marriage
because of her lack of social status, and her decision to auction many of
her husband's possessions after his death, including the Palmer family's
fine picture collection, it would appear her sources of income as a widow
were few. But one supposes that there was more than charity on Handel's mind and that, as with Donnellan and Delany, Palmer knew Handel
socially and had shared musical interests. The inventory of her father's
house at the time of his death included four violins in cases, providing
some evidence that Palmer had music in her life from childhood.

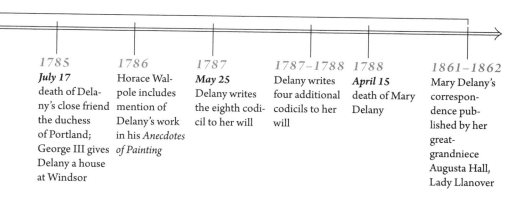

1785
July 17
death of Delany's close friend the duchess of Portland; George III gives Delany a house at Windsor

1786
Horace Walpole includes mention of Delany's work in his *Anecdotes of Painting*

1787
May 25
Delany writes the eighth codicil to her will

1787–1788
Delany writes four additional codicils to her will

1788
April 15
death of Mary Delany

1861–1862
Mary Delany's correspondence published by her great-grandniece Augusta Hall, Lady Llanover

After naming the maidservants, Handel continued remembering women with the inclusion of both Elizabeth Mayne and Anne Donnellan. That he did not include Delany is at first surprising. The reason for the omission may simply be the focus of this final codicil, in which Handel was specifically acknowledging those with whom he was still actively engaged. As Delany was living in Dublin, she was not a part of his immediate circle at the time of his death (see Chapter 6). The last bequest went to Johann Reiche, secretary for the affairs of Hanover in London. It is not known if, or how, Reiche was active in Handel's life during the composer's final years, but as with the other gifts Handel made, this one was probably given in both friendship and gratitude.

Handel's death on April 14, 1759 set in motion the legal actions necessary to prove the will. As the original will of 1750 was not witnessed at the time of writing, two witnesses swore an oath that they were "well acquainted with his Manner and Character of hand Writing" and testified that the "whole body and Contents of the said Will" were in his hand. The next day, Handel's servant Duburk testified that he was present when the will and all its codicils "were all found locked and sealed up together in a Cover" in a bureau in Handel's house, and that when it was found the "Bequest therein to Mr James Hunter" was partially obliterated (as it now appears). He stated that "he well knew the said James

Wills and Legacies continued

1818

thirteenth-century illuminated Bible and illuminated
twelfth-century commentary by
Hugh of Saint-Victor previously
owned by Ralph Palmer, Lord
Verney, and Charles Burney, passed
to the British Museum as part of
the Burney Collection

1901 (?)

Rubens's oil sketch for
The Elevation of the Cross,
previously owned by
Christopher Batt, and having
remained continuously in the
Batt-Buckley families, passed
to the Louvre

1911

George V deposits
Handel's autograph
manuscripts in the British
Museum as part of the
Royal Music Library

Hunter the Legatee and the said James Hunter died in the Life time of the said Mr Handel the Testator." Handel's bequest to Hunter, following the form of the other bequests in his original will, contained a gift of some material object followed by a monetary gift, but the former has been so inked over in both copies by Handel that it remains undecipherable today (even with digital technology). Either Handel gave Hunter the item or items during his lifetime, or he changed his mind about making the gift at all. What remained of the bequest was the very generous monetary gift of £500. However, Hunter had died a year and a half earlier in the autumn of 1757.

Hunter also left a will. His original testament, dated July 19, 1751, left everything to his wife, Catherine.[8] He only returned to the will after her death in June 1757, changing his heir and executor to his brother-in-law and leaving more specific directions about his musical instruments, music books, and dye house. None of these instructions was followed. Since Hunter had never been released from bankruptcy, his entire estate was put up for auction to pay his debts. An announcement for the auction of his household goods on November 30 appeared in the *Public Advertiser* on November 16, 1757:

> To be SOLD by AUCTION . . . ALL the genuine Houshold
> Goods, Plate, China, Linen and Books, likewise all the Stock
> of Dye Wares, Horses, Cart, Chaise, &c. of Mr. James Hunter,

1920

Rembrandt's *Man in Oriental Costume,*
previously owned by Ralph Palmer, Sir Paul
Methuen and his family, William II of the
Netherlands, and the Vanderbilt family,
passed to the Metropolitan Museum

1957

Queen Elizabeth II
presents the Royal Music
Library to the Trustees of
the British Museum

Scarlet Dyer, deceased, at his late Dwelling House at Old Ford,
near Bow, Middlesex. The Goods consist of all Sorts of very good
useful Kitchen and other Furniture; likewise a double-key'd
Harpsichord [called "curious" in later announcements], by Shudi,
a fine Violin, and sundry Sorts of Flutes, and a great Variety of
Manuscript and printed Music Books....

In April 1758, the "large commodious dyehouse and dwelling-house,
and the Dyehouse Plant in complete Repair . . . situated in Oldford, near
Bow, late in the Occupation of Mr. James Hunter" were advertised for
rent.[9] In June, all of Hunter's dyeing equipment was tendered at auction.[10] According to the Hand-in-Hand Insurance Company records,
Hunter's executors turned over the ownership of Hunter's dye house on
June 26, 1759, to one Jonathan Haggard, Esq., and Haggard renewed the
policy himself on July 10.[11] Finally on April 14, 1761, the "creditors of
James Hunter" were informed of what must have been a final dividend
based on the proceeds of the sale and auction of Hunter's property.[12]

Hunter's financial problems, as well as his removal from London to
Old Ford, might lead one to assume that he was an obscure bankrupt,
but in fact, he left a strong reputation behind him as a man who aspired
to excellence in music and collected at great expense manuscript copies
"of all the music of Handel that he could procure." At least John Hawkins described him this way at the end of the eighteenth century, when

he further identified him as one of Handel's few intimate friends and one
of only two who "seemed to possess most of his confidence" (the other
being Goupy).[13] In the mid-nineteenth century, the Handel manuscript
collection "of Mr. Hunter (the dyer)" was well enough known to be
listed, in the auction catalogue offering Bernard Granville's collection
for sale, as one of only six such collections made, but it was "believed
to have been broken up and lost."[14] When the Granville Collection was
purchased by the British Library in 1916 and subsequently listed in the
library's *Catalogue of Additions to the Manuscripts 1916–1920*, it still
was known that specific pages in the manuscripts were "in the hand of
James Hunter, described by Hawkins . . . as a 'dyer of Old ford,' and
an enthusiastic admirer of Handel and his works."[15] After this recognition, however, Hunter disappeared from history for more than eighty
years. When the first accounting was made of Handel's copyists in the
mid-1950s, the pages written by Hunter in both the Granville and the
so-called Lennard Collections were identified only by the anonymous
designation "S7" (Scribe 7).[16] My investigation into the lives of Handel's
legatees enabled the work of S7 to be reconnected with Hunter, and subsequently a further manuscript (signed with his initials) to be identified
as fully copied by him.[17]

In addition, the discovery that Hunter fell into bankruptcy in 1741
has offered a solution to a mystery of the Lennard Collection (named
for its nineteenth-century owner), whose initial collection of forty-nine
volumes was abruptly broken off in that year (see Chapter 7). That is,
it seems likely that this collection, now preserved at the Fitzwilliam
Museum, Cambridge, contains at its core Hunter's great legacy to posterity: a collection of Handel manuscripts, assembled on account of his
love of the music and purchased at so dear a price as to play a role in his
fall into the bankruptcy from which he was never released. Like Handel,
Hunter probably hoped to keep his manuscript collection intact by leaving it to a person who would have understood its worth. Although his
bankruptcy prevented the fulfillment of the specific bequest he made
of his music books to the publisher John Walsh, the collection was preserved nevertheless. Fortunately for posterity, whoever bought the music

books at auction, and it may have been Walsh, kept the Handel manuscripts together, as did the subsequent owners through Henry Barrett Lennard, whose son presented it to the Fitzwilliam Museum in 1902.[18]

Anne Donnellan died in May 1762. Her will offers something of a female counterpart to Handel's.[19] In her original will, of 1758, for example, she set up the necessary administration for enacting the will in two countries, appointing an executor in both Ireland and England, and she made sure that her wishes concerning her family were clearly laid out. The will can be parsed in three distinct sections. In the first, she addressed the "Mistake and Defect" in her younger brother Christopher's will that enabled their older brother Nehemiah to take possession of a lease on Christopher's property in Brannockstown, County Kildare. This had prevented her, Christopher's executrix, from selling the real estate as devised by him "towards the discharge of his several pious charitable and friendly Legacies." This defect and the resultant legal costs of carrying the will through the Court of Chancery had expended two-thirds of what her brother had wanted to bequeath. As a result, her first direction to her Irish executor was that he raise £1,000 through a mortgage she held on "my Brother Nehemiah's Lease of the aforesaid Brenockstown" and with that sum to "pay to every charitable and other Legatee in my said Brother Christopher's Will who shall be then living."

In the second section, she requested that her English executor "sell and dispose of my House and Stables and Coach House in Charles Street Berkley Square (which I built myself) towards the discharge of my several Legacies." These included monetary gifts of various sizes to family members and charitable institutions in Ireland, and very generous provisions for her nurse Anne Shuttleworth and servant Anne Philpot, including a life annuity to Shuttleworth and "all my wearing Apparel and Linnen" to Philpot (as Handel left "all my wearing apparel" to Duburk). She left further gifts to other named servants, possibly seven in all. Finally, in the third section, after using real estate in different ways to effect her first two sets of bequests, she referred to the personal estate of the late Capt. Thomas Whorwood, a first cousin of her stepfather, Philip

Percival, in which she would have a right after the death of the Percival cousin who held a life interest.[20] With the understanding that this would amount to at least £1,000, she left "whatever may come" from the estate to "the Provost and the Segnior Fellows of Trinity College Dublin" in whatever way they "shall judge most conducive towards promoting of Religion Learning and good manners in the said University."

A year later, practically on the anniversary of her original will, Donnellan added a codicil for the purpose of remembering friends. As her disposable income was minuscule—at her death she had £163 10s. 3d. in her account at Goslings Bank—these were mementoes and gifts of remembrance from among her possessions.[21] She left to her "dear Friend M[rs] Delany all my prints and Drawings in Books and Sheets also my Dressing Table japan and my old China Ware," and to her "dear Friend M[rs] Elizabeth Montague my great Indian Cabinet and also her picture which She gave me." These and other bequests in Donnellan's will indicate the value she placed on goods and furniture either imported from the Far East (the Indian Cabinet and China Ware) or modeled on eastern techniques (the "Dressing Table japan" was likely "japanned" to imitate Japanese black-lacquered furniture). Also significant, in terms of their personal value, are gifts of her artwork ("all my prints and Drawings"), art returned to the original giver (as Handel did also in returning the painting attributed to Rembrandt to Bernard Granville), and portraits of friends. For example, she left to her "dear Friend and Cousin Mary Forth . . . M[rs] Delany's picture set in Gold," to "my Kind Friend M[r] Bernard Granville his Sister Delany's Picture in Oyle and also his Choice of any two Pictures in my House," and to "M[rs] Dewes their Sister all the Pictures in my House done by M[rs] Delany." She concluded, "I hope all my Friends will accept of these triffles as tokens of my grateful Affection."

The death of her former nurse, Anne Shuttleworth, obliged her in July 1761 (as the death of his manservant LeBlond had earlier obliged Handel) to add a second codicil. Mostly this is taken up with a redistribution of her former gifts to Shuttleworth, but at the end of the codicil she added one new bequest: "I leave Handel's picture in Enamel to the British Museum." This gift is duly recorded among the accessions of the bourgeoning museum, which had been established only in 1753: "1762. June 11. An enameled picture by [Rupert] Barber, set in gold, of George Frederick Handel: left to this Museum by Mrs. Donnellan and presented by her Executor, Edward Legrand Esq."[22] Unfortunately, there is no trace of the picture today.

Wills were affected not only by issues of life and death but also by illness. In a final codicil written in November 1761, and prefiguring Goupy's will of 1769, Donnellan altered another one of her bequests on the news that her nephew Col. Nehemiah Donnellan "is under an Alienation of mind and is in Confinement for the same." As a result, she transferred his legacy into the hands of a relative "to be disposed of as he shall judge proper for the use of the said Col. Donnellan my Nephew and in case of his death . . . to his own use."

Although her bequest of Handel's portrait to the British Museum did not prove a lasting legacy, the gift of her interest in the Whorwood estate to Trinity College did. The relative who held a life interest in the estate did not die until 1785, and it was not until 1789 that Donnellan's legacy was paid out. An extract from the Registry of Trinity College, dated February 22, 1794, confirms the gift:

> Whereas a legacy of One thousand two hundred and forty-three Pounds, has been bequeathed to the College of Dublin by Mrs. Anne Donnellan for the encouragement of Religion, Learning, and good Manners; the particular mode of application being entrusted to the Provost and Senior Fellows:—
>
> Resolved,
>
> I. That a Divinity Lecture, to which shall be annexed a Salary, arising from the interest of One thousand two hundred Pounds, shall be established for ever, to be called *Donnellan's Lecture*.
>
> II. That the Lecturer shall be forthwith elected from among the Fellows of said College, and hereafter annually on the 20th of November.
>
> III. That the subject or subjects of the Lectures shall be

determined at the time of election by the board, to be treated of in six Sermons . . .

IV. That one moiety of the interest of the said £1200 shall be paid to the Lecturer, as soon as he shall have delivered the whole number of Lectures; and the other moiety as soon as he shall have published four of the said Lectures . . .[23]

Given the intense concern expressed by Handel's circle about the threat of Deism (with its belief in a clockwork universe devoid of divine intervention) and Donnellan's own turn to Hutchinsonianism (with its attempt to show, in opposition to modern Newtonian science, that all of natural history could be found explicated in the Bible), it seems appropriate that the first set of lectures in 1795 was delivered on the topic "The proof of Christianity derived from the miracles recorded in the New Testament."[24] In 1989, however, the home of the Donnellan Lectures shifted into the Department of Philosophy at Trinity College. Since that time, they have been offered every three years and dominated by eminent American philosophers, including Martha Nussbaum, Richard Rorty, and Stanley Cavell.

The two other women of Handel's will, Elizabeth Mayne and Elizabeth Palmer, died after Donnellan. Palmer passes out of the historical record in 1764 with the closing out of her account in 3 percent consolidated annuities at the Bank of England. Although there are no further accounts, there is also no evidence of her death or of a will. Her husband left her a life interest in the house on Curzon Street "together with all its offices and appurtenances," empowering her to sell any or all of it, but similarly giving her only a life interest in the proceeds, as also in his real estate holdings and his financial instruments of all kinds. Therefore, there was no reason for Elizabeth Palmer to make a will, as her husband had already bequeathed everything to his brother on her death. The inheritance that Elizabeth herself brought to the marriage from her father is valued differently in various sources. One newspaper report claimed that she had a fortune of £20,000. Lord Verney in a note to himself about the match wrote down that she received £500 from her father's will, and that the full estate was valued at £6,000 in monies and real estate. In fact, she received £2,500 from her father's will, but the early death of her brother brought her also her father's real estate, of unspecified value, in the counties of Suffolk, Oxford, and Durham. It is difficult to believe that Ralph and Elizabeth Palmer ran through all of these assets, as well as the inheritance Palmer had received in monies and real estate from his family, in their eight years of marriage, but Elizabeth's immediate auctioning of the Curzon Street house and its contents after her husband's death suggests this to have been the case. Given adequate funds she could have continued living well among its splendor and, if she had wanted to annoy the Palmer-Verney family, squandered the inheritance slowly. It seems, instead, that Ralph Palmer is the one who squandered the wealth he gained through both inheritance and marriage and that Elizabeth did what she needed to raise enough money to live and, probably, to pay debts.

Lord Verney bought back at least some of his maternal inheritance at the auction, choosing some of the most valuable books and pictures. It was his grandfather John Verney, whose wife was a Palmer, who had restored the Verney family's finances following the English Civil War (1642–1651) as a result of his work for the Levant Company as a merchant trader. His son, Ralph, the first earl Verney, used this inheritance to expand his land holdings, but did little otherwise to solidify the family's assets—although he was the Verney who so colorfully expressed his irritation at Ralph Palmer's marriage on the back of a letter. At his death in 1753, his son Ralph, the childhood comrade of Ralph Palmer, became the second earl Verney, and it was he who bought back his family's Palmer inheritance at the Curzon Street auction. Ironically, however, he seems to have had the same urge toward financial extravagance as his friend Palmer, and he ultimately bankrupted the Verney family, whose possessions were scattered. Lord Verney and his wife therefore spent their final years living quietly in the house on Curzon Street that Palmer had so richly furnished years before.

The valuable books and pictures in Palmer's collection were not maintained intact as a single collection, but Elizabeth's decision to auction them in 1756 set in motion the events that led to their survival in many libraries and museums today. The thirteenth-century illuminated Bible and the illuminated twelfth-century commentary by Hugh of Saint-Victor passed from Palmer to the second earl Verney to the music historian Charles Burney and finally, as part of Burney's library, to the British Museum in 1818. Rembrandt's *Man in Oriental Costume* (called the "Great Bashaw" in the Palmer auction) passed to Goupy's patron Paul Methuen and his family, thereafter to William II of the Netherlands, and then to the Vanderbilt family in New York, from whose collection it passed to the Metropolitan Museum (New York). If the Palmer collection had passed to Elizabeth's brother-in-law, Hamey Palmer, the most valuable books and pictures might not have been similarly preserved. Hamey served as a Gentleman Usher of the Privy Chamber at £200 per year and died in 1771 leaving what little he had to his two underage children. His son Hamey Palmer Jr., circling back to the life decisions made by his great-uncle John Verney, made his living with the East India Company and died as a major general in the Bengal Army at Barrackpore in 1811.

Elizabeth Mayne died in 1768 with £1,700 in her account of 3 percent consolidated annuities at the Bank of England. In her will, she left her daughter a life interest in all the dividends and interest from this account.[25] To her son, who had already inherited the manor estate at Teffont Evias from his father and significant monetary bequests and land holdings from his uncle Christopher Batt, she gave £400, and she also allowed £50 apiece to her daughter, her son, and his wife for mourning apparel. To the "Managers and Governeurs of the Incorporated Society for the propagation of the Gospel in Foreign Parts," she left £100. She made special arrangements of an annual annuity of £10 to her maidservant Elizabeth Newton, "who is most attendant on my person." To her other servants—an unnamed maid, a footman, and a coachman—she left a flat amount of £10 to £15. Other than these monetary gifts, she, like Donnellan, left personal items both large and small to family, friends, and servants. As neither her son nor her daughter had children, the Mayne family line through her husband died out with their son: thus the manor of Teffont Evias passed to a lateral branch.

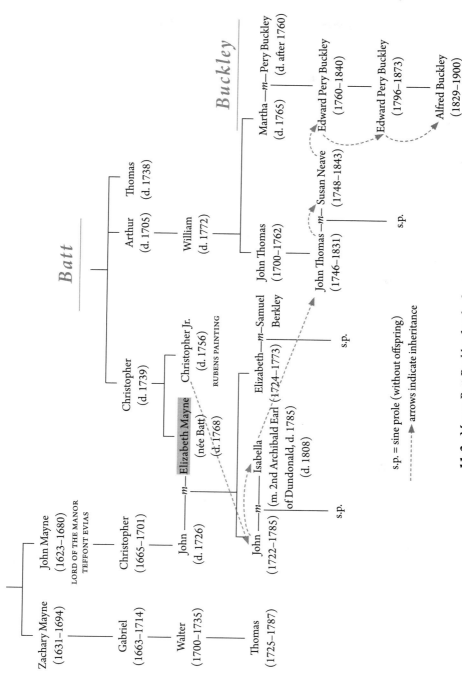

11.3 Mayne-Batt-Buckley family chart

The Batt family line through her father, Christopher Batt, also died out (her brother Christopher having died unmarried), and this had important ramifications for her brother's estate.

Christopher Batt Jr. left his Essex estates to his nephew John Mayne and his heirs. If, however, John Mayne left no living children, then the estate was to pass to Samuel Berkley, the husband of his niece and their heirs, unless the Berkleys also left no living children, in which case it was to pass to John Thomas Batt, the son of his first cousin William, and his heirs. Such an arrangement was not unusual. Batt and his cousin William also had been tied into a similar arrangement by their uncle Thomas Batt, who left half of his estate to William and a quarter of it to Christopher. He left the income on the final quarter to Christopher for life and the principal to his heirs, in lieu of which heirs it passed to William's sons. These complicated arrangements depended on knowing at the end of various lives whether or not an individual had left direct heirs and determining inheritance on that basis. Perhaps, then, it is not surprising that neither the estate of Thomas Batt, who died in 1738, nor that of his nephew Christopher Batt, Handel's friend, who died in 1756, was finally resolved until the death of John Mayne's widow (née Raymond), who by a second marriage had become Isabella, Countess of Dundonald, in 1808.

Leaving myriad further details aside, this tangle of residuary legatees, unraveled in the course of my investigation into the families of Handel's legatees, makes it possible to trace some of Batt's art collection to the present. One piece, now at the Louvre, is *Elevation of the Cross,* an oil sketch by Rubens for the great triptych he painted for St. Walburga Church, Antwerp. The provenance of this work has been traced back to an Alfred Buckley (1829–1900). Previously, the only known earlier reference appeared in a catalogue of Dutch and Flemish paintings in England published in 1830 by the art dealer John Smith (no relation to John Christopher Smith), where its owner was identified as a "J. T. Batts."[26] A continuous provenance can now be projected from 1750, the year in which the art dealers Charles Gouyn, a jeweler, and Thomas Major, an engraver, brought this work among others "purchased abroad" into England. Christopher Batt purchased it for £79 16s. at their auction

11.4 Peter Paul Rubens, *Elevation of the Cross,* c. 1609 (Louvre, Paris / Peter Willi / The Bridgeman Art Library)

in March 1750 on the same day that Handel bought *Moses in the Bulrushes* by Louis Parrocel. At this point the work is identified simply as *The Crucifixion* by Rubens. Batt's will named his nephew John Mayne as his executor and heir, but his failure to mention either his Kensington houses or his art collection, especially after he had specifically named his Essex estates, may have been the same kind of "defect" that allowed the will of Donnellan's brother to be contested. For whatever reason, Mayne did not simply take possession of the collection, but at the death of his uncle in 1756 had it auctioned and bought back most of the best pieces, including Rubens's "original Sketch for the Altar of ye Great Ch. Att Antwerp" for £85 1s.

John Mayne died in 1785 and by his will bequeathed "to my dearly beloved Wife Mrs Isabella Mayne the use of all my Pictures for and during her natural life and from and immediately after her decease I give and bequeath the same Pictures to the said John Thomas Batt [Jr]."[27] By this provision, Mayne fulfilled the requirement in his uncle Christopher Batt's will that if both he and his sister Elizabeth Berkley died childless, then the estate should pass to his cousin John Thomas Batt [Sr.] and his heirs. John Thomas Batt Jr., who is named incorrectly as "Batts" in the Smith catalogue of 1830 as the current owner of the Rubens sketch, died in 1831. By his will he left to his cousin Edward Pery Buckley, whose mother Martha Batt was sister to John Thomas Batt Sr., "All my Pictures commonly considered as my Collection of Pictures according to my Catalogue thereof and all my Books (after the decease of my Wife)."[28] Thereafter the collection passed from father to son, reaching Alfred Buckley on the death of his father in 1873. The collection was sold at auction by Christie, Manson & Woods on May 4, 1901, in a sale that included pictures from a number of collectors. According to a published report on this auction,

> Mr. Buckley's Collection, which comprised the first 73 entries in the catalogue, and realized a total sum of £9,000 6s., was by far the most important. The pictures were chiefly collected by Mr. J. T. Batt, and hung at New Hall, Salisbury.[29]

The Rubens sold for £3,360.

The quality of art in the large collections of Handel's friends—Palmer, Batt, Granville, and Jennens—dazzles even today. Handel's own smaller collection was also fine, and particularly so if the two paintings attributed to Rembrandt and now untraceable were actually by that artist. One strand in the fabric of their shared lives was having the finest art as a part of their daily environment. This was especially true, of course, of Goupy, who spent much of his professional life among the biggest and most important collections of the time, including those of the dukes of Chandos and Devonshire, the lords Sunderland and Burlington, and the royal family. Goupy's own collection of art, judging by the works he sold at auction in 1765 as well as the posthumous auction of the remaining items in 1769, was not lacking in great art, if it contained, as described, works by Titian, Rembrandt, and Poussin, among others.

Goupy died in 1769 out of favor, out of work, and impoverished. In his will, without any money of his own to bestow, he bequeathed his "Book of Nudities" to a Robert Thompson, his "Four Flutes in a case" to a Thomas Lewis, and his japanning equipment, palettes, and easels to the soprano La Francesina (Élisabeth Duparc), Handel's leading soprano soloist from 1738 to 1746.[30] With money he claimed as a debt from the estate of his late patron Henry Furnese and the proceeds from a sale of all his real and personal estate, including the artwork he had held back from the auction in 1765, he created a trust for the support and maintenance of Mrs. Wright, who had lived with him many years and was "now so unhappy as to be deprived of her reason" (see Chapter 10). The auctioneers of Langford and Son offered two separate sales of Goupy's collection in 1770, one of "Pictures [and] drawings" (mostly by Marco Ricci and Goupy), which raised £296 3s. 6d., and one of "prints, copper plates, and drawings," all by Goupy.[31]

Goupy's own work has, in general, not stood the test of time, but he left a lasting legacy in his etchings and in the drawings related to them, some of which can be found in private collections, as well as in the British Museum, Cleveland Museum of Art, and Indianapolis Museum of Art.[32] A fine example of his teaching is preserved in the etchings of the naturalist Mark Catesby, whose two-volume *The Natural History of Carolina, Florida, and the Bahama Islands*, published in parts between 1729 and 1747, marked a milestone in scientific illustration. Catesby described in his preface to the first volume how the project nearly came to naught when he realized that "the Expence of Graving [engraving his drawings] would make it too burthensome an Undertaking," forcing him to give up his plan of having the work done in Paris or Amsterdam. He then explained how the project was saved. "At length by the kind Advice and Instructions of that inimitable Painter Mr. *Joseph Goupy*, I undertook and was initiated in the way of Etching them myself, which, tho' I may not have done in a Graver-like manner, choosing rather to omit their method of cross-Hatching, and to follow the humour of the Feathers, which is more laborious, . . . I hope has proved more to the purpose."[33] It is precisely this avoidance of traditional cross-hatching and stipple in favor of a freer style that sets off Goupy's etching technique from that of his contemporaries, made his teaching so valuable, and recommends him most strongly to posterity.[34]

After Patrick Delany's death in 1768, Mary Delany lived on another twenty years, reaching the age of eighty-eight. During this second widowhood, she spent about half of each year at Bulstrode, the Buckinghamshire house of the duchess of Portland, and half in a small house in London near St. James's Palace. Through the duchess, she became increasingly close to George III and Queen Charlotte, and after the duchess's death in 1785, George III granted Delany a "grace and favour" house in Windsor, enabling her to continue dividing her time between town and country. Frances (Fanny) Burney, author and daughter of the music historian Charles Burney, was appointed "dresser" to the queen in 1786, and in the last years of Delany's life, the two women were close companions. At her death, on April 15, 1788, Delany left a will longer than Handel's or any of the other friends'. The original will is dated 1782, after which follow twelve codicils. The eighth codicil, with the notation "25th May 1787 my Birth Day," is the last to be dated. The next four codicils were written over the following year.[35]

Despite Delany's elevated social contacts, she had little in terms of monetary wealth. In a court decision following the death of her first husband, she was granted a jointure of £370 per annum for life.[36] The cash account Delany opened with Goslings Bank in 1747 shows payments of this jointure to have been made each year, sometimes in two installments of £185, until April 19, 1788, four days after her death (see Chapter 6). Delany added to this regular income by selling her London house in Spring Gardens. She converted the £1,900 she received from the sale a few days later into 3 percent consolidated stock of a value of £2,000, the account placed in the names of her brother and brother-in-law. Delany was able to add £1,000 to the capital of this account in 1770 with a remittance from Ireland, probably related to Patrick Delany's estate, but in 1772 and 1773 she withdrew £400 of capital to meet expenses. After these fluctuations, Delany received about £45 in dividends from this investment twice yearly, and these payments also continued regularly until her death. Her brother, who died in 1775, left her £100 a year, but this sum only came into her account from his estate in three years: 1775, 1776, and 1780. In general, then, her annual income from the early 1770s onward amounted to £460. On the day of her death, she had a little more than £134 in her cash account.[37]

Delany's long will, therefore, amounts to a litany in which she bestowed what seems to be every object, big or little, in her house to friends and relations. Like Handel, she began with her servants, and she treated them as generously as she could, giving to her maid, cook, and manservant one pound for each year of their service, and to her personal maid, Ann Motley, "twenty Guineas [and] all my wearing Apparel and Body Linen that has been washed and once worn." Larger monetary gifts were few and were limited to her closest relatives. Her total disposable wealth for paying debts and bequests seems to have been limited to the capital in her 3 percent consolidated annuity account, worth about £2,270. She gave to her goddaughter, Sarah (Sally) Sandford, who had been left a widow with four sons, £100, writing, "To my dear Mrs Sandford I bequeath one hundred Pounds[;] I had intended a much larger Sum not foreseeing a very unexpected disappointment of Fortune," a reference to the various financial setbacks she had suffered (see Chapter

7). To her nephews Bernard and Court Dewes she gave £300 and 100 guineas (£105) respectively. To her third nephew, John Dewes, who had inherited her brother's estate twenty years before, she gave no money, but bequeathed to him, as to the others, specific family portraits. In the first codicil to her will, she left another £500 to Court Dewes in trust to try to redress the debts of her niece Mary Port (née Dewes), as she puts it, "to be applied towards the payment of such of Mʳ Ports of Ilam debts as he the said Court Dewes shall think proper."

Like Donnellan, Delany hoped the sale of her property would provide for others. Thus she left the lease of the house in St. James's Place to Mary Port, "together with the Residue of my Personal Estate," giving various calculations depending on what the sale of the lease and contents of her house might raise in order to provide as much as a third of the proceeds to her great-niece Georgina Port, whom Delany had helped to raise and who had lived with her for many years. As the old Chancery suit filed against Dr. Delany by the family of his first wife was still active, despite the ruling in Dr. Delany's favor in the House of Lords, Delany provided £100 to create a trust for the "sole and separate" use by a niece of her husband should there be "a sufficient ballance in my favour after all Expenses and lawful demands on account of the Cause be paid and satisfied." She left her harpsichord and "written Musick Books" to her great-niece Georgina Port, and to her goddaughter, Sally Sandford, "the duplicates of my Musick."

Despite her meager estate, and her aversion to publicity, Mary Delany was widely recognized at the time of her death as a woman of intellect, a model of etiquette, and an artist. Between 1750 and 1752, she adamantly opposed George Ballard's proposal to dedicate to her the third "century" of his *Memoirs of Several Ladies of Great Britain, who have been celebrated for their Writings or Skill in the Learned Languages, Arts and Sciences.* Her first mention of it comes in a letter to her sister (September 28, 1750): "Apropos, did I tell you that Mr. Ballard has *picked me out* (a thing unknown to him, but from report of a few partial acquaintances) to subscribe his Third Century to. I am vexed at it, and positively refused, but D. D. [Dr. Delany] contradicted it, and says it will be using the man ill."[38]

She continued to protest as the project moved forward (November 4, 1752): "I don't know how to help myself, but *I am vexed* at the books being dedicated to me. If I am not too late, I wish it could still be avoided; if it cannot, I don't like '*Mrs. D. wife of Dr. D.*' and I like '*lady*' less, as it is *not proper*."[39] Delany's criticisms had little effect, and a month later she confessed that her husband "likes the last dedication mightily, [so] it is to no purpose for me to wish it undone." It finally read as follows:

To
Mʳˢ DELANY
THE TRUEST JUDGE
AND BRIGHTEST PATTERN
OF ALL THE ACCOMPLISHMENTS
WHICH ADORN HER SEX
THESE MEMOIRS OF
LEARNED LADIES
IN THE
SEVENTEENTH AND EIGHTEENTH
CENTURIES
ARE MOST HUMBLY INSCRIBED
BY HER OBEDIENT SERVANT
GEORGE BALLARD[40]

The value of her correspondence was also recognized in her lifetime, and some of it was published, much to her chagrin. When she discovered, for example, that some of her letters were included in the publication of Jonathan Swift's correspondence, she wrote to a friend: "I am *sick* with the account of Swift's last volume! The publisher has *done basely*, for he promised a friend of mine, who insisted on the letters of Mrs. Pendarves [that is, any of the letters she wrote to Swift during her first widowhood] being delivered to him, that if any were found they should [send them on]—It is a serious vexation."[41] Surely this fear of exposure is what led her repeatedly to tell her sister and other correspondents to burn her letters. That they didn't was a great gift to posterity. Over her eighty-eight years,

Delany's continued correspondence provides a detailed description of a changing society, including firsthand accounts of an early forced marriage, a later companionate marriage, family relations, legal issues, culture, and scientific exploration. It was published in six volumes (lightly edited and censored) in 1861–1862 by Augusta Hall, Lady Llanover, the daughter of Delany's great-niece Georgina Port.

At least equal to the importance of her letters to the history of eighteenth-century Britain, and arguably much better known, are the flower collages that Delany created in her second widowhood. Always fascinated by nature, as evidenced by her shell collection and interest in flowers, Delany engaged more deeply with the study of natural science during the time she spent with the duchess of Portland. At Bulstrode, Delany joined the duchess in a deep and systematic exploration of botany, instructed by some of the leading botanists, gardeners, and artists of the time who spent time at the Portland estate. Georg Dionysius Ehret, an outstanding botanical artist, was employed to teach the children of the duchess; the reverend John Lightfoot, a distinguished botanist, was the family chaplain; Philip Miller, a great botanical horticulturalist who oversaw the Chelsea Physic Garden, was a frequent visitor; and two eminent botanists who had sailed around the world with Captain Cook, Joseph Banks, and Daniel Solander, were long-term guests.[42]

Delany was quickly caught up in this atmosphere of investigation and exploration, and, on October 18, 1769, began her transcription of an English translation of the Latin treatise by William Hudson on English flowers, which used the new Linnaean system of classification. The result is a 474-page manuscript in her own hand entitled "A British flora after the sexual system of Linnaeus" (1769).[43] Three years later this intellectual interest blossomed into art. Always dexterous, and deft with scissors—even as a child she had cut out detailed figures and silhouettes in paper—she created a way of representing flowers in full detail by using cut paper of different colors to illustrate every nuance and shading. At first she thought of these as a version of dried flowers preserved in their full color, but later she referred to them as mosaics. Some of these, depicting a single flower, consisted of hundreds of paper slivers.[44] A special characteristic of the mosaics is the placement of flowers against a saturated black background. Her models

11.5 Mary Delany, *Aeschelus Hippocastanum* (Horse Chestnut), collage dated June 6, 1776, formerly Vol. 1, no. 7 of Delany's ten-volume *Flora Delanica* (© The Trustees of the British Museum)

for doing so were few, but may perhaps be found in the rage for japanning, which involved a shiny, black lacquer finish on which gold designs or more colorful botanic images or scenes might be painted; Delany first mentioned learning this process in 1729.[45] She used the same color scheme in about

1740 for the fancy dress she designed with a black satin background on which flowers were embroidered in meticulous detail and brilliant colors. Delany's flower mosaics are not merely beautiful, however. Because of her previous study of the Linnaean taxonomy, they are also highly accurate. She based them on actual flowers that she dissected, professional botanists providing her with some of the rarer specimens. Each of her finished paper mosaics was then labeled with its Linnaean classification.

Over the course of ten years, from the ages of seventy-two to eighty-two, Delany created ten albums of paper collages depicting 979 different flowering plants. She had hoped to reach 1,000, but failing eyesight made continuation impossible. George III and Queen Charlotte were keenly interested in her progress. The botanist Sir Joseph Banks declared her collages "*the only* imitations of nature that he had ever seen, from which he could *venture* to describe botanically any plant without the least fear of committing an error."[46] Horace Walpole thought it appropriate to include Delany's work in his *Anecdotes of Painting in England*, writing to her on November 28, 1786, to beg her forgiveness for "recording her name in vol. 2, p. 242." His reference describes her as "a lady of excellent sense and taste, who painted in oil, and who at the age of 74 *invented* the art of paper mosaic, with which material (coloured) she executed, in eight years, within 20 of 1000 various flowers and flowering shrubs with a *precision and truth unparalleled*."[47] The first biography of Mary Delany appeared five years after her death, and the ten volumes of her flower mosaics are preserved in the British Museum.[48]

HANDEL'S FRIENDS WERE not as famous as he was, but they were intelligent, cultured, and creative. They were collectors of music, art, and nature, and were high-achieving amateurs as musicians and artists. Through their collections, creative work, or generosity, they all left significant legacies to posterity. They were a sounding board for Handel's music; they listened to him sing newly composed work; and they attended rehearsals in his house. Conversations about work in progress surely occurred with many of them. Goupy and Handel would have discussed the operas at the Royal Academy of Music, especially those they worked on together, and Hunter also may have discussed music with the composer, given his ardent interest in collecting Handel's works. Hawkins describes Goupy and Hunter as the two friends who possessed most of Handel's confidence.[49] In addition, Handel probably discussed his work with Bernard Granville and the Harrises, and we know, for example, that Charles Jennens was not only openly critical of parts of *Messiah* but also offered important suggestions to Handel about his settings of his other librettos. Handel's music intersected with all of their lives in multiple ways, reflecting contemporary politics in the opera librettos and fascination with the East in their settings, resonating with personal issues of love and conflict, providing a large part of the music they played in their homes, offering religious inspiration, and giving solace to the ill and bereaved. For these friends—and for many, many others of the period—Handel's music in its vibrant color and striking juxtapositions resonated outward with the complexity of their lives, while its extraordinary beauty and emotional depth spoke to their innermost selves. Period and place have no stranglehold on Handel's music. Its inherent qualities have transcended the audience for which it was written and leapt the boundaries of time, a continuing legacy to future generations.

Currency, Living Costs, Wages, and Fees

1. Currencies*

Denomination	Value	Abbreviation
British		
penny (pl. pence)	smallest named unit	d. (*from the Latin "denarius"*)
derived forms		
farthing	¼d.	
ha'penny	½d.	
sixpence	6d.	
shilling	12d.	s.
intermediate forms		
half crown	2s. 10d.	
crown	5s.	
half guinea	10s. 6d. (see below)	
pound	240d. = 20s.	£
guinea	21s.	
German		*Approximate value in 18th-c £
taler (or reichstaler)	tlr. or rtlr.	4s. 6d.
Levant (Aleppo)		
Levant piastre	*𝓛𝓹*	2s. 11d.

2. Selected Cost-of-Living Figures for England (Primarily London) in the Mid-Eighteenth Century

Figures are drawn from the following sources:
 • James E. Thorold Rogers, *A History of Agriculture and Prices in England,*

---

*The Marteau Early Eighteenth-Century Currency Converter: A Platform of Research in Economic History (www.pierre-marteau.com/currency/converter.html)

vol. 7: 1703–1793 (Oxford: Clarendon Press, 1902), given with page references (this is the foundational study)

- Marjorie Penn, ed., "The Account Books of Gertrude Savile, 1736–58," *Thoroton Society Record Series* 24 (1967): 99–152; musical references given in bold with date of account entry; others identified "Savile"

Food and sundries

1d.	one lobster (1745), p. 343
4d.	lb. butter (1742), p. 309
5d.	lb. sugar (1744), p. 377
8d.	lb. salmon (1745), p. 343
	6 pigeons (1744), p. 304
10d.	dozen brass coat buttons (1740), p. 466
	quire writing paper (1756), p. 452
1s.	London mop (1741), p. 466
	lb. tobacco (1744), p. 377
	libretto at the opera (February 26, 1737) [*Giustino*]
1s. 7d.	4 chickens (1744), p. 304
1s. 10d.	lb. black pepper (1744), p. 377
2s.	pair kid gloves (1745), p. 468
2s. 3d.	4 dozen larks (1744), p. 304
3s.	dozen best pencils (1740), p. 466
	quire music paper (1755), p. 452
	ticket in the gallery for *Beggar's Opera* (January 22, 1737)
3s. 6d.	one barrel of beer (1747), p. 351
4s.	dozen gold buttons (1740), p. 466
5s. (=1 crown)	**ticket in the gallery for an opera at the Haymarket** (February 26, 1737) [*Giustino*]
	songs out of "the Oritorio *Saul*" (May 5, 1739), purchase of score
5s. 6d.	gallon port (1750), p. 358
7s.	dozen candles (1741), p. 315
	6 shovels (1742), p. 467
	iron hammer (1742), p. 467
8s.	lb. bohea tea (1740), p. 377
10s. 6d. (= ½ g.)	**single ticket (in the boxes or pit) for an "Oritoria"** (March 23, 1737) [*Il trionfo del Tempo*]
	Handel's Te Deum (May 8, 1739), purchase of score
12s.	ream writing paper (1748), p. 452
13s.	lb. green tea (1740), p. 367
14s.	copper warming pan (1741), p. 466

15s.	new wagon wheel (1741), p. 466
	2 new ploughs (1742), p. 467
	ruffled hat (1744), p. 467
16s.	lb. finest hyson tea (1740), p. 377
21s. (=1 g.)	hat with double rich strong gold lace (1744), p. 467
	hogshead of ale (1747), p. 351
£1 1s. (=1 g.)	**songs out of "*Alexanders Feats*" (May 5, 1739), purchase of score**
24s. (=£1 4s.)	new saddle with stirrups and leathers (1742), p. 467
	9x4 quilt (1743), p. 467
	large mattress (1754), p. 468
28s. (=£1 8s.)	3 fine blankets (1743), p. 467
30s. (=£1 10s.)	lb. cheese, various types, average (1720), p. 309
£1 11s. 6d.	bagwig (1741), p. 466
	punch bowl (1741), p. 466
£2	lodging at Bath for a week (1752), p. 534
£2 2s.	a coffin with double lid lined with flannel, & covered with white Russell tire (1752), p. 470
£2 15s.	double-gilt snuff box (1742), p. 467
£4 14s. 6d.	3 wigs (1741), p. 466
£5 5s.	pair of pocket pistols with bolts (1745), p. 468
£6	the cost of feeding one man for a year (1754), p. 534
£6 6s.	mahogany bureau, p. 467
£7 7s.	pair of hair pistols with bolt guards (1745), p. 468
£7 11s.	cost of funeral, including coffin, shroud, velvet pall, many pairs of kid gloves (1752), p. 470
£10	year's rent for house on Greek Street in Soho (Savile)
£12	the cost of boarding 1 working man for a year (1734), p. 678
£15–20	1 carriage horse, p. 306
£20	season ticket for the opera
£80	new landau (1745), p. 468
£240	leasehold for house on Greek Street in Soho (Savile)

Wages and Fees

3d.	daily wage for women farm workers (1742), p. 499 (assuming 300 working days in a year=£3 15s. annual wage)
4d.	daily wage for boy farm workers (1742), p. 499 (assuming 300 working days in a year=£5 annual wage)
8d.	daily wage for men farm workers (1742), p. 499 (assuming 300 working days in a year=£10 annual wage)

1s.	daily wage *without drink* for a carpenter, wheelwright, or mason (1732), p. 623 (assuming 300 working days in a year=£15 annual wage)
1s. 2d.	daily wage *with drink* for a carpenter, wheelwright, or mason (1732), p. 623 (assuming 300 working days in a year=£17 1s. annual wage)
1s. 4d.	daily wage for carpenter (1742), p. 499 (assuming 300 working days in a year=£20 annual wage)
6s.	payment to tailor for making coat and waistcoat (1739), p. 498
16s.	payment to tailor for making 2 suits (1739), p. 498
20s. (=£1)	paid for cleaning and dyeing a scarlet cloak (1739), p. 498
£3 10s.	year's wage for killing moles (1737), p. 704
£5–10	husbandman (1737), pp. 703–4
£6	year's wage of Gertrude Savile's maid (Savile)
£8	year's wage of Gertrude Savile's serving man (Savile) year's wage of head ploughman, wagoner, or seedman (1732), p. 623
£36	year's wage of person who was bailiff *and* shepherd (1737), p. 703

3. Selected Examples Drawn from Documents Consulted for This Book
Expenses

4d.	postage of letter from York (1737: Peacock inventory)
1s. 6d.	Hackney coach from London to Hackney and back (1737: Peacock inventory)
3s. 6d.	lb. of chocolate (1727: Delany)
4s.	lb. of chocolate (1728: Delany) lb. of worsted (a type of yarn) (1737: Delany)
5s.	good lodgings at Bath per day (1756: Delany)
6s.	lb. knotting thread (1766: Delany)
7s.	yard of pink damask (1731: Delany)
8s.	yard of blue-and-white material for an evening dress (1744: Delany)
8–9s.	set of white tassels—not able to find a set for less (1754: Delany)
13s.	lb. of tea (1727: Delany)
16–18s.	lb. green tea (1760: Delany)
18s.	cost of silk and worsted for "working" (embroidering) a chair (1734: Delany)

£1 10s.	yard of material without gold or silver used by Princess Amelia for a gown (1738: Delany, "30 shillings")
£8 4s. 6d.	2 months' schooling and board at Mr. Weston's Academy (1720: Sir Harcourt Masters)
£9 9s. (=9 g.)	Jacob Kirkman harpsichord (1755: Donnellan)
£10	carpet sold by Delany at "full value" (1771: Delany)
£10 9s.	11 mourning rings (1738: Peacock inventory)
£11 9s.	a piece of linen for shirts (1735: Henry Lannoy Hunter)
£12 12s.	1 plain gold watch with chain and seal (1738: Peacock inventory)
£13 17s. 6d.	10 chaldron of coals (1735: Henry Lannoy Hunter)
£16	gown and petticoat of fine blue satin (1731: Delany)
£21	2 steers (1720: Sir Harcourt Masters)
£26	cost of writing out a second conducting score of Handel's *Rinaldo* (1711)
£28 17s. 6d.	purchase price of Rembrandt's *Man in Oriental Costume* at the auction of Ralph Palmer's paintings (1755)
£34	value of Peacock's library, including "Two Folio Bibles, Three very large Books, being the Antiquities of Rome gilt with the Kings Arms in Leaf Gold, Twenty nine Folio's Sundrys, One Bible and about three hundred and eighty Quarto's Octavo's & Duodecimo's and one hundred and fifty old Books and Pamphlets" (1738: Peacock inventory)
£39 18s.	what Handel paid for a "Rembrandt" (1750)
£48	total valuation of the contents of Handel's house after the paintings, musical instruments, and library were removed (1759)
£50	required donation to become a director of the Foundling Hospital (waived in Handel's case)
£53 7s. 5s.	horse expenses for 3 months (1735: Henry Lannoy Hunter)
£65	100 sheep (1720: Sir Harcourt Masters)
£79 16s.	what Christopher Batt paid for Rubens oil sketch of the crucifixion (1750)
£100	1 year boarding with brother John (1735: Henry Lannoy Hunter)
£105 (=100 g.)	offer to Handel by Lord Middlesex for the use of an old opera (1743)
£250	John Percival's estimate of his monthly expenses in Paris for a family of 4 with servants (1725: Percival)
£500	musical clock that played 24 tunes (1725: Delany)

£504 18s. 2d.	total valuation of the contents of Richard Peacock's house (father of Elizabeth Palmer)
£1,000	estimate of the cost of "scenes & Coaths" for 1 season of opera at the Royal Academy of Music (1719)
£1,400	cost of apprenticing Henry Lannoy Hunter with the Levant Company (1726)
£14,962 4s. 11½d.	fortune bequeathed to Henry Lannoy Hunter by primogeniture (1733)

Wages, Pensions, Fees

4s.	salary of the organ blowers for performance of *Messiah* at the Foundling Hospital on May 15, 1754
£2 12s. 6d. (=2½ g.)	payment for "working" (embroidering) a chair (1734: Delany)
£4 11s.	estimate from Smith for copying out instrumental parts of *Alexander's Feast* for James Harris (1738)
£10	profit from a concert in Bath (1716: Percival)
£16	annual salary for a good, sought-after servant (1775: Delany)
£20	annual salary for a trusted servant of 34 years (1779: Delany)
£19 8s. 6d.	total cost for orchestra of 38 musicians for performance of *Messiah* at the Foundling Hospital on May 15, 1754
£26 5s. (=25 g.)	Handel's payment from Walsh for publishing an opera
£43 2s.	servants' wages and wearing apparel for 3 months (1735: Henry Lannoy Hunter)
£70	annual salary for a state trumpeter in Dublin (1716: Percival)
£100	fee budgeted for a new opera at the opening of the Royal Academy of Music (1719)
£220	Goupy's fee to Baron Kielmansegg for copies of the 7 Raphael cartoons (c. 1716–1717)
£225 (=1000 taler)	Handel's annual salary from Hanover (1710–1713)
£299 4s. 11d.	Handel's payment from the opera (1713)
£360 (=2500 ₤)	payment by Levant Company for embroglio caused by Henry Lannoy Hunter (1732)
£370	Delany's annual widow's portion
£525 (=500 g.)	Middlesex's offer to Handel for 1 new opera (1743)
£600	Handel's annual payment from the Royal Treasury

£1,000	appraisal of Hunter's dye house in terms of the value of its brick and timber (1745)
£1,500	top salary for the leading male and female singer at the Royal Academy of Music in the 1720–1721 season
£1,900	price for which Mary Delany sold her house in Spring Gardens (1766)
£6,000	Ralph Verney's profit from 6 years in Aleppo with the Levant Company (1668–1674)
£10,000	George Granville, Lord Lansdowne's losses in the South Sea crash (1720)

A Very Select Discography

There is no attempt here to offer a complete discography or to present the best or most recent recordings. Rather, this is a list of recordings from my own library that I have used and enjoyed. I offer it as a guide to readers who want to hear the music. Works are listed within sub-groupings in the order they appear in each chapter. The dates provided are those of the first performance or first publication and do not always represent the version on the recording. Space does not permit a similar listing of the many live performances that have similarly affected my understanding of Handel and his music; nor would such a listing be of benefit to the reader.

For two very good discographies by Philippe Gelinaud, one of Handel's operas and one of "oratorios, dramas, serenades, and odes," see www.gfhandel.org.

Chapter 3: Politics, Patronage, and Pension
CEREMONIAL AND RELIGIOUS PIECES

Eccheggiate, festeggiate! (1710?)
No recording

Ode for the Birthday of Queen Anne ("Eternal Source of Light Divine") (1712)
Utrecht Te Deum (1713)
Utrecht Jubilate (1713)
with *Anthem for the Foundling Hospital* (1749)
Decca (458 072-2) Academy of Ancient Music, Simon Preston (2 CDs)

Ode for the Birthday of Queen Anne
Coronation Anthems (1727)
EMI (5 57140 2) Academy of Ancient Music, Stephen Cleobury

Water Music (1717)
Archiv (410525-2) The English Concert, Trevor Pinnock (this recording offers the *Water Music* in the earliest known ordering of movements, rather than in the later version of three suites)

Chandos Anthems (1717–18)
Chandos (CHAN 0503, 0504, 0505, 0509) The Sixteen, Harry Christophers (4 CDs)

OPERA
POLITICAL STORIES

Floridante (1721)
Hungaroton (HCD 31304-06) Capella Savaria, Nicholas McGegan
Archiv Produktion (477 6566) Il Complesso Barocco, Alan Curtis

Riccardo primo (1727)
L'Oiseau-Lyre (452 201-2) Les Talens Lyriques, Christophe Rousset

Chapter 4: Commerce and Trade
OPERA AND ORATORIO
EAST-WEST DEPICTIONS

Rinaldo (1711)
Harmonia Mundi (HMC 901796.98), Freiburger Barockorchester, René Jacobs (improvised percussion parts for the "exotic" music, expanded continuo section, and harpsichord cadenzas based on contemporary sources add to the magic and virtuosity of the opera)

Esther (1720)
L'Oiseau-Lyre (414-423-1) Academy of Ancient Music, Christopher Hogwood

Athalia (1733)
L'Oiseau-Lyre (417-126-2) Academy of Ancient Music, Christopher Hogwood (with Emma Kirkby's Josabeth up against Joan Sutherland's Athalia)

Alexander Balus (1747)
Hyperion (CDA67241/2) Choir of New College Oxford, King's Consort, Robert King

Floridante (1721) see listing for Chapter 3

Giulio Cesare (1724)
Harmonia Mundi (HMC 901385.87) Concerto Köln, René Jacobs
Opus Arte (OA 0950 D) Glyndebourne production, Orchestra of the Age of Enlightenment, William Christie (3 DVD video)

Riccardo primo (1727) see listing for Chapter 3

Chapter 5: Music at Home
CHAMBER MUSIC

The Complete Chamber Music
(Philips 4700 893-2) Academy Chamber Ensemble (Trio Sonata in F Major, HWV 392, on CD 2) (6 CDs)

CONCERTOS

Op. 3 (complete) (1734)
Harmonia Mundi (HMU 907415) Academy of Ancient Music, Richard Egarr (Op. 3, no. 2 on CD 3)

KEYBOARD MUSIC

Eight Keyboard Suites (1720)
Somm (B003B3B1UQ) Laurence Cummings (recorded in Handel House Museum, London)

"Softly sweet, in Lydian measures," *Alexander's Feast* (sung by Harriet Byron in *The History of Sir Charles Grandison* by Samuel Richardson) see listing for *Alexander's Feast* under chapter 8

Chapter 6: Marriage, Wealth, and Social Status
WEDDING MUSIC

Wedding Anthem for Princess Anne ("This is the day which the Lord hath made") (1734)
No recording

Parnasso in festa (1734)
Hyperion (CDA67701/2) The King's Consort, Matthew Halls

"ORPHEUS" AND "APOLLO" CANTATAS

"Hendel, non può mia musa" (1707)
Stradivarius (STR 35701) Retablo Barocco, Roberta Invernizzi, soprano

Apollo e Dafne ("La terra é liberata") (1710)
Glossa (GCD 921527) La Risonanza, Fabio Bonizzoni

OPERA
LOVE STORIES

Radamisto (1720, first version)
Virgin (5 45673 2) Il Complesso Barocco, Alan Curtis

Radamisto (1720, second version)
Harmonia Mundi (HMU 907111.13) Göttinger Festival Production, Freiburger
Barockorchester, Nicholas McGegan

Rodelinda (1725)
Virgin Veritas (5 45277 2) Raglan Baroque Players, Nicholas Kraemer
NVC Arts (3984-23024-3) Glyndebourne production, Orchestra of the Age
of Enlightenment, William Christie (DVD video)

Scipione (1726)
FNAC (592245) Les Talens Lyriques, Christophe Rousset

Floridante (1721) see listing for Chapter 3

Amadigi (1715)
Erato (2292-45490-2) Les Musiciens du Louvre, Marc Minkowski

Alcina (1735)
EMI Angel (DSD-3985) City of London Baroque Sinfonia, Richard Hickox
(LP, now available on CD)
Erato (8573-80233-2) Les Arts Florissants, William Christie

Imeneo (1740)
VoxBox Classics (CDX 5135) Brewer Chamber Orchestra & Chorus, Rudolf
Palmer

Deidamia (1741)
Virgin Veritas (5 45550 2) Il Complesso Barocco, Alan Curtis

Chapter 7: Ambition, Law, and Friendship

ORATORIO

FRIENDSHIP

Saul (1739)
Naxos (8.554361-63) Junge Kantorei, Barockorchester Frankfurt, Joachim Carlos Martini

Samson (1743)
Coro (COR 16008) The Sixteen, Harry Christophers

MUSICAL CARICATURE

Semele (1744)
Deutsche Grammophon (435 782-2) Ambrosian Opera Chorus, English Chamber Orchestra, John Nelson

Belshazzar (1745)
Teldec (0630-10275-2) Stockholm Kammerkören, Concentus Musicus Wien, Nikolaus Harnoncourt

LAW

Solomon (1749)
Philips (412 612-1) Monteverdi Choir, English Baroque Soloists, John Eliot Gardiner

Susanna (1749)
Harmonia Mundi (HMU 907030.32) Chamber Chorus of the University of California, Berkeley, Philharmonia Baroque Orchestra, Nicholas McGegan

Chapter 8: Making and Collecting

ODE AND ORATORIO

THE MUSICAL DIVINE

Alexander's Feast (1736)
Philips (422 053-2) Monteverdi Choir, English Baroque Soloists, John Eliot Gardiner

Il trionfo del Tempo e del Disinganno (1707)
Opus 111 (OP 30321) Concerto Italiano, Rinaldo Alessandrini
Virgin Classics (3 63428 2) Le Concert d'Astrée, Emmanuelle Haïm

Il Trionfo del Tempo e della Verità (1737/9)
Naxos (8.554440-42) Junge Kantorei, Barockorchester Frankfurt, Joachim Carlos Martini

Ode for St. Cecilia's Day (1739)
Archiv Produktion (419 220-2) The English Concert, Trevor Pinnock

CONCERTOS

Op. 4, *Six Organ Concertos* (1738)
Harmonia Mundi (HMX 2908292.95) Academy of Ancient Music, Richard Egarr

Op. 6, *Twelve Grand Concertos* (1740)
Harmonia Mundi (HMX 2908292.95) Academy of Ancient Music, Andrew Manze

Chapter 9: Religion and Charity
ORATORIO
MIRACLES AND PROPHECY

Israel in Egypt (1739)
Decca (452 295-2) King's College Choir, Cambridge, The Brandenburg Consort, Stephen Cleobury (importantly, this recording includes all three parts of the oratorio, including Part I, "The Sons of Israel do mourn")

Messiah (1742)
Harmonia Mundi (HMU 907050.52) Chamber Chorus of the University of California, Berkeley, Philharmonia Baroque Orchestra, Nicholas McGegan (includes performances of the many variants made by Handel)

RELIGIOUS FREEDOM

Esther (1720) see listing for Chapter 4

Judas Maccabaeus (1747)
Hyperion (CDA 66641/2) Choir of New College, Oxford, The King's Consort, Robert King

Theodora (1750)
Harmonia Mundi (HMU 907060.62) Chamber Chorus of the University of California, Berkeley, Philharmonia Baroque Orchestra, Nicholas McGegan
Kultur (D2099) Glyndebourne production, Orchestra of the Age of Enlightenment, William Christie (DVD video)

Chapter 10: Sickness and Death
OPERA
ILLNESS

Admeto (1727)
Virgin Veritas (5 61369 2) Il Complesso Barocco, Alan Curtis

MUSICAL DISRUPTION

Apollo e Dafne (1710) see listing for Chapter 6

Semele (1744) see listing for Chapter 7

ORATORIO
MADNESS

Saul (1739) see listing for Chapter 7

Hercules (1745)
Archiv Produktion (469 532-2) Les Musiciens du Louvre, Marc Minkowski

BLINDNESS

Samson (1743) see listing for Chapter 7

FINAL WORKS

Jephtha (1751)
Philips (422 351-2) Monteverdi Choir, English Baroque Soloists, John Eliot Gardiner

The Triumph of Time and Truth (1757)
Hyperion (CDD 22050) The London Handel Choir and Orchestra, Denys Darlow

Acknowledgments

This book has been in progress for many years and has incurred many debts. I was honored to hold the MIT Class of 1949 Professorial Chair from 1996 to the time of my official retirement from MIT in 2011. The fund associated with this chair was the primary support for my archival research over that entire period. I am also indebted to the National Endowment for the Humanities for a Fellowship in 2006–2007 and to the Institute for Advanced Study in Princeton for a Fellowship in 2004, both of which gave me the time to work with the material I had gathered and to begin shaping it into a narrative.

I am extremely grateful to all the libraries, archives, and museums named in the bibliography where I spent many happy and exciting hours. The staffs of these repositories were unfailingly helpful, responding to my questions and supplying me with the many, many documents I requested.

I am especially grateful to Kim Sloan (curator, Prints and Drawing Room, British Museum), John Greenacombe (former general editor of the Survey of London), and the late Christopher Elrington (former general editor of the Victoria County History) for essential research advice at critical moments.

I am indebted to the research assistants who have worked with me at MIT over the years: Elizabeth Connors, Gerald Waldman, and Dr. Minji Kim. I am also grateful to Dr. Debbie Welham, and to Professor Chris Mounsey, who recommended her, for providing some crucial research on art auction catalogues.

I owe a special debt of gratitude to the many friends and colleagues who read parts or all of the book at various stages. Their criticisms improved my thinking and clarified my writing, while their enthusiasms gave me the encouragement I needed to keep on. Many thanks to Jane Bernstein, Samuel Jay Keyser, Eddie Kohler, Stephanie Leone, Dr. Abraham Lotan, Robert Marshall, Nancy Netzer, Michael Ouellette, Charles Shadle, John H. Roberts, Kay Shelemay, Kim Sloan, Ruth Smith, and

Rev. James Weiss. I hope each of you recognizes your importance to this project.

I am particularly indebted to Maribeth Payne, music editor at W. W. Norton, for her continued enthusiasm and persistence during the long gestation of this project. The finished shape of the book owes a great deal to our conversations over the years and to her keen insight into book publishing. Michael Fauver, music assistant editor, only came into this project in the six months before the manuscript was submitted, but in that short space of time has made invaluable contributions, and not only of an editorial nature. It was his clarity that guided me through the many hurdles of manuscript submission, editorial process, and design.

Above all, I am grateful to the direct and lateral descendants of Handel's friends who encouraged my work, gave me access to unique documents and portraits, and offered me gracious hospitality in their homes: S. Anthony Bosanquet, Jean Elrington, Ruth Hayden, Lynette Keating, James Lord Malmesbury, and Jacqui Mills.

Select Bibliography

PRIMARY SOURCES ON THE SIX FRIENDS
Abbreviations used for archives and libraries in the Notes given in brackets

The National Archives [TNA]
Commissioners of Bankrupts

B 4/10, no. 1222 (9 July 1741) commission of bankruptcy against James
Hunter ZJ 1/39: *London Gazette,* nos. 8030, 8052, 8074 (1 January 1741–
31 December 1742) public announcements of commission of bankruptcy

B 1/17, p. 11 (22 January 1742) petitions against James Hunter by both of his
brothers

B 1/17, pp. 36–40 (31 March 1742) financial accounting and petitions against
James Hunter by fifteen merchants

B 1/17, p. 95 (16 August 1742) addition of two further merchant petitioners
The General Advertiser, no. 3693 (27 August 1746) public notice of further
dividend to creditors of James Hunter
The Public Ledger, or The Daily Register of Commerce and Intelligence, nos.
390 and 393 (11 February 1761 and 14 April 1761) final notice of dividend
to creditors of James Hunter (deceased 1757)

B 4/10, no. 1834, p. 306 (26 January 1744) commission of bankruptcy against
John Hunter, brother of James Hunter

B 6/1 (24 May 1744) certificate of conformity for John Hunter (official discharge from bankruptcy)

Chancery

Delany-related

C 11/935/5 *Mary Pendarves v. Mary Bassett* [*sic*] (relating to the estate of
Alexander Pendarves; interrogatories and depositions only) 1727–1760

Decrees and Orders (not always in chronological order within volumes):
C 33/350/1, p. 175 (12 February 1727/8); C 33/354, p. 53 (8 December
1729); C 33/356/1, p. 40 (15 December 1730), p. 57 (21 December 1730),
p. 66 (12 January 1730/31), p. 144 (4 March 1730/31), p. 180 (12 March
1730/31); C 33/356/2, p. 242^r (8 May 1731), p. 244^v (20 May 1731),
p. 307^r (1 July 1731), p. 342^r (7 August 1731); C 33/358/1, p. 89^v (18
December 1731), p. 54^r–54^v (11 January 1731/2); C 33/360/1, p. 184^r (27
February 1732/3), p. 163^v (13 March 1732/3); C 33/360/2, p. 267^r (26

April 1733); C 33/362, p. 136^v (6 February 1733/4), p. 181^r (12 March 1733/4)

Goupy-related
C 12/726/4 *Hedges v. Goupy* 1739
Decrees and Orders: C 33/371, p. 171^v (8 February 1738/9), p. 204 (19 February 1738/9), p. 233^v (13 March 1738/9), p. 344 (9 April 1739), p. 454 (22 June 1739); C 33/373, p. 18^v (21 November 1739), p. 27^v (24 November 1739), pp. 665^v–666^v (11 July 1740); C 33/375, p. 470 [471] (15 July 1740)
Depositions: C 24/1541

Hunter-related
C 11/2384/44 *Hutchinson v. Lannoy* 1719 (bill and five answers)
C 11/369/15 *Hutchinson v. Lannoy* 1723 (new bill)
C 11/411/4 *Hutchinson v. Lannoy* depositions taken in Aleppo (1721)
C 11/411/8 *Hutchinson v. Lannoy* depositions taken in Cyprus (1723)
Decrees and Orders: C 33/333, p. 156 (19 February 1720), p. 310^v (6 May 1720 and 14 June 1720), p. 287^v (31 May 1720), p. 403 (5 July 1720 and 9 July 1720), p. 366 (13 July 1720); C 33/337, p. 226 (7 May 1722), p. 247 (22 May 1722), p. 324^v (4 June 1722), p. 355^v (28 June 1722); C 33/339, p. 204^r–204^v (6 May 1723), pp. 411^r–412^v (14 May 1723); C 33/341, p. 8^v (11 November 1723), p. 18^r–18^v (25 November 1723), p. 71 (7 December 1723), p. 245 (26 February 1724); C 33/343, p. 123 (4 March 1725)
(suit involving the children of Timothy Lannoy, who died intestate; the Hunter children are involved as descendants of the deceased Elizabeth Lannoy Hunter, their mother; the suit provides a précis of the marriage contract between Elizabeth Lannoy and John Hunter)
C 11/100/14 *Bank of England v. Hunter* 1733 (bill and three answers)
Decrees and Orders: C 33/361, p. 47 (6 December 1733), p. 99 (10 January 1734); C 38/418 Master's Report (4 February 1734)
(*Bank v. Hunter* for defaulting on a bill of exchange: see also Bank of England records, following)
C 11/1550/24 *Hunter v. Pryce* 1738 (bill only)
(James Hunter and partner Loth Speck v. ship captain for proceeds of voyage)

Palmer-related
C 11/528/44 *Palmer v. Peacock* 1737
C 11/866/4 *Palmer v. Peacock* 1743
C 127/55 *Palmer v. Peacock* Interrogatories and Depositions 1737/38
Decrees and Orders: C 33/370, f. 61^r (17 December 1737), f. 125^r (23 January

1738), f. 129ᵛ (3 February 1738), ff. 220ᵛ–221ᵛ (4 March 1738); C 33/372, f. 18ᵛ (28 November 1738), f. 33ʳ (8 December 1738)

(executors of Richard Peacock v. his son and heir James Peacock, brother of Elizabeth Peacock Palmer [no relation between executor and the family of Ralph Palmer])

C 107/87 an account of repairs necessary to Mrs. Mayne's house, 10 June 1776

C 109/25–27 account books of Thomas Wagg, ironsmith, showing extensive ironwork for the Palmers' Curzon Street house 1744–47

Oaths of Allegiance and test oaths

(various Royal Academy of Music directors, e.g.)

C 214/15 (Geo. I, 1–5, 11–13) Pulteney (1715), Fairfax (1718), Stanhope (1718)

C 214/16 (Geo. I, 1, 5–11) Burlington (1719)

C 224/30 (1719–1778) Portland (1719)

(taking the oaths at a central law court, such as Chancery, was required of major office holders; see also Metropolitan London Archives)

Forfeited Estates Commission

See Emma Jolly, "Jacobite Material: The Records of the Forfeited Estates Commission for England," *Genealogists' Magazine* 28/11 (2006): 493–98

FEC 1/635 Col. Bernard Granville (Mary Delany's father)

FEC 1/672 High Treason: Alphabetical list of all persons attainted by impeachments

FEC 2/52 Index of all against whom claims were made

Lord Chamberlain Papers

LC 5/158, ff. 403 and 439 Goupy's commission and payment to mend and repair Mantegna's *Triumphs of Caesar*

Prerogative Court of Canterbury (wills)

Delany-related

PROB 11/798 (proved 12 December 1752) Sir Anthony Westcombe

PROB 11/1015 (proved 25 November 1775 and 26 January 1776) Bernard Granville

PROB 11/1165 (proved 7 May 1788) Mary Delany

PROB 10/3078 Mary Delany's original will

Donnellan-related

PROB 11/875 (proved 22 May 1762) Anne Donnellan

PROB 10/2321 Anne Donnellan's original will

Goupy-related

PROB 11/684 (proved 13 July 1737) John Hedges

PROB 11/461 (proved 20 August 1701) William Hedges (father to John Hedges)

PROB 11/600 (proved 10 November 1724) Anne Hedges (mother to John Hedges)

PROB 11/370 (proved 10 August 1682) Col. John Searle (first husband to Anne Hedges)

PROB 11/949 (proved 22 June 1769) Joseph Goupy

PROB 10/2510 Joseph Goupy's original will

Hunter-related

PROB 11/545 (proved 29 March 1715) John Hunter (father of James Hunter)

PROB 11/572 (proved 5 February 1720) Joanna Hunter (grandmother of James Hunter)

PROB 11/595 (proved 18 January 1723) James Lannoy (uncle of James Hunter)

PROB 11/709 (proved 13 April 1741) Charles Master (first cousin of James Hunter)

PROB 11/716 (proved 6 March 1742) James Hunter (uncle of James Hunter)

PROB 11/739 (proved 1 April 1745) Sir Harcourt Master (uncle of James Hunter)

PROB 11/792 (proved 2 January 1752) Elizabeth Hunter (aunt of James Hunter)

PROB 11/833 (proved 12 October 1757) James Hunter

PROB 10/2217 James Hunter's original will

PROB 11/937 (proved 23 March 1768) Henry Lannoy Hunter (brother of James Hunter)

PROB 11/975 (proved 26 March 1772) John Ellicott (an executor of James Hunter's will)

Palmer-related

PROB 11/550 (proved 16 February 1716) Ralph Palmer (I)

PROB 11/746 (proved 20 March 1746) Ralph Palmer (II)

PROB 11/814 (proved 13 February 1755) Ralph Palmer (III)

PROB 11/685 (proved 10 October 1737) Richard Peacock (father to Elizabeth Palmer); summary in the Bank of England will register, Society of Genealogists

PROB 11/823 (proved 21 June 1756) Elizabeth Peacock (mother to Elizabeth Palmer)

Mayne-related

PROB 11/695 (proved 20 March 1739) Christopher Batt (father of Elizabeth Mayne)

PROB 11/742 (proved 25 October 1745) Eleanor Mayne (sister of John Mayne)

PROB 11/820 (proved 25 February 1756) Christopher Batt Jr. (brother of Elizabeth Mayne)

PROB 11/945 (proved 10 July 1769) Elizabeth Mayne

PROB 10/2501 Elizabeth Mayne's original will

PROB 11/1136 (proved 29 December 1785) John Mayne (son of Elizabeth Mayne)

PROB 11/1492 (proved 10 February 1809) The Rt. Hon. Isabella Countess of Dundonald (widow of John Mayne)

PROB 11/1783 (proved 19 April 1831) John Thomas Batt Jr. (son of John Thomas Batt, residuary legatee of Christopher Batt Jr.'s will should his nephew and niece die without issue)

PROB 11/1974 (proved 24 February 1843) Susan Batt (widow of John Thomas Batt)

General Register Office (Non-conformist Records)

RG 7/159, f. 35^v marriage record of Mary Dublois and George Peacock (brother to Elizabeth Peacock) 5 July 1737, Fleet Prison

RG 7/160, f. 40^r *ditto* Fleet Street

RG 4/3980, f. 61^r burial of Mary Peacock (wife of George Peacock?) 30 August 1742 Bunhill Fields

State Papers

SP 34/17/43A–F (December 1711) Petition of John Mayne to Queen Anne and supporting affidavits in relation to his murder of Margaret Richards of Exeter

Levant Company (documents relating to Henry Lannoy Hunter)

SP 105/117 (not paginated)

SP 110/25, ff. 179^r–179^v, 180^v

SP 110/27, ff. 2^r–4^r, 13^r–20^v

SP 110/57, Pt. 1: ff. 36^r, 53^v–54^r, 55^v–56^r, 65^r

SP 110/61, ff. 19^v–32^r, 40^r–44^v

War Office (documents relating to John Hunter's service as a Royal Dragoon)

SP 41/18 (21 July 1747)

SP 41/20 (24 January 1750)

(see also below, War Office)

War Office

documents relating to John Hunter's service as a Royal Dragoon
WO 25/21, p. 19
WO 25/22, p. 89
WO 25/22, p. 113

Parliamentary Archives (House of Lords Judicial Office)

House of Lords Appeal Cases

Delany v. Tenison

HL/PO/JO/10/3/251/2 (28 June 1757) petition and appeal
HL/PO/JO/10/4/30 (28 June 1757) answers of two respondents
HL/PO/JO/10/4/35 (16 June 1767) answer of one respondent
HL/PO/JO/10/7/101 (28 June 1757) full case and judgment
HL/PO/JU/4/3/13 appeal cases and writs of error 1758–1760: Delany,
      pp. 80–83
[HL/PO/JO/2/29] *Journals of the House of Lords* 29, pp. 135–85
[HL/PO/JO/2/31] _____ 31, p. 635 (16 June 1767) revival of *Delany v.*
      Tenison
[HL/PO/JO/2/32] _____ 32, p. 7 (25 November 1767) dismissal of
      revived case

South Sea Company

HL/PO/JO/10/5/57–63 (1720) subscriber lists
HL/PO/JO/10/2/156 (1720) Inventory of the real and personal estate of Sir
      Harcourt Masters (James Hunter's uncle and a director of the South Sea
      Company), published London: printed for Jacob Tonson, Bernard Lintot,
      and William Taylor, 1721

British Library [BL]

Correspondence

Add. MS. 4313 Letters of Benjamin Martyn to Thomas Birch (1737–1762), ff.
      101–69
Add. MS. 32556, ff. 170–71 Letter from Goupy to Cox Macro, Doctor in
      Divinity, with Macro's biography of Goupy (1728)
Add. MS. 33965, f. 204 chit signed by Handel authorizing the bearer to col-
      lect his South Sea Company dividend (1716)
Add. MSS. 46964–47000 Correspondence of John Percival, First Lord
      Egmont, mostly concerning his estates, but from 46867 a "conclusion"
      offering a chronology of the year with personal details
Add. MSS. 47025–47033 Correspondence of John Percival, First Lord
      Egmont, mostly personal

Add. MS. 70493 Letters of Elizabeth Montagu copied by the duchess of
Portland (pp. 1–73: letters to Donnellan)

East India Company Records
Cash journals (with annual accounting of James Hunter's dyeing for the company)
L/AG/1/5/15 (1742–1750), p. 208 (30 June 1746), p. 265 (30 June 1747), p.
306 (31 May 1748), p. 359 (31 May 1749), p. 424 (30 June 1750)
L/AG/1/5/16 (1750–1756), p. 54 (31 May 1751), p. 136 (31 May 1752), p. 213
(31 May 1753), p. 295 (31 May 1754), p. 364 (30 June 1755), p. 433 (30
June 1756)
L/AG/1/5/17 (1756–1763), p. 56 (30 June 1757), p. 115 (31 July 1758: "James
Hunter Dec^d in full for Dying and Setting")

Anne Donnellan's stock account:
L/AG/14/5/10-13 (1749–1762)

Fire Judgments (following London Fire, 1666)
Hunter family
Add. MS. 5063, #66, ff. 221–22
Add. MS. 5080, #19, ff. 175–81^r
Add. MS. 5092, #28 and 57, ff. 25–38 and 279–86

Inventory of Handel's household goods after his death
Eg. 3009, ff. 17–18

Music
Add. MS. 52363 collection of keyboard pieces owned by "Elizabeth Batt
1704"

Printed material
821.i.7(5) *The Library of Mr. Tho. Britton, Smallcoal-man. Being a curious collection of books in divinity, history, physick and chemistry . . . Also an extraordinary collection of manuscripts in Latin and English. Will be sold by auction . . . on . . . the 1st of November [1694], etc.*
011899.h.13 *The Library of Mr. Thomas Britton, Smallcoal-man, deceas'd. Being a curious collection of very ancient and uncommon books . . . Also a collection of MSS. chiefly on vellum. Which will be sold by auction . . . on . . . the 24th of January, 1714/15, etc.*
1509/1479 Thomas Weston, *A New and Compendious Treatise of Arithmetick, in whole numbers and fractions, vulgar and decimal*, 2nd ed. (London: Ward & Chandler, 1736)

9917.ccc.29 *A Copy of the Names of all the Marriages, Baptisms, and Burials . . . Somerset House . . . 1714 to 1776* (1862), p. 8, Hunter-Cooke (see Lambeth Palace, p. 402)

C.131.h.4.(9.) *A Catalogue of all the Genuine Collection of Italian, and other Pictures, belonging to Joseph Goupy, Esq; Cabinet-Painter to his late Royal Highness, Frederick Prince of Wales . . . Which will be Sold by Auction, by Mr. Hobbs . . . On Friday next, the 23d of March 1765,* etc.

C.131.ff.20.(10.) *A Catalogue of the Collection of Pictures, Drawings, and Several high-finish'd Drawings by Marco Ricci, and other Masters, of that eminent Painter, Mr. Joseph Goupy, deceas'd; which . . . will be sold by Auction, by Mr. Langford and Son . . . on . . . the third of April 1770,* etc.

C.131.ff.20.(11.) *A Catalogue of the Collection of Prints, Copper Plates, and Drawings of Mr. Joseph Goupy, deceas'd; which . . . will be sold by Auction, by Mr. Langford and Son . . . on . . . the 3d of April 1770,* etc.

M/636 (1–60) microfilm: Verney Papers from Claydon House, co. Bucks; Presented by the Gilbert Verney Foundation and the Friends of the Dartmouth Library

Bank of England
Anne Donnellan
accounts:

AC27/248 (p. 535) 4% Ann.s 1747 Lottery 2nd Subscription
  Transfers: AC28/964 #1793; AC28/962 #1075, #1786, #1787

AC27/6700 (p. 1439) Reduced Annuities, later reduced 3% Annuities
  Transfers: AC28/27593 #1625, #2965; AC28/27599 #4146; AC28/27595 #4550; AC28/27606 #5163; AC28/27617 #1742; AC28/27619 #1749; AC28/27640 #9311; AC28/27641 #2142

AC27/6716 (p. 1496)
  Transfers: AC28/27655 #2162; posthumous withdrawals: AC28/27673 #8637, #8638; AC28/27675 #8899; AC28/27674 #9612, #9613

Joseph Goupy
accounts:
South Sea Annuities (no transfers survive)
AC27/6442 (p. 555) 1723–1728 G
AC27/6455 (p. 926) 1728–1733 E–G
AC27/6463 (p. 676) 1733–1738 E–G

James Hunter
Stock accounts:
AC27/113 (p. 677) 3 % Ann.s 1726 (1732–33)
  Transfers (all with signatures): AC28/628 #12823, 12824, 12854

AC27/6456 (p. 629) South Sea Annuities '28–'33 (1732)
AC27/451 (p. 752) bank stock (1732–34)
  Transfers (all with signatures): AC28/1575 #2270; AC28/1576 #2815
  AC28/1579 #5270
Cash accounts:
C98/153, f. 2761 (1743–45); C98/160, f. 2613 (1745–47); C98/188, f. 2737
  (1753–54); C98/195, f. 2570 (1754–56)
Administration:
ADM9/22, f. 465 (7 and 18 May 1731) Hunter received £435 from bank by
  bill on Schultze
ADM7/11, f. 44 (28 November 1734) Hunter repaid bank in full for bill on
  Schultze (see legal case)
ADM7/11, f. 32 (6 November 1735) bank loaned Hunter £3,000 @ 4% per
  annum
ADM9/27, f. 383 (14 August 1740) Hunter repaid £2,701 5s.
ADM9/27, f. 410 (13 September 1740) Hunter repaid principal (£298 15s.)
  and interest (£573 17s. 1d.) in full

Elizabeth Mayne

accounts:
AC27/150 (p. 1950) 3% Ann.s 1743
  Transfers: AC28/698 #4699, #4700; AC28/702 #4913, #4920
AC27/162 (p. 1426) 3% Ann.s 1745 A–Z
  Transfers: AC28/733 #8351; AC28/716 #3727; AC28/715 # 3771
AC27/159 (p. 1414) 3% Anns. 1744 A–Z
  Transfer: AC28/724 #1576
AC27/1388 (p. 2987) Consols 3% 1752–1759 I–O
  Transfers: AC28/3686 #5993; AC28/3690 # 9986
AC27/1401 (p. 5260) Consol 3% 1759–1761 M–P
  Transfers: AC28/3696 #4121; AC28/3710 #797; AC28/3733 #3446
AC27/1417 (p. 5519) Consols 3% 1761–1764
  Transfers: AC28/3770 #5235; AC28/3805 #5544
AC27/1436 (p. 6290) Consols 3% 1764–1769 M–N
  Transfers: AC28/3831 #7830; AC28/3840 #4757; AC28/3880 #8831
AC27/1456 (p. 6857) Consols 3% 1769–1776 M–N
  Transfers; posthumous withdrawals: AC28/3936 #4515; AC28/4000
  #8908

Elizabeth Palmer

accounts:
AC27/167 (p. 2418) 3% Ann.s 1757 A–Z
  Transfers: AC28/747 #3349, #6080, #5071; AC28/744 #3304

AC27/1389 (p. 3671) 3% Consols 1752–1759 P–S
AC27/173 (p. 2571) 3% Ann.s 1759 L–Z
    Transfer: AC28/750 #5961
AC27/1401 (p. 6098) Consols 3% 1759–1761 M–P
    Transfer: AC28/3703 #6864
AC27/181 (p. 1577) 3½ % Ann.s 1756 A–Z
    Transfers: AC28/781 #6570 *signature*; AC28/782 #7112
AC27/1418 (p. 6877) Consols 3% 1761–1764 O–P
    Transfers: AC28/3786 #6905; AC28/3779 #8928; AC28/3816 #1937

Westminster City Archives (for Handel, Palmer, Delany, Donnellan, Goupy)

Scavengers and Highway rate books for St. George Hanover Square 1720–
    1750, City of Westminster Archives Centre

London Metropolitan Archives [LMA]
Image
SC/PZ/PP/02/011 *Dye Works Old Ford,* watercolor signed and dated A. G.
    Stout [18]90

Middlesex Deeds Register
Delany
MDR/1755/3/33 & 34 purchase of house in Spring Gardens

Goupy
MDR/1746/2/68 transfer of house on Savile Row

Palmer
MDR/1746/1/188 transfer of house on Curzon Street to Ralph Palmer
MDR/1746/1/298 further transfer of property abutting Curzon Street to
    Ralph Palmer
MDR/1746/2/325 register of will of Ralph Palmer II confirming Palmer III
    as heir
MDR/1746/2/467 transfer of Chelsea house from Palmer to Lord Verney
MDR/1755/3/470 transferred the leases of Curzon Street house to Elizabeth
    Verney
MDR/1758/2/591 transfer of Curzon Street house from Elizabeth Palmer to
    Lord Verney

Mayne
MDR/1750/1/251 sale or transfer of four row houses in Kensington from
    Christopher Batt Jr. and William Pannett to Frances Stone, widow

MDR/1750/1/252 confirmation by Pannett of his purchase of these houses in 1730

Oath rolls and certificates
(various Royal Academy of Music directors, e.g.)

County courts: Middlesex

MR/R/O/031 (January–September 1720) oath rolls: James Bruce, Thomas Smith, John Arbuthnot (14 January 1720); Joseph Eyles, Francis Whitworth (5 September 1720)

MR/R/S/053 (January 1719–December 1720) sacrament certificates: Bruce, Smith, Arbuthnot (10 January 1719); Whitworth (21 August 1720)

MR/R/O/029 (1715–1770) Register Book: Bruce, Smith, Arbuthnot (14 January 1720); Whitworth (5 September 1720); Brian Fairfax (8 July 1723)

County courts: Westminster

WR/R/O/012 (1716–1721) oath rolls: Halifax (1718)

WR/R/S/027 (January 1719–December 1720) sacrament certificates: John Vanbrugh, William Poulteney (3 March 1719)

City of London court

CLA/047/LR/02/01/005/005 (1719–January 1728) oath roll: John Percival (25 April 1720)

CLA/047/LR/02/03/033 (January 1720–January 1722) sacrament certificates: John Percival (13 March 1720, #642)

(See also the National Archive for central law courts)

Marriage license

DL/A/D/004/MS10091/087 Bishop of London Marriage Licenses: Palmer-Peacock (20 February 1746), f. 109^r

Inhabitants and land tax assessment records

CLC/W/FB/011/MS10835 Ward of Aldgate Book of Inhabitants List: James Hunter in Billiter Sq. (1732), f. 524^r

CLC/525/MS11316 Land tax assessment records for the third precinct in the Ward of Aldgate (1733–1742), James Hunter on Fenchurch St. in vols. 102, 105, 108, 111, 114, 117, 120, 123, 126

CLC/525/MS06002 Land tax assessment records for the Parish of St. Mary Stratford Bow for 1747 and 1755, Hunter's dye house in Old Ford (pt. 1, p. 9, and pt. 2, p. 16)

Hand-in-Hand Fire Office (fire insurance)

CLC/B/055/MS08674/067, policy no. 33314 (12 July 1745) James Hunter's insurance on dye house in Old Ford with details of property, continued to 1752

CLC/B/055/MS08674/079, policy no. 33314 (9 June 1752) renewal of above by Hunter; reassigned by Hunter's executors 26 June 1759

Guildhall Library
Levant Company Apprenticeships
MS 30719/4, f. 4ᵛ Henry Lannoy Hunter apprenticeship (12 August 1726)
MS 30719/4, f. 16ᵛ Henry Lannoy Hunter granted freedom of the city (19 December 1733)

London Directories 1677–1900
Vols. 1–18 (to 1760)

Tower Hamlets Local History Library and Archives (Bancroft Library)
Land tax assessments, Parish of St. Mary Stratford Bow
L/SMS/B/1/1–3 James Hunter bought his dye house from Wilson in 1745; it stood empty from his death in 1757 to 1759; new owner in 1760 (records for 1747 and 1755 at London Metropolitan Archive)

Lambeth Palace
Marriage licenses (Archbishop of Canterbury)
VMI/75 Vicar-General Marriage Allegations, Mayne-Batt (19 July 1722)
FMI/63 Faculty Office Marriage Allegations, Hunter-Cooke (17 December 1728)

Return of Papists
Terrick 22, f.16 (Fulham Papers) Return of Papists (3 August 1767), Goupy

National Art Library, Victoria and Albert Museum
23.L Sale Catalogue of Goupy's Pictures and Drawings (3 April 1770), typescript, from a bound volume in the Royal Library, Windsor, on microfiche
86.OO.18–19 *Sale Catalogues of the Principal Collections of Pictures (One Hundred & seventy one in number) Sold by Auction in England with the years 1711–1759, the greater part of them with the Prices and Names of Purchasers,* ms., 2 vols., compiled by Mr. (Richard) Houlditch
86.T.127 Thomas Weston, *A Copy-Book Written for the Use of the Young-Gentlemen at the Academy in Greenwich* (London, 1726)

Barclays Group Archives, Manchester

Archives of Goslings Bank

Mary Delany
Cash Account:
ACC 130/19 (p. 449) 1747
ACC 130/21 (p. 113) 1747–1751
ACC 130/23 (p. 133) 1751–1754
ACC 130/25 (p. 155) 1754–1756
ACC 130/27 (p. 133) 1757–1759
ACC 130/29 (p. 123) 1759–1760
ACC 130/31 (p. 99) 1760–1762
ACC 130/33 (p. 89) 1762–1763
ACC 130/35 (p. 81) 1763–1765
ACC 130/37 (p. 72) 1765–1766
ACC 130/39 (p. 208) 1766–1768
ACC 130/41 (p. 230) 1768–1769
ACC 130/43 (pp. 253, 258) 1769–1771
ACC 130/46 (pp. 290, 291) 1771–1773
ACC 130/49 (pp. 325, 326) 1773–1775
ACC 130/53 (pp. 342, 343) 1775–1777
ACC 130/57 (pp. 375, 376) 1777–1779
ACC 130/61 (pp. 364, 365) 1779–1781
ACC 130/65 (pp. 400, 401) 1781–1783
ACC 130/69 (pp. 423, 424) 1783–1785
ACC 130/74 (pp. 164, 165) 1785–1787
ACC 130/80 (p. 183) 1787–1789

Anne Donnellan
Cash Account:
ACC 130/25 (pp. 26, 92) 1754–1757
ACC 130/27 (pp. 22–23) 1757–1759
ACC 130/29 (p. 27) 1759–1760
ACC 130/31 (pp. 20, 405) 1760–1762
ACC 130/33 (p. 286) 1762 (account closed at her death)

Bodleian Library, Oxford

MSS Eng. Lett. c. 438 and d. 409 correspondence of Ralph Palmer II, mostly
    1720–1731

Berkshire Record Office, Reading (Hunter Papers)

D/EHR E1 Henry Lannoy Hunter cash journal (with record of payments to and from James Hunter)

D/EHR F1/2 marriage contract of James Hunter's parents (1708)

D/EHR F3 settling of father's estate on Henry Lannoy Hunter (1734)

D/EHR F7 & 11 marriage contract of Henry Lannoy Hunter (1736)

D/EZ5/B6/2 loans in cash and bonds from Henry Lannoy Hunter to James Hunter (1734)

East Sussex Record Office, Lewes

FRE 8353–8364 Palmer property in Leicestershire with précis of Palmer wills and marriage contracts

Herefordshire Record Office (Kentchurch Court Estate)

AL40/1050 (10 January 1745) assignment of lease of dye house in Old Ford to James Hunter by Thomas Wilson

Newport Public Libraries, Newport, Wales

Mrs. Delany's letters, mounted in nine volumes (1720–1788): these original letters contain bits of material omitted for various reasons by Lady Llanover in her nineteenth-century edition; further, the collection does not include all the letters published by Llanover

Houghton Library, Harvard University (Cambridge, MA)

*EB7.A100.739a *Advice to Mr. Handel . . .* [April 1739]

F EC7 H100 738g J. H. [?John Hedges], *Guido's Ghost: a tale* (London: printed for John Brindley . . . , 1738) about Joseph Goupy

MS Eng. 1254 letter to Mary Pendarves (later Delany) (1724) from Lord Lansdowne

MS Eng. 1365 (46) letter to Elizabeth Robinson Montagu (1764) from Mary Delany

MS Eng. 1365 (50) two letters to Elizabeth Robinson Montagu (1742 and 1752) from Anne Donnellan

Private Collections

John Mayne marriage settlement on Elizabeth Batt (12 July 1722)

Christopher Batt covenant with cousin William Batt concerning will of their uncle Thomas Batt (18 May 1739)

Deeds and indentures relating to the Manor House at Teffont Evias (Mayne)

Papers and correspondence of the Bosanquet family (Hunter)

SELECTED SECONDARY SOURCES ON THE SIX FRIENDS

(There are many more publications on Delany and the Verney family, and many, many more sources on the eighteenth century, but I have listed only those that had a direct influence on my research or thinking for this book. See the Notes for specific references, and consult the sources listed here for further bibliography)

Delany

Cahill, Katherine. *Mrs. Delany's Menus, Medicines and Manners*. Dublin: New Island, 2005.

Fortescue, Mary Teresa. *The History of Calwich Abbey*. London: Simpkin & Co., 1914.

Granville, Roger. *The History of the Granville Family*. Exeter: William Pollard & Co., 1895.

Handasyde, Elizabeth. *Granville the Polite: The Life of George Granville, Lord Lansdowne, 1666–1735*. London: Oxford University Press, 1933.

Hayden, Ruth. *Mrs Delany and Her Flower Collages*. London: British Museum Press, 1980.

Kippis, Andrew, and Joseph Towers. *Biographia Britannica: or, the Lives of the Most Eminent Persons Who Have Flourished in Great Britain and Ireland*. 5 vols. London: W. and A. Strahan, 1778–1793).

Laird, Mark, and Alicia Weisberg-Roberts, eds. *Mrs. Delany and Her Circle*. New Haven, CT: Yale University Press, 2009.

McLean, Hugh. "Bernard Granville, Handel and the Rembrandts." *The Musical Times* 126/1712 (1985): 593–601.

———. "Granville, Handel and 'Some Golden Rules.'" *The Musical Times* 126/1713 (1985): 662–65.

Peacock, Molly. *The Paper Garden: An Artist Begins Her Life's Work at 72*. New York: Bloomsbury, 2010.

The Autobiography and Correspondence of Mary Granville, Mrs. Delany: with Interesting Reminiscences of King George the Third and Queen Charlotte. 6 vols. Edited by Lady Llanover [Augusta Hall]. London: Richard Bentley, 1861–1862, cited as DELANY CORRESPONDENCE. Originally published in two series of three volumes, the set will be cited here as a continuous six-volume series, as it is treated in the comprehensive index in the final volume.

Correspondence (to and about):

"Correspondence with Dr. and Mrs. Delany, Mrs. Donnellan, and Mrs. Dewes." In *The Correspondence of Samuel Richardson*, vol. 4, edited by

Anna Laetitia Barbauld, 1–119. London: Richard Phillips, 1804, cited as
     RICHARDSON CORRESPONDENCE.
The Correspondence of Jonathan Swift, vol. 5: 1737–1745. Edited by Harold
     Williams. Oxford: Clarendon Press, 1965. (Delany and Donnellan)

Donnellan

Diary of Viscount Percival, Afterwards First Earl of Egmont. 3 vols. Edited by
     R. A. Roberts. Manuscripts of the Earl of Egmont: Historical Manuscripts
     Commission. London: His Majesty's Stationery Office, 1920–23, cited as
     PERCIVAL DIARY.
Kelly, Patrick. "Anne Donnellan: Irish Proto-Bluestocking." *Hermathena—A
     Trinity College Dublin Review* 54 (Summer 1993): 39–68.
Popkin, Richard H. "Bishop Berkeley and Anne Donnellan." In *The High
     Road to Pyrrhonism*, edited by Richard A. Watson and James E. Force,
     363–67. San Diego, CA: Austin Hill Press, Inc., 1980.

Correspondence (to and about):

DELANY CORRESPONDENCE (see under Delany or Abbreviated References)
*Elizabeth Montagu—The Queen of the Blue Stockings: Her Correspondence from
     1720 to 1761.* 2 vols. Edited by Emily J. Climenson. London: John Murray,
     1906, cited as MONTAGU CORRESPONDENCE.
John, 5th Earl of Orrery. *The Orrery Papers*. 2 vols. Edited by Countess of
     Cork and Orrery. London: Duckworth and Company, 1903.
The Correspondence of Edward Young (1683–1765). Edited by Henry Pettit.
     Oxford: Clarendon Press, 1971.
*The Letters of Mrs. Elizabeth Montagu, with Some of the Letters of Her
     Correspondents.* 3 vols. Edited by Matthew Montagu. Boston, MA: Wells
     and Lilly, 1825.

Goupy

Andrews, Jonathan, and Andrew Scull. *Customers and Patrons of the Mad-
     Trade.* Berkeley: University of California Press, 2003. (Goupy's consulta-
     tion with a mad doctor about a woman living with him)
Harris, Ellen T. "Joseph Goupy and George Frideric Handel: From
     Professional Triumphs to Personal Estrangement." *Huntington Library
     Quarterly* 71/3 (2008): 397–452, cited as HARRIS-GOUPY.
Robertson, Bruce, and Robert Dance. "Joseph Goupy and the Art of the
     Copy" and "Joseph Goupy: Checklist of Prints, Drawings and Paintings."
     The Bulletin of the Cleveland Museum of Art 75/10 (December 1988):
     354–75 and 376–82.
Simon, Jacob. "New Light on Joseph Goupy." *Apollo* 138 (February 1994):
     15–18.

Hunter

Burrows, Donald. "'Something Necessary to the Connection': Charles Jennens, James Hunter and Handel's *Samson.*" *The Handel Institute Newsletter* 15/1 (Spring 2004): 1–3.

Gwynn, Grace Lawless. *The Story of the Bosanquets.* London: Eglise Protestante de Londres, 1970.

Harris, Ellen T. "James Hunter, Handel's Friend." *Händel-Jahrbuch* 46 (2000): 247–64.

Mayne

McBain, Audrey, and Lynette Nelson. *The Bounding Spring: A History of Teffont in Wiltshire.* Teffont: Black Horse Books, 2003.

Palmer

Brownbill, J. "Palmer of Little Chelsea." *The Genealogists' Magazine* 2 (1926): 67–72.

Davies, Randall. *Chelsea Old Church.* London: Duckworth and Company, 1904.

Keevil, John J. *The Stranger's Son.* London: Geoffrey Bles, 1953.

Lady Verney, Margaret Maria. *Verney Letters of the Eighteenth Century from the MSS. At Claydon House.* 2 vols. London: Ernest Benn Ltd., 1930.

Whyman, Susan E. *Sociability and Power in Late-Stuart England: The Cultural Worlds of the Verneys 1660–1720.* New York: Oxford University Press, 1999.

ABBREVIATED REFERENCES (ALL OTHER REFERENCES APPEAR IN NOTES WITH A FULL CITATION AT THE FIRST MENTION IN EACH CHAPTER):

BURNEY COLLECTION *17th and 18th Century Burney Collection Database.* British Library Newspapers.

BURNEY-COMMEMORATION Burney, Charles. *An Account of the Musical Performances in Westminster-Abbey and the Pantheon in Commemoration of Handel.* London: printed for the benefit of the Musical Fund, 1785.

BURROWS-HANDEL Burrows, Donald. *Handel.* New York: Schirmer Books, 1994.

BURROWS-HANOVER Burrows, Donald. "Handel and Hanover." In *Bach, Handel, Scarlatti: Tercentenary Essays,* edited by Peter Williams. Cambridge: Cambridge University Press, 1985.

BURROWS-CHAPEL Burrows, Donald. *Handel and the English Chapel Royal.* Oxford: Oxford University Press, 2005.

BURROWS-RONISH Burrows, Donald, and Martha J. Ronish. *A Catalogue of Handel's Musical Autographs.* Oxford: Clarendon Press, 1994.

CAMBRIDGE COMPANION Burrows, Donald, ed. *The Cambridge Companion to Handel*. Cambridge: Cambridge University Press, 1997.

CHE Landgraf, Annette, and David Vickers, eds. *The Cambridge Handel Encyclopedia*. Cambridge: Cambridge University Press, 2009.

COLLECTIONS Best, Terence, ed. *Handel Collections and Their History*. Oxford: Clarendon Press, 1993.

COXE Coxe, William. *Anecdotes of George Frederick Handel and John Christopher Smith*. 1799, repr. Richmond, Surrey: Tiger of the Stripe, 2009.

DELANY CORRESPONDENCE *The Autobiography and Correspondence of Mary Granville, Mrs. Delany: With Interesting Reminiscences of King George the Third and Queen Charlotte*. 6 vols. Edited by Lady Llanover [Augusta Hall]. London: Richard Bentley, 1861–1862.

DEUTSCH Deutsch, Otto Erich. *Handel: A Documentary Biography*. 1955, repr. New York: Da Capo Press, 1974.

ECCO *Eighteenth Century Collections Online.*

GROVE MUSIC ONLINE *The New Grove Dictionary of Music and Musicians*, 2nd edition. London: Macmillan, 2001; online edition at www.oxford musiconline.com.

HARRIS CORRESPONDENCE Burrows, Donald, and Rosemary Dunhill, eds. *Music and Theatre in Handel's World: The Family Papers of James Harris 1732–1780*. Oxford: Oxford University Press, 2002.

HARRIS-GOUPY Harris, Ellen T. "Joseph Goupy and George Frideric Handel: From Professional Triumphs to Personal Estrangement." *Huntington Library Quarterly* 71/3 (2008): 397–452.

HAWKINS Hawkins, Sir John. *A General History of the Science and Practice of Music*. 5 vols. London: printed for T. Payne and Son, 1776.

HHB4 Eisen, Walter, and Margaret Eisen, eds. *Händel-Handbuch*, vol. 4: *Dokumente zu Leben und Schaffen*. Kassel: Bärenreiter, 1985.

MAINWARING Mainwaring, John. *Memoirs of the Life of the Late George Frederic Handel*. London: R. and J. Dodsley, 1760; facs. Buren: Frits Knuf, 1975.

MONTAGU CORRESPONDENCE *Elizabeth Montagu—The Queen of the Blue Stockings: Her Correspondence from 1720 to 1761*. 2 vols. Edited by Emily J. Climenson. London: John Murray, 1906.

ODNB *Oxford Dictionary of National Biography*. Oxford: Oxford University Press, 2004; online edition at www.oxforddnb.com.

PERCIVAL DIARY *Diary of Viscount Percival, Afterwards First Earl of Egmont*. 3 vols. Ed. R. A. Roberts. Manuscripts of the Earl of Egmont: Historical Manuscripts Commission. London: His Majesty's Stationery Office, 1920–1923.

RICHARDSON CORRESPONDENCE "Correspondence with Dr. and Mrs. Delany, Mrs. Donnellan, and Mrs. Dewes." In *The Correspondence of Samuel Richardson*, vol. 4, edited by Anna Laetitia Barbauld, 4–119. London: Richard Phillips, 1804.

SIMON-CELEBRATION Simon, Jacob, ed. *Handel: A Celebration of His Life and Times (1685–1759)*. London: National Portrait Gallery, 1985.

Notes

1. INTRODUCTIONS: HANDEL AND HIS FRIENDS

1. My first published discussion of Handel's will appeared as Ellen T. Harris, "Handel and His Will," in *Handel's Will: Facsimiles and Commentary*, ed. Donald Burrows (London: The Gerald Coke Handel Foundation, 2008), 9–20.
2. Printed in Lady Llanover [Augusta Hall], ed., *The Autobiography and Correspondence of Mary Granville, Mrs. Delany: With Interesting Reminiscences of King George the Third and Queen Charlotte*, 6 vols. (London: Richard Bentley, 1861–62), 3:549–50; hereafter DELANY CORRESPONDENCE.
3. Thomas Harris to James Harris (13 February 1757) in Donald Burrows and Rosemary Dunhill, eds., *Music and Theatre in Handel's World: The Family Papers of James Harris 1732–1780* (Oxford: Oxford University Press, 2002), 321; hereafter HARRIS CORRESPONDENCE.
4. Sir Richard Colt Hoare, *The History of Modern Wiltshire*, 6 vols. (London: J. Nichols, 1822–1844), 4:112.
5. DELANY CORRESPONDENCE, 2:267.
6. Charles Burney, *A General History of Music: From the Earliest Ages to the Present Period*, 4 vols. (London: printed for the author, 1776–1789), 4:110.

2. BEFORE LONDON

1. Otto Erich Deutsch, *Handel: A Documentary Biography* (1955; repr. ed., New York: Da Capo Press, 1974), 1; hereafter DEUTSCH.
2. John Mainwaring, *Memoirs of the Life of the Late George Frederic Handel* (London: printed for R. and J. Dodsley, 1760); hereafter MAINWARING. See pp. 1–28 for the stories of Handel's youth. In my discussion of these years in Handel's life, I take the liberty of quoting from these wonderful stories.
3. For Handel's probable education and curriculum in Germany, see John Butt, "Germany–education and apprenticeship," in *The Cambridge Companion to Handel*, ed. Donald Burrows (Cambridge: Cambridge University Press, 1997), 11–23; hereafter CAMBRIDGE COMPANION.
4. Christoph Wolff, *Johann Sebastian Bach: The Learned Musician* (New York: W. W. Norton & Company, 2000), 183–84.
5. Georg Philipp Telemann [autobiography], in Johann Mattheson, *Grun-*

dlage einer Ehren-Pforte, ed. Max Schneider (Kassel: Bärenreiter-Verlag, 1969), 354–69, at 359: "Die Feder des vortreflichen Hn. Johann Kuhnau diente mir hier zur Nachfolge in Fugen und Contrapuncten; in melodischen Sätzen aber, und deren Untersuchung, hatten Händel und ich, bey öfftern Besuchen auf beiden Seiten, wie auch schrifftlich, eine stete Beschäfftigung."

6. Wolff makes a point of the importance of a university degree as a qualification for an important cantorial position, pointing out that Bach was exceptional in lacking a university education (*Bach*, 221): "all his predecessors in the St. Thomas cantorate since the sixteenth century and all of his successors until well into the nineteenth century were university trained."

7. Mattheson, *Grundlage*, 93, as translated in Donald Burrows, *Handel* (New York: Schirmer Books, 1994), 17; hereafter BURROWS-HANDEL.

8. On Keiser's absence from Hamburg and the commission of Handel to compose an opera on the libretto of *Almira*, see John H. Roberts, "Keiser and Handel at the Hamburg Opera," *Händel-Jahrbuch* 36 (1990): 63–87, and Dorothea Schröder, "Zu Entstehung und Aufführungsgeschichte von Händels Oper 'Almira': Anmerkungen zur Edition des Werkes in der Hallischen Händel-Ausgabe," *Händel-Jahrbuch* 36 (1990): 147–53. Many details of this story need to be supposed.

9. DEUTSCH, 11–12.

10. *Das neu-eröffnete Orchestre* (Hamburg, 1713), 211: "Wer bey diesen Zeiten etwas in der *Music* zu *praestiren* vermeinet, der begibt sich nach *Engelland*."

11. MAINWARING, 32–37, preserves Handel's version of this story. For Mattheson's version, see Mattheson, *Grundlage*, 94–95; English translation in BURROWS-HANDEL, 18.

12. MAINWARING, 39 and 41.

13. MAINWARING, 51–52.

14. Ursula Kirkendale, "Orgelspiel im Lateran," *Die Musikforschung* 41 (1988): 1–9; Werner Braun, "Händel und der 'römische Zauberhut' (1707)," *Göttinger Händel-Beiträge* 2 (1989): 71–86.

15. This chronology, long assumed, has been proven correct in Rashid-S. Pegah, "'anno 1707': Neue Forschungsergebnisse zur Tätigkeit von G. F. Händel in Rom und Florenz," *Die Musikforschung* 62 (2009): 2–13.

16. Carlo Vitali and Antonello Fùrnari, "Händels Italienreise—neue Dokumente, Hypothesen und Interpretationen," *Göttinger Händel-Beiträge* 4 (1991): 41–66, and Juliane Riepe, "Händel in Neapel," in *Ausdrucksformen der Musik des Barock. Passionoratorium–Serenata–Rezitativ*, ed. S. Schmalzried (Karlsruhe: Laaber-Verlag, 2002), 77–128.

17. TNA C 12/726/4 (1739), lawsuit of *Hedges v. Goupy*.

18. *A Catalogue of all the Genuine Collection of Italian, and other Pictures, belonging to Joseph Goupy, Esq; Cabinet-Painter to his late Royal Highness, Frederick Prince of Wales . . . Which will be Sold by Auction, by Mr. Hobbs . . . On Friday next, the 23d of March*, etc. (London, 1765), BL C.131.h.4.(9.). The spelling of the cardinal's name as "Ottobani" was common in England at this time and probably can be attributed to the English printer. It appears this way, for example, in the "Memoirs of the Life of Sig. Agostino Steffani" by John Hawkins when it was reprinted in *The Gentleman's Magazine* (October 1772).

19. No painting attributed to Carracci appears in the inventory of Cardinal Ottoboni's collection made at his death in 1740. See Edward J. Olszewski, *The Inventory of Paintings of Cardinal Pietro Ottoboni (1667–1740)* (New York: Peter Lang, 2004). A painting of Saint Catherine of similar description and size (to the extent that "palmi" can be converted into inches or centimeters) appears in the inventory made in 1690 of the collection of Ottoboni's uncle, Pope Alexander VIII, where it is attributed (weakly) to "Vanni"; this collection passed to the cardinal on the death of the pope in 1691. The original painting by Carracci is now in the collection of the National Gallery of Art, Washington, DC, and its provenance can only be traced back to Louis-Jacques-Aimé-Théodore de Dreux, Marquis de Nancré, who died in 1719. After passing through a number of hands in France, it was sold at auction in London in 1798. The Samuel H. Kress Foundation, New York, purchased it in 1950 and gave it to the National Gallery of Art, Washington, DC, in 1952. If the *St. Catherine* by Carracci can be equated with the "Vanni" painting in the inventory of 1690, then it passed out of the Ottoboni collection sometime after Goupy left Rome around 1710, perhaps as part of the cardinal's campaign to become Cardinal-Protector of France. Another possibility, of course, is that the "Vanni" and Carracci paintings are not equivalent and that Ottoboni acquired Carracci's painting independently of his uncle and then disposed of it before his death.

20. Carlo Vitali, "Italy—political and musical contexts," in Cambridge Companion, 43.

21. *Disinganno*, which means "undeceit," or, when used as an abstract personification, "The Undeceiver," cannot literally be translated as Truth. In later versions of the work in England, however, the difficult Italian word *Disinganno* in the title is replaced at first by "Verità," and then in the English version by "Truth." I use "Truth" here for simplicity and to make the connection to the later London revisions.

22. Mainwaring, 53.

23. Ibid., 64–65.
24. Ibid., 65.
25. *A Dictionary of British and Irish Travellers in Italy 1701–1800*, compiled from the Brinsley Ford Archive by John Ingamells (New Haven, CT: Yale University Press, 1997), 633.
26. Giordano's *Galatea* was owned by the Samminiati family of Florence by at least 1677. It descended by marriage to the Pazzi family in the eighteenth century and through them at the end of the nineteenth century to the collection of the Pitti Palace, Florence. See Oreste Ferrari and Giuseppe Scavizzi, *Luca Giordano,* 3 vols. (Naples: Edizioni scientifiche italiane, 1966), 2:86. Goupy can only have seen this painting in Florence.
27. Edward Croft-Murray, *Decorative Painting in England 1537–1837,* 2 vols. (Feltham, Middlesex: The Hamlyn Publishing Group, 1970), 2:264–65.
28. Donald Burrows, "Handel and Hanover," in *Bach, Handel, Scarlatti: Tercentenary Essays,* ed. Peter Williams (Cambridge: Cambridge University Press, 1985), 39; hereafter BURROWS-HANOVER.
29. The following section on the probable terms of Handel's employment by the elector of Hanover draws in part on Ellen T. Harris, "Handel Is Fired," in *I Wish I'd Been There: European History,* eds. Byron Hollinshead and Theodore K. Rabb (New York: Random House, 2008), 169–86.
30. MAINWARING, 71–72.
31. James Macpherson, *Original Papers; Containing the Secret History of Great Britain, from the Restoration, to the Accession of the House of Hannover,* 2 vols. (Dublin: Printed for Messrs. J. Exshaw et al, 1775), 2:93; in English translation only.
32. See, for example, on Noël Coward's intelligence work for England: Stephen Koch, "The Playboy Was a Spy," *The New York Times Book Review* (Sunday, April 13, 2008), 31.
33. For the complete letter in the original Italian, see Walter and Margaret Eisen, eds., *Händel-Handbuch,* vol. 4: *Dokumente zu Leben und Schaffen* (Kassel: Bärenreiter, 1985), 43, hereafter HHB4: "dotato di onorati sentimenti, di Civili maniere, di gran pratica delle lingue e di talento più che mediocre nella musica . . ."
34. English translation of both letters in DEUTSCH, 43.

3. POLITICS, PATRONAGE, AND PENSION

1. As quoted in Donald Burrows, *Handel and the English Chapel Royal* (Oxford: Oxford University Press, 2005), 43; hereafter BURROWS-CHAPEL.
2. The Gordian knot presented by this contemporary report was beautifully unraveled by Olive Baldwin and Thelma Wilson, "Handel, Eccles and the

Birthday Celebrations for Queen Anne in 1711," *The Musical Times* 154 (2013), 77–84. I am grateful to the authors for providing me with a copy of their work before publication.

3. Quoted in Baldwin and Wilson, "Handel, Eccles and the Birthday Celebrations," 82.

4. The paper on which *Echeggiate, festeggiate!* is written limits the period of composition to Handel's first year in London; see Donald Burrows and Martha J. Ronish, *A Catalogue of Handel's Musical Autographs* (Oxford: Clarendon Press, 1994), 112–13; hereafter BURROWS-RONISH. Further, it cannot have been written after April 17, 1711, when Charles, the Habsburg claimant to the throne of Spain, identified in *Echeggiate, festeggiate!* as Charles III of Spain, became Charles VI, Holy Roman Emperor, on the death of his older brother. John Roberts has argued persuasively that *Echeggiate, festeggiate!* was commissioned by and first performed for Johann Wenzel, Count Gallas, the Imperial ambassador, at his residence in Leicester House in November 1710. He associates the performance with the victories of the Grand Alliance at Almenara and Saragossa the previous summer, for which Queen Anne had declared a national day of Thanksgiving on November 7 (see John Roberts, "'At His First Coming to England': Handel's Habsburg Serenata," in *Händel's Weg von Rom nach London: Tagungsbericht Engers 2009; In memoriam Christoph-Hellmut Mahling*, ed. Wolfgang Birtel, *Schriften zur Musikwissenschaft* 21 [Mainz: Are-Musikverlag, 2012], 31–61).

5. For details of the emendations and disorder, see BURROWS-RONISH: 112–13. John Roberts has proposed a theoretical reconstruction of the first version of the serenata (neither the music nor text survives complete) and suggested that excerpts of the work could have been performed at Queen Anne's birthday celebration (see Roberts, "'At His First Coming to England'").

6. Translation of the Italian text by Terence Best in Georg Friedrich Händel, *Kantaten mit Instrumenten II*, ed. Hans Joachim Marx, *Hallische Händel-Ausgabe*, series 5, vol. 4 (Kassel: Bärenreiter, 1995), xxxvii–xl.

7. The text of the Birthday Ode by Tate survives at the Houghton Library, Harvard University: *EC65 T1878 711s.

8. DELANY CORRESPONDENCE, 1:5–6.

9. The evidence concerning Handel lodging at Barn Elms has been expertly sifted by John Greenacombe, "Mr Andrews, Handel and Barn Elms," a paper presented at the Handel Institute Conference (November 24, 2002). I am grateful to Mr. Greenacombe for giving me a copy of this unpublished paper. A summary appears in John Greenacombe, "Barn Elms," in *The Cambridge Handel Encyclopedia*, eds. Annette Landgraf

and David Vickers (Cambridge: Cambridge University Press, 2009), 83, hereafter CHE.

10. All quotations from Handel's operatic librettos taken from Ellen T. Harris, ed., *The Librettos of Handel's Operas*, 13 vols. (New York: Garland Publishing, 1989).

11. George Granville, Lord Lansdowne, *The Genuine Works in Verse and Prose, of the Right Honourable George Granville, Lord Lansdowne*, 2 vols. (London: printed for J. Tonson and L. Gilliver, 1732), 1:[194].

12. MAINWARING, 78.

13. Handel was a careful conservator of his manuscripts. It might seem unlikely at first that he would bother to take the score of *Rinaldo* with him on his return to Hanover, but he did not know at that time what his future held. It is rather more unlikely that he would have left his newest and most spectacular composition behind.

14. DEUTSCH, 40.

15. Ibid., 44.

16. James A. Winn, "Style and Politics in the Philips-Handel Ode for Queen Anne's Birthday, 1713," *Music & Letters* 89/4 (2008): 547–61.

17. See Winn, "Style and Politics."

18. Harold E. Samuel, "A German Musician Comes to London in 1704," *The Musical Times* 122 (1981): 591.

19. William was the only one of eighteen children borne by Anne to survive infancy, and he died in 1700 at the age of eleven. Note that "Sound the trumpet and beat the warlike drum" bears no relation to the better-known duet "Sound the trumpet, 'til around / You make the list'ning shores resound" from *Come ye sons of Art*, Purcell's Birthday Ode for Queen Mary in 1694.

20. BURROWS-HANOVER, 42–43.

21. BURROWS-CHAPEL, 78.

22. The following sections on Handel's firing, the Utrecht Te Deum and Jubilate, and the Water Music draw in part on Ellen T. Harris, "Handel Is Fired," in *I Wish I'd Been There: European History*, eds. Byron Hollinshead and Theodore K. Rabb (New York: Random House, 2008), 169–86.

23. BURROWS-HANOVER, 43–44.

24. Ibid., 45.

25. David Hunter, "Royal Patronage of Handel in Britain: The Rewards of Pensions and Office," in *Handel Studies: A Gedenkschrift for Howard Serwer*, ed. Richard G. King (Hillsdale, NY: Pendragon Press, 2009), 127–53; for a clear discussion of the title given to Handel as Composer of Music to the Chapel Royal, see BURROWS-CHAPEL, 175–80.

26. Jane Clark, "'Lord Burlington Is Here,'" in *Lord Burlington: Architecture,*

Art and Life, eds. Toby Barnard and Jane Clark (London: The Hamble-don Press, 1995), 251–96; see also the collection of essays in Edward Corp, ed., *Lord Burlington—the Man and His Politics: Questions of Loyalty* (Lewiston, NY: Edwin Mellen Press, 1998).

27. The quotation comes from a letter written by John Percival, listing the rumors associated with the new king (26 January 1715): BL Add. MS. 47028, p. 14 (f. 7ᵛ).

28. Duncan Chisholm has also argued that the opera has a Jacobite meaning, but by associating Silla with the duke of Marlborough, not the elector Georg Ludwig ("Handel's 'Lucio Cornelio Silla': Its Problems and Context," *Early Music* 14 [1986]: 64–70).

29. BURROWS-CHAPEL, 138–39.

30. The performance of Handel's *Water Music* in 1717 is well documented. See Howard Serwer, "The World of the Water Music," *Händel-Jahrbuch* 42–43 (1996/1997): 101–11.

31. MAINWARING, 89–92.

32. Emma Jolly, "Jacobite Material: The Records of the Forfeited Estates Commission for England," *Genealogists' Magazine* 28/11 (2006): 493–98.

33. For additional interpretations, see Ellen T. Harris, *Handel as Orpheus: Voice and Desire in the Chamber Cantatas* (Cambridge, MA: Harvard University Press, 2001), 210–39.

34. Details on Goupy's patronage come from a suit in Chancery: *Hedges v. Goupy* (TNA C 12/726/4); see Ellen T. Harris, "Joseph Goupy and George Frideric Handel: From Professional Triumphs to Personal Estrangement," *Huntington Library Quarterly* 71 (2008): 397–452, here-after HARRIS-GOUPY.

35. Goupy's copy of Raphael's *The Death of Ananias*, showing Ananias being struck down after misrepresenting the amount of the gift he and his wife, Sapphira, have offered to the Apostles (*Acts* V), is preserved in the Yale Center for British Art. Bruce Robertson and Robert Dance, "Joseph Goupy: Checklist of Prints, Drawings and Paintings," *The Bulletin of the Cleveland Museum of Art* 75/10 (December 1988): 376–82, at 380.

36. Carracci's frescos for the Farnese Gallery in Rome include two scenes from this story: *Polyphemus Playing His Pipes for Galatea* and *Polyphemus Attacking Acis and Galatea*.

37. Burlington bought Giordano's *Galatea* in Paris in 1715. I am grateful to Eleanor Brooke, documentation assistant, The Devonshire Collection, Chatsworth, for clarifying the provenance of this painting.

38. Two letters from Goupy to Oxford are printed in Richard W. Goulding and C. K. Adams, eds., *Catalogue of the Pictures Belonging to His Grace the*

Duke of Portland, K. G. (Cambridge: Cambridge University Press, 1936), 446.

39. F. M. Scherer, *Quarter Notes and Bank Notes: The Economics of Music Composition in the Eighteenth and Nineteenth Centuries* (Princeton, NJ: Princeton University Press, 2004), 208.

40. BL Add. MS. 32556, ff. 170–71.

41. Sir John Hawkins, *A General History of the Science and Practice of Music*, 5 vols. (London: printed for T. Payne and Son, 1776), 5:411–12; hereafter HAWKINS.

42. DEUTSCH, 86–88.

43. On Handel and Bononcini, see Judith Milhous and Robert D. Hume, "New Light on Handel and The Royal Academy of Music in 1720," *Theatre Journal* 35 (1983): 149–67, at 152; for Ariosti, see Lowell Lindgren, "Parisian Patronage of Performers from the Royal Academy of Musick (1719–28)," *Music & Letters* 58 (1977): 4–28, at 8.

44. The original libretto, by Francesco Silvani, was titled *La costanza in trionfo* and first composed by Marc'Antonio Ziani for Venice in 1696.

45. Percival correspondence (4 February 1716–1717): BL Add. MS. 47028, p. 358 (f. 179ᵛ).

46. The production took place in Fano: Winton Dean and John Merrill Knapp, *Handel's Operas 1704–1726* (Oxford: Clarendon Press, 1987), 387, n. 5.

47. Elizabeth Gibson, *The Royal Academy of Music 1719–1728* (New York: Garland Publishing, 1989), 155–56 (citing *MSS of the Duke of Portland VII*, "Harley MSS V, 1701–29," *Historical Manuscripts Commission* 29 [London: Mackie & Co., 1901], 311, where *Floridante* is misprinted as "*Horidante*" [but given correctly in the index]).

48. BL Add. MS. 46971, p. 241 (Conclusion: f. iiʳ).

49. This type of perjury was sometimes openly admitted and encouraged. See Eveline Cruickshanks and Howard Erskine-Hill, *The Atterbury Plot* (Basingstoke, Hampshire: Palgrave Macmillan, 2004), 4–6. On Burlington and the Atterbury Plot, see p. 108.

50. William C. Smith, "George III, Handel, and Mainwaring," *The Musical Times* 65 (1924): 789–95, at 790.

51. Charles Burney, *An Account of the Musical Performances in Westminster-Abbey and the Pantheon in Commemoration of Handel* (London: printed for the benefit of the Musical Fund, 1785), 34; hereafter BURNEY-COMMEMORATION.

52. See Hunter, "Royal Patronage."

4. COMMERCE AND TRADE

1. Ruth Smith, "*Opera in tempore belli*: English Traditions in *Rinaldo* Revisited," *Handel Institute Newsletter* 23/2 (2012): [2–6], at [6]. Smith here

argues that, despite its fantastical elements and close connection to Hill's experiences in Jerusalem, *Rinaldo* also may have reminded audience members of the "successful siege of Port Royal (5–13 October 1710) by British regular and colonial forces [which] marked . . . the beginning of permanent British control over the peninsula of Nova Scotia . . ." [5].

2. George Frideric Handel, *Rinaldo*, with the Freiburger Barockorchester, René Jacobs, conductor (Harmonia Mundi Fr., 2003).
3. It has been argued, for example, that in the Passions of Johann Sebastian Bach, sharp and flat keys are deployed allegorically to differentiate Christian understanding and Jewish law. See Eric Chafe, "J. S. Bach's 'St. Matthew Passion': Aspects of Planning, Structure, and Chronology," *Journal of the American Musicological Society* 35 (1982): 49–114. On the crux of the sharp-flat conflict in the *St. John Passion*, see Eric Chafe, "Key Structure and Tonal Allegory in the Passions of J. S. Bach: An Introduction," *Current Musicology* 31 (1981): 39–54, especially 43.
4. The choice of key was closely related to instrumentation. In the Baroque era, the trumpet was largely restricted to the key of its lowest or fundamental note, so that the use of a D trumpet, the most common of the period, was linked to the key of D major. If Handel had chosen to use trumpets for both marches, as described in the libretto, he could not as easily have differentiated the movements in key as he did.
5. See Susan E. Whyman, *Sociability and Power in Late-Stuart England: The Cultural Worlds of the Verneys 1660–1720* (New York: Oxford University Press, 1999).
6. Mainwaring, 10.
7. TNA PROB 11/545 (will of John Hunter, father of James Hunter).
8. The inventory of the Sir Harcourt Master's possessions and debts from 1720 appears in manuscript at the Parliamentary Archives HL/PO/JO/10/2/156 and in print as *The Particular and Inventory of All and Singular the Lands, Tenements, and Hereditaments, Goods, Chattels, Debts, and Personal Estate whatsoever, of Sir Harcourt Master, Knt. Late one of the Directors of the South-Sea Company . . .* (London: printed for Jacob Tonson, Bernard Lintot, and William Taylor, 1721). The son who attended Weston's Academy was Charles Masters (1712–1741).
9. Thomas Weston, *A New and Compendious Treatise of Arithmetick in whole Numbers and Fractions, Vulgar and Decimal . . . With a Large and Copious Appendix Containing several useful Tables of Monies, Weights, and Measures . . .* (2nd edition, London: printed for Ward and Chandler, 1736), 402.
10. TNA C 11/1550/24 (1738), *Hunter v. Pryce.*
11. "The great business flotations of the 1690s required hundreds of copyists and tellers. The organization of these large clerical operations, and the

time they took, were among the most important limiting factors on the business ingenuity of the age . . . It was not accidental that this was the great period of the English writing-master": John Carswell, *The South Sea Bubble* (London: The Cresset Press, 1960), 12–13.

12. *The London Journal* (23 December 1721), a clipping preserved at the Greenwich Heritage Centre (formerly the Greenwich Local History Library), London.

13. From the first set of school regulations (1719), as quoted in H. D. Turner, *The Cradle of the Navy: The Story of the Royal Hospital School at Greenwich and at Holbrook, 1694–1988* (York: William Sessions Limited, 1990), 12.

14. Elizabeth Handasyde, *Granville the Polite: The Life of George Granville, Lord Lansdowne, 1666–1735* (London: Oxford University Press, 1933), 175–76.

15. TNA PROB 11/709 (will of Charles Master, first cousin of James Hunter).

16. TNA PROB 11/739 (will of Sir Harcourt Master, uncle of James Hunter).

17. TNA PROB 11/792 (will of Elizabeth Hunter, aunt of James Hunter).

18. Burrows-Hanover, 40.

19. David Hunter, "Royal Patronage of Handel in Britain: The Rewards of Pensions and Office," in *Handel Studies: A Gedenkschrift for Howard Serwer*, ed. Richard G. King (Hillsdale, NY: Pendragon Press, 2009), 127–53, at 132.

20. Judith Milhous and Robert D. Hume, *Vice Chamberlain Coke's Theatrical Papers 1706–1715* (Carbondale: Southern Illinois University Press, 1982), 198–202.

21. Ibid., 237.

22. David Hunter, "Patronizing Handel, Inventing Audiences," *Early Music* (2000): 33–49, at 34, citing the eighteenth-century economic historians Gregory King and Joseph Massie, whose writings are accessible on EEBO (Early English Books Online) and ECCO (Eighteenth-Century Collections Online). See also Roy Porter, *English Society in the 18th Century* (rev. ed., London: Penguin Books, 1991), 48–97.

23. Deutsch, 90.

24. On the ratio of librettos with Eastern and Western settings at this time, see Angelo Michele Piemontese, "Persia e persiani nel dramma per musica veneziano," in *Opera e libretto*, 2 vols., eds. Gianfranco Folena, Maria Teresa Muraro, and Giovanni Morelli, *Studi di musica Veneta* (Florence: Olschki, 1990–1993), 2:1–34.

25. For further detail and references on the Ostend crisis, see Ellen T. Harris, "With Eyes on the East and Ears in the West: Handel's Orientalist Operas," *Journal of Interdisciplinary History* 36/3 (2006): 419–43.

26. Both statutes printed in F. Russell, ed., *A Collection of Statutes concerning the Incorporation, Trade, and Commerce of the East India Company, and the Government of the British Possessions in India, With the Statutes of Piracy* (London: printed by Charles Eyre and Andrew Strahan, 1794), 61–63, 76–83. Statutes are identified using a specific abbreviated format that provides, in order: the year of the reign, the abbreviated name of the monarch, and the chapter number—that is, the chronological position of the statute among all those passed in that year. Thus 5 Geo I c. 21 refers to the twenty-first chapter (statute) passed in the fifth year of the reign of George I (14 August 1719–13 August 1720) as determined by the specific date of succession.

27. *Cobbett's Parliamentary History of England from the Norman Conquest, in 1066, to the Year 1803*, 36 vols. (London: printed by T. C. Hansard, 1806–1820), 8:492.

28. *The Political State of Great Britain*, 38 vols., ed. Abel Boyer (London: printed for J. Baker, 1711–1729), 31:377.

29. See Harris, "With Eyes on the East"; see also Paul Monod, "The Politics of Handel's Early London Operas, 1711–1719," *The Journal of Interdisciplinary History* 36/3 (2006): 445–72.

30. The tangled chronology of *Esther*'s creation and performance for the duke of Chandos at Cannons has been sorted out in John H. Roberts, "The Composition of Handel's *Esther*, 1718–1720," *Händel-Jahrbuch* 55 (2009): 353–90. Roberts dates the two choruses discussed here to 1718. See Chapter 10 for further discussion of this oratorio.

31. See Harris, "With Eyes on the East," 436–41, where I first discussed *Riccardo primo* in light of the Ostend East India crisis.

32. For further on the rivalry of Cuzzoni and Bordoni and their factions, see Suzana Ograjensek, "Francesca Cuzzoni and Faustina Bordoni: 'The Rival Queens'?" *Handel and the Divas* (exhibition catalogue) (London: Handel House Museum, 2008), 3–7; Suzanne Aspden, "The 'Rival Queens' and the Play of Identity in Handel's *Admeto*," *Cambridge Opera Journal* 18 (2006), 301–31; and "'An Infinity of Factions': Opera in Eighteenth-Century Britain and the Undoing of Society," *Cambridge Opera Journal* 9 (1997): 1–19.

33. The librettist of the original version was Giovanni Sebastiano Brillandi; see John H. Roberts, "The Riddle of *Riccardo primo*," *Händel-Jahrbuch* 58 (2012): 473–94.

34. Thomas McGeary, "Handel as Art Collector: His Print Collection," *Göttinger Händel-Beiträge* 8 (2000): 157–80, at 161; see also McGeary, "Handel as Art Collector: Art, Connoisseurship and Taste in Hanoverian Britain," *Early Music* 37 (2009): 533–74, at 539, and Alison Meyric

Hughes and Martin Royalton-Kisch, "Handel's Art Collection," *Apollo* 146 (September 1997): 17–23, at 20.

35. The documents on the imbroglio caused by Henry Lannoy Hunter in Aleppo may be found in TNA SP 110/27, SP 110/57, and SP 105/117.

36. *Giulio Cesare,* produced at the English National Opera (2012), about which Andrew Clark in the *Financial Times* (October 2, 2012) wrote, "If the production team had intended to suck the soul out of one of Handel's greatest creations, they could hardly have done better." Full text at www .ft.com/intl/cms/s/2/8cecbcac-0c82-11e2-a73c-00144feabdc0.html. *Rinaldo,* produced at the Lyric Opera of Chicago (2012), about which Lawrence A. Johnson wrote in *Chicago Classical Review* (March 1, 2012), "For all its postmodern kitsch, the Lyric's new production has a certain sardonic goofy charm that eventually wins you over. The staging only occasionally got in the way of the singing." Full text at www.chicagoclas sicalreview.com/2012/03/stellar-vocalism-and-goofy-charm-make-for-an-engaging-rinaldo-at-lyric-opera.

37. Delany to Anne Granville (9 September 1729), DELANY CORRESPON-DENCE, 1:213.

38. TNA PROB 11/1165 (will of Mary Delany).

39. TNA PROB 11/949 (will of Joseph Goupy).

40. See Ray Desmond, *Kew: The History of the Royal Botanic Gardens* (Kew: The Harvill Press, 1995), 28. See also HARRIS-GOUPY, 431.

5. MUSIC AT HOME

1. Shaftesbury to James Harris (24 January 1736), HARRIS CORRESPON-DENCE, 12.

2. Mary Delany to her mother (12 April 1735), DELANY CORRESPON-DENCE, 1:533–34.

3. HAWKINS, 5:127.

4. I have previously written about the interplay of printed and manuscript scores during this period, and parts of this chapter are based on that work. See Ellen T. Harris, "Music Distribution in London During Handel's Lifetime: Manuscript Copies Versus Prints," in *Mediating Music from Hildegard of Bingen to The Beatles,* eds. Craig Alan Monson and Roberta Montemorra Marvin, *Eastman Studies in Music* (Rochester, NY: University of Rochester Press, 2013), 95–117.

5. On Handel's relationship with Walsh, see Donald Burrows, "Walsh's Editions of Handel's Opera 1–5: The Texts and Their Sources," in *Music in Eighteenth-Century England: Essays in Memory of Charles Cudworth,* eds. Christopher Hogwood and Richard Luckett (Cambridge: Cambridge University Press, 1983), 79–102, and "John Walsh and His Handel

Editions," in *Music and the Book Trade from the Sixteenth to the Twentieth Century*, eds. Robin Myers, Michael Harris, and Giles Mandelbrote (London: Oak Knoll Press and the British Library, 2008), 69–104.

6. HAWKINS, 5:74.

7. Ralph Thoresby in his diary entry of June 5, 1712, quoted in Jacob Simon, ed., *Handel: A Celebration of His Life and Times (1685–1759)* (London: National Portrait Gallery, 1985), 91; hereafter SIMON-CELE-BRATION.

8. Curtis Price, "The Small-Coal Cult," *The Musical Times* 119/1630 (1978): 1032–34, at 1034, n. 9.

9. DEUTSCH, 44; Roner's letter to Hughes passing on this information is dated 31 July 1711 (DEUTSCH, 45).

10. *The Library of Mr. Tho. Britton, Smallcoal-man. Being a curious collection of books in divinity, history, physick and chemistry . . . Also an extraordinary collection of manuscripts in Latin and English. Will be sold by auction . . . on . . . the 1st of November [1694]*, etc. Exemplar consulted: BL 821.i.7(5).

11. *The Library of Mr. Thomas Britton, Smallcoal-man, deceas'd. Being a curious collection of very ancient and uncommon books . . . Also a collection of MSS. chiefly on vellum. Which will be sold by auction . . . on . . . the 24th of January, 1714/15*, etc. Exemplar consulted: BL 011899.h.13.

12. Michael Tilmouth and Simon McVeigh, "Britton, Thomas," in *The New Grove Dictionary of Music and Musicians*, 2nd edition (London: Macmillan, 2001); *Grove Music Online* at *Oxford Music Online*. See www.oxford musiconline.com/subscriber/article/grove/music/04017 (accessed June 11, 2012), hereafter GROVE MUSIC ONLINE.

13. MAINWARING, 56–57.

14. George Berkeley to John Percival (1 March 1717), BL Add. MS. 47028, p. 364 (f. 182^v).

15. John Percival to Daniel Dering (7 August 1724), BL Add. MS. 47030, p. 146 (f. 74^v).

16. The HWV numbers for Handel function like the more familiar Koechel (K) numbers for Mozart or the BWV (Bach-Werke-Verzeichnis) numbers for Bach. The HWV numbers provide no indication of overall chronology but in general are grouped by genre: the trio sonatas are HWV 380–405.

17. Thematic material from the first movement was later used in the Trio Sonata in B Flat, Op. 2, no. 3; the last three movements were revised and reused in two different trio sonatas published by Walsh in 1738, the second and third movements in no. 6 and the finale in no. 4. See Terence Best, "Handel's Chamber Music: Sources, Chronology and Authenticity," *Early Music* 13 (1985): 476–99, at 487.

18. Hawkins, 5:75 and 127.
19. Ibid., 128; see also James Mosley, "Caslon, William, the elder (1692–1766)," *Oxford Dictionary of National Biography* (Oxford: Oxford University Press, 2004); online edition, January 2008, www.oxforddnb.com/view/article/4857 (accessed June 11, 2012), hereafter ODNB.
20. L. M. Middleton, "Needler, Henry (*bap.* 1685, *d.* 1760)," rev. K. D. Reynolds, ODNB, accessed June 12, 2012.
21. Hawkins, 5:126.
22. Mary Delany to Anne Granville (5 December 1729), Delany correspondence, 1:228.
23. Hans Joachim Marx, "The Origins of Handel's Opus 3: A Historical Review," in *Handel Tercentenary Collection,* eds. Stanley Sadie and Anthony Hicks (Houndmills, Basingstoke: Macmillan Press for The Royal Musical Association, 1987): 254–70.
24. Winton Dean, "The Malmesbury Collection," in *Handel Collections and Their History,* ed. Terence Best (Oxford: Clarendon Press, 1993), 29–38, hereafter Collections.
25. BL Sloane 4034, f. 71; see also Howard Serwer and William A. Frosch, "The Trouble with Elizabeth Legh," *Göttinger-Händel-Beiträge* 7 (1998): 258–66; facsimile published in William A. Frosch, "A Bonesetter's Contract," *The Handel Institute Newsletter* 17/2 (Autumn 2006): [4].
26. Mary Delany [to Anne Granville (1729)], Delany correspondence, 1:185.
27. See Ellen T. Harris, "Paper, Performing Practice, and Patronage: Handel's Alto Cantatas in the Bodleian Library MS Mus. d. 61–62," in *Festa Musicologica: Essays in Honor of George J. Buelow,* eds. Thomas J. Mathiesen and Benito V. Rivera (Stuyvesant, NY: Pendragon Press, 1995), 53–78.
28. Dean, "The Malmesbury Collection," in Collections, 36.
29. Mary Delany to Anne Granville (January 26, 1727), Delany correspondence, 1:129. Although the name of the opera is not given, *Admeto* opened on January 31, 1727, and Mary Delany writes of attending the first rehearsal "yesterday" (25 January 1727) of "Mr. Handel's opera performed by Faustina, Cuzzoni and Senesino."
30. See Harris, "Music Distribution in London," 142–46.
31. See Charles Humphries and William C. Smith, *Music Publishing in the British Isles from the Beginning Until the Middle of the Nineteenth Century; A Dictionary of Engravers, Printers, Publishers and Music Sellers* (Oxford: Blackwell, 1970).
32. John Percival to Philip Percival (17 April 1714), BL Add. MS. 47027, p. 194 (f. 97ᵛ).

33. Philip Percival to John Percival (10 May 1715), BL Add. MS. 47028, p. 48 (f. 24^v).

34. Philip Percival to John Percival (24 June 1718), BL Add. MS. 47028, p. 466 (f. 233^v).

35. Philip Percival to John Percival (15 March 1715), BL Add. MS. 47028, pp. 29–30 (f. 15^{r-v}).

36. John Percival to Philip Percival (25 April 1721), BL Add. MS. 47029, pp. 110–11 (f. 56^{r-v}).

37. Philip Percival to John Percival (5 May 1721), BL Add. MS. 47029, p. 115 (f. 58^v).

38. Philip Percival to John Percival (3 June 1714), BL Add. MS. 47027, p. 240 (f. 120^v).

39. Philip Percival to John Percival (18 July 1717), BL Add. MS. 47028, p. 389 (f. 195^r).

40. Philip Percival to John Percival (17 April 1714), BL Add. MS. 47027, p. 196 (f. 98^v).

41. John Percival to Philip Percival (1 August 1717), BL Add. MS. 47028, p. 395 (f. 198^r).

42. John Percival to Philip Percival (3 May 1714), Add. MS. 47027, pp. 213–14 (f. 107^{r-v}); John Percival to Philip Percival (2 February 1720), Add. MS. 47029, p. 15 (f. 8^v).

43. HAWKINS, 5:270–71.

44. Ibid., 253 (in footnote).

45. On the relation among these sources, see Terence Best, ed., *Klavierwerke I:Erste Sammlung von 1720, Hallische Händel-Ausgabe* IV/1 (Kassel: Bärenreiter, 1993): xiv–xx.

46. Mary Delany to Anne Granville (27 November 1736), DELANY CORRESPONDENCE, 1:579.

47. Anne Granville to Lady Throckmorton (22 August 1739), DELANY CORRESPONDENCE, 2:61.

48. See Harris, "Music Distribution in London," 149.

49. *Diary of Viscount Percival, Afterwards First Earl of Egmont*, ed. R. A. Roberts, 3 vols., Historical Manuscripts Commission (London: His Majesty's Stationery Office, 1920–23), 2:50, hereafter PERCIVAL DIARY. In the performances mounted by Handel in Oxford in July 1733, a Mr. Mattis is listed among the musicians; H. Diack Johnstone ("Oxford," in CHE, 476) associates this person with the violinist John-Nicola Matteis, which identification seems likely for Percival's "Mr. Mathies" as well.

50. Orrery to the Bishop of Cork (11 December 1736) in John, 5th Earl of Orrery, *The Orrery Papers*, ed. Countess of Cork and Orrery, 2 vols. (London: Duckworth and Company, 1903), 1:177.

51. Mary Delany to Anne Granville Dewes (16 November 1751), DELANY CORRESPONDENCE, 3:59; Delany is referring to the first edition of songs from *Theodora* published by Walsh in 1751.

52. Mary Delany to Anne Granville (4 April 1734), DELANY CORRESPONDENCE, 1:454.

53. For a different interpretation of this painting, see Jeremy Barlow, *The Enraged Musician: Hogarth's Musical Imagery* (Aldershot: Ashgate, 2005), 35–36.

54. Delany to Anne Granville (13 July 1731), DELANY CORRESPONDENCE, 1:283. Richard (Colley) Wesley was grandfather to the Duke of Wellington.

55. Delany to Anne Granville (30 March 1732), DELANY CORRESPONDENCE, 1:345–46.

56. *Gazetteer and London Daily Advertiser,* no. 5052 (28 November 1757), 17th and 18th Century Burney Collection Database; hereafter BURNEY COLLECTION. See also the will of James Hunter, proved 12 October 1757 (TNA PROB 11/833).

57. TNA PROB 11/695 (proved 20 March 1739), will of Christopher Batt Sr.

58. Barbara Small, "Smith, John Christopher," in GROVE MUSIC ONLINE, accessed June 12, 2012. See also on Handel teaching, David Hunter, "Handel's Students, Two Lovers, and a Shipwreck," *Early Music* 39/2 (2011): 157–66.

59. William Coxe, *Anecdotes of George Frederick Handel and John Christopher Smith* (1799; repr. Richmond, Surrey: Tiger of the Stripe, 2009): 45; hereafter COXE.

60. Isabella Mayne (née Raymond) was widowed in 1785 and afterward married the ninth earl of Dundonald. When the couple separated, Isabella returned to her family home in Sudbury, Belchamp Hall. She bequeathed her remaining estate to her brother. There is an eighteenth-century organ at Belchamp today.

61. C. H. Collins Baker and Muriel I. Baker, *The Life and Circumstances of James Brydges—First Duke of Chandos* (Oxford: Clarendon Press, 1949), 130.

62. Jacob Wilhelm Lustig, *Inleiding tot de Muzykkunde* [Introduction to the Art of Music], 2nd ed. (Groningen: Hindrik Vechnerus, 1771), 172, as quoted and cited in DEUTSCH, 360.

63. Richard G. King, "Anne of Hanover and Orange (1709–59) as patron and practitioner of the arts," in *Queenship in Britain 1660–1837*, ed. Clarissa Campbell Orr (Manchester: Manchester University Press, 2002), 162–92, at 186–87. On the nature of the revisions and additions in this set of cantatas, see John Mayo, "Einige Kantatenrevisionen Händel,"

Händel-Jahrbuch 27 (1981): 63–77, and Ellen T. Harris, "Handel's London Cantatas," *Göttinger Händel-Beiträge* 1 (1984): 86–102.

64. DEUTSCH, 380.

65. The arias from *Ottone* are contained in Bodleian Library MS Don. C. 69.

66. James S. Hall and Martin V. Hall proposed that the ornamentation was written for the famous alto castrato Gaetano Guadagni ("Handel's Graces," *Händel-Jahrbuch* 3 [1957]: 25–43), and Winton Dean (ed., *G.F. Handel: Three Ornamented Arias* [Oxford: Oxford University Press, 1973], iii) suggested that in a public performance Handel "would no doubt have made adjustments at rehearsal" to correct for any clashes of the ornamentation with the orchestral parts. For a discussion of their probable relation instead to Elizabeth Legh, see Ellen T. Harris, "Paper, Performing Practice, and Patronage," in *Festa Musicologica: Essays in Honor of George J. Buelow*, eds. Thomas J. Mathiesen and Benito V. Rivera (Stuyvesant, NY: Pendragon Press, 1995), 53–78. John H. Roberts ("Three Arias in Search of an Author," *Händel-Jahrbuch* (2013): 393–403, at 401) makes a strong case for the alto version of "Deh! v'aprite, o luci belle" having been composed for Anastasia Robinson in the role of Agilea in *Teseo* following the drop in her voice from soprano to contralto. Even so, the added ornamentation in Legh's score suggests that this copy of the aria was intended specifically for Legh's use; Robinson is not likely to have needed her ornamentation written out. I am grateful to Professor Roberts for sharing his article with me before publication.

67. George Frideric Handel, *Crudel tiranno amor*, facsimile and first edition, eds. Berthold Over and the Bavarian State Library, Munich, *Documenta musicologica. 2. Reihe, Handschriften-Faksimiles*, 34 (Kassel: Bärenreiter, 2006).

68. A keyboard reduction in Handel's hand of a soprano aria from the opera *Amadigi*, "O caro mio tesor," also incompatible with the orchestral version in the opera and with added vocal ornamentation, survives in the Fitzwilliam Museum, Cambridge. Like *Crudel tiranno amor*, it was probably prepared for an English student. See Winton Dean, "Vocal Embellishment in a Handel Aria," in *Essays on Opera* (Oxford: Clarendon Press, 1990), 22–29; orig. in *Studies in Eighteenth-Century Music: A Tribute to Karl Geiringer on His Seventieth Birthday*, ed. H. C. Robbins Landon (London: George Allen & Unwin, 1970), 151–59.

69. Terence Best, "Handel's keyboard music," *The Musical Times* 112 (1971): 845–48, at 847; these two suites are now numbered HWV 447 and 452.

70. (London: J. Fuller et al., 1759), 215–16, as quoted and cited in Ilias Chrissochoidis, "Early Reception of Handel's Oratorios, 1732–1784:

Narrative-Studies-Documents" (PhD dissertation: Stanford University, 2004), 881.

71. See, for example, Samuel Richardson, *Pamela: or, Virtue Rewarded*, 4th ed., 2 vols. (London: printed for C. Rivington, 1741), 1:92–93, and 2:96–98 (sourced from the British Library on ECCO).

72. Samuel Richardson, *Clarissa. Or, the History of a Young Lady: Comprehending the Most Important Concerns of Private Life*, 3rd ed., 8 vols. (London: printed for S. Richardson, 1751), 2:50; text of song, pp. 51–54; engraving of the music included between pp. 54 and 55 (sourced from the British Library on ECCO).

73. Letter from Donnellan to Richardson (14 July 1750): *The Correspondence of Samuel Richardson*, ed. Anna Laetitia Barbauld, 4 vols. (London: Richard Phillips, 1804), 4:9; hereafter RICHARDSON CORRESPONDENCE.

74. Richardson, *Clarissa*, 8:102.

75. See RICHARDSON CORRESPONDENCE, 4:1–119. See also T. C. Duncan Eaves and Ben D. Kimpel, *Samuel Richardson: A Biography* (Oxford: Clarendon Press, 1971).

76. Richardson to Donnellan (22 February 1752), RICHARDSON CORRESPONDENCE, 4:61.

77. Donnellan to Richardson (26 March 1752), RICHARDSON CORRESPONDENCE, 4:68.

78. Samuel Richardson, *The History of Sir Charles Grandison*, "a piracy," 7 vols. ([Dublin] London: printed by S. Richardson, 1753), 2:21–22 (sourced from Houghton Library, Harvard University, on ECCO); see also Samuel Richardson, *The History of Sir Charles Grandison*, ed. Jocelyn Harris (Oxford: Oxford University Press, 1986: 1st paperback in 1 vol., in 3 separately paginated parts [orig. 7 vols. in 3, 1972]), Part 1:238–39.

79. Delany to Anne Granville (4 April 1734), DELANY CORRESPONDENCE, 1:454.

80. Delany to Anne Granville (12 April 1734), DELANY CORRESPONDENCE, 1:457–58.

81. Delany to Anne Granville Dewes (4 December 1755), DELANY CORRESPONDENCE, 3:383.

82. Delany to Anne Granville Dewes (12 December 1756), DELANY CORRESPONDENCE, 3:454.

6. MARRIAGE, WEALTH, AND SOCIAL STATUS

1. John West, Earl of De La Warr to Charles, Duke of Richmond (January 1733), as quoted in DEUTSCH, 303–4.

2. On Anne's patronage of Handel, see Richard G. King, "Anne of Hanover and Orange (1709–59) as Patron and Practitioner of the Arts," in *Queen-*

ship in Britain 1660–1837: Royal Patronage, Court Culture and Dynastic Politics, ed. Clarissa Campbell Orr (Manchester: Manchester University Press, 2002), 162–92. For a concise overview, see Richard G. King, "Anne, Princess, of Hanover and Orange," in CHE: 37–38.

3. Lord Hervey, *Some Materials Toward Memoirs of the Reign of King George II*, ed. Romney Sedgwick (London, 1931), 273, as quoted in King, "Anne of Hanover," 170–71.

4. BURROWS-CHAPEL, 321.

5. BURROWS-CHAPEL, 320.

6. As quoted in King, "Anne of Hanover," 164.

7. Lord Hervey, as quoted in King, "Anne of Hanover," 172.

8. On Handel's finances, see Ellen T. Harris, "Handel the Investor," *Music & Letters* 85/4 (2004): 521–75, and "Courting Gentility: Handel at the Bank of England," *Music & Letters* 91/3 (2010): 357–75.

9. See Ellen T. Harris, "Pamphilj as Phoenix: Themes of Resurrection in Handel's Italian Works," in *The Pamphilj and the Arts: Patronage and Consumption in Baroque Rome*, ed. Stephanie C. Leone (Chestnut Hill, MA: McMullen Museum of Art, 2011), 189–97; see also Ellen T. Harris, *Handel as Orpheus: Voice and Desire in the Chamber Cantatas* (Cambridge, MA: Harvard University Press, 2001), 25–48.

10. MAINWARING, 50–51, 54.

11. COXE, 12.

12. As quoted in BURROWS-HANOVER, 39.

13. William C. Smith, "George III, Handel, and Mainwaring," *The Musical Times* 65 (1924): 793.

14. COXE, 32–33.

15. TNA SP 34/17/43A-F (December 1711), Petition of John Mayne to Queen Anne and supporting affidavits in relation to his murder of Margaret Richards of Exeter.

16. Elizabeth Montagu to Anne Donnellan (1 January 1741), BL Add. MS. 70493, pp. 19–20.

17. Queen Charlotte to Delany (7 November 1784) and George III to Delany (7 November 1784), DELANY CORRESPONDENCE, 6:236–37.

18. Alexandra Coghlan, "Radamisto, English National Opera: A Sexy, Postmodern Take on Handel's Orientalism," October 8, 2010, *The Arts Desk*, www.theartsdesk.com/opera/radamisto-english-national-opera, accessed September 21, 2011.

19. Amazon.com editorial review, www.amazon.com/Handel-Rodelinda-George-Frideric/dp/B000007TKL, accessed September 21, 2011.

20. Amazon.com product description, www.amazon.co.uk/Handel-Amadigi-Gaula-Opera-Acts/dp/B000WHBTBU, accessed September 21, 2011.

21. Stephen Smoliar, "Jeffrey Thomas' Handel Master Class at the Conservatory," February 17, 2011, *Examiner,* www.examiner.com/classical-music-in-san-francisco/jeffrey-thomas-handel-master-class-at-the-conservatory, accessed September 21, 2011.

22. Delany Autobiography, Letter IV, DELANY CORRESPONDENCE, 1:24.

23. Delany Autobiography, Letter V, DELANY CORRESPONDENCE, 1:27.

24. Delany Autobiography, Letter IX, DELANY CORRESPONDENCE, 1:61.

25. Delany to Anne Granville (29 November 1720), DELANY CORRESPONDENCE, 1:57.

26. Review of the Chandos recording of *Floridante*, Answers.com, www.answers.com/topic/handel-flavio-re-di-longobardi, accessed June 19, 2012.

27. Handel had previously used the heaviness of this music to depict weeping at the cross in "Piangete, si, piangete," *La resurrezione* (1708).

28. Delany Autobiography, Letter V, DELANY CORRESPONDENCE, 1:29.

29. Lansdowne to Delany (5 April 1725), DELANY CORRESPONDENCE, 1:114–15.

30. Delany to Anne Granville (15 August 1734), DELANY CORRESPONDENCE, 1:488.

31. TNA C 33/354 (8 December 1729), p. 53; abbreviations written out and spelling modernized.

32. Delany to Anne Granville (28 March 1734), DELANY CORRESPONDENCE, 1:446.

33. Editorial comment, DELANY CORRESPONDENCE, 1:117.

34. Barclays Group Archives ACC 130/19 (17 June 1747), opening of the account.

35. See Harris, "Courting Gentility."

36. Jacob Vanderlint, *Money answers all Things: Or, An Essay to make Money Sufficiently plentiful Amongst all Ranks of People, and Increase our Foreign and Domestick Trade; Fill the Empty Houses with Inhabitants, Encourage the Marriage State* . . . (London: printed for T. Cox, 1734), 145. I am grateful to Robert D. Hume for directing me to this publication.

37. Anne Salisbury to Lady Percival (8 or 9 January 1737 and undated subsequent letters), BL Add. MS. 47000, ff. 91^r–93^r.

38. Delany to Anne Granville Dewes (31 March 1759), DELANY CORRESPONDENCE, 3:544–45.

39. Montagu to Gilbert West (28 January 1753) in *Elizabeth Montagu—The Queen of the Blue Stockings: Her Correspondence from 1720 to 1761*, ed. Emily J. Climenson, 2 vols. (London: John Murray, 1906), 2:25–26; hereafter MONTAGU CORRESPONDENCE. See also Richard H. Popkin, "Bishop Berkeley and Anne Donnellan," in *The High Road to Pyrrhonism,*

eds. Richard A. Watson and James E. Force (San Diego, CA: Austin Hill Press, Inc., 1980), 363–67.

40. Dean Berkeley to Percival (3 September 1728), BL Add. MS. 47032, p. 159 (f. 82ʳ).
41. Delany to Anne Granville Dewes (28 February 1751), DELANY CORRE-SPONDENCE, 3:21.
42. Patrick Kelly, "Anne Donnellan: Irish Proto-Bluestocking," *Hermathena —A Trinity College Dublin Review* 54 (Summer 1993): 39–68, at 53.
43. Delany to Anne Granville Dewes (18 February 1752), DELANY CORRE-SPONDENCE, 3:90.
44. The ledgers documenting Donnellan's cash account at Goslings Bank from 1749 to her death in 1762 survive in Barclays Group Archives, Manchester. The Bank of England Archive holds the records of most of her various investments. Her stock account with the East India Company is preserved in the company's stock ledgers at the British Library. See the Bibliography for details.
45. TNA PROB 11/545 (proved 29 March 1715), will of John Hunter.
46. Faculty Office Marriage Allegations: Lambeth Palace Library FMI/63 (17 December 1728), Hunter-Cooke.
47. *London Evening Post,* no. 4646 (Tuesday, 7 June 1757).
48. *Verney Letters of the Eighteenth Century from the MSS. at Claydon House,* ed. Margaret Maria Lady Verney, 2 vols. (London: Ernest Benn Ltd., 1930), 2:174.
49. Verney Papers from Claydon House, microform, 60 reels; read at the British Library and at Firestone Library, Princeton University.
50. TNA C 127/55.
51. TNA PROB 11/685 (proved 10 October 1737), will of Richard Peacock.
52. TNA RG 7/159.
53. TNA C 127/55.
54. TNA C 11/588/44 (1737), *Palmer v. Peacock.*
55. TNA C 11/866/4 (1743), *Palmer v. Peacock.*
56. LMA MDR/1746/1/188 and 298 (purchase of house on Curzon Street); TNA C 109/25–7 (Thomas Wagg accounts).
57. TNA PROB 11/823 (written 11 July 1746; proved 21 June 1756), will of Elizabeth Peacock.
58. London Metropolitan Archives DL/A/D/004/MS10091/087, Bishop of London Marriage Licenses: Palmer-Peacock (20 February 1746), f. 109ʳ.
59. *St. James's Evening Post,* no. 5789 (Tuesday, 24 February 1747), BURNEY COLLECTION.
60. Announcement of her death in the *St. James's Evening Post,* no. 5631 (Thursday, 20 February 1746), BURNEY COLLECTION.

61. On the map by Richard Horwood, *Plan of the Cities of London and Westminster, the Borough of Southwark and Parts adjoining Shewing every House* (London, 1792–1799), the Palmers' double house can be identified on Curzon Street as Nos. 29 and 28.
62. LMA MDR 1755/3/470; MDR 1758/2/591.
63. Westminster City Archives: St. George Hanover Square rate books, C327–330.
64. East Sussex Record Office: FRE 8352–8364, quotation from FRE 8356.
65. The Palmer and Verney correspondence concerning the securing of the bride's inheritance is quoted in Susan E. Whyman, *Sociability and Power in Late-Stuart England: The Cultural Worlds of the Verneys 1660–1720* (New York: Oxford University Press, 1999), 135.
66. Delany to Anne Granville (19 January 1728), DELANY CORRESPONDENCE, 1:154–55.
67. Delany to Anne Granville (17 January 1732), DELANY CORRESPONDENCE, 1:333.
68. Delany to Anne Granville Dewes (16 March 1751), DELANY CORRESPONDENCE, 3:25.
69. DEUTSCH, 413–15. Deutsch mistakenly gives 1736 rather than 1731 as the year on this letter; the wedding took place on 6 December 1731; see HHB4, 192. See also Klaus-Peter Koch, "Handel's German Relatives," in *Handel's Will: Facsimiles and Commentary,* ed. Donald Burrows (London: The Gerald Coke Handel Foundation, 2008), 21–24, at 22.
70. PERCIVAL DIARY, 2:68.

7. AMBITION, LAW, AND FRIENDSHIP

1. See Ellen T. Harris, "Handel the Investor," *Music & Letters* 85/4 (2004): 521–75, and "Courting Gentility: Handel at the Bank of England," *Music & Letters* 91 (2010): 357–75.
2. DEUTSCH, 299.
3. Burney writes that Gibson "would not grant permission for [*Esther*] being represented on that stage [the opera house], even with books in the children's hands" (BURNEY-COMMEMORATION, 100–101). This statement has generally been taken to mean that Gibson, as dean of the Chapel Royal, would not allow the children of the Chapel Royal Choir to perform in a staged representation. As John Roberts has argued, however, the phrase "even with books in the children's hands," suggests rather that the children were prohibited altogether from performing in the opera house. Roberts maintains that there is "no evidence" that the boys participated at all in Handel's production of *Esther.* See John H. Roberts, "Christ of the Playhouse: Indirect

Narrative in Handel's *Messiah*," *Händel-Jahrbuch* 55 (2009): 107–24, at 116–18.

4. PERCIVAL DIARY (27 March 1733), 1:345.
5. DEUTSCH, 310.
6. Ibid., 367.
7. Donald Burrows, *Handel* Messiah (Cambridge: Cambridge University Press, 1991), 11.
8. DEUTSCH, 516.
9. BURROWS-HANDEL, 262–63.
10. *The Universal Spectator* (19 March 1743); see also Burrows, *Messiah*, 26.
11. DEUTSCH, 602; HHB4, 383–84.
12. See Harris, "Handel the Investor."
13. Bank of England ADM9/22, f. 465.
14. TNA C 11/100/14 (1733), *Bank of England v. Hunter*, bill of complaint.
15. Giles Jacob, *A New Law-Dictionary* . . . (London: printed by E. and R. Nutt, and R. Gosling, 1729), n.p. (sourced from the British Library on ECCO).
16. TNA C 38/418 (4 February 1734), *Bank of England v. Hunter*, Master's Report.
17. Bank of England ADM7/11, f. 44.
18. Berkshire Record Office D/EHR E1: Henry Lannoy Hunter cash journal.
19. Bank of England ADM7/11, f. 32.
20. TNA C 11/1150/24 (1736), *Hunter v. Pryce.*
21. Bank of England ADM9/27, f. 383; ADM7/12, f. 36; ADM9/27, f. 410.
22. *London Gazette*, no. 8030 (7 to 11 July 1741), TNA ZJ 1/39.
23. TNA B 1/17 (31 March 1742), pp. 36–40.
24. On bankruptcy in this period, see Sheila Marriner, "English Bankruptcy Records and Statistics Before 1850," *Economic History Review* 33 (1980): 351–66, and Julian Hoppit, *Risk and Failure in English Business: 1700–1800* (Cambridge: Cambridge University Press, 1987).
25. Berkshire Record Office D/EHR E1, Henry Lannoy Hunter cash journal.
26. Herefordshire Record Office AL40/1050.
27. LMA CLC/B/055/MS 08678/067 (1745), 079 (renewed 1752), Hand-in-Hand Fire and Life Insurance Society, policy no. 33314. A watercolor by A. G. Stout, dated 1890, *Dye Works at Old Ford* (London Metropolitan Archives: SC/PZ/PP/02/011), despite showing the buildings in derelict condition, provides a good illustration of the sheer size of such an operation.
28. HAWKINS, 5:412.

29. *Catalogue of the Very Important and Interesting Musical Collections of a Distinguished Amateur . . . to which are added the well known and very important Series of Handel's Works written by the Composer's Amanuensis, J. C. Smith, for his Friend and Patron, Bernard Granville, Esq . . . which will be sold by Auction, by Messrs. Puttick and Simpson . . . on Friday, January 29st [sic], 1858, and following day,* p. 12.

30. Hunter worked on a handful of volumes for both the Granville and Lennard (his own) Collections. In fact, there seems to be a particularly close connection between these two sets as the two volumes in the Lennard Collection that include Hunter's hand (Fitzwilliam Museum, Cambridge, MU MS 794 and 813) may be rejects from the Granville Collection. See Burrows, "The Barrett Lennard Collection," in COLLECTIONS, 120.

31. Montagu to Donnellan (1 January 1740 [1741]), BL Add. MS. 70493, p. 19.

32. Percival to William Byrd (3 December 1729), BL Add. MS. 47032, p. 257 (f. 145^r).

33. John Hawkins uses the phrase "intimate friends" without any apparent sexual overtone (HAWKINS, 5:412). Molly Peacock considers the question of sensuality/sexuality in the relationship of Delany and Donnellan in *The Paper Garden: An Artist Begins Her Life's Work at* 72 (New York: Bloomsbury, 2010), 142–44, 158–59. On Delany's female friendships, see also Lisa L. Moore, *Sister Arts: The Erotics of Lesbian Landscapes* (Minneapolis: University of Minnesota Press, 2011).

34. On the broad range of sexual activity in London in the eighteenth century, see Dan Cruickshank, *The Secret History of Georgian London: How the Wages of Sin Shaped the Capital* (London: Random House Books, 2009).

35. See Donald Burrows, "'Something Necessary to the Connection': Charles Jennens, James Hunter and Handel's *Samson*," *Handel Institute Newsletter* 15/1 (2004): 1–3.

36. See Ruth Smith, "Love between Men in Jennens' and Handel's *Saul*," in *Queer People: Negotiations and Expressions of Homosexuality, 1700–1800,* eds. Chris Mounsey and Caroline Gonda (Lewisburg, PA: Bucknell University Press, 2007), 226–45.

37. The King James Version reads: "I am distressed for thee, my brother Jonathan: very pleasant hast thou been unto me: thy love to me was wonderful, passing the love of women."

38. The poem survives at Harvard University, Houghton Library, *EB7. A100.739a. See Ilias Chrissochoidis, "Handel at the Crossroads: His 1737–1738 and 1738–1739 Seasons Re-Examined," *Music & Letters* 90/4 (2009): 599–635; and David Hunter, "Margaret Cecil, Lady Brown:

"'Persevering Enemy to Handel' but 'Otherwise Unknown to History,'" *Women & Music* 3 (1999): 43–58.

39. Radnor to Harris (6 November [1744]), HARRIS CORRESPONDENCE, 204.
40. DEUTSCH, 500.
41. Ibid., 584.
42. Handel to Jennens (9 September 1742), DEUTSCH, 554.
43. DEUTSCH, 560.
44. Betty Matthews, "Unpublished Letters concerning Handel," *Music & Letters* 40 (1959): 261–68, at 263.
45. Horace Walpole to Horace Mann (4 May 1743), DEUTSCH, 569.
46. TNA C 12/726/4 (1739), *Hedges v. Goupy*. See HARRIS-GOUPY for further details and sources.
47. Pepys wrote descriptive accounts in his diary of his sexual relations with his wife and his sexual encounters with other women. See, for example, Claire Tomalin, *Samuel Pepys: The Unequalled Self* (London: Penguin Books, 2003), 201–3.
48. Romney Sedgwick, *The History of Parliament: The House of Commons 1715–1754*, 2 vols. (London: Oxford University Press, 1970), 1:444.
49. Reed Browning, "Hervey, John, second Baron Hervey of Ickworth (1696–1743)," ODNB, accessed December 21, 2011. See also HARRIS-GOUPY.
50. John Robartes (later Earl of Radnor) to Harris (19 July 1740), HARRIS CORRESPONDENCE, 100
51. HARRIS CORRESPONDENCE, 117 and 119.
52. DEUTSCH, 574.
53. Delany to Anne Dewes (24 January 1744), DELANY CORRESPONDENCE, 2:254.
54. Delany to Anne Dewes (21 February 1744), DELANY CORRESPONDENCE, 2:266.
55. Winton Dean, "Charles Jennens's Marginalia to Mainwaring's Life of Handel," *Music & Letters* 53 (1972): 162 and facsimile (n.p.).
56. Delany to Anne Dewes (21 February 1744), DELANY CORRESPONDENCE, 2:267.
57. Delany to Anne Dewes (11 February 1744), DELANY CORRESPONDENCE, 2:262.
58. Reported by "W" in *St. James's Chronicle; Or, British Evening-Post*, no. 2411 (Tuesday, 20 August to Thursday, 22 August 1776).
59. DEUTSCH, 610.
60. Sir Richard Colt Hoare, *The History of Modern Wiltshire*, 6 vols. (London: J. Nichols, 1822–1844), 4:112.

61. Delany to Anne Dewes (21 February 1744), DELANY CORRESPON-
    DENCE, 2:267.
62. Delany to Anne Dewes (3 April 1744), DELANY CORRESPONDENCE,
    2:290.
63. Dr. Delany to Delany (23 April 1743), DELANY CORRESPONDENCE,
    2:210–11.
64. Delany to Anne Dewes (3 January 1745) and (9 March 1745), DELANY
    CORRESPONDENCE, 2:333 and 343.
65. Delany to Anne Dewes (23 March 1745), quoting a letter she had written
    to her cousin William Monk, DELANY CORRESPONDENCE, 2:345–46.
66. Parliamentary Archives HL/PO/JU/4/3/13, pp. 80–83 (1758–1760) and
    HL/PO/JO/10/7/101 (1757), *Delany v. Tenison.*
67. Delany to Anne Dewes (23 and 30 December 1752), DELANY COR-
    RESPONDENCE, 3:185–90; TNA PROB 11/798 (proved 12 December
    1752), will of Sir Anthony Westcombe.
68. Delany to Anne Dewes (23 December 1752), DELANY CORRESPON-
    DENCE, 3:185.
69. Delany to Anne Dewes (30 December 1752), DELANY CORRESPON-
    DENCE, 3:189–90.
70. Delany to Anne Dewes (7 March 1758), DELANY CORRESPONDENCE,
    3:490–91.
71. Delany to Anne Dewes (21 January 1747), DELANY CORRESPONDENCE,
    2:451.
72. Lady Shaftesbury's letter is quoted in DEUTSCH, 657.
73. See Harris, "Handel the Investor."
74. *Susanna* and *Solomon* were the first two volumes added to Hunter's col-
    lection some ten years after it had been abruptly discontinued in 1741.
    See Burrows, "Lennard," in COLLECTIONS, 132.

8. MAKING AND COLLECTING

1. *The General Advertiser,* no. 4071 (Monday, 13 November 1747), BURNEY
   COLLECTION; see also DEUTSCH, 642.
2. *The General Advertiser,* no. 4088 (Tuesday, 5 December 1747), BURNEY
   COLLECTION; see also DEUTSCH, 643.
3. See Berta Joncus, "Handel at Drury Lane: Ballad Opera and the Production of Kitty Clive," *Journal of the Royal Musical Association* 131/2
   (2006): 179–226. Joncus demonstrates "the large extent to which
   Handel's tunes infiltrated English ballad-style musical theatre of the
   mid-eighteenth century, not only in the number of ballad farces that
   featured his music, but more significantly in the sheer number of performances of his music in farces" (180) and provides a Table of Handel
   melodies in ballad opera from 1728 to 1750 (181–91).

4. See David Bindman, "Roubiliac's Statue of Handel and the Keeping of Order in Vauxhall Gardens in the Early Eighteenth Century," *The Sculpture Journal* 1 (1997): 22–31; and Suzanne Aspden, "'Fam'd Handel Breathing, tho' Transformed to Stone': The Composer as Monument," *Journal of the American Musicological Society* 55/1 (2002): 39–90.

5. DEUTSCH, 456.

6. An example of a gold ticket with this image is at the British Museum (registration no. MG.681).

7. Although the concerto (without its choral conclusion) was composed for performance at the first London production in 1735 of *Athalia*, it became associated with *Il trionfo* after 1737.

8. Suzanne Aspden also mentions the connection to the Roubiliac statue ("'Fam'd Handel Breathing,'" 54–55).

9. See, for example, Craig Ashley Hanson, *The English Virtuoso: Art, Medicine, and Antiquarianism in the Age of Empiricism* (Chicago: The University of Chicago Press, 2009), and Ken Arnold, *Cabinets for the Curious: Looking Back at Early English Museums* (Aldershot: Ashgate Publishing, 2006). The classic study is Walter E. Houghton Jr., "The English Virtuoso in the Seventeenth Century: Parts I and II," *Journal of the History of Ideas* 3 (1942): 51–73 and 190–219.

10. Lowell Lindgren, "The Accomplishments of the Learned and Ingenious Nicola Francesco Haym (1678–1729)," *Studi Musicali* 16/2 (1987): 247–380, at 327–28.

11. Ibid., 327.

12. Ibid., 328.

13. Hazelle Jackson, *Shell Houses and Grottoes* (Princes Risborough: Shire, 2001) [40 pp]. See also Maria Zytaruk, "Mary Delany: Epistolary Utterances, Cabinet Spaces & Natural History," in *Mrs. Delany and Her Circle*, eds. Mark Laird and Alicia Weisberg-Roberts (New Haven, CT: Yale University Press, 2010), 130–49.

14. Delany (Pendarves) to Anne Granville (later Dewes) (30 June 1734), DELANY CORRESPONDENCE, 1:484–85.

15. Delany (Pendarves) to her mother (12 April 1735), DELANY CORRESPONDENCE, 1:534.

16. Delany (Pendarves) to Dean Swift, DELANY CORRESPONDENCE, 1:570.

17. Dering to Percival (18 June 1728), BL Add. MS. 47032, 125 (f. 64^r). On Hans Sloane and his wide-ranging collections, see Alison Walker, Arthur MacGregor, and Michael Hunter, eds., *From Books to Bezoars: Sir Hans Sloane and His Collections* (London: The British Library, 2012); and Arthur MacGregor, ed., *Sir Hans Sloane: Collector, Scientist, Antiquary, Founding Father of the British Museum* (London: British Museum Publications, 1994).

18. Anecdote in *The London Literary Gazette, and Journal of Belle Lettres, Arts, Sciences, &c.* no. 296 (Saturday, 21 September 1822), 603, available online in Google Books. This source pre-dates that from 1860 previously identified as the earliest: see Arthur MacGregor, "The Life, Character and Career of Sir Hans Sloane," in *Sir Hans Sloane*, 44, n. 202. (I have not yet stumbled upon any manuscript at the British Library with the mark of a buttered muffin.)

19. On the foundation collections of the British Museum and eighteenth-century collecting in general, see Kim Sloan and Andrew Burnett, eds., *Enlightenment: Discovering the World in the Eighteenth Century* (London: British Museum Publications, 2003).

20. *The Library of Mr. Thomas Britton, Smallcoal-man, Deceased…* (London: Thomas Ballard, 1715), British Library 011899.h.13.

21. F. G. E., "Thomas Britton: The Musical Small-Coal Man (1654?–1714)," *The Musical Times* 47/762 (1906): 534.

22. Percival (in Paris) to Ned Southwell (in Venice) (7 May 1726): BL Add. MS. 47031, p. 344 (f. 169^v).

23. See Burrows-Ronish and Hans Dieter Clausen, "The Hamburg Collection," in Collections, 10–28.

24. Richard G. King, "New Light on Handel's Musical Library," *The Musical Quarterly* 81/1 (1997): 109–38, at 121; his translation from Friedrich Chrysander, "Victor Schoelcher: Eine Erinnerung," *Die Zukunft* 6 (20 January 1894): 119.

25. David Charlton and Sarah Hibberd, "'My Father Was a Poor Parisian Musician': A Memoir (1756) concerning Rameau, Handel's Library and Sallé," *Journal of the Royal Musical Association* 128/2 (2003): 161–99.

26. Simon-Celebration, 286–88.

27. The foremost expert on Handel's borrowings is John H. Roberts; see his *Handel Sources: Materials for the Study of Handel's Borrowings*, 9 vols. (New York: Garland Publishing, 1986), in which he provides facsimiles of the scores from which Handel borrowed and lists of borrowings keyed to the Complete Works of Handel. For a historical perspective, see George J. Buelow, "The Case for Handel's Borrowings: The Judgment of Three Centuries," in *Handel Tercentenary Collection*, eds. Stanley Sadie and Anthony Hicks (London: Macmillan Press, 1987): 61–82. For an analysis of Handel's compositional process, see David Hurley, *Handel's Muse: Patterns of Creation in His Oratorios and Musical Dramas 1743–1751* (Oxford: Oxford University Press, 2001).

28. *Duets… Agostino Steffani*, BL Add. MS. 37779.

29. *Il Xerse… Sig. Gio. Bononcini*, BL Add. MS. 22102; for a facsimile of this manuscript and commentary, see Roberts, ed., *Handel Sources*, vol. 8: *Il Xerse / Giovanni Bononcini*.

30. "Sketch of Life," Burney-Commemoration, 34.
31. Books identified with Palmer's library include: British Library: Add. MS. 33244, Burney 2, Burney 308, Egerton 666, and Stowe 4; Royal College of Physicians: MS-PALMR/310 and MS-PALMR/37; Bodleian Library: MSS Eng lett c 438 and d 409 (letters of the Palmer family); Worcester College, Oxford: MS 213 and 213*.
32. The succession of owners gives some indication of how closed a community London society was in the mid-eighteenth century. The thirteenth-century annals of Reading Abbey (Oxford, Worcester College, MS. 213 and 213*) passed from Palmer to Verney to Sir Francis Basset, the grandson of Alexander Pendarves's niece who had received the bulk of Pendarves's estate (rather than his wife Mary, later Delany) when he died intestate. The younger Baldwin Hamey's notes on the life and medical practice of his father in manuscript, *Universa Medicina* (Royal College of Physicians), passed from Palmer to Verney to Dr. John Monro, the physician who treated a female member of Goupy's household for madness (see Chapter 10).
33. The volumes, compiled by a Richard Houlditch, are preserved in the National Art Library (86.OO.18–19); the Palmer auction in 86.OO.18, pp. 349–51. For a brief overview of these volumes, see Frank Simpson, "Dutch Paintings in England before 1760," *The Burlington Magazine* 95/599 (1953): 39–42.
34. Delany to Bernard Granville (27 and [29] April 1758), Delany Correspondence, 2:495–97. On Delany as an artist, see Kim Sloan, "Mrs. Delany's Paintings & Drawings: Adorning Aspasia's Closet," in Laird and Weisberg-Roberts, eds., *Mrs. Delany and Her Circle*, 110–29.
35. Anthony Blunt, *The Paintings of Nicolas Poussin: Critical Catalogue* (London: Phaidon, 1966), 19–21, nos. 22, 23, and 24.
36. Another version of this scene by Poussin is at the Kunsthistorische Museum, Vienna. See Blunt, *The Paintings of Nicolas Poussin*, 29–30, no. 37, especially p. 30, where Blunt identifies the then lost version (L9, pp. 158–59) with the copy in the Palmer collection. For the rediscovery of the "Palmer version," see Denis Mahon, *Nicholas Poussin: Works from His First Years in Rome* (Jerusalem: Israel Museum, 1999).
37. [Thomas Martyn], *The English Connoisseur . . .* (London: printed for L. Davis and C. Reymers, 1766), 133.
38. This is not laid out clearly in published discussions of Handel's buying at auction. Handel's purchases are as follows (with artists' names as given in Houlditch and corrections only where there might be confusion): Rembrandt, *A Large Landscape and Fig.s* (£39 18s.) at Mr. Cousein's sale (8–9 February 1750); Rysdael, *A Landscape* (£6 16s. 6d.) at Bragge's sale (15–16 February 1750); Caracci, *A Small History* (£2 3s.) at Mr.

Humphrey Edwin's sale (16 March 1750); Parocelle Sen., *A Landskip with Moses in the Bulrushes* (£12 12s.) at the Major and Gouijns sale (22–23 March 1750); Cortona, *The Sacking of Troy* (£7) and Prelemburch [Poelembrugh], *A Landskip with a Bacchanalian* (£10 10s.) at Lady Sunderland's sale ([March] 1750); Watteau, *A Conversation* (£9 9s.) at Mr. Vanhacchen's [Vanhaecken's] sale (1750, before 25 March). Jacob Simon (Simon-Celebration, 289) puts the Ruysdael into the Major and Gouijns sale (rather than Lady Sunderland's sale) and leaves out the Vanhaecken sale. Thomas McGeary, "Handel as Art Collector: His Print Collection," *Göttinger Händel-Beiträge* 8 (2000): 157–80, follows Simon. A thorough search of the Houlditch volumes produces the likelihood of further purchases by Handel, given that a buyer is not always listed for each painting. At Bragge's sale, for example, where Handel purchased a Ruysdael, he may also have purchased his landscape by Roelant Savery (there were three on offer). Hugh McLean ("Bernard Granville, Handel and the Rembrandts," *The Musical Times* 126/1712 [October 1985]: 593–601) has already suggested that Handel may have purchased his Ricci watercolors at the Cousein sale (#27), where he acquired his large Rembrandt, and the lack of named purchaser for the Ricci in the Houlditch volumes leaves open this possibility. McLean's other suggestions must be discounted, however, as Houlditch named purchasers for the other items he suggests.

39. An advertisement for this auction appears in *The General Advertiser,* no. 4805 (Friday, 16 March 1750), Burney Collection.

40. Jérôme Delaplanche, *Joseph Parrocel, 1646–1704: la nostalgie de l'héroïsme* (Paris: Arthéna, 2006), lists this work among the rejected paintings of Joseph Parrocel as *PR 63* and describes it as "an excellent example of the characteristic style of Louis Parrocel." Nevertheless, a painting entitled *The Finding of Moses* and attributed to Joseph Parrocel and not Louis was sold at Sotheby's in 2008. See Thomas McGeary, "Handel as Art Collector: Art, Connoisseurship and Taste in Hanoverian Britain," *Early Music* 37/4 (2009): 533–74, at 568.

41. Shaftesbury to Harris (13 February 1750), Harris correspondence, 264.

42. The catalogue is preserved in a unique copy at the Frick Art Reference Library, New York. See Simon-Celebration, 289–90.

43. On Handel's art collection see Thomas McGeary, "Handel as Art Collector," and "Handel as Art Collector: His Print Collection."

44. George Vertue notebooks (British Library Add. MS. 23074, f. 10) as printed in "Vertue Note Books, Volume III," *The Walpole Society* 22 (1933–1934): 152.

45. On marketing art see: David H. Solkin, *Painting for Money: The Visual Arts and the Public Sphere in Eighteenth-Century England* (New Haven: Yale University Press, 1996); Iain Pears, *The Discovery of Painting: The Growth of Interest in the Arts in England, 1680–1768* (New Haven: Yale University Press, 1988); and Louise Lippincott, *Selling Art in Georgian London: The Rise of Arthur Pond* (New Haven, CT: Yale University Press, 1983).

46. On the earnings of a typical craftsman, see F. M. Scherer, *Quarter Notes and Bank Notes: The Economics of Music Composition in the Eighteenth and Nineteenth Centuries* (Princeton, NJ: Princeton University Press, 2004), 208.

47. On the rise of prints as a luxury commodity, see Sheila O'Connell, "Curious and Entertaining: Prints of London and Londoners," in *London 1753* (London: British Museum Press, 2003), 39–43.

48. See Bruce Robertson and Robert Dance, "Joseph Goupy and the Art of the Copy," *The Bulletin of the Cleveland Museum of Art* 75/10 (1988): 354–75, at 371.

49. Oliver Millar, *The Tudor, Stuart, and Early Georgian Pictures in the Collection of Her Majesty the Queen*, 2 vols. (London: Phaidon Press, 1963), text vol., 184.

50. "Department of Antiquities and Coins. Donations 1756–1836" (British Museum: manuscript in the Medieval and Later Antiquities Department); see Chapter 11.

51. See "The Image of Handel," in SIMON-CELEBRATION, 32–47, at 38.

52. See "Handel," in John Kerslake, *Early Georgian Portraits*, 2 vols. (London: Her Majesty's Stationery Office, 1977), 1:120–32, at 130.

53. Roubiliac to Harris (16 April 1741); Thomas Harris to Harris (21 April 1741); Countess of Shaftesbury to Harris (27 June 1741); Roubiliac to Harris (10 July 1741), HARRIS CORRESPONDENCE, 113–16.

54. Judith Milhous and Robert D. Hume, "New Light on Handel and The Royal Academy of Music in 1720," *Theatre Journal* 35 (1983): 149–67.

55. DEUTSCH, 235.

56. See Burrows, "John Walsh and His Handel Editions," in *Music and the Book Trade from the Sixteenth to the Twentieth Century*, eds. Robin Myers, Michael Harris, and Giles Mandelbrote (New Castle: Oak Knoll Press, 2008), 69–104, at 98–99.

57. British Library D.310.b(1.).

58. British Library g.274.a.

59. On the identification of Prince Frederick's Handel collection, see Donald Burrows, "The 'Granville' and 'Smith' Collections of Handel Manuscripts," in *Sundry Sorts of Music Books: Essays on the British Library*

Collections: Presented to O. W. Neighbour on His 70th Birthday, eds. Chris Banks, Arthur Searle, and Malcolm Turner (London: British Library, 1993), 231–47.

60. Shaftesbury to Harris (20 May 1756); Shaftesbury to Harris (27 May 1756), HARRIS CORRESPONDENCE, 313–14.

61. Harris to Robartes (later Radnor) (13 January 1740), HARRIS CORRESPONDENCE, 86.

9. RELIGION AND CHARITY

1. See, for example, Delany to Bernard Granville (18 December 1750), DELANY CORRESPONDENCE, 2:629. See also Lady Llanover's list of Delany's paintings (DELANY CORRESPONDENCE, 6:499–501).

2. See Stephanie Leone, "Cardinal Benedetto Pamphilj's Art Collection: Still-Life Painting and the Cost of Collecting," in *The Pamphilj and the Arts: Patronage and Consumption in Baroque Rome*, ed. Stephanie Leone (Chestnut Hill, MA: McMullen Museum of Art, 2011), 113–38.

3. Although religion played a major role in the events of 1688, it was not the only issue. For a detailed argument about (and fulsome discussion of) the social, political, and economic causes and outcomes, see Steve Pincus, *1688: The First Modern Revolution* (New Haven, CT: Yale University Press, 2009).

4. The full line of succession at the death of the last Stuart monarch, Queen Anne, can be found online on *Wikipedia*: "Jacobite line of succession to the English and Scottish thrones in 1714." Arthur Charles Addington, *The Royal House of Stuart*, 3 vols. (London: Charles Skilton Ltd., 1966–1976).

5. The statutes mentioned are: the Act of Toleration, 1 Will & Mary c. 18 (1689); Occasional Conformity Act, 10 Anne c. 6 (1711); Act for Strengthening the Protestant Interest, 5 Geo 1 c. 4 (1719).

6. "House of Lords Journal Volume 23 (14 February 1727)" in *Journal of the House of Lords* (London: 1767–1830), vol. 23 (1727–1731), www.british-history.ac.uk/report.aspx?compid=11390&strquery=36. Date accessed: 24 March 2014. See also DEUTSCH, 203.

7. Quoted in Luke Tyerman, *The Life and Times of the Rev. John Wesley, M.A., Founder of the Methodists*, 3 vols. (London: Hodder and Stoughton, 1870–1871), 1:77.

8. DELANY CORREPONDENCE, 3:94.

9. As quoted by Pierre Jean Grosley, who was in London in 1765: *A Tour to London: Or, New Observations on England, and Its Inhabitants*, trans. Thomas Nugent, 3 vols. (Dublin: printed for J. Exshaw, E. Lynch, J. Williams, R. Moncrieffe, T. Walker, and D. Jenkin, 1772), 2:37 (sourced from the British Library on ECCO).

10. The author(s) of the libretto of *Esther* cannot be firmly identified. Pope

was said to be the author, but there is no definite proof of this. Arbuthnot and John Gay probably were contributors. The text was based on Thomas Brereton's play *Esther; or Faith Triumphant* (1715), itself based on Jean Racine's play *Esther.* See Graydon Beeks, "Handel and Music for the Earl of Carnarvon," in *Bach, Handel, Scarlatti: Tercentenary Essays,* ed. Peter Williams (Cambridge: Cambridge University Press, 1985), 1–20, and John H. Roberts, "The Composition of Handel's *Esther,* 1718–1720," *Händel-Jahrbuch* 55 (2009): 353–90.

11. See Ruth Smith, *Handel's Oratorios and Eighteenth-Century Thought* (Cambridge: Cambridge University Press, 1995), 276–87. Smith's book is essential to the understanding of Handel's oratorios in terms of their own time and provides the foundation for my own thinking.

12. MAINWARING, 64–65.

13. HAWKINS, 5:409–10.

14. Percival to Taylor (24 November 1723), BL Add. MS. 46974, pp. 83–84 (f. 50^{r-v}).

15. *The History and Proceedings of the House of Commons from the Restoration to the Present Time . . .* 14 vols. (London: printed for Richard Chandler, 1742–1744), 10:320.

16. *The London Daily Post, and General Advertiser,* no. 1696 (Tuesday, 1 April 1740), [1–2], BURNEY COLLECTION. The original review appears in *The Daily Advertiser,* no. 2570 (Thursday, 19 April 1739); see HHB4, 308–9 (this issue is not included in the Burney Collection, nor is it cited in Deutsch). The two versions are reprinted and compared in Ilias Chrissochoidis, "Handel at the Crossroads: His 1737–1738 and 1738–1739 Seasons Re-examined," *Music & Letters* 90/4 (2009): 599–635, in Appendix V, 631–35.

17. George Bernard Shaw, *The Great Composers: Reviews and Bombardments by Bernard Shaw,* ed. Louis Crompton (Berkeley: University of California Press, 1978), 77–78.

18. Katherine Knatchbull to Harris (postscript of 9 December in a letter of 5 December 1738), HARRIS CORRESPONDENCE, 66.

19. See Ruth Smith, "The Meaning of Morell's Libretto of 'Judas Maccabaeus,'" *Music & Letters* 79/1 (1998): 50–71, for a thorough discussion of the historical context in which the oratorio was written and its relationship to the construction of Morell's libretto.

20. As reported in Laetitia-Matilda Hawkins, *Anecdotes, Biographical Sketches and Memoirs* (London: F.C. and J. Rivington, 1822), 195 (as quoted in a review of this volume in *The British Critic,* New Series, 19 [January 1823]: 61).

21. Percival to Bishop of St. David's (18 November 1729), BL Add. MS. 47032, p. 253 (f. 143^{r}).

22. Berkeley to Percival (2 March 1731), BL Add. MS. 47033, pp. 61–62 (f. 32^{r-v}).

23. Percival to Charles Dering (9 October 1722), BL Add. MS. 47029, p. 269 (f. 136^r).

24. Jennens's authorship of the libretto for *Israel in Egypt* cannot be fully documented, but his reference to the preparation of the libretto of *Messiah* in a letter of 10 July 1741 as "another Scriptural Collection" he hoped to persuade Handel to set makes it as sure as it can be without proof. These are Handel's only two librettos based entirely on scriptural texts.

25. Letter of Jennens to his friend Edward Holdsworth (10 July 1741), as quoted in Donald Burrows, *Handel* Messiah (Cambridge: Cambridge University Press, 1991), 11.

26. Burrows, *Messiah*, 24, 32.

27. Jennens's letter to Holdsworth quoted in Ruth Smith, "The Achievements of Charles Jennens (1700–1773)," *Music & Letters* 70 (1989): 161–90, at 184. For the description of Jennens's Christianity, see Ruth Smith, *Charles Jennens: The Man Behind Handel's* Messiah (London: The Gerald Coke Handel Foundation, 2012), 18. Although Jennens was critical, Handel listened and in many cases altered his scores as a result. As Smith has shown in *Charles Jennens*, the negative historical opinion of Jennens and his abilities was trumped up in his lifetime and until now has been accepted at face value.

28. As quoted from the minutes of the General Committee of the Foundling Hospital (10 May 1749) in DEUTSCH, 670.

29. BURROWS-HANDEL, 360; Donald Burrows, "Handel and the Foundling Hospital," *Music & Letters* 58 (1977): 269–84.

30. Burrows, "Foundling," 279.

31. HAWKINS, 5:359.

32. See Ellen T. Harris, "Handel and His Will," in *Handel's Will: Facsimiles and Commentary*, ed. Donald Burrows (London: The Gerald Coke Handel Foundation, 2008), 9–20; the immediately following examples and discussion derive from this article.

33. TNA PROB 11/684 (proved 13 July 1737), will of John Hedges; on Hedges's patronage of Goupy, see HARRIS-GOUPY.

34. The will exists in two autograph copies: (1) Foundling Museum, London, Gerald Coke Handel Collection 5193, and (2) TNA PROB 1/14. Both are printed in facsimile in *Handel's Will*.

35. TNA PROB 11/1022 (proved 3 August 1776), will of John Gowland.

36. Lord Justice Conolly to Percival (5 March 1729), BL Add. MS. 47032, p. 192 (f. 103^v).

37. Address to His Royal Highness the Prince of Wales in a letter from

Henry Newman to Percival (14 December 1726), BL Add. MS. 47031, p. 437 (f. 216ʳ).

38. Marquis of Blandford (Paris) to Percival (19 February 1727), BL Add. MS. 47032, p. 11 (f. 6ʳ).

39. William Byrd (Virginia) to Percival (10 June 1729), BL Add. MS. 47032, pp. 207–8 (f. 117ʳ⁻ᵛ).

40. Ruth Smith, "Thomas Morell and His Letter about Handel," *Journal of the Royal Musical Association* 127/2 (2002): 191–225, at 221.

41. Ibid., 218; Morell's entire letter is transcribed on pp. 216–19.

42. Anne Dewes to Bernard Granville (3 December 1750): DELANY CORRESPONDENCE, 2:624.

43. For a detailed study of the issues in *Theodora*, see Ruth Smith, "Comprehending *Theodora*," *Eighteenth-Century Music* 2/1 (2005): 57–90.

44. Dorothea Schröder, "'A Sect, Rebellious to the Gods, and Rome': Händels Oratorium *Theodora* und der Methodismus," *Göttinger Händel-Beiträge* 6 (1996): 101–14, but see Smith, "Theodora," 208.

45. 1 Will & Mary c. 18 (1689).

46. Smith, "Theodora," 218; BURROWS-HANDEL, 334.

47. See Jennens's letter of 19 September 1738: DEUTSCH, 465–66.

10. SICKNESS AND DEATH

1. Berkeley to Percival (9 September 1724), BL Add. MS. 47030, p. 186 (f. 95ʳ).

2. Delany to Anne Dewes (7 November 1751), DELANY CORRESPONDENCE, 3:53 and note.

3. Delany to Anne Dewes (1 March 1744), DELANY CORRESPONDENCE, 2:273.

4. Delany (Pendarves) to Anne Granville (later Dewes) (24 December 1736), DELANY CORRESPONDENCE, 1:582.

5. See Daniel Statt, *Foreigners and Englishmen: The Controversy over Immigration and Population, 1660–1760* (Newark: University of Delaware Press, 1995).

6. [T. Birch, ed.], *A Collection of the Yearly Bills of Mortality from 1657 to 1758 Inclusive* (London: printed for A. Millar, 1759).

7. DEUTSCH, 394.

8. Shaftesbury to Harris (26 April 1737), HARRIS CORRESPONDENCE, 26.

9. Shaftesbury to Harris (30 April 1737), HARRIS CORRESPONDENCE, 27.

10. Harris to Shaftesbury (5 May 1737), HARRIS CORRESPONDENCE, 27–28.

11. The Hon. Mrs. Boscawen to Delany (29 May 1775), DELANY CORRESPONDENCE, 5:130.

12. Shaftesbury to Harris (30 April 1737), HARRIS CORRESPONDENCE, 27.

13. Shaftesbury to Harris (26 April 1737), HARRIS CORRESPONDENCE, 26.

14. Upton to Harris (1 September 1737), HARRIS CORRESPONDENCE, 36.

15. Shaftesbury ("Memoirs of Handel"; see DEUTSCH: 844–48, at 846) and Hawkins (HAWKINS, 5:326), in which both describe the necessity of persuading Handel to go to Aix.

16. MAINWARING, 122–23.

17. BURROWS-RONISH, 249: Handel writes only, "Mr. Duval medecin in Poland St." Although he doesn't give the physician's first name, the address on Poland Street is sufficient to supply the full identification. See Munk's Roll of the Royal College of Physicians of London (www.munks roll.rcplondon.ac.uk/) and P. J. and R. V. Wallis, *Eighteenth-century Medics: Subscriptions, Licenses, Apprenticeships* (Newcastle upon Tyne: Project for Historical Biobibliography, 1988), 178.

18. Thomas Harris to Harris (17 May 1740), HARRIS CORRESPONDENCE, 98.

19. Robartes (later Radnor) to Harris (19 July 1740), HARRIS CORRESPONDENCE, 100.

20. Richard G. King, "Handel's Travels in the Netherlands in 1750," *Music & Letters* 72 (1991): 372–86, at 374.

21. MONTAGU CORRESPONDENCE, 1:52, 56–59. There is no mention in the printed correspondence of a meeting with Handel.

22. Radnor to Harris (8 August 1741), HARRIS CORRESPONDENCE, 119.

23. Philip Percival to John Percival (1 September 1718), BL Add. MS. 47028, p. 497 (f. 249^r).

24. Philip Percival to John Percival (24 December 1720), BL Add. MS. 47029, p. 90 (f. 46^r).

25. Percival to Mr. Foster (21 December 1722), BL Add. MS. 47029, p. 285 (f. 144^r).

26. See Anita Guerrini, *Obesity & Depression in the Enlightenment: The Life and Times of George Cheyne* (Norman: University of Oklahoma Press, 2000).

27. George Cheyne, *An Essay of Health and Long Life* (London: printed for George Strahan, 1724); all quotations of Dr. Cheyne taken from this book (sourced from the British Library on ECCO).

28. The list of medics in Wallis, *Eighteenth-century Medics,* includes fifty-four by the name of Parry, none of whom is an obvious fit with the reference in Shaftesbury's letter in terms of date and place of practice. The closest match is a surgeon named Parry (no first name given), who is associated with the county of Wiltshire, where Harris lived, and was active in 1748.

29. George Harris to Harris (13 September 1743), HARRIS CORRESPONDENCE, 166.

30. Cfm MU MS 260, p. 40; see Burrows-Ronish, 242.
31. Medical investigation into Handel's physical illness has largely disproved previous suggestions that he suffered a series of small strokes; see William A. Frosch, M.D., "The 'Case' of George Frideric Handel," *The New England Journal of Medicine* 321/11 (1989): 765–68. The theory that saturnine gout was the root cause has now been further reinforced by David Hunter, "Handel's Ill-Health: Documents and Diagnoses," *Royal Musical Association Research Chronicle* 41 (2008): 69–92.
32. Cheyne, *An Essay of Health*, 155.
33. Ibid., 156.
34. Ibid., 159.
35. Jennens to Edward Holdsworth (29 April 1743), HHB4, 362–63.
36. Thomas Harris to Harris (18 June 1743), Harris correspondence, 163.
37. Radnor to Harris (?Summer, 1745), Harris correspondence, 216.
38. Shaftesbury to Harris (24 October 1745): Harris correspondence, 219.
39. The reference for the attack in Dublin is provided by Alfred Mann, "An Unknown Detail of Handel Biography," *Bach: The Quarterly Journal of the Riemenschneider Bach Institute* 16/2 (1985): 3–5 and Plate 1 (p. 20).
40. Martyn to Thomas Birch (27 November 1738), BL Add. MS. 4313, f. 110^{r-v}.
41. Percival Diary (5 September 1739), 3:81.
42. Dr. John Monro, "1766 Case Book," C-2, in Jonathan Andrews and Andrew Scull, *Customers and Patrons of the Mad-Trade* (Berkeley: University of California Press, 2003).
43. Ibid., C-24.
44. Ibid., C-7 and 8.
45. Goupy's will is preserved in TNA PROB 11/949 (proved 22 June 1769).
46. The series of recollections of Handel and Goupy appear in *St. James's Chronicle or, British Evening-Post*, no. 2411 (Tuesday, 20 August to Thursday, 22 August 1776), [1], and no. 2416 (Saturday, 31 August to Tuesday, 3 September 1776), 4, and are followed by a rebuttal in *The Public Advertiser*, no. 14647 (Thursday, 12 September 1776), [1]. All may now be searched in the Burney Collection. See Harris-Goupy and Ilias Chrissochoidis, "Handel, Hogarth, Goupy: Artistic Intersections in Early Georgian England," *Early Music* 37/4 (2009): 577–96.
47. Burrows-Handel, 202–3; see also Deutsch, 465–66; but see especially Ruth Smith, "Early Music's Dramatic Significance in Handel's *Saul*," *Early Music* 35 (2007): 173–89, at 175–76. Smith is the first scholar to have taken Jennens's remarks about madness seriously and to under-

stand Handel's instrumentation in *Saul* as an attempt to evoke the music of the Old Testament.

48. The text of *Saul* is given from the libretto printed for Handel's performance of the work in Ireland (Dublin: printed by George Faulkner in Essex-street, 1742).

49. See Winton Dean, *Handel's Dramatic Oratorios and Masques* (London: Oxford University Press, 1959), 287, where he describes the construction and impact of this scene and describes Handel's alteration of the libretto as "a stroke of genius."

50. The remarkable mad scenes in Handel's *Orlando* and *Hercules* have attracted scholarly attention. On *Hercules,* see David Ross Hurley, "Dejanira and the Physicians: Aspects of Hysteria in Handel's *Hercules,*" *The Musical Quarterly* 80 (1996): 548–61. For a discussion of Handel's *Orlando* in the context of Italian operatic precedents, see Ellen Rosand, "Operatic Madness: A Challenge to Convention," in *Music and Text: Critical Inquiries*, ed. Steven Paul Scher (Cambridge: Cambridge University Press, 1992), 241–87.

51. See Hurley, "Dejanira and the Physicians," 555.

52. Shaftesbury to Harris (24 October 1745), Harris correspondence, 219.

53. See Ellen T. Harris, "Handel the Investor," *Music & Letters* 85/4 (2004): 521–75.

54. I previously considered the various events leading up to Handel's writing his will in Ellen T. Harris, "Handel and His Will," in *Handel's Will: Facsimiles and Commentary*, ed. Donald Burrows (London: The Gerald Coke Handel Foundation, 2008), 9–20, at 9.

55. Deutsch, 693; HHB4, 442.

56. BL RM 20. e. 9, ff. 91 and 92; Burrows-Ronish, 125. See also Donald Burrows, "Handel's Last Music Autograph," *Händel-Jahrbuch* 40–41 (1994–1995): 155–68.

57. Deutsch, 703.

58. Samuel Sharp, *A Treatise on the Operations of Surgery, with a Description and Representation of the Instruments Used in Performing Them* (London: n.p., 1739), 128–31 and following (sourced from the British Library on ECCO).

59. Montagu correspondence, 1:196–97.

60. Hawkins, 5:408.

61. Sharp, *A Treatise on the Operations of Surgery*, 164.

62. Ibid., 165–67.

63. Delany to Anne Dewes (25 November 1752), Delany correspondence, 3:177; see also *The General Advertiser*, no. 5622 (4 November 1752), Burney Collection.

64. Hawkins, 5:408.
65. Countess of Shaftesbury to Harris (13 March 1753), Harris correspondence, 287.
66. Thomas Harris to Harris (20 March and 31 March 1753), Harris correspondence, 288.
67. Shaftesbury to Harris (3 April 1753), Harris correspondence, 288.
68. Delany to Anne Dewes (25 November 1752), Delany Correspondence, 3:177.
69. C. Gilbert to Elizabeth Harris (21 May 1753), Harris correspondence, 291.
70. Hawkins, 5:408.
71. Shaftesbury to Harris (8 February 1757), Harris correspondence, 321; Thomas Harris to Harris (21 July 1757), Harris correspondence, 326; Upton to Harris (4 March 1758), Harris correspondence, 331.
72. Thomas Harris to Harris (27 March 1756), Harris correspondence, 310.
73. Delany to Anne Dewes (4 December 1755), Delany correspondence, 3:383; Delany to Anne Dewes (12 December 1756), Delany correspondence, 3:454.
74. Thomas Harris to Harris (17 May 1740), Harris correspondence, 98–99; Diary of George Harris (29 May 1756), Harris correspondence, 314.
75. Handel refused because the Ode had already been set by Maurice Greene. See Burney-Commemoration, 33.
76. Thomas Harris to Harris (21 November 1758), Harris correspondence, 335.
77. Christoph Wolff, *Johann Sebastian Bach: The Learned Musician* (New York: W. W. Norton & Co., 2000), 448–49.
78. Percival to Mr. Bearcroft (11 January 1731), BL Add. MS. 47033, p. 3 (f. 2^r).
79. Sir Philip Parker to Percival (16 January 1731), BL Add. MS. 47033, p. 8 (f. 4^v).
80. Percival to Parker (25 January 1731), BL Add. MS. 47033, p. 13 (f. 7^r).
81. Shaftesbury to Harris (8 February 1757), Harris correspondence, 321; Shaftesbury to Harris (31 December 1757), Harris correspondence, 327.
82. Thomas Harris to Harris (21 November 1758), Harris correspondence, 335; Burrows and Dunhill suggest that the "new" oratorio was probably the reworking of *Solomon*.
83. Deutsch, 814.
84. Thomas Morell based his libretto broadly on a conflation of the biblical

story of Jephtha told in the Book of Judges and the classical story of Iphigenia, who was offered as a sacrifice by her father in exchange for success
in the Trojan War. These primary sources (which included the biblical
story of Abraham and Isaac as well as that of Jephtha) were further mod-
ified by intermediary sources, the principal among these being the play
Jephthes sive Votum, written in 1544 by the Scottish historian George
Buchanan. Morell even borrowed the text of Jephtha's aria "Open thy
marble jaws, O Tomb" directly from *The British Enchanters* by George
Granville, Lord Lansdowne, Mary Delany's uncle. As Lansdowne's
play had been an important model for Handel's *Rinaldo,* it thus became
an important source for Handel's first and last dramatic works written
for London. See for a thorough examination of Morell's text in light of
contemporary biblical commentary and for further bibliography, Ruth
Smith, "Why Does Jephtha Misunderstand His Own Vow?" in *Handel
Studies: A Gedenkschrift for Howard Serwer,* ed. Richard G. King (Hillsdale, NY: Pendragon Press, 2009), 59–85.

85. See Ellen T. Harris, "Silence as Sound: Handel's Sublime Pauses," *Journal of Musicology* 22/4 (2005): 521–58, at 549, and 552–54, where I
placed the role of silence in *Jephtha* within a broader discussion of silence
in Handel's works.

86. Ruth Smith identifies the recipient of Morell's letter as John Nichols,
dates it to 1779–1780, and provides a full and accurate transcription.
See Smith, "Thomas Morell and His Letter About Handel," *Journal of the
Royal Musical Association* 127/2 (2002): 191–225.

87. The substitution of "Truth" (*Verità*) for "Undeceiver" (*Disinganno*) in the
title allowed for greater ease of understanding; however, the name of the
character remained Disinganno to distinguish him, one assumes, from
universal truths mentioned in the text.

88. See Roland Dieter Schmidt, "Die drei Fassungen von Händels Oratorium *Il trionfo del Tempo / The Triumph of Time and Truth* (HWV 46a,
46b, 71)," *Göttinger Händel-Beiträge* 7 (1998): 86–118.

89. I am indebted to Irving and Marilyn Lavin for animated conversations
at the Institute for Advanced Study in Princeton on the possible relationship between Bernini's sculpture and Handel's oratorio.

90. Domenico Bernini, *Vita del Cavalier Gio. Lorenzo Bernino, descritta da
Domenico Bernino, suo figlio* (Rome, 1713), 80–82, as quoted in Marilyn
Aronberg Lavin, "Bernini and the Truthful Self," in *Artists' Art in the
Renaissance* (London: The Pindar Press, 2009), 179–91, at 181, n. 9.

11. WILLS AND LEGACIES

1. COXE, 62–63.
2. BURROWS-RONISH, x–xii.

3. On Handel's will, see *Handel's Will: Facsimiles and Commentary*, ed. Donald Burrows (London: The Gerald Coke Handel Foundation, 2008), containing facsimiles of both copies of Handel's will (Foundling Museum, London: Gerald Coke Handel Collection 5193, and PROB 1/14).

4. Shaftesbury to Harris (12 February 1745), HARRIS CORRESPONDENCE, 214.

5. Thomas Harris to Harris (13 February 1757), HARRIS CORRESPONDENCE, 321.

6. DEUTSCH, 818–19.

7. For the early identification of the angel as David, see Suzanne Aspden, "'Fam'd Handel Breathing, tho' Transformed to Stone': The Composer as Monument," *Journal of the American Musicological Society* 55 (2002): 39–90, at 74; Aspden leaves open the question of what music, if any, is implied.

8. TNA PROB 11/833 (proved 12 October 1757), will of James Hunter.

9. *The Whitehall Evening Post*, no. 1889 (27 April 1758), BURNEY COLLECTION.

10. *The Public Advertiser*, no. 7368 (6 June 1758), BURNEY COLLECTION.

11. London Metropolitan Archives: CLC/B/055/MS 08674/079, no. 33314, f. 213 (left: each page number refers to an opening).

12. *The Public Ledger*, no. 393 (14 April 1761), BURNEY COLLECTION.

13. HAWKINS, 5:412.

14. *Catalogue of the Very Important and Interesting Musical Collections of a Distinguished Amateur . . . to which are added the well known and very important Series of Handel's Works written by the Composer's Amanuensis, J. C. Smith, for his Friend and Patron, Bernard Granville, Esq . . . which will be sold by Auction, by Messrs. Puttick and Simpson . . . on Friday, January 29st [sic], 1858, and following day*, p. 12.

15. *Catalogue of Additions to the Manuscripts in the British Museum 1916–1920 . . .* (London: The Trustees of the British Museum, 1933), 293.

16. Jens Peter Larsen, *Handel's Messiah: Origins, Composition, Sources*, 2nd ed. (New York: W. W. Norton & Co., 1972; orig. 1957), 270.

17. See Ellen T. Harris, "James Hunter, Handel's Friend," *Händel-Jahrbuch* 46 (2000): 247–64, and Donald Burrows, "'Something Necessary to the Connection': Charles Jennens, James Hunter and Handel's *Samson*," *The Handel Institute Newsletter* 15/1 (Spring 2004): 1–3.

18. Burrows, "The Barrett Lennard Collection," in COLLECTIONS, 109.

19. TNA PROB 11/875 (proved 22 May 1762), will of Anne Donnellan.

20. See Patrick Kelly, "Anne Donnellan: Irish Proto-Bluestocking," *Hermathena—A Trinity College Dublin Review* 54 (Summer 1993): 56.

21. Donnellan's accounts at Goslings Bank are preserved in Barclays Group Archive: ACC 130/33, p. 286.

22. "Department of Antiquities and Coins. Donations 1756–1836," MS. in the Medieval and Later Antiquities Department, British Museum.

23. Extract from the Registry of Trinity College, published as a frontispiece to the publication of the lectures given in 1795 by the second Donnellan lecturer: Rev. Richard Graves, *Lectures on the Four Last Books of the Pentateuch ... Delivered in the Chapel of Trinity College Dublin at the Lecture Established by the Provost and Senior Fellows, Under the Will of Mrs. Anne Donnellan*, 3rd ed. (Dublin: William Curry, Jun. and Company, 1829).

24. Thomas Elrington, *Sermons Preached in the Chapel of Trinity College, Dublin, in the Year 1795, at the Lecture Established by the Provost and Senior Fellows, under the Will of Mrs. Anne Donnellan* ... (Dublin: George Bonham, 1796), the extract from the Registry of Trinity College on the establishment of the lectures appears on pp. [v]–vii.

25. TNA PROB 11/945 (proved 10 July 1769), will of Elizabeth Mayne.

26. John Smith, *A Catalogue Raisonné of the Works of the Most Eminent Dutch, Flemish, and French Painters*, Part II: *Containing the Life and Works of Peter Paul Rubens* (Reprint of the 1830 edition; London: Sands and Company, 1908), 2, no. 3, gives the name of the owner as J. T. Batts, and this form of the name has been repeated in all modern sources: see Julius S. Held, *The Oil Sketches of Peter Paul Rubens: A Critical Catalogue* (Princeton, NJ: Princeton University Press, 1980), 479–81, no. 349. Smith describes the sketch as "a second Sketch, with considerable variations, [compared with one he previously listed] painted with a *bravura* freedom and a rich *impasto* of colour" (p. 2, no. 3).

27. TNA PROB 11/1136 (proved 29 December 1785), will of John Mayne, son of Elizabeth Mayne.

28. TNA PROB 11/1783 (proved 19 April 1831), will of John Thomas Batt Jr., son of John Thomas Batt, a nephew of Christopher Batt and Elizabeth Mayne.

29. *Art Sales of the Year 1901* ..., ed. J. Herbert Slater (London: H. Virtue and Company, 1902), 229, 232–33. The catalogue entry (p. 233) describes the sketch as "on panel—the centre 26 in. by 20 in.; the wings, each 26 in. by 10 ½ in." It then quotes the Smith catalogue and adds: "This work is one of several known studies executed by Rubens for the altar-piece in Antwerp Cathedral; but in some respects, especially in the drawing, is superior to many of the artist's finished works. Rubens is said to have received 2,600 florins (about £335) for painting the altar-piece at Antwerp."

30. TNA PROB 11/949 (proved 22 June 1769), will of Joseph Goupy.

31. Jacob Simon, "New Light on Joseph Goupy (1689–1769)," *Apollo* 139 (February 1994): 15–18, at 16.

32. Bruce Robertson and Robert Dance, "Joseph Goupy: Checklist of Prints,

Drawings and Paintings," *The Bulletin of the Cleveland Museum of Art* 75/10 (December 1988): 376–82.

33. Mark Catesby, *The Natural History of Carolina, Florida, and the Bahama Islands*, 2nd ed. (London: printed for Charles Marsh, Thomas Wilcox, and Benjamin Stichall, 1754), xi.

34. Both Horace Walpole and George Vertue made this point in their contemporary assessments of Goupy. See Bruce Robertson and Robert Dance, "Joseph Goupy and the Art of the Copy," *The Bulletin of the Cleveland Museum of Art* 75/10 (December 1988): 354–75, at 363 and 366.

35. TNA PROB 11/1165 (proved 7 May 1788), will of Mary Delany.

36. TNA C 33/356 (8 December 1730), p. 53, *Pendarves v. Bassett*, Orders and Decrees.

37. TNA PROB 11/1015 (proved 25 November 1775), will of Bernard Granville; Barclays Group Archive: ACC 130/80, p. 183.

38. Delany to Anne Dewes (28 September 1750), DELANY CORRESPONDENCE, 2:595.

39. Delany to Anne Dewes (4 November 1752), DELANY CORRESPONDENCE, 3:171.

40. Ballard (Oxford: printed by W. Jackson, 1752), [241] (sourced from the British Library on ECCO).

41. Delany to Viscountess Andover (4 September 1766), DELANY CORRESPONDENCE, 4:77.

42. See Mark Laird and Alicia Weisberg-Roberts, eds., *Mrs. Delany and Her Circle* (New Haven, CT: Yale University Press, 2010), with 265 color illustrations, for Mary Delany's interwoven interests in the visual arts (including embroidery) and botany.

43. Dumbarton Oaks Research Library and Collection, Rare Book Collection, Washington, DC.

44. Ruth Hayden counts 230 paper petals in the bloom alone of the "Passeflora Laurifolia, Bay Leaved" (*Mrs. Delany and Her Flower Collages* [London: British Museum Press, 1980], 134 [text] and 72 [colored plate]).

45. Delany to Anne Granville (9 September 1729), DELANY CORRESPONDENCE, 1:213.

46. As quoted by Lady Llanover, DELANY CORRESPONDENCE, 6:95.

47. Horace Walpole to Delany (28 November 1786), Delany to Walpole (30 November 1786), and editorial note, DELANY CORRESPONDENCE, 6:416–17.

48. Delany's biography appears in Andrew Kippis and Joseph Towers, *Biographia Britannica: or, The Lives of the Most Eminent Persons Who Have Flourished in Great Britain and Ireland*, 5 vols. (London: W. and A. Strahan, 1778–1793), 5:88–93.

49. HAWKINS, 5:412.

Index

Page numbers in *italics* indicate an illustration or chart.